Mini
Thai
Dictionary

**English-Thai
Thai-English**

Comp...
Updat...

D1359977

TUTTLE Publishing

Tokyo | Rutland, Vermont | Singapore

Published by Tuttle Publishing, an imprint of Periplus
Editions (HK) Ltd.

www.tuttlepublishing.com

© 2018 by Periplus Editions (HK) Ltd

ISBN 978-0-8048-5002-5

Distributed by:

North America, Latin America and Europe
Tuttle Publishing
364 Innovation Drive, North Clarendon,
VT 05759-9436 USA.
Tel: 1(802) 773-8930 Fax: 1(802) 773-6993
info@tuttlepublishing.com; www.tuttlepublishing.com

Asia Pacific
Berkeley Books Pte. Ltd.
3 Kallang Sector #04-01, Singapore 349278
Tel: (65) 6741-2178 Fax: (65) 6741-2179
inquiries@periplus.com.sg; www.periplus.com

22 21 20 19   5 4 3 2   1907RR
Printed in China

TUTTLE PUBLISHING® is a registered trademark of
Tuttle Publishing, a division of Periplus Editions (HK) L

CONTENTS

INTRODUCTION

This Mini Thai Dictionary gives entries that are based on everyday colloquial Thai although more "polite" or "formal" ones are also included, where appropriate. To ensure that you are aware of these distinctions both "colloquial" and "formal" entries are clearly indicated, as is the case with various idioms and slang terms listed.

In compiling this work we have done our best to include the most commonly used Thai words. It should be emphasized, however, that in a book of such limited scope, it has been impossible to provide a totally comprehensive listing of vocabulary items. Even so we believe that this dictionary will meet the needs of users who would like to develop a proficiency in the language and a better understanding of a distinctively different socio-cultural world.

To help you get a better sense of how different Thai words function there are also a number of specific examples of usage provided. Merely providing lists of words and their Thai or English equivalents does not really give the user enough to work with if they are interested in moving beyond a rudimentary, and often unsatisfactory, level of communication.

Numerous examples of how the particular meanings

Introduction

of Thai words/expressions are formed are also provided. These examples are given in parentheses and appear as follows: (literally, 'word A'-'word B' and so on). A case in point is the way the Thai word for "river" is formed. In English "river" is a single word. In Thai, however, "river" — **mâeh-náam** แม่น้ำ — is a combination of two distinct and completely different words. The first of these is **mâeh**, or "mother," and the second is **náam**, or "water." In other words "river" in Thai is literally "mother"-"water" (or "mother of water(s)"). Similarly, the English word "tear(s)" (i.e. the tears of someone crying) in Thai is **náam-taa** (literally, "water"-"eye[s]") น้ำตา, the word **taa** here meaning "eye(s)."

From examining the examples provided in the English-Thai section of the dictionary you should be able to not only extend your vocabulary and improve your facility with the language, but also develop a better understanding of the type of English typically spoken by many Thai people. Regardless of your language background it is natural to use your mother tongue as a type of template when speaking another language. That is until you begin to make a serious effort to understand the underlying nature of the language you are trying to learn and develop a fuller sense of it in its own terms.

The basics of Thai might be considered simple enough for you to quickly pick up the language, especially when compared to some European languages, for example:

1. Words are not modified or conjugated for tense, person, possession, number (singular/plural), gender, or subject-verb agreement.
2. Determiners such as "a, an," or "the" are not used.

Hence many Thai speakers of English speak in what is usually referred to as "broken English" (or "Tinglish" as some would have it)—this being strongly influenced by their native Thai language template. And, obviously, non-Thais do much the same thing when speaking Thai.

Here it should be mentioned that there are a significant, and ever increasing, number of English words in Thai, many concerned with technological advances and innovation. At the same time there is also a growing body of "non" technical words and expressions that have been incorporated into Thai. Such instances are clearly indicated by the inclusion of the marker (from English) next to such entries. Inevitably, English borrowings into Thai have been "Thai-ified" and, at times, are not immediately clear or comprehensible to the native English speaker. In all cases an attempt has been made to provide a usable form of pronunciation for these various English "loan" words.

A final note: In addition to "polite," "formal," "colloquial" terms and a smattering of widely used "idioms," a number of common crude, vulgar words are included and clearly marked. These particular entries are for the benefit of the curious reader—a form of FYI, as it were. However, it is strongly advised that you avoid using any such words until you have gained a good level of familiarity with Thai society and the way Thai people interact. Under no circumstances experiment using such language with strangers as the consequences of doing so could, potentially, be very unpleasant.

General overview of some key aspects of Thai

In one very basic sense Thai is like English—it has an alphabet. Thai words, like those in English, are composed of particular combinations of letters—both consonants and vowels. In the Thai case, however, different vowels are written before, above, below or after consonants, or a combination of these positions. And in a very small number of cases, the vowel sound, while the same as other written forms, is not written at all; rather it is "inherent" and has to be learned.

Thai has its own distinctive script which is similar to the closely related language of neighboring Laos. Thai, like Lao, is written without spaces between the words. In written Thai, however, spaces do occur between what we might loosely call "grouped associated ideas."

It should be emphasized that there is no ideal way of writing—that is romanizing or transliterating—Thai words in English. There are a number of "systems" for romanizing Thai and, regrettably, none of them (including that used in this dictionary) is ideal. In fact, at times, some of the systems used to romanize Thai words are rather unhelpful when it comes to getting the pronunciation correct. For example, you may have seen the common, polite everyday greeting for "hello" **sàwàt dii** written as **sawasdii/dee** or **sawas dii/dee**. There is no issue with the **dii/dee** which simply sounds like the English letter 'd.' As for the **sawas** what has occurred is that the writer has employed one of the romanization systems which adhere strictly to the actual Thai spelling. In written Thai, the final 's' in **sawas** is indeed spelled with an 's' letter, but what needs to be understood is that when 's' (and in Thai there are a number of different letters representing 's') appears at the end of a syllable or word it is pronounced as a 't' sound (although some consider this to be closer to a 'd' — hence you will sometimes see **sawad dii/dee**, or, for the popular noodle dish, **pad/phad thai** rather than the more accurate **phàt thai** — the word **phàt** actually sounding closer to the English golfing term "putt"). In a following section all of the syllable-final consonant sounds in Thai are provided.

In summary, while Thai and English share many of the same sounds there are a number of instances where there are no comparable sounds between the two languages. Hence it is a good idea, whenever possible, to ask a Thai friend or acquaintance to look at a particular word or phrase in the Thai script provided and help you with your pronunciation.

Introduction

Romanized Thai

English pronunciation is often very confusing to non-native speakers as individual letters do not correspond to a single unchanging sound. Take the vowel sound 'e,' for example, which is pronounced in a number of ways. Consider the 'e' sounds in the following: "mother," "women," "they," "he," and so on. Thai pronunciation, by contrast, is much more "phonetic," that is, vowels and consonants have but one sound which does not change in different words as is the case in English.

Consonants

The majority of Thai consonants are similar to those in English, although there are a number of important differences. The consonants listed below are in the "initial" position, that is, at the beginning of a word.

Romanized letters	Sounds like	as in
k	g	"s<u>k</u>in"
kh	k	"<u>k</u>ing"
*ng	ng	"singi<u>ng</u>"
j	j	"<u>j</u>et"

Romanized letters	Sounds like	as in
ch	ch	"<u>ch</u>at"
d	d	"<u>d</u>o"
t	t	"s<u>t</u>op"
th	t	"<u>t</u>ime"
n	n	"<u>n</u>ame"
b	b	"<u>b</u>ar"
p	p	"s<u>p</u>a"
ph	p	"<u>p</u>ass"
f	f	"<u>f</u>ar"
m	m	"<u>m</u>e"
y	y	"<u>y</u>ou"
r	r	"<u>r</u>at"
l	l	"<u>l</u>ove"
w	w	"<u>w</u>ine"
s	s	"<u>s</u>ee"
o	o	"<u>o</u>n"

*Note: The English sound **ng** only occurs (with a slight exception—see below) in the syllable-final position of a word, as in "si*ng*," "bri*ng*," etc. However, **ng** occurs both at the beginning and end of Thai words and syllables. The closest comparable English sound to the syllable initial 'ng' in Thai is the sound that occurs at the beginning of the second syllable of words such as "si*nger*" (i.e. si*ng-ng*ing), or "wri*nger*" (i.e. wri*ng-ng*ing). You may find it useful to practice pronouncing the **ng** sound at the beginning of various Thai words by trying the following: say "sing," "sing," "singing, singing," then "nging, nging."

Syllable-final Consonant Sounds

In Thai only eight consonant sounds occur in the syllable-final position. These eight sounds can be divided into two groups—stops and sonorants. Stops are sounds whose pronunciation ends abruptly, while sonorants are sounds whose pronunciation can be sustained for some time. For example, the 't' in "hot" is a stop while the 'n' in "bin" is a sonorant. It is possible to sustain the 'n' in "bin" for a long time—"bin*nnnn*....," but the 't' in "hot" has a short, sharp sound which brings the pronunciation of that word to a sudden stop once it has been spoken.

The eight final consonant sounds in Thai are:

Stops	**Comparable English Sound**
k	sic<u>k</u>
t	fla<u>t</u>
p	si<u>p</u>

Sonorants	Comparable English Sound
ng	wi<u>ng</u>
n	bi<u>n</u>
m	ja<u>m</u>
y	<u>j</u>oy
w	<u>n</u>ow

Syllable-initial Consonant Clusters

Only a relatively small number of consonant clusters (i.e. two or more consonants together) occur in Thai, compared to English. All Thai consonant clusters occur in syllable-initial position. No consonant clusters occur at the end of Thai words. The consonant clusters are as follows:

kr, kl, kw, khr, khl, khw, tr, pr, pl, phr, phl.

Also 'fr' and 'fl' which only occur in English loan words.

'R' and 'L' sounds in Thai

The pronunciation of 'r' and 'l' sounds in Thai varies according to the speech style or register. In the formal style 'r' and 'l' are usually pronounced quite clearly and distinctly. However, in casual and informal conversation,

Introduction

'r' and 'l' both tend to be pronounced as 'l' in the syllable-initial position. In consonant clusters in informal Thai 'r' is often replaced by 'l' and sometimes both 'r' and 'l' sounds are omitted altogether from consonant clusters. Note that the change of 'r' sound to 'l' in casual spoken Thai does not alter the tones of words, which remain unchanged. Compare the following examples:

Formal style pronunciation	Informal style pronunciation
khráp (Male polite particle)	kháp
plaa (a fish)	paa
ruai (to be rich)	luai (luu-ay)
à-rai (What?)	à-lai
krà-thá (a pan)	kà-thá

Vowels

In Thai there are both "long" and "short" vowels. This distinction between long and short vowels is very important. In the short form used in this dictionary the following are written the same as in English, but the sound is very short:

Short vowels	Sounds like
a	a as in "<u>a</u>h"
e	e as in "l<u>e</u>t"
i	i as in "h<u>i</u>t"
o	o as in "<u>o</u>h!"
u	u as in "p<u>u</u>t"

As for the "long" vowels, they are written as follows:

Long vowels	Sounds like
aa	ar as in "f<u>ar</u>"
eh	ey as in "h<u>ey</u>"
ii	ee as in "fr<u>ee</u>"
oh	o as in "g<u>o</u>ld"
uu	oo as in "g<u>oo</u>d"
am	um as in "dr<u>um</u>"
ai	ai as in "Th<u>ai</u>"
ao	ow as in "c<u>ow</u>"

Introduction

The following vowel sounds have both a "long" and a "short" form. However, in the instances below the "short" form is not as abrupt as in the selection of vowels listed above, yet there is a clear distinction between "long" and "short" vowel sound which is best demonstrated by a native speaker with good, clear enunciation.

Long/short vowels	Sounds like
ae	**air** as in "p<u>air</u>"
aw	**aw** as in "l<u>aw</u>"
oeh	**er** as in "h<u>er</u>"
ia	**ea** as in "n<u>ear</u>"
iu	**ew** as in "n<u>ew</u>"
oi	**oy** as in "b<u>oy</u>"
ua	**our** as in "t<u>our</u>"
ueh	**on** as in "pris<u>on</u>" (longer)
uea	**ure** as in "c<u>ure</u>" (longer)

Tones

Thai is a "tonal" language, which means variations in tone or pitch determine the meaning of a word. Thus the assistance of a native Thai speaker to help you approximate the correct tones would be invaluable.

Some people find the idea of "tones" particularly daunting but, in fact, tones in Central Thai (the name of the official language in Thailand) are not as impenetrable as these individuals imagine. Indeed, there are a relatively small number of words where it is vital to get the tone absolutely correct to be understood (for example, see the entries for "near" and "far"). These days with a large and growing number of foreigners visiting Thailand, Thais are becoming accustomed to non-native speakers "mangling" their language to one degree or another when trying to speak it. So often meaning can be conveyed, partially through context, even if one's tones are slightly off kilter. To say this is not to reduce the significance of tones, for ultimately they are crucial; rather it is to encourage you, the learner, to use the language as much as you can and develop your confidence, and hopefully your interest, so as to help you move on to another level.

Thai has five tones: mid, low, falling, high and rising. In the system of romanization used in this dictionary the mid-tone is unmarked. The other tones are represented by the following symbols written above the relevant syllable (in

Introduction

the case of words with a number of syllables) or the word if it is monosyllabic: low tone `; falling tone ^; high tone ´; and rising tone ˇ.

Here are some examples of the tones with words given in romanized form—their English meaning and in Thai script. Try having a Thai friend or acquaintance pronounce the words written in Thai to get some idea of the differences in tone, then practice saying them yourself.

Tone Level	Tone symbol	Example	Meaning
mid	No mark	**mai** ไมล์	a mile (from English)
low	`	**mài** ใหม่	new
falling	^	**mâi** ไม่	No/not
high	´	**mái** ไม้	wood
rising	ˇ	**măi** ไหม	silk

In closing it should be pointed out that many of the words in this dictionary with two or more syllables have hyphens included to help you with your pronunciation. Here, for example, is the word for the month of August: **sĭng-hăa-khom**.

We wish you "Good luck" on your journey into the Thai language or, as the Thais would say, โชคดี **"Choke dee"**.*

---

* While this particular rendering of Thai might cause some to laugh, make jokes or bad puns it's very close to what the Thai for "Good luck" actually sounds like.

English–Thai

A

abandon v (leave – a car, a girlfriend, etc.) láthíng ละทิ้ง, or simply thíng ทิ้ง

abbreviation N kham-yâw คำย่อ

abbot N jâo-aa-wâat เจ้าอาวาส

abdomen N chûawng-tháwng ช่องท้อง

abduct v lák-phaa ลักพา

able to ADJ sǎa-mâat สามารถ

ability N khwaam sǎa-mâat ความสามารถ

abnormal ADJ phìt-pòk-kà-tì ผิดปกติ

aboard See 'on board'

abolish v lêrk-lóm เลิกล้ม

abort, an abortion v, N tháeng แท้ง, tham tháeng ทำแท้ง

about (approximately) ADV prà-maan ประมาณ, or raaw raaw ราวๆ

about (regarding, concerning) PREP kìao-kàp เกี่ยวกับ,

or rûeang เรื่อง (used in a meaning of 'subject/topic' for informal expression)

above, on top (of) ADV khâang bon ข้างบน

abroad, overseas ADV, ADJ tàang prà-thêht ต่างประเทศ, or mueang nâwk เมืองนอก; to be abroad/overseas—to be living abroad/overseas—either of these equally common expressions: yùu tàang prà-thêht อยู่ต่างประเทศ, or yùu mueang nâwk อยู่เมืองนอก

absence N **absent** ADJ (not be here/there) mâi yùu ไม่อยู่, e.g. he/she is not here khǎo mâi yùu เขาไม่อยู่

absent-minded ADJ jai-loi ใจลอย

absolute ADJ, **absolutely** ADV nâe-nawn แน่นอน

absorb v dòut-suem ดูดซึม

abstain (to give up something) v lôek เลิก

abstract N naam-má-tham นามธรรม

absurd ADJ rái-săa-rá ไร้สาระ

abundance N, **abundant** ADJ ù-dom-sŏm-buun อุดม สมบูรณ์

abuse V (mistreat/hurt) tham ráai ทำร้าย; to abuse (verbally, to scold/berate) dàa (somebody) ด่า, or, equally common — wâa (somebody) ว่า

abyss N thá-leh-lúek ทะเลลึก

academic (an academic – a university lecturer) aajaan (pronounced like 'ah-jarn') อา จารย์; (the general term for) things 'academic' wíchaa-kaan วิชาการ

academy N rohng-rian โรงเรียน

accelerate V rêng เร่ง

accent N (when speaking) săm-niang สำเนียง

accept V yawm ráp ยอมรับ

acceptable ADJ yawm ráp dâi ยอมรับได้

access V (get access to) khâo เข้า e.g. I can't get access to the Internet khâo in-toe-nèt mâi-dâi เข้าอินเตอร์เน็ตไม่ได้

accessories N (accompanying item of dress) khrûeang-prà-dàp เครื่องประดับ

accidentally, by chance ADV dohy bang-oehn โดยบังเอิญ (COLLOQUIALLY) bang-oehn บังเอิญ

accommodation N thîi phák ที่พัก

accompany V pai pen phûean ไปเป็นเพื่อน (literally, 'go'-'be'-'friend')

accomplish, achieve V tham săm-rèt ทำสำเร็จ

accomplishment, achievement N khwaam-săm-rèt ความสำเร็จ

according to (what he/she said) PREP taam thîi... ตามที่...

account (e.g. bank account) N ban-chii บัญชี; an accountant N nák ban-chii นักบัญชี

accumulate V sà-sŏm สะสม

accuracy N **accurate** ADJ mâen yam แม่นยำ

accuse V klàow hăa กล่าวหา

accustom V khún khoei คุ้น เคย

ache (as in 'headache/

2

toothache, etc.) N pùat ปวด

acid N kròt กรด

acne (pimple/s) N rán สิว

acquaintance (not a friend as such) N khon rúu jàk คนรู้จัก

acquainted/familiar (e.g. to be acquainted with something) ADJ khún khoei kàp คุ้นเคยกับ

acquire v dâi rian-róu ได้เรียนรู้ (to gain knowledge)

across from... PREP trong khâam kàp... ตรงข้ามกับ

act (do) v (COLLOQUIAL) tham ทำ, or (in more formal, bureaucratic language) pàtìbàt ปฏิบัติ

action N kaan kràtham การกระทำ

active ADJ khlâwng-khlâew คล่องแคล่ว

activity N kìt-jà-kam กิจกรรม

activist N (i.e. a social activist) nák kìt-jà-kam นักกิจกรรม

actor/actress (general term for 'performer') N nák sà-daehng นักแสดง

actual (real) ADJ pen jing เป็นจริง

actually (as in 'actually he

doesn't have a car') ADV thîi jing ที่จริง

acupuncture N fǎng-khěm ฝังเข็ม

adapt/adjust v pràp ปรับ; pràp-tua ปรับตัว (as to a new environment)

add v phôehm เพิ่ม, bùak บวก (plus, i.e. +)

addict (drug) N khon tìt yaa คนติดยา

addicted v (to drugs, sex, types of food, soap operas, etc.) (COLLOQUIAL) tìt ติด

additional ADJ thîi phôehm-toehm ที่เพิ่มเติม

address thîi yùu ที่อยู่

administer v jàt kaan จัดการ, baw-rí-haan บริหาร (manage as an administrator)

admire/praise v chom ชม

admit/confess v yawm ráp ยอมรับ

adolescent N wai rún วัยรุ่น

adopt v ráp líang รับเลี้ยง; an adopted child bùt bun tham บุตรบุญธรรม

adorable (lovable) ADJ nâa rák น่ารัก

adore v rák mâak รักมาก

3

adult N phûu yài ผู้ใหญ่

adultery N (for someone to engage in adultery – an affair with a 'married' man/woman) pen chúu เป็นชู้ (Note: for an adulterer often just the single word chúu ชู้ is used. *Also see* entry under 'womanizer')

advance, go/move forward v kâw nâa ก้าวหน้า

advance money, a deposit N ngoehn mát jam เงินมัดจำ

advantage (benefit) N phôn prà-yòht ผลประโยชน์; to take advantage (of someone) ao prìap เอาเปรียบ

adventure N phà-jon-phai ผจญภัย, **adventurous** ADJ châwp phà-jon-phai ชอบผจญภัย

advertise v **advertisement** N khôht-sà-naa โฆษณา (Note: this word also means 'propaganda')

advice N kham náe nam คำแนะนำ, **advise/suggest** v náe nam แนะนำ

aerobics (from English) N ae-rohbìk แอโรบิก; to do aerobics lên ae-rohbìk เล่น

(literally, 'dance'-'aerobics') เต้นแอโรบิกส์

aeroplane/airplane N khrûeang bin เครื่องบิน

affair N (as in that's 'my affair/ my business' – the word for 'story' is used) rûeang เรื่อง, (for a married person to have a lover, i.e. an affair) (COLLOQUIAL) mii chúu มีชู้

affect v mii phôn tàw มีผลต่อ

affection N khwaam rák khrâi ความรักใคร่

affirm/confirm v yuehn yan ยืนยัน

afford v săa-mâat mii dâi (literally, 'able'-'have'-'can') สามารถมีได้

afraid/scared, to be ADJ klua กลัว

Africa N (from English) áep-fríkaa แอฟริกา

after CONJ lăng jàak หลังจาก; (later) ADV thii lăng ทีหลัง

afternoon N (after midday till 4 p.m.) tawn bàai ตอนบ่าย, late afternoon (4 p.m. to dusk) tawn yen ตอนเย็น

afterwards, then ADV lăng jàak nán หลังจากนั้น

again ADV (another – person, bottle of beer, etc.) ...ìik ...อีก: e.g. 'play (name of game) again' lên ìik เล่นอีก; 'can I have another bottle of beer?' khǎw bia ìik khùat (literally, 'request/ask for'- 'beer'-'another'-'bottle') ขอ เบียร์อีกขวด

against PREP tàw tâan ต่อต้าน

age N aa-yú อายุ; to ask someone's age, i.e. 'How old are you?' khun aa-yú thâo-rài (literally, 'you'-'age'-'how much?') คุณอายุเท่าไร

agency N (company) bawrísàt tua thaen บริษัทตัวแทน

agent/representative N tua thaen ตัวแทน (NOTE: often the English word 'agent' is used with Thai pronunciation 'a yên' เอเย่นต์)

aggression N rúk raan รุกราน

aggressive ADJ kâaw ráaw ก้าวร้าว; (COLLOQUIAL) someone looking for trouble khon hǎa rûeang (literally, 'person'- 'looking for'-'a story/an issue') คนหาเรื่อง; to look for trouble hǎa rûeang หาเรื่อง

agile ADJ wâwng-wai ว่องไว

ago ADV thî láew ที่แล้ว; two years ago sǎwng pii thî láew (literally, 'two'-'year'- 'ago') สองปีที่แล้ว

agony N jèp เจ็บ, pùat ปวด

agree V (with someone) hěn dûai เห็นด้วย

agree to do something V tòk-long tham ตกลงทำ

agreed! ADJ tòklong ตกลง

agreement N khâw tòklong ข้อตกลง

agriculture N kà-sèht-trà-kam เกษตรกรรม

ahead ADV lûang nâa ล่วงหน้า

aid V See 'help'

AIDS N rôhk èhds โรคเอดส์

aim N pâo-mǎai เป้าหมาย

aimless ADJ mâi-mii jùt-mǎai ไม่มีจุดหมาย

air N aa-kàat อากาศ

air conditioned ADJ ...pràp aa-kàat (literally, 'adjust'- 'air') ...ปรับอากาศ, or (MORE COLLOQUIALLY) ...ae แอร์

aircraft, airplane N khrûeang-bin เครื่องบิน

air force N kawng tháp aa-kàat กองทัพอากาศ

5

air hostess N (COLLOQUIAL, from English) ae แอร์; the term naang fáa (literally, 'woman'- 'sky') นางฟ้า is also used colloquially

airline N sǎai kaan bin สายการบิน

airmail N mehl aa-kàat เมล์ อากาศ

airport N (COLLOQUIAL) sà-nǎam bin สนามบิน

airsick ADJ mao khrûeang-bin เมาเครื่องบิน

aisle N thaang-doehn ทางเดิน

alarm tuean phai (literally, 'warn'-'danger') เตือนภัย; alarm clock naalí-kaa plùk (literally, 'clock'-'wake') นาฬิกาปลุก

alcohol, liquor N (spirits) lâo เหล้า

alcoholic ADJ tìt lâo ติดเหล้า

alert v tuean เตือน, ADJ tùehn tua ตื่นตัว

alien N (as in strange, different, unusual) plàehk แปลก; alien (from outer space) má-nút tàang daow (literally, 'human'-'different'-'planet') มนุษย์ต่างดาว

alienate v hǒehn hàang เหิน ห่าง

alike, the same ADV mǔean เหมือน

alive ADJ yang mii chii-wít yùu ยังมีชีวิตอยู่

all ADJ (the whole lot), altogether ADV tháng mòt ทั้งหมด

all-around ADJ râwp rúu รอบรู้

allergic (to something) ADJ

allergy N pháeh แพ้

alley, lane, side street N (in Bangkok, in particular, can also refer to a substantial road) soi ซอย

alligator N See 'crocodile'

all-out ADJ tem thîi เต็มที่

allow/give permission v à-nú-yâat hâi อนุญาตให้

allow v (let someone) yawm ยอม

allowed/permitted to ADJ dâi ráp à-nú-yâat ได้รับอนุญาต

all right ADJ See 'okay'

almost ADV kùeap เกือบ

alone ADV (be by oneself) khon diao คนเดียว

along ADV taam ตาม (i.e. walk

6

along the path), dûai ด้วย
(i.e. as company)

alongside ADV yùu khâang
อยู่ข้าง

a lot ADV yér เยอะ

aloud ADV dang ดัง

alphabet N àk-sǎwn อักษร

already ADV láew แล้ว (a term
that indicates completion);
'gone' pai láew (literally, 'go'-
'already') ไปแล้ว

although, even though
CONJ thǔeng máeh wâa
ถึงแม้ว่า

also (as well) ADV dûai tûai:
e.g. he/she will go also/as
well khǎo pai dûai (literally,
'he'/'she'-'go'-'also/as well')
เขาไปด้วย

alternative/choice N mii
thîi lûeak มีที่เลือก, or mii
thaang lûeak มีทางเลือก

altogether ADV See 'all'

alumni N sìt kào ศิษย์เก่า

always ADV sà-mǒeh เสมอ

amateur N sà-màk-lên สมัคร
เล่น

amaze V plàek jai แปลกใจ

amazing ADJ (as in 'that's
unbelievable!' 'incredible')

mâi nâa chûea ไม่น่า
เชื่อ, also má-hàt sà-jan
มหัศจรรย์

ambassador, diplomat
(general term) N thûut ทูต

amber ADJ sǐi lǔeang-thawng
สีเหลืองทอง

ambulance N rót phá-yaa-
baan รถพยาบาล

ambush N lâwp tham-ráai
ลอบทำร้าย

America N à-meh-rí-kaa
อเมริกา

American N khon à-meh-rí-
kan คนอเมริกัน

among, between PREP
rá-wàang ระหว่าง

amount N jam-nuan จำนวน

amphetamine N (COLLOQUIAL)
yaa bâa (literally, 'drug/
medicine'-'crazy/mad') ยาบ้า;
ice yaa ái ยาไอซ์

amputate V tàt àwk ตัดออก

amulet N (i.e. the ubiquitous
Buddha image amulets
worn by many Thai people,
both male and female) phrá
khrûeang พระเครื่อง

amusement park N sǔan
sà-nùk สวนสนุก

7

amusing/funny ADJ tà-lòk ตลก, or tà-lòk khòpkhǎn ตลกขบขัน

analyze v wí-khràw วิเคราะห์

ancestor N banphá-bu-rùt บรรพบุรุษ

ancient ADJ bohraan โบราณ; very old kào kàe เก่าแก่

and CONJ láe (pronounced with a very short sound of 'air') และ, or kàp กับ (most common and informal word)

anemia N loh-hìt-jaang โลหิต จาง

angel N naang fáa นางฟ้า (female), the-wá-daa เทวดา (male)

anger N khwaam kròht ความ โกรธ

Angkor/Angkor Wat ná-khawn wát (literally, 'city'-[of] 'temple(s)') นครวัด

angry ADJ kròht โกรธ, also moh-hǒh โมโห

animal N sàt สัตว์

ankle N khâw tháo ข้อเท้า

anklet N kamlai khâw tháo กำไลข้อเท้า

anniversary N khróp rawp ครบรอบ

announce v prà-kàat ประกาศ

annoy/bother v róp kuan รบกวน

annoyed ADJ ramkhaan รำคาญ

annual ADJ prà-jam pii ประจำปี

another (more) ADJ ìik… อีก…: e.g. 'another one' (as in 'another plate of food' etc. ìik jaan nùeng อีกจานหนึ่ง); a second word for 'another' is ùehn อื่น (which is used in this sense: 'another person' khon ùehn คนอื่น)

answer (response) N kham tàwp คำตอบ

answer (respond) v tàwp ตอบ

answer the phone v ráp thoh rá sàp รับโทรศัพท์

answering machine N khrûeang ràp thoh-rá-sàp เครื่องรับโทรศัพท์

ant(s) N mót มด

antenna (TV, radio) N sǎo aa-kàat เสาอากาศ

anthem N phleng cháat เพลง ชาติ

anti- PREFIX tàw-tâan ต่อต้าน

antibiotic N yaa khâa-chúea ยาฆ่าเชื้อ

8

anticipate v khâat wàng
คาดหวัง

antique(s) N khǎwng kào
ของเก่า

anus (polite/medical term)
N thawaan nàk ทวารหนัก;
(vulgar, common term) ruu
tùut (literally, 'hole'-'arse')
รูตูด

anxiety N khwaam kang-won
ความกังวล

anxious ADJ kang-won กังวล

any ADJ (the equivalent of
the English word 'any' is
generally implied in Thai
questions and responses
without any specific word as
such. For example, to say
'do you have any money?'
is khun mii ngoehn mái
[literally, 'you'-'have'-'money'-
'question marker'] คุณมีเงิน
ไหม; here there is no word
that specifically means 'any',
it is understood. To respond
'yes, I do' is simply mii มี
which means 'have'. To
answer 'no, I don't have any'
you can say either mâi mii
[literally, 'no'-'have'] ไม่มี or,

mâi mii loei [literally, 'no'-
'have'-'at all'] ไม่มีเลย. The
idea of 'any' is understood,
but not expressed as a word.
In certain limited cases,
however, there is a Thai
word that means 'any/some'.
This is used in the following
example, the same English
question asked above but
in another form in Thai: 'do
you have any/some money?'
khun mii ngoehn bâang mái
[literally, 'you'-'have'-'money'-
'any/some'-'question marker']
คุณมีเงินบ้างไหม. Here the
word bâang บ้าง may be
translated as 'any/some')

anybody, anyone (at all)
PRON (the word kâw ก็ is
pronounced very similar to
the English word 'gore', but
short and with a falling tone)
khrai kâw dâi ใครก็ได้

anyhow, anyway ADV yang-
ngai kâw taam ยังไงก็ตาม

anything (at all) ADV àrai kâw
dâi อะไรก็ได้

anywhere (at all) ADV thîi nǎi
kâw dâi ที่ไหนก็ได้

apart (from....), in addition to... PREP náwk jàak.... นอกจาก

apartment N (from English) à-páatméhn อะพาร์ตเมนต์

ape/monkey N ling ลิง

apologize to v (e.g. for stepping on someone's foot) kǎw thôht ขอโทษ

apology N (e.g. 'my apologies' – on hearing of someone's serious illness/death) sà-daeng khwaam sǐajai แสดงความเสียใจ

apparently ADV yàang hěn dâi chát อย่างเห็นได้ชัด; apparently (it seems as if...) praa-kòt wâa ปรากฏว่า

appear/become visible v praa-kòt ปรากฏ

appearance/attitude, looks N thâa thaang ท่าทาง

appendicitis N sâi-tìng àk-sèp ไส้ติ่งอักเสบ

appetizer/entrée/starter N khǎwng wâang ของว่าง

applaud v pròp-mueh ปรบมือ

apple N (from English) áep-pôen แอปเปิล

appliance N (electrical)

khrûeang fai fáa เครื่อง ไฟฟ้า

apply v (for permission) kǎw à-nú-yâat ขออนุญาต

apply v (for work/a job) sà-màk สมัคร

appointment N nát-mǎai นัด หมาย, or simply nát นัด; to have an appointment mii nát มีนัด

apprehend v (to arrest) jàp จับ, (to understand) khâo jai เข้าใจ

approach v (in space) khâo hǎa เข้าหา

approach v (in time) klâi wehlaa ใกล้เวลา

appropriate/suitable ADJ màw-sǒm เหมาะสม

approve (of something) v hěn sǒmkhuan เห็นสมควร; to approve (something) à-nú-mát อนุมัติ

approximately ADV prà-maan ประมาณ

April N meh-sǎa-yon เมษายน

apron N phâa-kan-pûean ผ้า กันเปื้อน

aquarium N phí-phít-thá-phan sàt-nám พิพิธภัณฑ์สัตว์น้ำ

10

aquatic ADJ nai náam ในน้ำ
architect N s à-tǎa-pà-ník สถาปนิก
architecture N sà-tǎa pàt-tà-yá-kam สถาปัตยกรรม
area N phúehn thîi พื้นที่, or bawrí-wehn บริเวณ
area code, post code N rá-hàt รหัส
Are you busy? PHR khun wâang mái? คุณว่างไหม
argue V thá lá-w ทะเลาะ
(NOTE: a very common Thai term meaning 'to argue/dispute an issue/contradict/talk back' is thǐang เถียง)
argument N kaan thòk thǐang การถกเถียง
arm N khǎen แขน
armpit N rák-rác รักแร้
army N kawng thá-hǎan กอง ทหาร, or commonly kawng tháp กองทัพ
aroma N (pleasant smell) klìn hǎwm กลิ่นหอม
around ADV (approximately) raow raow ราวๆ
around PREP (here, nearby) thǎew níi แถวนี้
around ADV (surrounding)

râwp râwp รอบๆ
arouse V krà-tûn กระตุ้น
arrange V jàt kaan จัดการ
arrangements N kaan jàt kaan, การจัดการ; to make plans waang phǎehn วางแผน
arrest V jàp จับ, or jàp kum จับกุม; to be arrested dohn jàp โดนจับ
arrive/reach V maa thǔeng มาถึง, or simply thǔeng ถึง
arrogant ADJ yìng หยิ่ง, or jawng hǎwng จองหอง
art N sǐnlápà ศิลปะ, or simply sǐn ศิลป์; artist sǐnlápin ศิลปิน
arthritis N rôhk kǎo โรคเกาต์
article N (in newspaper) bòt khwaam บทความ
artificial ADJ (as in an artificial limb, or copy of a brand name product) thiam เทียม
artist N sǐn-lá-pin ศิลปิน
artistic ADJ mii sǐn-lá-pà มี ศิลปะ
as ADV taam-thîi ตามที่, CONJ tawn-thîi ตอนที่
ashamed, embarrassed ADJ nâa lá-aai น่าละอาย
ashtray N thîi khìa bùrìi ที่ เขี่ยบุหรี่

11

Asia N eh-chia เอเชีย

Asian N khon eh-chia คนเอเชีย

ask V (a question) thăam ถาม,

ask about V thăam kìao kàp ถามเกี่ยวกับ, or simply thăam rûeang ถามเรื่อง

ask for, request V khăw ขอ

asleep ADJ V nawn làp นอนหลับ, or nawn นอน

ass/arse N (bottom) (COLLOQUIAL) tùut ตูด

assault V tham-rái ทำร้าย

assemble/gather together V rûap ruam รวบรวม

assemble, put together V (e.g. a bicycle) prà-kàwp ประกอบ

assess V prà-moehn ประเมิน

asset N sáp-sĭn ทรัพย์สิน

assist V chûai ช่วย

assistance N khwaam chûai lŭea ความช่วยเหลือ

association N sà-maa-khom สมาคม

as soon as CONJ (COLLOQUIAL) phaw พอ

assume V (suppose, imagine) sŏmmút สมมุติ/สมมติ

asthma N (medical condition) rôhk hàwp hùeht โรคหอบ หืด (COLLOQUIALLY) hàwp หอบ

astonished ADJ prà-làat jai ประหลาดใจ

as well ADV dûai ด้วย

at PREP thîi ที่; at home thîi bâan ที่บ้าน

athlete N (sports person, male/female) nák kii-laa นักกีฬา

athletic ADJ khăeng-raeng แข็งแรง

ATM (from English) eh-thii-em เอทีเอ็ม

atmosphere/ambience N ban-yaa-kàat บรรยากาศ

at night, nighttime N tawn klaang khuehn ตอนกลาง คืน, or simply klaang khuehn กลางคืน

atom N (from English) à-tawm อะตอม

at once, immediately ADV than thîi ทันที

at the latest, the latest ADJ lâa sùt ล่าสุด

attached file, attachment N fai thîi nâep maa ไฟล์ที่แนบ มา (NOTE: the most commonly used English terms related to computers, the Internet, etc. are generally also used in Thai – the word 'file', for example, is fai ไฟล์)

attack v (in war) johm tii โจมตี

attack v (with words) dàa wâa ด่าว่า

attain, reach, arrive v thǔeng ถึง

attempt N khwaam phá-yaa-yaam ความพยายาม

attempt/try v phá-yaa-yaam พยายาม

attend v (a party/meeting, etc.) khâo rûam เข้าร่วม

attire N chút ชุด

attitude N (opinion – formal) thàt sà ná khá tì ทัศนคติ

attorney N thá-naai-khwaam ทนายความ

attractive ADJ (appealing to the eye) nâ dueng dùut น่าดึงดูด

aubergine/eggplant N má-khǔea มะเขือ

auction v (to tender) prà-muun ประมูล

auction off v prà-muun khǎai ประมูลขาย

audience N (looking at a performance) phûu chom ผู้ชม, or phûu fang (listening to a radio broadcast, etc.) ผู้ฟัง

August N sǐng-hǎa-khom สิงหาคม

aunt N (elder sister of mother or father) pâa ป้า

aunt N (mother's younger sister) náa น้า (also 'uncle' – mother's younger brother)

aunt N (father's younger sister) aa อา (also 'uncle' – father's younger brother)

aunt N (respectful address to a mature lady) khun pâa คุณป้า

Australia N àwt sà treh lia ออสเตรเลีย

Australian N khon àwt sà treh lia คนออสเตรเลีย

authentic ADJ tháe แท้, jing จริง

author N See 'writer'

authority N (official) jâo nâa thîi เจ้าหน้าที่

authority N (power) amnâat อำนาจ

autograph N laai sen ลายเซ็น

automatic ADJ àt-tà-noh-mát อัตโนมัติ

automobile/car N rót yon รถยนต์; sedan rót kěng รถเก๋ง

autumn N rúeduu bai mái rûang ฤดูใบไม้ร่วง

available ADJ **to have** V (e.g. to sell/rent) mii มี

available, to make V jàt hâi mii... จัดให้มี...

avenue N thà-nŏn ถนน

average N (numbers) chàlìa เฉลี่ย

average, to feel V (so-so, just OK) yang-ngán ยังงั้น

avoid V lìik-lîang หลีกเลี่ยง

awake ADJ (to have woken up) tùehn láew ตื่นแล้ว

awaken V tùehn ตื่น

aware ADJ rú'n tua รู้ตัว

awareness N khwaam rúp rú'n ความรับรู้

away ADV: either the same word as 'go' pai ไป or 'leave' jàak pai จากไป

awesome ADJ sùt-yâwt สุดยอด

awful ADJ nâa-klua น่ากลัว, yâe-mâak แย่มาก (badly)

awkward ADJ ùeht-àt-jai อึดอัดใจ

ax, axe N khwăan ขวาน

B

babble V phûut phlâam พูด พล่าม

baby N thaa-rók ทารก (generally used in formal or written language; colloquially the term lûuk ลูก is used. This word is also used to refer to one's own or somebody else's children no matter their age)

babysitter N phîi lîang dèk พี่ เลี้ยงเด็ก

back N (part of body) lăng หลัง

back, rear ADJ lăng หลัง

back, to go ADV klàp pai กลับไป

backache N pùat lăng ปวดหลัง

backbone N krà-dùuk-săn-lăng กระดูกสันหลัง

background N khwam-pen-maa ความเป็นมา

back up/reverse V thŏi pai ถอยไป

backpack N (bag) pêh เป้

backward ADV thŏi lăng ถอย หลัง

bad ADJ lehw เลว, bad (e.g. food that has gone off) sĭa
เสีย

เสีย; no good mâi dii ไม่ดี;
awful/terrible/atrocious
(e.g. person, film, situation)
yâeh แย่

bad luck N (unlucky, accursed)
suai ซวย, (alternatively)
chôhk ráai โชคร้าย

bag N (paper or plastic) thǔng
ถุง

bag N (general term for bags;
also used for 'pocket' in a
garment) krà-pǎo กระเป๋า;
bag (suitcase) krà-pǎo doehn
thaang กระเป๋าเดินทาง

bake V (to be baked) òp อบ

balance N sǒm-dun สมดุล
(NOTE: the English word
'balance' is often used
with Thai pronunciation,
something like baa láan
บาลานซ์)

balcony, verandah N rá
biang ระเบียง

bald ADJ hǔa láan (literally,
'head'-'million') หัวล้าน

ball N bawn บอล (also the
common colloquial word
used to refer to football/
soccer)

balloon N lûuk pòhng ลูกโป่ง

bamboo N mái phài ไม้ไผ่

ban V hâam ห้าม

banana N klûai กล้วย

band N (of musicians) wong
don-trii วงดนตรี

bandage N phâa phan phlǎeh
ผ้าพันแผล

Bangkok N krung-thêp
กรุงเทพฯ

bank N (financial institution)
thá-naa-khaan ธนาคาร

bank N (of river) rim fàng mâeh
náam ริมฝั่งแม่น้ำ

bank account N banchii thá-
naa-khaan บัญชีธนาคาร

banknote N See 'note'

bankrupt, to go N (a
business) lóm lá-laai ล้ม
ละลาย (COLLOQUIAL) jéng เจ๊ง
(NOTE: this is also used as a
slang term meaning to be
'broken/worn out' as in 'my
mobile/cell phone is broken')

banquet N ngaan líang งาน
เลี้ยง

bar N (serving drinks) baa บาร์

barber N châang tat phǒm
ช่างตัดผม

barefoot ADJ tháo plào เท้า
เปล่า

15

barely ADV nói mâak น้อยมาก

bargain V tàw rawng ต่อรอง

bark (dog bark) V hào เห่า; to howl hăwn หอน

barren ADJ (arid, dry environment) hâeng-láeng แห้งแล้ง

barrier N sìng-kìit-khwăang สิ่งกีดขวาง, ùp-pà-sàk อุปสรรค

base, foundation N thăan ฐาน; military base thăan tháp ฐานทัพ

basic ADJ (the beginning level, elementary) bûeang tôn เบื้องต้น, or phúen-thăan พื้นฐาน

basis N thăan ฐาน

basket N tà-krâa ตะกร้า

basketball N (from English) báat-sàkèht-bawn บาสเก็ตบอล, (COLLOQUIAL) báat บาส

bastard (as in 'you bastard!' – the term given here is, in fact, considerably stronger and far more vulgar in meaning so you can use your imagination) âi-hîa ไอ้เหี้ย

bat N (animal) kháang-khaow ค้างคาว

bathe/take a bath/have a wash V àap náam อาบน้ำ

bathrobe N sûea khlum àap náam เสื้อคลุมอาบน้ำ

bathroom N hâwng náam ห้องน้ำ

bathtub N àang àap náam อ่างอาบน้ำ

battery N thàan ถ่าน, or (from English) bàet-toeh-rîi แบตเตอรี่ (COLLOQUIAL) bàet แบต

battle N kaan sûu róp การสู้รบ

bay (or gulf) N àow อ่าว (NOTE: the 'Gulf of Thailand' is àow thai อ่าวไทย)

be (at) V yùu thîi อยู่ที่

beach N chaai hàat ชายหาด

bean(s) N thùa ถั่ว

beancurd N tâo hûu เต้าหู้

bear N mĭi หมี

beard N khrao เครา

beat N (to defeat) ao cháná เอาชนะ

beat V (to strike) tii ตี

beat N (as in music, rhythm) jang-wà จังหวะ

beautiful ADJ (in appearance) sŭai สวย

beauty parlor/beauty salon N ráan sŏehm sŭai (literally, 'shop/store'-'enhance'-

16

'beauty') ร้านเสริมสวย

because conj phráw wâa เพราะว่า, or simply phráw เพราะ

become v klaai pen กลายเป็น

bed n tiang เตียง

bedbug n rûet เรือด

bedding, bedclothes n khrûeang nawn เครื่องนอน

bedroom n hâwng nawn ห้องนอน

bedsheet n phâa puu thîi nawn ผ้าปูที่นอน

bee n phûeng ผึ้ง

beef, meat/flesh n (in general) núea เนื้อ (NOTE: also common slang word for marijuana)

beehive n rang phûeng รังผึ้ง

beer n bia เบียร์

before PREP (in front of) khâang nâa ข้างหน้า

before ADV (in time) kàwn ก่อน

beg v khǎw ráwng ขอร้อง

beggar n khǎw-thaan (literally, 'request'-'things given') ขอทาน

begin v rôehm เริ่ม

beginning n tawn rôehm tôn ตอนเริ่มต้น; (COLLOQUIAL) in the beginning/at first tawn râehk

ตอนแรก

behave v (FORMAL) prà-phrúet ประพฤติ; **behavior** n khwaam prà-phrúet ความ ประพฤติ

behind PREP (location) khâang lǎng ข้างหลัง

belated ADJ lâa cháa ล่าช้า

belief, faith n khwaam chûea ความเชื่อ

believe v chûea เชื่อ

bell n rá-khang ระฆัง, krà dìng กระดิ่ง (i.e. bicycle bell)

bellboy n phá-nák-ngaan yók-krà-pǎo พนักงานยก กระเป๋า

belly n (stomach) tháwng ท้อง (NOTE: also the general way of referring to a woman falling pregnant/being pregnant)

belongings n (personal) khǎwng sùan tua ของ ส่วนตัว, (COLLOQUIAL) khâow khǎwng (literally, 'rice/food'- 'things') ข้าวของ

belong to v pen khǎwng เป็นของ: e.g. 'it belongs to him/it's his' pen khǎwng khǎo (literally, 'belong'-'him') เป็นของเขา

17

below, downstairs, beneath PREP khâang lâang ข้างล่าง

belt N khěm khàt เข็มขัด; safety belt/seatbelt (in a car) khěm khàt níráphai เข็มขัดนิรภัย

beneficial ADJ mii prà-yòht มีประโยชน์

benefit N phŏn-prà-yòht ผลประโยชน์

beside PREP khâang ข้าง, or khâang khâang ข้างๆ

besides ADV (in addition, apart from) nâwk jàak... นอกจาก

best ADJ (i.e the best) dii thîi sùt ดีที่สุด

best wishes dûai khwaam pràat-thà-nǎa dii ด้วยความปรารถนาดี

bet/gamble V lên kaan phá-nan เล่นการพนัน, or simply lên phá-nan เล่นพนัน

betel nut N màak หมาก

betray V hàk lǎng หักหลัง

better ADJ (than something else) dii kwàa ดีกว่า

better, to get ADJ (improve) dii khûen ดีขึ้น, (from an illness) khôi yang chûa ค่อยยังชั่ว

between PREP rá-wàang ระหว่าง

beverage (refreshment) N khrûeng-dùehm เครื่องดื่ม

bias N à-khá-tì อคติ

Bible N (Christian) phrá khamphii พระคัมภีร์

bicycle N (rót) jàk-krà-yaan (รถ) จักรยาน

big ADJ yài ใหญ่

bikini N (from English) chút bì-kì-nii ชุดบิกินี

bill N (as in a restaurant – from English) bin bìn บิล *Also see* under the entry for 'pay'

billion ADJ phan láan (literally, 'thousand'-'million') พันล้าน

billionaire N sèht-thǐi phan láan เศรษฐีพันล้าน (the word sèht-thǐi เศรษฐี means a 'wealthy man')

bind V phùuk ผูก, mát มัด

binoculars N klâwng sǎwng taa กล้องสองตา

biology N chii-wá-wít-thá-yaa ชีววิทยา

bird N nók นก

birth, to give V khlâwt lûuk คลอดลูก

birth certificate N sǔu-ti-bàt สูติบัตร

18

birth control pill N See 'contraceptive pill'

birthday N wan kòeht (pronounced like 'one gurt') วันเกิด

birthplace N thîi kòeht ที่เกิด

biscuit N (sweet, cookie) (from English) khúk-kîi คุกกี้

bit N (just a bit, a little bit) nìt nòi นิดหน่อย

bite v kàt กัด

bitter (taste) sǐi dam สีดำ

black ADJ sǐi dam สีดำ

black beans N thùa dam ถั่วดำ (also part of a Thai slang expression meaning gay 'anal sex' àt thùa dam อัดถั่วดำ, àt อัด = 'stuff/compress')

black eye N taa chám ตาช้ำ

black magic N See 'voodoo'

blackout, faint N pen lom เป็นลม

bladder N krà-páw phàt-sǎa-wá กระเพาะปัสสาวะ

blame v thôht โทษ

bland/tasteless ADJ jùeht จืด

blanket N phâa hòm ผ้าห่ม

bleed v sǐa lûeat (literally, 'lose'-'blood') เสียเลือด

blemish N (flaw e.g. in a jewel, a person's complexion) tam nì ตำหนิ

blend/mix v (a drink) phàsǒm ผสม

bless v ouai phawn อวยพร

blind N (person) taa bàwt ตาบอด

blink v kà phríp taa กะพริบตา

blog N/V (from English) bláwk บล็อก

blood N lûeat เลือด

blood group N mùu lûeat หมู่เลือด

blood pressure N khwaam dan lûeat ความดันเลือด, (COLLOQUIALLY, SIMPLY) khwaam dan ความดัน (NOTE: 'high blood pressure' is khwaam dan sǔung ความดันสูง; 'low blood pressure' khwaam dan tàm ความดันต่ำ)

blood test N kaan trùat lûeat การตรวจเลือด

blossom N dàwk-mái baan ดอกไม้บาน

blouse N sûea sà trii เสื้อสตรี

blow v (the wind) phát พัด

blue ADJ (sky blue) sǐi fáa สีฟ้า

Also see 'navy blue'

blunt ADJ (not sharp) thûeh ทื่อ

blur v mua มัว

blush v nâa daeng หน้าแดง

board N kràdaan กระดาน; blackboard kràdaan dam (literally, 'board'-'black') กระดานดำ *Also see* 'surfboard'

board v (bus, train) khûen ขึ้น

boarding pass N bàt khûehn khrûeang บัตรขึ้นเครื่อง

boast v (brag) ùat อวด, or ('talk big') khui móh คุยโม้

boat/ship N ruea เรือ

body N râang kaai ร่างกาย; dead body, corpse sòp ศพ

bodybuilding N (COLLOQUIAL) lên klâam (literally, 'play'-'muscle') เล่นกล้าม

boil v tôm ต้ม (NOTE: also used as slang meaning 'cheat' or 'swindle')

boiling/boiled ADJ (e.g. water) dùeat เดือด

bomb/hand grenade N lûuk rá-bòet ลูกระเบิด

bon voyage! (Have a safe trip) doehn thaang plàwt phai ná เดินทางปลอดภัยนะ

bone N krà-dùuk กระดูก

bong N (bamboo water pipe for smoking tobacco or marijuana) bâwng บ้อง, or bâwng kan-chaa บ้องกัญชา

book N nǎngsǔeh หนังสือ

bookstore N ráan nǎng-sǔeh ร้านหนังสือ

boost v phôehm เพิ่ม (FORMAL) sǒehm เสริม

boot N rawng-tháo búut รองเท้าบูท

border, edge N khàwp ขอบ

border N (between countries) chaai daehn ชายแดน

bored ADJ bùea เบื่อ

boring ADJ (a film, a person) nâa bùea น่าเบื่อ

born v kòeht (pronounced like 'gurt') เกิด

borrow v khǎw yuehm ขอยืม, or simply yuehm ยืม

boss, master N jâo-naai เจ้านาย (in short) naai นาย

bossy ADJ (COLLOQUIAL) jâo-kîi jâo-kaan เจ้ากี้เจ้าการ

both PRON (of them) tháng khûu ทั้งคู่

bother/disturb v róp-kuan รบกวน

bother, disturbance N kaan róp-kuan การรบกวน

bottle N khùat ขวด

bottom ADJ (at the bottom) khâang tâi ข้างใต้

bottom N (buttocks; also used in the broader sense to mean 'the deepest or lowest part') kôn ก้น

bouquet N châw dàwk-mái ช่อดอกไม้

bow V khóhng โค้ง (i.e. to bend the head or body to express greeting), kôm ก้ม (i.e. to lower the head quickly, as in greeting or acknowledgment)

bowl N chaam ชาม

bowling N lêhn boh-lîng เล่น โบว์ลิ่ง

box N (general term) klàwng กล่อง, (cardboard) klàwng krà-dàat กล่องกระดาษ

box V, **boxing** N (fighting) muai มวย; Thai boxing muai thai มวยไทย

boy N dèk chaai เด็กชาย

boyfriend/girlfriend N faehn แฟน

bra, brassiere N yók song ยกทรง

bracelet N kamlai mueh กำไลมือ

brag V See 'boast'

braid V thàk ถัก, N phŏm pia ผมเปีย (i.e. a length of hair that has been braided)

brain N sà-măwng สมอง

brainwash V láang sà-măwng ล้างสมอง

brake N (in a vehicle) (from English) brèhk เบรก, V yìap brèhk เหยียบเบรก (to reduce the speed)

branch N (of a bank, business franchise) săa-khăa สาขา, (of a tree) kìng-mái กิ่งไม้

brand N yîi-hâw ยี่ห้อ: also 'brand name' (from English) bran nehm แบรนด์เนม

brandy N (from English) bà-ràn-dii บรั่นดี

brass N thawng lŭeang (literally, 'gold'-'yellow') ทองเหลือง

brave/daring ADJ klâa hăan กล้าหาญ

bread, bun N khànŏm pang ขนมปัง

break V (glasses, plates) tàehk แตก; break (a leg, bones) hàk หัก

break apart v tàehk yâehk แตกแยก

break down v (car, machine) sĭa เสีย

breakfast, morning meal n aa-hăan cháo อาหารเช้า

breakfast, to eat v kin aa-hăan cháo กินอาหารเช้า

breakup n lôehk kan เลิก กัน (the discontinuance of a relationship)

breast(s) n (also chest, male or female) nâa òk หน้าอก; breasts/tits (COLLOQUIAL; also the word for 'milk') nom นม

breathe v hăai-jai หายใจ; breathe in hăai-jai khâo หายใจเข้า; breathe out hăai-jai àwk หายใจออก

breed v (of cat or dog) phan พันธุ์; 'what sort of breed is it (dog/cat etc.)?' phan àrai พันธุ์อะไร

breeze n lom àwn àwn (literally, 'wind'-'gentle') ลมอ่อนๆ

bribe n sĭn bon สินบน

bride n jâo sǎow เจ้าสาว

bridegroom n jâo bàow เจ้าบ่าว

bridge n sà-phaan สะพาน

(NOTE: the same word is used for 'bridge' in dental work); footbridge (over a busy road) sà-phaan loi (literally, 'bridge'-'float') สะพานลอย

brief ADJ sân-sân สั้นๆ

briefcase n krà-pǎo tham ngaan กระเป๋าทำงาน

bright ADJ (of light) sà-wàang สว่าง

brighten v tham hâi sà-wàang ทำให้สว่าง

bring v ao maa (literally, 'take'-'come') เอามา (Often used like this: when the object, say an umbrella (rôm ร่ม), is understood. Otherwise if you wished to say the full sentence 'bring an umbrella' it would be ao rôm maa เอา ร่มมา, i.e. ao–'umbrella'–maa)

bring up v (e.g. a topic/submit plans) sà-nǒeh เสนอ, (raise children) líang เลี้ยง

British ADJ angkrìt อังกฤษ; a British person khon angkrìt คนอังกฤษ

broad/wide/spacious ADJ kwâang กว้าง

broadcast, program n raai-

22

kaan krà-jaai sĭang รายการ
กระจายเสียง

broadcast v krà-jaai sĭang
กระจายเสียง

broadminded ADJ jai kwâang
ใจกว้าง

broccoli N (from English)
bráwk-koh-lîi บรอกโคลี

broke ADJ (SLANG; meaning 'to
have no money') See 'money'

**broken, does not work,
spoiled** ADJ sĭa เสีย,
(COLLOQUIAL) jéng เจ๊ง

broken, shattered ADJ tàehk
แตก

broken, snapped ADJ (of
bones, etc.) hàk หัก

broken hearted ADJ
(COLLOQUIAL) òk-hàk อกหัก

bronze N thawng sǎmrít ทอง
สัมฤทธิ์

broom N mái kwàat ไม้กวาด

broth, soup N náam súp
น้ำซุป

brothel N sâwng ซ่อง, or sâwng
sŏh-pheh-nii ซ่องโสเภณี

brother N (older) phîi chaai พี่
ชาย, (younger) náwng chaai
น้องชาย

brother-in-law N (older)

phîi khŏei พี่เขย, (younger)
náwng khŏei น้องเขย

brow N khíw คิ้ว

brown ADJ sĭi náamtaan สี
น้ำตาล

bruise N, to be bruised ADJ
chám ช้ำ

brush N (for scrubbing)
praehng แปรง

brush N (paint brush) phû-kan
พู่กัน

bubble N fawng ฟอง

bucket/bin N thǎng ถัง

Buddha N (The Lord) phrá
phút-thá-jâo พระพุทธเจ้า

Buddhism N sàat-sà-nǎaphút
ศาสนาพุทธ

Buddhist(s) N chaow phút
ชาวพุทธ

buddy N (friend) phûean เพื่อน

budget N ngóp prà-maan งบ
ประมาณ

buffalo N (water buffalo)
khwaai ควาย

buffet N (from English) búp-
fêh บุฟเฟ่ต์

bug N má-laeng แมลง

build v sâang สร้าง

building N (made of brick/
stone) tùek ตึก

23

bull N wua tua phûu วัวตัวผู้

bully V klâeng แกล้ง (treat somebody badly), N nák leng นักเลง (a thug)

bump V chon ชน

burden N phaa-rá ภาระ

bureaucrat/public servant N khâa râat-chákaan ข้าราชการ

burglar N khà-mohi ขโมย

Burma N phá-mâa พม่า; also Myanmar mian-mâa เมียนมาร์

Burmese N (person) chaow phá-mâa ชาวพม่า, or khon phá-mâa คนพม่า; Burmese (language) phaa-sǎa phá-mâa ภาษาพม่า

burn N (injury) phlǎeh mâi แผลไหม้, V phǎo เผา

burp V roeh เรอ

bury V fǎng ฝัง

bus N (the general term for bus, non-airconditioned, is either) rót meh รถเมล์ or rót bút (from the English 'bus') รถบัส. An airconditioned bus or coach is commonly referred to as a rót thua รถทัวร์, or 'tour bus'.

bush N phûm-mái พุ่มไม้

bus station N (COLLOQUIAL) sá-thǎa-nii-khǒn-sòng สถานีขนส่ง (literally, 'transport'- 'send')

business N thú-rá-kìt ธุรกิจ

businessperson N nák thú-rá-kìt นักธุรกิจ

busy ADJ (bothersome – e.g. in a busy work environment where there is no let up) yûng ยุ่ง, (crowded and noisy) wûn waai วุ่นวาย, (telephone) sǎai mâi wâang สายไม่ว่าง

but CONJ tàeh แต่

butter N noei เนย

butterfly N phǐi sûea ผีเสื้อ

button N krà-dum กระดุม

buy V súeh ซื้อ

by PREP (created by name of author/artist) dohy โดย

bye, goodbye INTERJ (from English) báai-baai บ้ายบาย, sà-wàt-dii สวัสดี

by means of PREP dûai wíthii... ด้วยวิธี

by the way, in addition ADV nâwk jàak níi นอกจากนี้ furthermore iik yàang nùeng อีกอย่างหนึ่ง

C

cab N (taxi cab) rót tháek-sîi รถแท็กซี่

cabbage N kàlàm plii กะหล่ำปลี, (Chinese cabbage) phàk kàat khǎow ผักกาดขาว

café N ráan kaa-faeh (literally, 'shop'-'coffee') ร้านกาแฟ

cafeteria N rohng aa-hǎan โรงอาหาร

cake N khànǒm khéhk (khéhk from English 'cake') ขนมเค้ก

calculate V khamnuan คำนวณ

calculator N khrûeang khít lêhk เครื่องคิดเลข

calendar N pà-tì-thin ปฏิทิน

calf N (lower leg) nâwng น่อง

call, summon V rîak เรียก

called, named V chûeh ชื่อ

calm, peaceful ADJ sà-ngòp สงบ

Cambodia N khà-měhn เขมร

Cambodian/Khmer N chaow khà-měhn ชาวเขมร, or khon khà-měhn คนเขมร, (language) phaa-sǎa khà-měhn ภาษาเขมร

camel N ùut อูฐ

camera N klâwng thài rûup กล้องถ่ายรูป

camp N khâai ค่าย, (from English) kháem แคมป์; V khâo khâai เข้าค่าย, tâng kháem ตั้งแคมป์

campus N wít-thá-yaa-khèht วิทยาเขต (other institution), má-hǎa-wít-thá-yaa-lai มหาวิทยาลัย (a college or university)

can, be able to, capable sǎa-mâat สามารถ, (COLLOQUIAL) …dâi …ได้ (put at the end of a sentence)

can/tin N krà-pǎwng กระป๋อง

canal N khlong คลอง

cancel V yók lôehk ยกเลิก

cancer N má-reng มะเร็ง

candid ADJ jing-jai จริงใจ

candidate N phûu sà-màk ผู้สมัคร

candle N thian เทียน

candy, toffee, sweets N (from English) táwp-fîi ทอฟฟี่; a sweet/lolly you suck on lûuk om ลูกอม

cane N mái tháo ไม้เท้า

canvas N phâa bai ผ้าใบ

canyon N hùp khǎo หุบเขา

25

cap N mùak หมวก

capability N khwaam săa mâat ความสามารถ

capital N (money, funds for investment) thun ทุน; capitalist/entrepreneur naai thun นายทุน

capitol N (city of a country, state) mueang lŭang เมืองหลวง

captain N kàp tan กัปตัน

caption N kham ban yaai phâap คำบรรยายภาพ

capture V (arrest) jàp จับ

car, automobile N rót รถ

card N (as in a credit card, name card, etc.) bàt บัตร (pronounced in a very similar way to the English word 'but'). *Also see* 'ID (identity card)'

cardboard N krà-dàat khăeng กระดาษแข็ง

cards N (game) phâi ไพ่; to play cards lên phâi เล่นไพ่

career N aa-chîip อาชีพ

care for, to love and V rák láe ao-jai sài รักและเอาใจ ใส่, also: take care ték khae (from English; COLLOQUIAL) เทค แคร์ (Also note: 'I don't care'

phŏm/chăn mâi khae ผม/ ฉันไม่แคร์)

care of (a child), to take V duu-laeh ดูแล

careful, cautious ADJ ra-wang ระวัง

careless ADJ mâi rá-mát rá-wang ไม่ระมัดระวัง, or sà-phrâo สะเพร่า

carpenter N châang máai ช่างไม้

carpet N phrom พรม

carrot N (from English) khaeràwt แครอต

carry V (largish or heavy objects, e.g. suitcase) hîu หิ้ว

cart N (street vendor pushcart, supermarket trolley, pram) rót khĕn รถเข็น

cartoon N (from English) kaa tuun การ์ตูน

carve V (a piece of meat) cham-làe ชำแหละ, or simply lâeh แล่, (a statue) kàe sàlàk แกะสลัก

case N (box) klàwng กล่อง

cash N (money) ngoehn sòt เงินสด

cash a check V lâehk chék แลกเช็ค

26

cashew N (nut) mét má-mûang hǐm-má-phaan เม็ดมะม่วงหิมพานต์; (COLLOQUIALLY) mét má-mûang เม็ดมะม่วง

cast N fùeak เฝือก

casual ADJ (for informal wear) lam-lawng ลำลอง, (without formality) mâi pen thaang kaan ไม่เป็นทางการ

cat N maew แมว

catch N (a ball; to arrest) jàp จับ

category N prà phêht ประเภท

catfish N plaa-dùk ปลาดุก

cauliflower N dàwk kà-làm ดอกกะหล่ำ

cause N (the cause of something) sǎa-hèht สาเหตุ

cave N thâm ถ้ำ

cavity N (hole) lǔm หลุม, (a pit in a tooth) fan-phù ฟันผุ

CD N (from English) sii dii ซีดี

ceiling N pheh-daan เพดาน

celebrate V chà-lǎwng ฉลอง

celebrity N khon dang คนดัง

celery N ceh-loeh-rîi เซเลอรี่

cell phone N thoh-rá-sàp-mueh thǔeh โทรศัพท์มือถือ, commonly referred to in speech as mueh thǔeh มือถือ

censor V (from English) sen-sôeh เซ็นเซอร์

center/centre, middle N trong klaang ตรงกลาง, or simply klaang กลาง

center N (of city) klaang mueang กลางเมือง

central N sǔun klaang ศูนย์กลาง (Note the use of central in 'central Thailand' – i.e. the middle and most populous region of Thailand spreading out in all directions from Bangkok. The 'central region' as it is known is referred to as phâak klaang ภาคกลาง.) *Also see* 'region'. It should be pointed out that Central Thai, also referred to as Bangkok Thai, is the official national language used in all forms of media and the education system. 'Central Thai' is known as phasǎa klaang (literally, 'language'-'centre/middle') ภาษากลาง

century N sàtà-wát ศตวรรษ

27

cereal N (from English) sii-
rîaw ซีเรียล, than-yá-phûeht
ธัญพืช

ceremony N phí-thii พิธี

certain, sure ADJ nâeh jai
แน่ใจ, or nâeh nawn แน่นอน

certainly ADV nâeh nawn
แน่นอน

certificate N prà-kàat-sànii-
yábàt ประกาศนียบัตร

chain N sôh โซ่

chair N kâo-îi เก้าอี้

challenge V tháa thaai ท้าทาย

champion N (from English)
cháehm-pîan แชมเปี้ยน

chance, opportunity N
oh-kàat โอกาส

chance, by ADV dohy bang-
oen โดยบังเอิญ

change, small N sèht
sà-taang เศษสตางค์, (MORE
COLLOQUIAL) sèht tang เศษตังค์

change V (conditions,
situations, clothes, plans)
plìan เปลี่ยน

change, exchange
(money) lâehk plìan แลก
เปลี่ยน (NOTE: for 'change or
exchange money' you would
say lâehk ngoehn แลกเงิน,

and for 'change clothes'
plìan sûeaphâa เปลี่ยน
เสื้อผ้า)

change one's mind V plìan
jai เปลี่ยนใจ

channel N châwng thaang
ช่องทาง

chaos N khwaam wûn waai
ความวุ่นวาย

chapter N bòt บท, tawn ตอน

character N (personality)
(FORMAL) bùk-khá-lík
ลักษณะ บุคลิกลักษณะ, (MORE
COLLOQUIALLY) ní-sǎi นิสัย

character, letter N (from an
alphabet) tua àksǎwn ตัว
อักษร, also (COLLOQUIALLY) tua
nǎngsǔeh ตัวหนังสือ

characteristic, qualities N
láksana ลักษณะ

charge V (to energize a
storage battery) cháat bàet
ชาร์จแบต, (demand a price)
khít-ngoehn คิดเงิน

charity N kaan kùson การกุศล

charming ADJ mii sà-nèh มี
เสน่ห์

chase V lâi taam ไล่ตาม

chase away/chase out V lâi
pai ไล่ไป

28

chat v khui คุย

cheap ADJ (in price) thùuk ถูก

cheat v kohng โกง

cheat, cheater N khon kohng คนโกง; someone who habitually cheats khon khîi kohng คนขี้โกง

check/verify v trùat sàwp ตรวจสอบ

checked N (pattern) laai màak rúk ลายหมากรุก

checkup N trùat râang-kaai ตรวจร่างกาย

cheek N kâem แก้ม

cheers! INTERJ (Hooray!) chai yoh ไชโย

cheese N noei khǎeng เนยแข็ง

chef N phâw khrua (literally, 'father'-'kitchen') พ่อครัว FEM mâeh khrua (literally, 'mother'-'kitchen') แม่ครัว

chemist N (pharmacy) ráan khǎai yaa ร้านขายยา; chemist (proprietor of pharmacy) phehsàt-chá-kawn เภสัชกร; chemist (scientist) nák khehmii นักเคมี

chess N màak rúk หมากรุก

chest N (box) hìip หีบ, (breast) nâa òk หน้าอก

chew v khíao เคี้ยว; chewing gum màak fàrang หมากฝรั่ง (NOTE: the choice of words: literally, 'betel nut' - 'foreign/western' – i.e. 'foreign betel nut')

chicken N kài ไก่

child N dèk เด็ก (NOTE: also generally used to refer to very junior staff in a work environment i.e. subordinates), offspring lûuk ลูก

chili N (pepper) phrík พริก

chili sauce N sáwt phrík ซอสพริก

chilled ADJ châeh yen แช่เย็น

chilly ADJ (weather) nǎow หนาว

chin N khaang คาง

China N mueang jiin (pronounced like 'jean') เมืองจีน

Chinese N khon jiin คนจีน, (language) phaa-sǎa jiin ภาษาจีน

Chinese New Year (celebrated on differing dates from later January until around the middle of February) trùt jiin ตรุษจีน

chip N (as in computer chip) (from English) chip ชิป

chip(s) N *See* 'French fries'

chocolate N (from English) cháwk-koh-láet ช็อกโกแลต

choke v (on something) sǎm-lák สำลัก, (someone) bìip khaw (literally, 'squeeze' –'neck/throat') บีบคอ

cholera N rôhk à-hì-waa โรค อหิวาต์

cholesterol N khǎi man nai lûeat (literally, 'fat'-'in'- 'blood') ไขมันในเลือด

choose v lûeak เลือก; choice thaang lûeak ทางเลือก

chop/mince v sàp สับ

chopsticks N tà-kìap ตะเกียบ

chore N ngaan bâan งานบ้าน

Christ, Jesus N phrá yeh-suu พระเยซู

Christian N khrís-tian คริสเตียน; Christian(s) chaaw khrít ชาวคริสต์

Christianity N sàatsà-nǎa khrít ศาสนาคริสต์

Christmas N khrít-sà-mâat คริสต์มาส

church N bòht โบสถ์

cigar N síkâa ซิการ์

cigarette N bùrìi บุหรี่

cigarette lighter N fai cháek ไฟแช็ค

cinema N rohng nǎng โรงหนัง

cinnamon N (spice) òb-choei อบเชย

circle N (shape) wong klom วงกลม

circle N (traffic) wong-wian วงเวียน

circumstance N sà-thǎan-ná-kaan สถานการณ์

citizen N prà-chaachon ประชาชน, or phon-lá-mueang พลเมือง

citrus: orange N sôm ส้ม; lemon má-naow มะนาว

city, large town N mueang เมือง

civilization N (from English) sìwílai ศิวิไลซ์, or aa-ráyá-tham อารยธรรม

claim v rîak ráwng เรียกร้อง (to demand), âang อ้าง (to state to be true)

clap v tòp mueh ตบมือ

class, category N chán ชั้น, or prà-phêht ประเภท

classroom N hâwng rian ห้องเรียน

clean ADJ sà-àat สะอาด

clean v (e.g. the bathroom) tham khwaam sà-àat ทำความสะอาด

cleanliness N khwaam sà-àat ความสะอาด

clear ADJ (water, soup, liquid) săi ใส, (of weather) plàwt pròhng ปลอดโปร่ง

clearly ADV (to see something clearly, to speak clearly) chát ชัด (NOTE: it is a genuine compliment in Thai when someone says you speak the language 'clearly' phûut thai chát (literally, 'speak'-'Thai'- 'clear[ly]') พูดไทยชัด

clever ADJ chà-làat ฉลาด, or kèng เก่ง

client/customer N lûuk-kháa ลูกค้า

climate N ban-yaa-kàat บรรยากาศ

climb v (a tree, a hill, a mountain) tài ไต่, or piin ปีน

clinic N (from English) khlii- nìk คลินิก

clitoris N mét lá-mút เม็ด

ละมุด, (SLANG) mét tháp-tim เม็ดทับทิม, (EXTREMELY VULGAR) tàet แตด

clock N (or a watch) naalí- kaa นาฬิกา (NOTE: also term meaning 'hour' in the 24 hour system of time keeping i.e. 15 hours = 3 p.m.)

close/near ADJ klâi ใกล้

close v (to close a door), **cover** v (to cover something, to put a lid on a jar) pìt ปิด

closet N tûu sûea phâa ตู้เสื้อผ้า

close together, stuck together ADV tìt kan ติดกัน

cloth N phâa ผ้า

clothes, clothing N sûea phâa เสื้อผ้า

cloud N mêhk เมฆ

cloudy, overcast ADJ mûeht khrúem มืดครึ้ม, or simply mii mêhk (literally, 'have'- 'cloud[s]') มีเมฆ

cloves N kaan phluu กานพลู

club, association N sà-moh- sǎwn สโมสร

clumsy ADJ sûm sâam ซุ่มซ่าม

coach N (a bus used for long- distance service) rót thua รถ

31

coarse ADJ (to the touch) yàap หยาบ, (vulgar, crude manner) yàap khaai หยาบคาย

coast N (of the sea) chaai tháleh ชายทะเล

coat N (jacket) sûea jáek-kèt เสื้อแจ็คเก็ต, (overcoat) sûea nâwk เสื้อนอก

cockroach N (COLLOQUIAL) má-laehng-sàap แมลงสาบ

cocky ADJ yîng หยิ่ง

cocoa N koh-kôh โกโก้

coconut N má-phráo มะพร้าว; young coconut má-phráo àwn มะพร้าวอ่อน; coconut milk/cream (used in curries) kà-thí กะทิ

coffee N kaa-faeh กาแฟ: black coffee kaa-faeh dam (literally, 'coffee'-'black') กาแฟดำ; white coffee kaa-faeh sài nom (literally, 'coffee'-'put'-'milk') กาแฟใส่นม

coin N rían เหรียญ

cold ADJ (drink) yen เย็น

cold N (common cold) wàt หวัด; to have a cold pen wàt เป็นหวัด

cold ADJ (weather) năow หนาว

collapse V phang พัง (break down), lôm ล้ม (fall down)

colleague, coworker N phûean rûam ngaan เพื่อนร่วมงาน

collect N (a parcel, a present, etc.) ráp รับ

college N wít-thá-yaa-lai วิทยาลัย

collide V chon ชน

collision N kaan chon การชน

color N sĭi สี (also the word for the noun 'paint')

colorblind ADJ taa bàwt sĭi ตาบอดสี

colorful ADJ mii sĭi săn มีสีสัน

comb N wĭi หวี

combine V ruam รวม; combine with ruam kàp รวมกับ; join together rûam kan ร่วมกัน

come V maa มา

come back V klàp maa กลับมา

come in V (enter) khâo maa เข้ามา

comedian N tua tà-lòk ตัวตลก

comedy N rûeang tà-lòk เรื่องตลก, or simply tà-lòk ตลก

(which also means 'funny')

comfortable ADJ sàbaai สบาย (a key Thai term which means something like 'relaxed and comfortable', a highly desirable state [often also used with the implicit sense of without worry or concern]). Two very common expressions meaning 'Are you feeling comfortable/ Are you feeling well/How do you feel? [generally asked with the expectation that the answer will be yes] are khun sàbaai dii rǔeh คุณสบายดี หรือ, khun sàbaai dii mái คุณสบายดีไหม

command, order N kham sàng คำสั่ง

command v (or, to order food in a restaurant) sàng สั่ง

commercial N khôht-sà-naa โฆษณา

common, ordinary ADJ tham-màdaa ธรรมดา

communicate v (with someone) sùeh-sǎan สื่อสาร

community N chum chon ชุมชน

company, firm N bawrí-sàt บริษัท

compare v prìap thîap เปรียบ เทียบ

compared with v prìap kàp เปรียบกับ

compel v (to force) bangkháp บังคับ

compensate v (to make up for) chót choei ชดเชย

compete v khàeng แข่ง

competition N (contest) kaan khàeng khǎn การแข่งขัน

complain v bòn บ่น; a grouchy/cranky person given to complaining khon khîi bòn คนขี้บ่น

complaint N kham ráwng thúk คำร้องทุกข์

complete ADJ (accomplished) sǎmrèt สำเร็จ, or simply sèt เสร็จ, (thorough) dohy sîn choehng โดยสิ้นเชิง, (to make whole) sǒmbuun สม บูรณ์, or khróp thûan ครบ ถ้วน

complete v tham hâi sèt ทำให้เสร็จ

completely ADV yàang sǒmbuun อย่างสมบูรณ์

33

complicated/complex ADJ (a piece of machinery, a relationship) sáp sáwn ซับซ้อน

compose, write V (letters, books, music) tàeng แต่ง, or khĭan เขียน

composition, writings N kaan tàeng การแต่ง, kaan khĭan การเขียน

compromise V prà-nii prà-nawm ประนีประนอม

compulsory/mandatory ADJ bangkháp บังคับ

computer N (from English) khawm-phiu-tôeh คอมพิวเตอร์, or (COLLOQUIALLY) khawm คอม (NOTE: a laptop computer is [from the English 'notebook'] notébúk โน้ตบุ๊ค.) Also see 'tablet PC'

concentrate V (think) mii sà-maa-thí มีสมาธิ, or ao jai sài เอาใจใส่

concentrated ADJ (liquid, substance) khêm khôn เข้มข้น

concept N khwaam khít ความคิด

concern N khwaam kang

won ความกังวล

concerned ADJ pen hùang เป็นห่วง,

concerning PREP kìao kàp เกี่ยวกับ

conclude V sà-rùp สรุป

concrete N rûup-pà-tham รูปธรรม, khawn krìt คอนกรีต (construction material)

condition/proviso N ngûean-khăi เงื่อนไข

condition N (of a secondhand car) sà-phâap สภาพ, (symptom, indication, state, e.g. when discussing sickness, illness) aa-kaan อาการ

condom N thŭng yang ถุงยาง, (from English) khawn-dâwm คอนดอม

condominium N (condo) (from English) khawndoh-mi-nîam (khondo) คอนโดมิเนียม (คอนโด)

confectionery/sweets N khànŏm wǎan ขนมหวาน

confess V (admit something) yawm ráp ยอมรับ

conference N See 'meeting'

confidence N khwaam mân-

jai ความมั่นใจ (i.e. having confidence mii khwaam mân-jai มีความมั่นใจ)

confident ADJ mân-jai มั่นใจ

confirm v yuehn yan ยืนยัน

Confucianism N lát-thí khǒng júeh ลัทธิขงจื๊อ

confuse v sàp sŏn สับสน

confused ADJ (in a mess) yûng yǒehng ยุ่งเหยิง, (filled with confusion) sàp sŏn สับสน, (perplexed) ngong งง

confusing ADJ nâa sàpsŏn น่าสับสน

congratulations! INTERJ (I congratulate you) khǎw sà-daehng khwaam yin-dii dûai ขอแสดงความยินดีด้วย, or (in short) yin-dii-dûai ยินดีด้วย

connect v tàw ต่อ, (together) tìt tàw kan ติดต่อกัน

connection(s) N (SLANG) sên เส้น, (COLLOQUIAL) to have connections with people of influence mii sên มีเส้น, (FORMAL) khwaam sǎm phan ความสัมพันธ์

conscious ADJ mii sà-tì มีสติ; be aware rúu tua รู้ตัว

conscious of, to be rúu sǎmnúek รู้สำนึก

consent v yin yawm ยินยอม

consider v (consider an issue) phí-jaa-rá-naa พิจารณา, (to think over) phí-jaa-rá-naa พิจารณา, or trài trawng ไตร่ตรอง

considerate ADJ khreng-jai เกรงใจ

constipation N to be constipated ADJ tháwng phùuk (literally, 'stomach'-'tie/tied') ท้องผูก

constitution N rát-thá-thammá-nuun รัฐธรรมนูญ

construct v sâang สร้าง

consult, talk over with v prùek sǎa ปรึกษา

contact, get in touch with v tìt tàw ติดต่อ

content N nûea hǎa เนื้อหา

contest v prà-kùat ประกวด

context N bawrí-bòt บริบท

continent N thá-wîip ทวีป

continue v tham tàw pai ทำต่อไป

contraceptive N (pill) (COLLOQUIAL) yaa khum ยาคุม

contract N (legal) sǎn-yaa

สัญญา (Note: the same word also means 'to promise')

contrast N khwaam taek tàang ความแตกต่าง

control v (something) khûapkhum ควบคุม

convenient ADJ sà-dùak สะดวก

conversation N (COLLOQUIAL) phûut khui พูดคุย

converse v (FORMAL) sŏn-thá-naa สนทนา, (COLLOQUIAL) to chat khui คุย

convince v tham hâi chûea ทำให้เชื่อ

cook N (person) khon tham aa-hăan คนทำอาหาร; also (from English) khúk กุ๊ก, or simply (COLLOQUIAL) M phâw krua พ่อครัว F mâeh krua แม่ครัว

cook v tham aa-hăan ทำอาหาร

cooked ADJ (also, of fruit, 'to be ripe') sùk สุก

cooker N (charcoal)/**stove** N (oven) tao เตา

cookie, sweet biscuit N (from English) khúk-kîi คุกกี้

cool ADJ yen เย็น

cool v (e.g. in a fridge) châeh yen แช่เย็น

cool ADJ (COLLOQUIAL – as in 'hip', 'trendy') têh เท่, or kĕh เก๋

cop N (police) tam-rùat ตำรวจ

copper N (metal) thawng daehng ทองแดง

copy v (imitate) lian bàep เลียนแบบ

copy N (e.g. a photocopy) sămnao สำเนา; v make a photocopy thàai èkkà-săan ถ่ายเอกสาร, or simply (from English) 'copy' kóp-pîi ก๊อปปี้

copyright N lík-khá-sìt ลิขสิทธิ์

coral N hĭn pà-kaa-rang หิน ปะการัง, or simply pà-kaa-rang ปะการัง

coriander, cilantro N phàk chii ผักชี

corn N khâaw phôht ข้าวโพด

corner N mum มุม

cornstarch N pâeng khâaw phôht แป้งข้าวโพด

corpse N (dead body) sòp ศพ

correct/to be right ADJ (answer to a question) thùuk tâwng ถูกต้อง

correct v (a mistake/error) kâeh แก้

correspond v (write letters, email) khĭan jòtmăai เขียน จดหมาย, khĭan ii-mehl เขียนอีเมล์

correspondent/reporter/ journalist N phûu sùeh khàaw ผู้สื่อข่าว, or nák khàaw นักข่าว

corridor N thaang doehn nai tùek ทางเดินในตึก

corrupt v thút-jà-rìt ทุจริต

cosmetics N See 'makeup'

cosmetic surgery N See 'plastic surgery'

cost(s) N (i.e. expenses) khâa chái jàai ค่าใช้จ่าย, (price) raa-khaa ราคา: How much does it/this cost?/What's the price? raa-khaa thâo-rài ราคาเท่าไร

costume N sûea phâa เสื้อผ้า

cotton N fâai ฝ้าย

cotton wool N săm-lii สำลี

couch, sofa N (from English) soh-faa โซฟา

cough v ai ไอ

could, might AUX v àat jà อาจ จะ: (e.g. he could/might go

khăo àat jà pai เขาอาจจะไป)

count, to v náp นับ

country (nation) prà-thêht ประเทศ; Thailand prà-thêht thai ประเทศไทย

country/countryside N (FORMAL) chon-ná-bòt ชนบท, (COLLOQUIAL) bâan nâwk บ้าน นอก

coup d'etat N rát-prà-hăan (literally, 'state'-'execute') รัฐประหาร

courgette, zucchini N suu-kì-nii ซูกินี

court N (of law) săan ศาล

cousin N lûuk phîi lûuk náwng ลูกพี่ลูกน้อง

cover v pìt ปิด, or khlum คลุม

cow N wua วัว

coworker, colleague N phûean rûam ngaan เพื่อน ร่วมงาน

cozy ADJ sà-baai สบาย

crab N puu ปู

cracked ADJ roi tàehk รอยแตก

cracker/salty biscuit N khà-nŏmpang kràwp ขนม ปังกรอบ

crafts N ngaan fĭi-mueh งาน ฝีมือ

craftsperson/craftsman N châang fǐi-mueh ช่างฝีมือ

cramp N (muscle pain in arm/ leg) tà-kriu ตะคริว; to have a cramp tà-kriu kin ตะคริว กิน; a stomach cramp tháwng jùk ท้องจุก

cranky ADJ aa-rom-sǐa อารมณ์เสีย

crash/bump V (into) chon ชน; car crash rót chon รถ ชน; crash helmet/motorcycle helmet (COLLOQUIAL) mùak kan nók หมวกกันน็อก

crate N lang mái ลังไม้

crazy, mad ADJ bâa-bâa baw-baw บ้าๆ บอๆ, or simply bâa บ้า, also (COLLOQUIAL TERM) ting-táwng ติงต๊อง (NOTE: a crazy/mad person is khon bâa คนบ้า)

cream N (from English) khriim ครีม

create/build V sâang สร้าง

creature N (an animal) sàt สัตว์, (a human) khon คน

credit N (from English) khreh-dìt เครดิต, nâa chûeae thǔeh น่าเชื่อถือ

criminal N (FORMAL) àat-yaa- kawn อาชญากร, (COLLOQUIAL) phûu-rái ผู้ร้าย

crisis N wí-khrìt วิกฤต

critical ADJ sǎm khan สำคัญ

criticism N kaan wí jaan การ วิจารณ์

crocodile/alligator N jawrá-khê จระเข้

crook N (a cheat) khon khîi kohng คนขี้โกง

cross/angry ADJ kròht โกรธ, or moh hǒh โมโห

cross, go over V (the road) khâam ข้าม

crosswalk N (COLLOQUIAL) thaang máa laai ทางม้าลาย

crow N (bird) kaa กา

crowded/congested; tight ADJ (to grip someone's hand tightly, to feel stuffed after eating a lot of food, etc.) nâen แน่น

crown N (as in dental work) khrâwp fan ครอบฟัน (NOTE: fan ฟัน or 'tooth' is pronounced like the English word 'fun')

cruel ADJ hòht rái โหดร้าย

crush V bòt บด, bìip-àt บีบอัด

crush on V (SLANG) àep-châwp

แอบชอบ

cry v (with tears) ráwng hâi
ร้องไห้, (cry out) ráwng ร้อง,
(shout) tà-kohn ตะโกน

cucumber N taeng kwaa
แตงกวา

cuisine, food N aa-hăan
อาหาร; style of cooking/
cuisine, e.g. Chinese food/
cuisine aa-hăan jiin อาหาร
จีน

culture N wát-thá-ná-tham
วัฒนธรรม

cup N thûai ถ้วย

**cupboard, wardrobe, chest
of drawers** N tûu ตู้

cure/treat v (an illness) ráksăa
รักษา

cured, preserved, pickled
ADJ (fruit) dawng ดอง

curious ADJ yàak rúu yàak
hĕn (literally, 'want know'-
'want see') อยากรู้อยากเห็น,
or simply sŏng-săi สงสัย

curly ADJ (as in 'curly hair') See
'frizzy'

currency (FORMAL) ngoehn traa
เงินตรา, (SIMPLY COLLOQUIAL)
ngoehn 'money' เงิน

curry N kaeng แกง

curtains, drapes N mâan
ม่าน

curve N (a line) sên khôhng
เส้นโค้ง, (a road) thaang khóhng
ทางโค้ง

cushion N (pillow) măwn
หมอน

custom/tradition N prà-
pheh-nii ประเพณี, or tham-
niam ธรรมเนียม

customer/client N lûuk kháa
ลูกค้า

cut/slice v hàn หั่น

cut v tàt ตัด, N phlăe (a wound
cut by a knife) See 'knife'

cute/appealing ADJ nâa rák
น่ารัก

cycling N khìi jàk-krà-yaan
ขี่จักรยาน

D

dad/father N (COLLOQUIAL) phâw
พ่อ, (MORE FORMAL) bì-daa บิดา

daily ADV (in the sense of a
regular activity) prà-jam-wan
ประจำวัน, (every day) thúk
wan ทุกวัน

dam N khùean เขื่อน

damage v (i.e. to be damaged)

chamrút ชำรุด, or sĭa hăi เสียหาย, (SIMPLY COLLOQUIAL) phang พัง, (to cause damage to) tham hâi chamrút ทำให้ชำรุด

damp/humid ADJ chúeh ชื้น

dance v tên ram เต้นรำ, or simply tên เต้น

dandruff v rang-khaeh รังแค

danger/dangerous ADJ an-tà-raai อันตราย

dark ADJ mûehd มืด

dark blue ADJ See 'navy blue'

dark skin N (in colloquial Thai it is common to use the abbreviated word for 'black' dam ดำ even for someone many westerners would consider to have a moderate tan) 'Dark skin' phĭu dam ผิว ดำ or phĭu klám ผิวคล้ำ

darling/my love N (expression of affection) thîi rák ที่รัก

date N (of the month) wan thîi วันที่

date of birth N wan duean pii kòeht (literally, 'day'-'month'- 'year'-'birth') วันเดือนปีเกิด

daughter N lûuk săow ลูกสาว

daughter-in-law N lûuk

sà-phái ลูกสะใภ้

dawn N cháo trùu เช้าตรู่

day N wan วัน; today wan níi วันนี้; yesterday mûea waan (níi) เมื่อวาน(นี้)

day after tomorrow ADV mà-ruehn (níi) มะรืน(นี้)

day before yesterday ADV mûeawaan suehn níi เมื่อ วานซืน (นี้)

day-care center N sà-thăan-líang-dèk สถานเลี้ยงเด็ก

daydream v făn klaang wan ฝันกลางวัน

daylight N săeng dàet แสงแดด

day off N (also used for 'holiday', i.e. day off work) wan yùt วันหยุด

daytime N klaang wan กลาง วัน

dead ADJ (COLLOQUIAL) taai láew ตายแล้ว, (MORE FORMAL) sĭa láew เสียแล้ว; death khwaam taai ความตาย

deaf ADJ hŭu nùak หูหนวก

dear N thîi rák ที่รัก

debate v tôh waa thii โต้วาที, tôh yáeng โต้แย้ง

debt(s) N nîi sĭn หนี้สิน

decade N thót-sà-wát ทศวรรษ

decay v nâo pùeay เน่าเปื่อย
(rot), phù ผุ (i.e. tooth decay)

deceive v làwk-luang หลอก
ลวง (in colloquial speech
the single word làwk หลอก
is used)

December N than-waa-khom
ธันวาคม

decide v tàt-sĭn jai ตัดสินใจ

decision N kaan tàt-sĭn jai
การตัดสินใจ

decisive ADJ (to act decisively)
dèt-khàat เด็ดขาด

decline/decrease/get less v
lót long ลดลง

decline/refuse/deny v pàtì-
sèht ปฏิเสธ

decorate v tòk tàeng ตกแต่ง

deejay N (DJ or 'disk jockey'
playing music on the radio
or in a club etc.) dii jeh
(pronounced very similar to
the English) ดีเจ

deep ADJ lúek ลึก

defeat v (someone else, i.e.
to win) ao chá-ná เอาชนะ, or
simply chá-ná ชนะ

defeated ADJ (beaten, lose a
contest) pháeh แพ้

defecate v (POLITE) thàai ถ่าย,
(COLLOQUIAL; the first of the
following two terms is more
appropriate in general) ùeh อึ,
khîi ขี้ (NOTE: the word khîi ขี้
which is the common way of
referring to feces should not
be thought of as equivalent
to the English term 'shit'; khîi
is not a vulgar word and such
bodily functions are often
talked of by Thai people in an
unself-conscious, matter-of-
fact way)

defect N (or fault in something)
khâw bòk phrâwng ข้อ
บกพร่อง

defend v (in war), protect
v (oneself or somebody
else), also to prevent v (the
outbreak of disease) pâwng
kan ป้องกัน

define v hâi khwaam măai
ให้ความหมาย

definite ADJ nâeh nawn แน่นอน

**deformed/crippled/
disabled** ADJ phí-kaan พิการ

degree, level, standard N
(e.g. 'high standard') rá-dàp
ระดับ

41

degree N (awarded by college or university) pà-rin-yaa ปริญญา

degree(s) N (temperature) ongsǎa องศา

dehydrate V khàat náam ขาดน้ำ

delay V tham hâi lâa cháa ทำให้ล่าช้า

delayed ADJ lâa cháa ล่าช้า

delete/rub out V lóp àwk ลบออก

delicate ADJ (fine, detailed work/craftsmanship) lá-ìat ละเอียด, prà-nìit ประณีต, (constitution/not strong) àwn-aeh อ่อนแอ

delicious/tasty ADJ àròi อร่อย

delinquent N (SLANG) dèk wáen เด็กแว้น, or dèk sakói เด็กสก๊อย (young members of motorcycle gangs); jìk-kǒh จิ๊กโก๋ (more general types of delinquents), and kúi กุ๊ย (a distinct low-life variety)

deliver V sòng ส่ง

demand V rîak ráwng เรียกร้อง

democracy N prà-chaa-thíp-pà-tai ประชาธิปไตย

demonstrate V (show how to) sǎa-thít สาธิต

dense ADJ nǎa nâen หนาแน่น, thùe ทึบ

dental floss N mǎi khàt fan ไหมขัดฟัน

dentist N (MORE FORMAL) thantà-phâet ทันตแพทย์, (COMMON) mǎw fan (literally, 'doctor'-'tooth') หมอฟัน

depart V àwk jàak ออกจาก; departure àawk doehn thaang ออกเดินทาง; department (in bureaucracy) phà-nàek แผนก

department store V hâang sàpphá-sĭn-kháa ห้างสรรพสินค้า, (SIMPLY COLLOQUIAL) hâang ห้าง

departure N (boarding at the airport) khǎa àwk ขาออก, (leaving) àwk doehn thaang ออกเดินทาง

depend V (on somebody for help) phôeng พึ่ง, (it depends on...) khûen yùu kàp... ขึ้นอยู่กับ..., or alternatively láew tàeh แล้วแต่

deposit V (money in a bank, to leave something somewhere) fàak ฝาก (NOTE: it is also very common to use this word in the following sense – e.g. to ask somebody going out to the shops to buy something in particular for you 'Can you get (buy) me some bread as well?' – fàak súeh [= buy] khanǒm pang [= bread] dûai ฝากซื้อขนมปังด้วย)

deposit N (of payment on a car, a house) ngoehn mát jam เงินมัดจำ, (money deposited in the bank) ngoen fàak เงินฝาก

depression N (mental condition) rôhk suem sâo โรคซึมเศร้า

depressed ADJ klûm jai กลุ้มใจ

descendant, heir/heiress N thaà-yâat ทายาท

describe V banyaai บรรยาย; description kham banyaai คำบรรยาย, or kaan banyaai การบรรยาย

desert N (arid land) thá-leh saai (literally, 'sea'-'sand') ทะเลทราย

desert V (abandon) thíng ทิ้ง

deserve V sǒm khuan dâi ráp สมควรได้รับ

design V (a house) àwk bàehp ออกแบบ

designer N (from English) dii saai nôeh, (MORE FORMAL) nák àwk baep นักออกแบบ

desire V (to do something) khwaam pràat-thànǎa ความปรารถนา; to desire (to do something) yàak อยาก

desire N (sexual) khwaam khrâi ความใคร่, tan-hǎa ตัณหา (NOTE: the word yàak อยาก (previous entry) can also convey this particular meaning)

desk, table N tó โต๊ะ

desperate ADJ mòt wǎng หมดหวัง

dessert N khǎwng wǎan (literally, 'thing'-'sweet') ของหวาน

destination N plaai thaang ปลายทาง

destiny N chôhk chá-taa โชคชะตา

destroy, devastate V tham-laai ทำลาย

destroyed/ruined ADJ thùuk

43

tham-laai ถูกทำลาย

destruction N kaan tham-laai การทำลาย

destructive ADJ châwp tham-laai ชอบทำลาย

detail(s) N (e.g. in a contract – 'the fine print') raai-lá-îat รายละเอียด

detect V (to spy) sùehp สืบ, (to find out) khôn-hǎa ค้นหา

detective N nák-sùehp นักสืบ

detention N kaan khum tua การคุมตัว

detergent N (washing powder) phǒng sák fâwk ผงซักฟอก; detergent (liquid – for washing plates etc.) náam-yaa láang jaan น้ำยาล้างจาน, (for washing clothing) náam-yaa sák phâa น้ำยาซักผ้า

determined, intent on getting something done/ accomplished ADJ tâng-jai ตั้งใจ

detour N thaang âwm ทางอ้อม

develop V phát-thá-naa พัฒนา; development kaan phát-thá-naa การพัฒนา, (grow) tòep toh เติบโต

device N ùp-pà-kawn อุปกรณ์

devilish ADJ hòht ráai โหดร้าย

dial V (telephone) kòt กด

diabetes N rôhk bao-wǎan โรคเบาหวาน

diagnose V wí-nít-chǎi-róhk วินิจฉัยโรค

diagram N phǎn phâap แผนภาพ

dialect N phaa-sǎa thìn ภาษา ถิ่น

diamond N phét เพชร

diaper N (baby's diaper) phâa-âwm ผ้าอ้อม

diarrhea, diarrhoea N tháwng sǐa ท้องเสีย, tháwng doehn (literally, 'stomach'-'walk') ท้องเดิน, tháwng rûang ท้องร่วง

diary N sà-mùt dai aa-rîi สมุด ไดอารี่

dictate, command V sàng สั่ง

dictionary N phót-jà-naanúkrom พจนานุกรม, (COLLOQUIAL) dìk (from English 'dictionary') ดิก

die V (COLLOQUIAL) taai ตาย, or (POLITE) sǐa เสีย

diesel N (petrol, gasoline) (petrol = náam-man) náam-man dii-sel น้ำมันดีเซล

diet v lót náamnàk ลดน้ำหนัก,
(also from English) dai-èt
ไดเอท

difference N (e.g. in quality)
khwaam tàehk tàang ความ
แตกต่าง

different ADJ tàehk tàang แตก
ต่าง; other ùehn อื่น

difficult ADJ (i.e. a difficult task)
yâak ยาก, difficult in the
sense of not being easy to do
things (e.g. going somewhere,
etc. or 'having a hard/difficult
life') lambàak ลำบาก

dig v (a hole in the ground)
khùt ขุด

digest v (food) yôi (aa-hăan)
ย่อย (อาหาร)

digit N tua-lêhk ตัวเลข

digital ADJ (from English) dí-jì-
tâwn ดิจิตอล

diligent ADJ khà-yăn ขยัน

dilute v juea jaang เจือจาง

dimple N lák yím ลักยิ้ม

dinner N aa-hăan yen; to
eat dinner (POLITE) thaan
aa-hăan yen ทานอาหารเย็น,
(COLLOQUIAL) kin khâaw yen
กินข้าวเย็น

dinosaur N (from English) dai-
noh-săo ไดโนเสาร์

dip v jùm จุ่ม

diploma N (from college or
school – also see 'degree')
à-nú-parin-yaa อนุปริญญา

dipper, ladle N (implement
used when cooking stir-fry
dishes) tháp-phii ทัพพี

direct ADJ (directly, non-stop)
trong ตรง

direct v (somebody to do
something) sàng สั่ง

direction N (according to the
compass) thít thaang ทิศทาง

director N (of company) phûu
jàt-kaan ผู้จัดการ

dirt N din ดิน, (dust) fùn ฝุ่น

dirty, filthy ADJ sòk-kà-pròk
สกปรก

disability N phí-kaan พิการ

disadvantage N khâw sĭa
ข้อเสีย, khwaam sĭa prìap
ความเสียเปรียบ

disagree v (with someone)
mâi hĕn dûai ไม่เห็นด้วย

disappear v See 'vanish'

disappointed ADJ phìt wăng
ผิดหวัง

disapprove v mâi à-nú-mát
ไม่อนุมัติ

45

disaster N phai phíbàt ภัย พิบัติ

discard v thing ทิ้ง

discipline N wí-nai วินัย

disco N (from English) dis-kôh ดิสโก้, (COLLOQUIAL) ték เทค; nightclub (from English) nái-khláp ไนท์คลับ

discomfort N khwaam ùet-àt ความอึดอัด

disconnect v (to shut off an appliance) dueng-àwk ดึง ออก, (to sever) yâek แยก

discount v, N (in the price of something) lót raa-khaa ลด ราคา

discover v khón phóp ค้นพบ

discredit v tham-hâi sîa chûeh-sîang ทำให้เสียชื่อ เสียง

discuss v (ways to solve a problem) thòk panhăa ถกปัญหา; discuss (exchange ideas) lâek-plìan khwaam khít hěn แลกเปลี่ยนความ คิดเห็น

disease N (general term) rôhk โรค

disguise v plawm plaeng ปลอมแปลง

disgusting ADJ nâa rangkìat น่ารังเกียจ; to be disgusted (COLLOQUIAL) màn sâi หมั่นไส้

dish/plate N jaan จาน

dishonest ADJ mâi sûeh-sàt ไม่ซื่อสัตย์

dishwasher N khrûeang láang-jaan เครื่องล้างจาน

disk N (CD, DVD) phàen dís แผ่นดิสก์

dislike v mâi châwp (literally, 'no'-'like') ไม่ชอบ

dissolve/melt v lá-laai ละลาย

display v (a show, a performance) kaan sà-daehng การแสดง

display v sà-daehng แสดง

distance N (from one place to another) rá-yá thang ระยะ ทาง

distribute v jàek แจก

district N (in Bangkok) khèht เขต, (in other provinces) amphoeh อำเภอ

disturb v róp-kuan รบกวน

disturbance N khwaam mâi sà-ngòp ความไม่สงบ

dive v (into the sea, go diving) dam náam ดำน้ำ

divide v (up – e.g. between

different people) bàeng แบ่ง;
separate/split up yâehk แยก

divided by v hǎan dûai (e.g.
twenty divided by five, 20
hǎan dûai 5) หารด้วย

divorce v yàa หย่า

divorced ADJ yàa láew หย่าแล้ว

do v (to perform an action)
tham ทำ

don't! v (do something) yàa อย่า

don't mention it PHR (or 'it
doesn't matter', 'that's OK,
don't worry about it') mâi
pen rai ไม่เป็นไร

do one's best tham dii thîi
sùt ทำดีที่สุด

doctor N (COLLOQUIAL) mǎw
หมอ, (MORE FORMAL) phâeht
แพทย์

document N èhkka-sǎan
เอกสาร

dog N (COMMON, COLLOQUIAL) mǎa
หมา, (MORE GENTEEL, FORMAL)
sù-nák สุนัข

doll N (toy) tùkka-taa ตุ๊กตา

dollar N (from English) dawn-
lâa ดอลลาร์, (COLLOQUIAL)
dawn ดอล

dolphin N plaa-loh-maa ปลา
โลมา

domestic ADJ (involving one's
own country) nai prà-thêht
ในประเทศ, (involving the
family) nai khrâwp-khrua ใน
ครอบครัว

donate v baw-rí-jàak บริจาค

done ADJ (cooked) sùk láew
สุกแล้ว

done ADJ (finished) sèt láew
เสร็จแล้ว

donut N (from English) doh-nát
โดนัท

door/gate N prà-tuu ประตู

doorbell N àwt ออด

dormitory N hǎw-phák
หอพัก

double N (a pair, or as in
'double' bed) pen khûu
เป็นคู่, (twice in amount)
sǎwng thâo สองเท่า

doubt/suspect/curious v
sǒng-sǎi สงสัย

down, downward ADV long
maa ลงมา

downstairs ADV khâang lâang
ข้างล่าง

down-to-earth ADJ (to be
natural, unpretentious)
pen tham-má-châat เป็น
ธรรมชาติ

47

downtown N nai mueang ใน
เมือง

dozen N lŏh โหล

drag V lâak ลาก

dragon N mang-kawn มังกร

drama N (as in TV soap opera)
lá-khawn ละคร; TV soap
opera lá-khawn thii-wii
ละครทีวี

drapes, curtains N mâan
ม่าน

draw V (a picture) wâat วาด;
draw a picture wâat rûup
วาดรูป; a drawing rûup wâat
รูปวาด

drawer N (in a desk) línchák
ลิ้นชัก

dream N khwaam fǎn ความฝัน

dream V fǎn ฝัน; Dream on!
(as in 'In your dreams!' or 'You
must be kidding!') fǎn pai
thóeh ฝันไปเถอะ

dress, frock N chút krà-
prohng ชุดกระโปรง

dressed, to get V tàeng tua
แต่งตัว

dressing N náam sà-làt น้ำ
สลัด

dressing gown N sûea khlum
เสื้อคลุม

drill N (tools) sà-wàan สว่าน,
(repetitious exercise) kaan
fùek การฝึก

drink V (in formal situations)
dùehm ดื่ม, (COLLOQUIAL)
gin-náam กินน้ำ (literally:
'eat water' is used in casual
conversations)

drink/beverage N khrûeang
dùehm เครื่องดื่ม

drive V (a car) khàp ขับ

driver N khon khàp คนขับ

driving license N (for either
car or motorcycle) (COLLOQUIAL)
bai khàp khìi ใบขับขี่

drop V yòt หยด

drought ADJ (very dry weather
conditions, land, etc.) hâehng
láehng แห้งแล้ง

drown V jom náam taai จม
น้ำตาย

drug N (medicine) yaa ยา,
drug (narcotic) yaa sèhp tìt
(literally, 'drug/medicine'-
'consume'-'stuck') ยาเสพติด

**drugstore, pharmacy,
chemist** N ráan khǎai yaa
ร้านขายยา

drunk/intoxicated ADJ mao
เมา; a drunk (drunkard) khîi

mao ขี้เมา. (NOTE: the word mao เมา is not only used to refer to someone being drunk on alcohol, it is also used to refer to someone being 'high' or 'stoned' on any type of drug. Stoned on marijuana, for example, is mao kan-chaa เมากัญชา. A habitual user of illegal drugs is referred to as khîi yaa ขี้ยา. The word khîi ขี้ in this instance means 'habitual', 'being prone to' some type of behavior)

dry ADJ hâehng แห้ง, (weather) hâehng láehng แห้งแล้ง

dry V tham hâi hâehng ทำให้แห้ง, tàak ตาก; to dry clothing tàak phâa ตากผ้า

dry clean(ing) V sák hâehng ซักแห้ง

dryer N (clothes dryer) khrûeang òp-phâa เครื่องอบผ้า, (hair dryer) dai-pào-phǒm ไดร์เป่าผม

dry out V (in the sun) tàak dàet ตากแดด

duck N pèt เป็ด

dull ADJ (boring) nâa bùea น่า

เบื่อ, (weather) khà-mùk-khà-mǔa ขมุกขมัว

dumb ADJ (COLLOQUIAL) ngôh โง่

dump V thîng ทิ้ง

dumpling N (meat) saa lá pao ซาละเปา

duplicate, make a copy V tham sǎm-nao ทำสำเนา

durable ADJ châi-thon ใช้ทน

durian N (fruit) thú-rian ทุเรียน

during, in between PREP nai rá-wàang ในระหว่าง

dusk ADJ klâi mûeht (literally, 'close'–'dark') ใกล้มืด

dust N fùn ฝุ่น; dustbin/rubbish bin/garbage bin thǎng khà-yà ถังขยะ

duty N (tax) phaa-sǐi ภาษี, (responsibility) nâa thîi หน้าที่

DVD N (from English) dii wii dii ดีวีดี

dye V yáwm ย้อม

dysentery N rôhk bìt โรคบิด

49

E

each ADJ (as in 'each particular person', 'each particular book') tàeh lá แต่ละ; every... thúk... ทุก

eager, enthusiastic ADJ krà-tueh-rueh-rón กระตือรือร้น

eagle N nók in-sii นกอินทรี

ear N hǔu หู; earphone(s), headphones hǔufang หูฟัง; ear wax khîi hǔu (literally, 'excrement'-'ear') ขี้หู

earlier, beforehand ADJ & ADV lûang nâa ล่วงหน้า

early ADV (come before usual time) kàwn weh-laa ก่อนเวลา

early in the morning ADV cháo trùu เช้าตรู่

earn V (a wage) dâi khâa jâang ได้ค่าจ้าง

earrings N tûm hǔu ตุ้มหู

earth, soil N din ดิน

Earth, the world N lôhk โลก

earthenware N khrûeng din-phǎo เครื่องดินเผา

earthquake N phàen din wǎi แผ่นดินไหว

east ADJ (direction) tà-wan àwk ตะวันออก

ease V tham-hâi ngâai ทำให้ง่าย easy ADJ ngâai ง่าย

easygoing ADJ sà-baai sà-baai สบายๆ, rûeay rûeay เรื่อยๆ

eat V—there are a number of words in Thai that mean 'to eat'. These range from the colloquial to more formal. They include: kin กิน or more fully kin khâaw (literally, 'eat'-'rice') กินข้าว (NOTE: the colloquial term kin กิน is also used as slang to refer to corrupt practices such as taking bribes); thaan ทาน; ráp prà-thaan (FORMAL) รับประทาน; chǎn (for monks) ฉัน. When animals 'eat' another word is often used: dàek แดก. If dàek is used to refer to people eating, it is extremely rude and should be avoided. It is generally used in informal settings among intimate male friends, and rougher, rowdier elements of Thai society.

ecology N nîwêt-wít-thá-yaa นิเวศวิทยา; **ecologist** nák ní-wêht-wít-tháyaa นัก นิเวศวิทยา

economical/frugal ADJ prà-yàt ประหยัด

economy, the N sèht-thà-kìt เศรษฐกิจ

ecstasy N khwaam sùk mâak ความสุขมาก; **ecstasy (the drug)** yaa ii yaa อี

edge N khàwp ขอบ

edible ADJ kin dâi กินได้

edit V kâe-kǎi แก้ไข

educate V sùek-sǎa ศึกษา

education N kaan sùek-sǎa การศึกษา

effect, result N phǒn ผล

effective ADJ dâi phǒn ได้ผล

effort N khwaam phá-yaa-yaam ความพยายาม

effort, to make an; try V phá-yaa-yaam พยายาม

egg N khài ไข่

eggplant, aubergine N (general term) má-khùea มะเขือ

eight NUM (the number) pàeht แปด

eighteen NUM sìp pàeht

(literally, 'ten'-'eight') สิบแปด

eighty NUM pàeht sìp (literally, 'eight'-'ten') แปดสิบ

either...or CONJ mâi... kâw... ไม่...ก็...

ejaculate/to come V (COLLOQUIAL; used for both men and women) sèt เสร็จ, or sèt láew เสร็จแล้ว. (The word sèt เสร็จ also means 'finished')

elbow N khâw sàwk ข้อศอก

elder ADJ (i.e. 'older than') kàeh kwàa แก่กว่า

elder N (older person) khon kàe คนแก่

election N kaan lûeak tâng การเลือกตั้ง

electric, electricity ADJ, N fai-fáa ไฟฟ้า

electrician N châang fai-fáa ช่างไฟฟ้า

electronic ADJ (from English) i-lék thraw-ník อิเล็กทรอนิก

elegant ADJ sǔai-ngaam สวยงาม

elementary ADJ (basic) phúehn-thǎan พื้นฐาน, prà-thǒm ประถม (i.e. an elementary school)

elephant N cháang ช้าง; a white elephant (regarded as auspicious in Thailand) cháang phùeak (literally, 'elephant'-'albino') ช้างเผือก

elevator N (from English 'lift') líp ลิฟต์

eleven NUM sìp èt สิบเอ็ด

eligible ADJ màw-sŏm เหมาะสม

eliminate V tàt-àwk ตัดออก

elite N khon chán sŭung (literally, 'person/people'-'class/level'-'high') คนชั้นสูง

else ADJ (as in 'anything else?') àrai ìik อะไรอีก

elsewhere ADV thîi-ùehn ที่อื่น

email N (message) (from English) ii-mehl อีเมล

email V (send an email) sòng ii-mehl ส่งอีเมล

email address N thîi yùu ii-mehl ที่อยู่อีเมล

embarrassed/shy ADJ aai (pronounced like 'eye') อาย

embarrassing ADJ nâa lá-aai น่าละอาย

embassy N sà-thăan thûut สถานทูต

embrace/hug V kàwt กอด

embroider V pàk ปัก

embroidery N yép pàk thàk rói เย็บปักถักร้อย

emerald N mawra-kòt มรกต

emergency N chùk chŏehn ฉุกเฉิน

emotion, feeling N khwaam rúu-sèuk ความรู้สึก

emotional ADJ àwn-wăi อ่อนไหว

empathy N khwaam-hĕn-jai ความเห็นใจ

emphasize/stress something V nén เน้น

employ V (to hire someone) jâang จ้าง

employee N (generally used with unskilled or lowly skilled workers) lûuk jâang ลูกจ้าง

employer N (boss) naai jâang นายจ้าง

empty, to be V wâang plào ว่างเปล่า

enchanted ADJ mii-sà-nèh มีเสน่ห์

encounter V phà-choehn-nâa เผชิญหน้า, pà-thá patá ปะทะ

end N (ending) jòp จบ, (the tip, e.g. of the tongue, nose, etc.) plaai ปลาย

52

end v sèt sîn เสร็จสิ้น, also jòp จบ

endless ADJ mâi-sîn-sùt ไม่สิ้นสุด

endure v òt-thon อดทน

enemy N sàt-truu ศัตรู

energy N phá-lang ngaan พลังงาน

engaged, busy ADJ (telephone) sǎai mâi wâang สายไม่ว่าง, (to be married) mân หมั้น

engine/motor N khrûeang yon เครื่องยนต์, or (simply and more colloquially) khrûeang เครื่อง

engineer N wítsà-wá-kawn วิศวกร

England N angkrìt อังกฤษ

English N (people) khon angkrìt คนอังกฤษ; (language) phaa-sǎa angkrìt ภาษาอังกฤษ

engrave v (to carve a piece of stone, wood, etc.) kàe-sà-làk แกะสลัก

enjoy v (to be fun/pleasurable) sà-nùk สนุก (This is a quintessential Thai word and the full sense of the

term is not really adequately conveyed by the English word 'enjoy'. In Thai being sà-nùk is 'highly desirable')

enjoyable ADJ nâa sà-nùk น่าสนุก

enjoy oneself v tham tua hâi sà-nùk ทำตัวให้สนุก (sometimes the English word 'enjoy' is also used in Thai: en-joy เอ็นจอย)

enlarge v khà-yǎai ขยาย

enormous ADJ má-hùe-maa มหึมา

enough, sufficient ADJ phaw พอ

enquire/ask v thǎam ถาม

enroll v long thá-bian ลงทะเบียน

enter v khâo เข้า (NOTE: this word is frequently used in conjunction with either the word 'come' maa มา, or 'go' pai ไป; e.g. 'come in [here]' khâo maa เข้ามา, or 'go in [there]' khâo pai เข้าไป)

entertain v tham-hâi sà-nùk ทำให้สนุก

entire, whole N tháng mòt ทั้งหมด

53

entrance, way in N thaang khâo ทางเข้า

entrée N aa-hǎan jaan-râek อาหารจานแรก

entrepreneur, business person N nák thúrá-kìt นักธุรกิจ

envelope N sawng ซอง

environment N sìng wâeht láwm สิ่งแวดล้อม

envy V ìtchǎa อิจฉา; **envious** ADJ nâa ìtchǎa น่าอิจฉา

episode N tawn ตอน

equal ADJ thâo kan เท่ากัน

equality N khwaam thâo thiam ความเท่าเทียม

equipment/implement N ù-pà-kawn อุปกรณ์

era N sà-mǎi สมัย, yúk ยุค

errand N thú-rá ธุระ

error, mistake N khwaam phìt ความผิด

escalator N bandai lûean บันไดเลื่อน

escape/flee V nǐi หนี

especially ADV dohy chà-phá-w โดยเฉพาะ

essay N (e.g. term essay at university) riang khwaam เรียงความ, (or essay/article in a newspaper) bòt khwaam บทความ

establish, set up V kàw tâng ก่อตั้ง

estate N thîi din ที่ดิน

estimate V prà-maan ประมาณ; estimate the price/give a quote tii raa-khaa ตีราคา

ethnic group, minority group N chon klùm nói ชนกลุ่มน้อย

Eurasian N (the offspring of an Asian and European/Caucasian parent) lûuk khrûeng (literally, 'child'-'half') ลูกครึ่ง

Euro N (currency) ngoehn yuù-roh เงินยูโร

Europe N yú-ròhp ยุโรป

evacuate V òp-phá-yóp อพยพ

evaluate V prà-moehn ประเมิน

even ADV (e.g. even young people like it) máeh tàeh แม้แต่

even ADJ (smooth) rîap เรียบ, (evenly matched, equal in a race/competition, e.g. a tie in a football game) sà-mǒeh kan เสมอกัน

evening N tawn yen ตอนเย็น

event N hèht kaan เหตุการณ์

ever ADV (e.g. 'have you ever been to...?') khoei เคย (NOTE: for fuller description of how this word is used *see* 'have'.)

every ADJ thúk ทุก

everybody, everyone PRON thúk khon ทุกคน (NOTE: common idiom - 'everybody for themselves/every man for himself' tua khrai tua man ตัวใครตัวมัน

every day ADJ thúk wan ทุกวัน

every kind of... N thúk chá-nít ทุกชนิด

everything PRON thúk sìng ทุกสิ่ง, also thúk-yàang ทุกอย่าง

every time ADV thúk khráng ทุกครั้ง

everywhere ADV thúk thîi ทุกที่

evidence, proof N làk thăan หลักฐาน

evil ADJ chûa ráai ชั่วร้าย N khwaam chûa ความชั่ว

exact ADJ (COLLOQUIAL) trong péh ตรงเป๊ะ, (or in short) péh เป๊ะ

exactly! just so! ADV

(COLLOQUIAL) nân lâe นั่นแหละ

exaggerate V phûut koehn jing พูดเกินจริง

exam, test N (knowledge or skill) sàwp สอบ

examine, inspect V trùat-sàwp ตรวจสอบ

example N tua yàang ตัวอย่าง

example, for CONJ chên... เช่น

exceed V koehn kwàa เกินกว่า

excellent ADJ yâwt yîam ยอดเยี่ยม; great, (COLLOQUIAL) 'that's great!' sùt yâwt สุดยอด

except CONJ, **to be exempt** ADJ (e.g. 'everyone can go except him') yók wéhn ยกเว้น; an exception khâw yók wéhn ข้อยกเว้น

except PREP (i.e. in the sense of being 'apart from' or 'in addition to') nâwk jàak นอกจาก

exchange V (money, opinions) lâehk plìan แลกเปลี่ยน

exchange rate N àttraa lâehk plìan อัตราแลกเปลี่ยน

excited ADJ tùehn tên ตื่นเต้น

exciting ADJ nâa tuehn tên น่าตื่นเต้น

excrement/feces N (FORMAL MEDICAL TERM) ùt-jaará อุจจาระ, (COLLOQUIAL) khîi ขี้ (in English the common colloquial for this is 'shit' of course, but the Thai word does not have the same type of crude/vulgar sense to it and, while not exactly polite, is not particularly rude. Thus khîi ขี้ is not used in situations, common in English, when someone is angry or has made a mistake, etc.)

excuse me! PHR (attracting attention) used as an apology, e.g. 'I'm sorry' (for bumping into you) khǎw thôht ขอโทษ (literally, 'request/ask for'-'punishment')

excuse me! PHR (said when trying to get past someone in a crowded place) khǎw thaang nòi ขอทางหน่อย

excuse N khâw kâe tua ข้อแก้ตัว

exercise v àwk kamlang kaai ออกกำลังกาย

exhausted ADJ nùeay เหนื่อย

exhibition N ní-thát-sà-kaan นิทรรศการ

exist v (to be alive) mii chiiwít yùu มีชีวิตอยู่

exit, way out N thaang àwk ทางออก

expand, grow larger v khà-yǎai ขยาย

expect v khâat wâa... คาดว่า

expel v lâi àwk ไล่ออก

expense(s), expenditure N raai jàai รายจ่าย, khâa chái jàai ค่าใช้จ่าย

expensive ADJ phaehng แพง

experience N prà-sòp-kaan ประสบการณ์

experience v (to have experienced something) mii pràsòp-kaan มีประสบการณ์

expert ADJ & N (have expertise) cham-naan ชำนาญ; an expert (in a particular field) phûu chîaw-chaan ผู้เชี่ยวชาญ

expire v (e.g. a driving license) mòt aa-yú หมดอายุ

explain v à-thí-baai อธิบาย (NOTE: the first two syllables of this word à and thí are

56

very short); '(I) can't explain'
à-thí-baai mâi dâi athibaai
ไม่ได้; explanation kham
à-thí-baai คำอธิบาย

explode v (e.g. a bomb)
rá-bòet ระเบิด

explore v sǎm-rùat สำรวจ

export v sòng àwk ส่งออก

express, urgent ADJ dùan
ด่วน

express v (emotion, one's
feelings) sà-daehng แสดง

expressway, freeway N
thaang dùan ทางด่วน

extend v (make larger/longer,
add to) tàw ต่อ; extension
(telephone) tàw ต่อ (NOTE: to
'extend a visa' is tàw wii-sâa
ต่อวีซ่า)

extinguisher N khrûeang dàp
phloehng เครื่องดับเพลิง

extra, additional ADJ phôehm
เพิ่ม

extraordinary ADJ (special)
phí-sèht พิเศษ

extravagant ADJ (spendthrift)
fûm fueai ฟุ่มเฟือย

extremely ADV (COLLOQUIAL) sùt
khìit สุดขีด, or (in short) sùt
sùt สุดๆ (e.g. 'extremely hot'

ráwn sùt sùt ร้อนสุดๆ, 'hot' =
ráwn ร้อน)

extrovert N châwp khâo sang
khom ชอบเข้าสังคม

eye N taa ตา

eyebrow N khíu คิ้ว (it is pronounced like 'cute' in English)

**eyeglasses, glasses,
spectacles** N wâen taa
แว่นตา

eyelash N khǒn taa ขนตา

eyelid N plùeak taa เปลือกตา

eyesight N sǎi taa สายตา

eyewitness N phá-yaan
พยาน

F

fable/legend N ní-thaan
นิทาน

fabric/textile/cloth N phâa ผ้า

face N nâa หน้า; lose face
(dignity, to be embarrassed)
khǎai nâa (literally, 'sell'-
'face') ขายหน้า, or sǐa nâa
(literally, 'ruined/spoiled'-
'face') เสียหน้า

face/confront v phà-choehn
nâa เผชิญหน้า

fact, facts N khâw thét jing ข้อเท็จจริง

factory N rohng ngaan โรงงาน

fail V (to be unsuccessful) mâi sǎmrèt ไม่สำเร็จ; to fail a test/exam sàwp tòk (literally, 'test'-'fall') สอบตก

failure N khwaam lóm lĕow ความล้มเหลว

faint/swoon V pen lom เป็นลม

fair ADJ (to be just)/fair-minded yút-tì-tham ยุติธรรม (NOTE: the English word 'fair' is commonly used in Thai but generally in the negative sense, i.e. something that's 'not fair' mâi fae ไม่แฟร์)

faith N khwaam chûea ความเชื่อ, (MORE FORMAL) sàt-thaa ศรัทธา

fake N (an imitation) plawm ปลอม, e.g. referring to a fake Rolex – 'it's a fake!' khǎwng plawm ของปลอม

fall, autumn N (season) rúe-duu bai mái rûang ฤดู ใบไม้ร่วง

fall V (drop, decrease) tòk ตก

fall/fell over V hòk-lóm

หกล้ม, or simply lóm ล้ม

false ADJ (not genuine) plawm ปลอม, (not true) mâi jing ไม่จริง; wrong phìt ผิด

familiar ADJ khún-kheoi คุ้นเคย

family N khrâwp khrua ครอบครัว

famine N khwaam òt yàak ความอดอยาก

famous ADJ mii chûeh sǐang (literally, 'have'-'name'- 'sound/voice') มีชื่อเสียง, (COLLOQUIAL) 'to be famous' dang ดัง; a famous/well- known person khon dang คน ดัง (NOTE: dang ดัง is also the word for a 'loud' sound/noise)

fan N (of a singer/movie star) faehn แฟน (from English: also colloquial term for either girl or boyfriend), (a machine for cooling) phát-lom พัดลม

fancy/luxurious/opulent ADJ rŭurǎa หรูหรา

fantasy N (from English) faen- taa-sii แฟนตาซี, jin-tà-naa- kaan จินตนาการ

far/distant ADJ klai ไกล See 'note' under the entry for 'near' to help differentiate

58

these two terms

fare N khâa dohy-sǎan ค่า โดยสาร (for buses and minivans), or simply, and more colloquially khâa rót ค่ารถ

farewell N am-laa อำลา (i.e. a farewell party is 'ngaan-líang am-laa' งานเลี้ยงอำลา)

farm N (from English) faam (is commonly used with a unit of land for rearing animal or fish or livestock, for example; chicken farm is faam kài ฟาร์มไก่), (a paddy field) râi naa ไร่นา

farmer N chaow naa (literally, 'people'-'rice field') ชาวนา

fart N & V (COLLOQUIAL) tòt ตด

fascinate V chûehn châwp ชื่นชอบ

fashion N (clothing) In Thai the English word is commonly used but with slightly different pronunciation fae-chân (NOTE: unfashionable/old-fashioned/out-of date choei เชย)

fast, rapid ADJ rew เร็ว; the expression to tell someone

to 'go faster' or 'hurry up' is rew-rew เร็วๆ

fast V (go without food) òt aa-hǎan อดอาหาร

fat, grease N khǎi man ไขมัน (NOTE: the word for cholesterol is khǎi man nai lûeat (literally, 'fat'-'in'-'blood') ไขมันในเลือด)

fat, plump, obese ADJ ûan อ้วน (NOTE: the word 'fat' does not have the same negative connotations in Thai conversation as it does in the west, although this could be changing. A more polite word to refer to someone who is carrying a few extra kilograms is sǒmbuun สมบูรณ์ which means 'healthy', 'complete', 'perfect')

fate N chôhk chá-taa โชค ชะตา

father N (COLLOQUIAL) phâw พ่อ, (FORMAL) bì-daa บิดา

father-in-law N phâw taa พ่อตา

fatigued, tired ADJ nùeay เหนื่อย

fault N khwaam phìt ความผิด

favorite N (to like the most) châwp mâak thîi sùt ชอบมากที่สุด

fax N (machine/message) fáek(s) แฟกซ์; to send a fax sòng fáek(s) ส่งแฟกซ์

fear N khwaam klua ความกลัว

fearful ADJ nâa klua น่ากลัว

fearless ADJ mâi klua ไม่กลัว, (brave) jai klâa ใจกล้า

feasible, possible ADJ pen pai dâi เป็นไปได้

feast N ngaan-líang งานเลี้ยง

feather N khŏn nòk ขนนก

feature N jùt dèhn จุดเด่น

February N kum-phaa-phan กุมภาพันธ์

federal N sà-hà-phan สหพันธ์

federation N sà-hà-phâap สหภาพ

fee N (generally for a public sector service) khâa tham-niam ค่าธรรมเนียม; service fee khâa bawrí-kaan ค่าบริการ

feeble ADJ mâi mii raeng ไม่มีแรง

feeble-minded, stupid ADJ (COLLOQUIAL) ngôh โง่

feed V hâi aa-hăan ให้อาหาร

feel V rúu-sùek รู้สึก

feeling N khwaam rúù-sùek ความรู้สึก

feet/foot N (for humans) tháo เท้า, foot/feet (for animals) tiin ตีน (NOTE: in central Thai the word tiin, when applied to people, is extremely rude)

felicity N khwaam sùk ความ สุข

fellow N phûean เพื่อน

female N (human being) yĭng หญิง, female (animal) tua mia ตัวเมีย

fence N rúa รั้ว

fend V pâwng kan ป้องกัน

feng shui N huang jûi ฮวงจุ้ย

ferry N ruea khâam fâak เรือ ข้ามฟาก

fertile ADJ (of land) ù-dom sŏmbuun อุดมสมบูรณ์

festival N (very common in Thailand) thêht-sàkaan เทศกาล; also 'temple fair' (similarly very common) ngaan wát งานวัด

fetch V (to go and get) pai ao maa (literally, 'go'-'take'- 'come') ไปเอามา

fever N khâi ไข้; to have a fever pen khâi เป็นไข้

60

few ADJ mâi kìi... ไม่กี่

few N sǎwng sǎam (literally, 'two'-'three') สองสาม

fiancé, fiancée N khûu mân คู่หมั้น

fiction N ní yaai นิยาย

fidelity N khwaam sûeh sàt ความซื่อสัตย์

field N (a sporting field, a parade ground) sà-nǎam สนาม; a rice field thûng naa ทุ่งนา, or simply naa นา

fierce, vicious ADJ (to describe either an animal or person) dù ดุ

fifteen NUM sìp hâa (literally, 'ten'-'five') สิบห้า

fifth ADJ thî hâa ที่ห้า

fifty NUM hâa sìp (literally, 'five'-'ten') ห้าสิบ

fight V (physically) sûu สู้

fight over V (e.g. the control of a piece of land, a child, etc.) yâehng แย่ง

figure N (number) tua lêhk ตัวเลข, (body shape) hùn หุ่น: e.g. 'a good figure' hùn dii หุ่นดี

fill V (e.g. up a car with petrol) toehm เติม

fill out V (a form) kràwk กรอก (also see 'form')

film, movie N (COLLOQUIAL) nǎng หนัง, (MORE FORMAL) phâap-phá-yon ภาพยนตร์

filthy ADJ See 'dirty'

final N & ADJ sùt tháai สุดท้าย

finally ADV ...nai thîi sùt ในที่สุด (in Thai, usually used at the end of a sentence)

finance N kaan-ngoehn การเงิน

find V phóp พบ; trying to find/ to look for something hǎa หา

fine ADJ (okay) dii ดี, OK (from English) oh-kheh โอเค

fine N (for some type of infringement) khâa pràp ค่าปรับ. (In the 'entertainment scene' in Thailand there is also something known as a 'bar fine' – the English words pronounced in the Thai manner. This is the 'fee' a patron has to pay to take a woman (dancer, hostess) out of the premises. A separate 'fee' for 'services rendered' is negotiated between these two individuals)

finger N níu นิ้ว; fingernail lép mueh เล็บมือ

finish, finish off v (stop doing an activity or task) sèt เสร็จ

finished ADJ (complete) sèt láew เสร็จแล้ว, (used up) mòt láew หมดแล้ว

fire N fai ไฟ; 'there's a fire (burning)!' fai mâi ไฟไหม้

fire alarm N săn-yaan fai-mâi สัญญาณไฟไหม้

fire someone v lâi àwk ไล่ออก

fireworks N prà-thát ประทัด

firm, company N bawrí-sàt บริษัท

firm ADJ (skin, muscles) nâen แน่น; firm (mattress) khăeng แข็ง; firm (secure) mânkhong มั่นคง

first ADJ râehk แรก; at first thii râehk ทีแรก, or tawn râehk ตอนแรก

first, earlier, beforehand ADV kàwn ก่อน

first ADJ thîi nùeng ที่หนึ่ง

fish N plaa ปลา

fish v (to go fishing) tòk plaa ตกปลา

fish ball N lûuk chin plaa ลูกชิ้นปลา

fisherman N (FORMAL) chaow prà-mong ชาวประมง, (INFORMAL) khon hăa plaa คนหาปลา

fish sauce N náam plaa (literally, 'water'-'fish') น้ำปลา

fist N kam pân กำปั้น

fistfight N chók tòi ชกต่อย

fit v (clothing; 'it fits perfectly') sài phaw dii ใส่พอดี

fitting, suitable, appropriate ADJ màw-sŏm เหมาะสม

five NUM hâa ห้า

fix v (a time, appointment) nát นัด, (repair) kâeh แก้, sâwm ซ่อม

flag N thong ธง; national flag thong châat ธงชาติ

flake N klèt เกล็ด

flame N pleow fai เปลวไฟ

flashlight/torch N fai chăai ไฟฉาย

flat, apartment N (from English) flàet แฟลต

flat, smooth ADJ (e.g. the sea) rîap เรียบ; flat (e.g. a flat tire/ tyre) baen แบน

flavor N rót รส

flaw N roi รอย, tam-nì ตำหนิ

flea N màt mǔt มัด หมัด

flea market N tà-làat khǎwng-kào ตลาดของเก่า

flee V nǐi หนี

fleece N khǒn kàe ขนแกะ

flesh, meat N núea เนื้อ

flexible/adaptable ADJ yûet yùn ยืดหยุ่น

flight N (on an airline) thîao bin เที่ยวบิน

flip V plík พลิก

flip flops/thongs N See 'slipper'

flippers N (fins – used for snorkeling, diving, etc.) tiin kòp (literally, 'feet'-'frog') ตีนกบ, also (from English) fin ฟิน

flirt V jìip (pronounced like the word 'jeep' with a low tone) จีบ

float V loi ลอย

flock N fǔung ฝูง

flood N & V náam thûam น้ำ ท่วม

floor N phúehn พื้น

flour N pâehng แป้ง (Note: the same word pâehng แป้ง also means 'face powder', 'baby powder' etc.)

flow V lǎi ไหล

flower N dàwk mái ดอกไม้

flu/influenza N khâi wàt yài ไข้หวัดใหญ่

fluent ADJ (to do something – e.g. speak a language – fluently) khlâwng คล่อง

fluid/liquid N khǎwng lěhw ของเหลว

flute N khlùi ขลุ่ย

fly N má-laehng-wan แมลงวัน

fly V bin บิน

foam N fawng ฟอง, (from English) fohm โฟม (is mostly used to refer to a facial foam)

fog N màwk หมอก

fold V (e.g. a piece of paper) pháp พับ

folk ADJ phúehn mueang พื้น เมือง

folk music N don-trii phúehn mueang ดนตรีพื้นเมือง

folktale N ní-thaan phúehn mueang นิทานพื้นเมือง

follow along V taam ตาม

follow behind V taam lǎng ตามหลัง

fond of ADJ (to like someone) châwp ชอบ

food N aa-hǎan อาหาร (NOTE: the word 'rice' khâaw ข้าว is often colloquially used to refer to 'food')

fool N (COLLOQUIAL) khon ngôh คนโง่

foolish, stupid ADJ (COLLOQUIAL) ngôh โง่

foot/feet N tháo เท้า (NOTE: the word used for animals' foot/feet is tiin ตีน. It is extremely rude and inappropriate to use this term when referring to humans in polite, or even informal, conversation)

footprint N (FORMAL) roi-tháo รอยเท้า, (VERY INFORMAL) roi-tiin รอยตีน (see note on 'foot/feet' above)

for PREP sǎmràp สำหรับ, also pûea เพื่อ

forbear v liil lîang หลีกเลี่ยง

forbid v hâam ห้าม

forbidden ADJ tâwng hâam ต้องห้าม, or simply hâam ห้าม

force, energy N kamlang กำลัง

force/compel v bangkháp บังคับ

forecast/predict v (as in weather forecast) phá-yaa-kawn พยากรณ์

forefinger N níu chíi นิ้วชี้

forehead N nâa phàak หน้าผาก

foreign/overseas ADJ tàang prà-thêet ต่างประเทศ

foreigner N chaow tàangchâat ชาวต่างชาติ. Also the common word fàràng ฝรั่ง. This can be an ambiguous term (meaning 'foreigner – westerner-caucasian') that, for some, has negative connotations. The term chaow tàangchâat ชาวต่างชาติ – noted above – does not have such connotations.

forest, jungle N pàa ป่า

forever N & ADV tà-làwt pai ตลอดไป

forget v luehm ลืม

forgetful ADJ khîi-luehm ขี้ลืม

forgive v hâi à-phai ให้อภัย

forgiveness, mercy N kaan hâi à-phai การให้อภัย

forgotten ADJ thùuk luehm ถูกลืม

fork N (utensil) sâwm ส้อม

form N (shape) rûup râang รูปร่าง

form V (to organize or arrange) jàt จัด

formal, official ADJ **officially** ADV thaang kaan ทางการ

format N rûup bàep รูปแบบ

former ADJ khon kàwn คนก่อน

formula N sùut สูตร

fortress, fort N pâwm ป้อม

fortunately/luckily... ADV chôhk dii thîi... โชคดีที่...

fortune teller N măw duu หมอดู; to have one's fortune told (COLLOQUIAL) duu măw ดูหมอ

forty N sìi sìp สี่สิบ

forward, to go V pai khâang nâa ไปข้างหน้า

foster V líang duu เลี้ยงดู

foul ADJ (bad odor) měn เหม็น, (rotten) nâo เน่า; **foul-mouth(ed)** ADJ (to speak rudely/coarsely) pàak ráai ปากร้าย, (slang; very rude, best left unsaid) pàak măa (literally, 'mouth'–'dog')

ปากหมา

foundation N muun ní-thí มูลนิธิ

fountain N náam phú น้ำพุ

four NUM sìi สี่

fourteen NUM sìp sìi สิบสี่

fraction N (a fraction of something) sèht-sùan เศษ ส่วน (NOTE: to make fractions in Thai the 'formula' is sèht เศษ (top number), sùan ส่วน (bottom number), e.g. ¾ – three quarters sèht săam sùan sìi เศษสามส่วน สี่. Also see the entry under a 'quarter')

fragile ADJ (delicate) bàwp-baang บอบบาง, (easily broken) tàek ngâai แตกง่าย

fragrance N náam hăwm น้ำหอม

fragrant ADJ hăwm หอม

frame N (e.g. picture frame) kràwp กรอบ

France N (country) prà-thêht fà-ràngsèht ประเทศ ฝรั่งเศส; French (person) khon fà-ràngsèht คน ฝรั่งเศส; (language) phaa-săa fà-ràngsèht ภาษาฝรั่งเศส

65

fraud N kaan kohng การโกง;
a fraud/fraudster khon khîi
kohng คนขี้โกง

free ADJ (of charge) mâi khít
ngoen ไม่คิดเงิน, (also
commonly used – from
English) frii ฟรี

free of commitments ADJ
mâi mii khâw phùuk mát
ไม่มีข้อผูกมัด

free/independent ADJ ìtsàra
อิสระ

freedom N ìtsàra-phâap
อิสรภาพ

freewill N sà-màk jai สมัครใจ

freeze V (as with frozen food)
châeh khǎeng แช่แข็ง

French fries/chips N (from
English) frén fraai เฟรนช์-
ฟราย, or man fàràng thâwt
มันฝรั่งทอด

frequent ADJ bòi bòi บ่อยๆ;
frequently bòi-bòi บ่อยๆ

fresh ADJ sòt สด

freshwater N náam jùeht
น้ำจืด

Friday N wan sùk วันศุกร์

fried V (deep fried), fry V thâwt
ทอด; stir-fry/stir-fried phàt
ผัด

friend N phûean เพื่อน. NOTE:
friends phûean-phûean
เพื่อนๆ; a close friend phûean
sànìt เพื่อนสนิท, (COLLOQUIAL/
SLANG) phûean síi เพื่อน
ซี้. Also note the following
idiomatic expressions:
phûean kin เพื่อนกิน (casual,
fair-weather friends) (literally,
'friend'-'eat'); phûean taai
เพื่อนตาย (friends who will
do anything for you) (literally,
'friend'-'die')

friendly, outgoing ADJ pen
kan ehng เป็นกันเอง (This
expression also means
'take it easy, make yourself
at home')

friendship N mít-tà-phâap
มิตรภาพ

frightened ADJ tòk jai ตกใจ
(NOTE: often said as tòk-kà-jai)

frizzy/curly/kinked ADJ yìk
หยิก (i.e. frizzy hair is phǒm
yìk ผมหยิก)

frog N kòp กบ

from PREP jàak จาก: e.g. 'what
country do you come from?'
khun maa jàak prathêht arai
(literally, 'you'-'come'-'from'-

66

'country'-'what'?) khun maa jàak prathêet arai

front ADJ (in front of) khâang nâa ข้างหน้า

frontier N phrom daen พรมแดน

frost N náam kháang khǎeng น้ำค้างแข็ง, or mâeh khá-náng แม่คะนิ้ง

frown N khà-mùat khíu ขมวดคิ้ว

frozen V & ADJ châeh khǎeng แช่แข็ง

frugal ADJ See 'economical'

fruit N phǒnlá-mái ผลไม้

fry V See 'fried'

fuel oil N náam man น้ำมัน

fugitive N lòp nǐi หลบหนี

fulfill V (to complete something successfully) sǎmrèt สำเร็จ

full ADJ tem เต็ม, (having consumed enough food or drink) ìm อิ่ม; to be full already ìm láew อิ่มแล้ว

fume N khwan ควัน

fun, to have ADJ sà-nùk สนุก

function/work V tham ngaan ทำงาน

funds, funding, capital N thun ทุน

funeral N ngaan sòp งานศพ

fungus/mould N chúea raa เชื้อรา; to be mouldy (COLLOQUIAL) raa khûen ราขึ้น

funny ADJ tà-lòk ตลก, or khǎm ขำ

fur N khǒn-sàt ขนสัตว์

furious ADJ kròht โกรธ

furniture N (from English) foeh-ní-jôeh เฟอร์นิเจอร์

further, additional ADJ phôehm toehm เพิ่มเติม

fussy ADJ (COLLOQUIAL) rûeang mâak (literally, 'issues'-'many') เรื่องมาก, or (alternatively) jûu jîi จู้จี้

future N à-naa-khót อนาคต; in (the) future nai à-naakhót ในอนาคต

G

gain V dâi ráp ได้รับ

gallery N (from English) kael-loeh-lîi แกลเลอรี่

gallon N (from English) kael-lawn แกลลอน

gallstone N kâwn nǐu ก้อนนิ่ว; gallstones nǐu นิ่ว

67

gamble v lên kaan phá-nan
เล่นการพนัน

game N (from English) kehm
เกม

gang N (from English) káeng
แก๊ง, klùm กลุ่ม

gangster N nák lehng นักเลง

gap N châwng wâang ช่องว่าง

garage N (for car repairs)
ùu sâwm rót อู่ซ่อมรถ, (for
parking) rohng rót โรงรถ

garbage/rubbish/trash N
khà-yà ขยะ

garden, yard N (also
'plantation') sŭan สวน

gardens (public), park N
sŭan săa-thaa rá-ná สวน
สาธารณะ

garland N (garlands of flowers
are very common in Thailand)
phuang maa-lai พวงมาลัย
(NOTE: the same word is also
used for 'steering wheel'),
garland – also simply maalai
มาลัย

garlic N kra-thiam กระเทียม

garment, clothing N sûea
phâa เสื้อผ้า

gas N (from English, for
cooking etc.) káet แก๊ส

gasoline, petrol N náam-
man น้ำมัน

gasoline/gas/petrol station
N pám náam-man ปั๊มน้ำมัน

gasp v hàwp หอบ

gate, door N prà-tuu ประตู

gateway N thaang khâo ทาง
เข้า

gather v rûap ruam รวบรวม

gauze N (from English) phâa
káwt ผ้าก๊อซ

gay N (homosexual) (from
English) keh เกย์, (SLANG)
effeminate homosexual
tút ตุ๊ด

gaze v jáwng mawng จ้องมอง

gazette N năng-sŭeh-pim
หนังสือพิมพ์

gecko N túk-kae ตุ๊กแก

gem N pét phloi เพชรพลอย

gender N (sex – i.e. male/
female) phêht เพศ

general, all-purpose N & ADJ
thûa pai ทั่วไป

generally, in general ADV
dohy thûa pai โดยทั่วไป

generation N (used for people,
the particular year/vintage of
a car etc.) rûn รุ่น

generous ADJ jai kwâang

(literally, 'heart'-'broad/wide') ใจกว้าง

gentle, graceful ADJ (behavior, movement) àwn yohn อ่อน โยน; to do something (e.g. like a massage) gently bao-bao เบาๆ

gentleman N sù-phâap bùrùt สุภาพบุรุษ

genuine/authentic/real ADJ (the opposite of an imitation/ fake) tháeh แท้; the genuine article/the real thing khǎwng tháeh ของแท้

germ N chúea rôhk เชื้อโรค

German N (person) khon yoeh-rá-man คนเยอรมัน; German (language) phaa-sǎa yoeh-rá-man ภาษาเยอรมัน; Germany (the country) prà-thêht yoeh-rá-má-nii ประเทศเยอรมนี

gesture, manner, expression, bearing, attitude N (i.e. the way one appears to another – friendly, unfriendly, disinterested) thâa thaang ท่าทาง

get V (receive) dâi ได้, or dâi ráp ได้รับ

get off V (e.g. a bus) long ลง

get on V (e.g. a bus) khûen ขึ้น

get up/stand up V lúk khûen ลุกขึ้น

get well soon! hǎai wai-wai หายไวๆ

ghost N phǐi ผี

giant N yák yài ยักษ์ใหญ่

gift/present N khǎwng khwǎn ของขวัญ

giggle V hǔa ráw khík khák หัวเราะคิกคัก

ginger N khǐng ขิง

girl (child) N dèk phûu yǐng เด็กผู้หญิง, or simply dèk yǐng เด็กหญิง

girlfriend/boyfriend (steady) faehn แฟน; (SLANG) a casual girlfriend, mainly for sex and a bit of fun without much, if any, commitment N kík กิ๊ก

give V hâi ให้ (NOTE: this important word is also used in a variety of ways with various meanings – see the Thai-English section)

give in/give up V (as in 'I give in, you can go out if you want to' or, 'I give up, I can't fix it')

69

yawm pháeh (literally, 'allow/ permit'-'defeat') ยอมแพ้

glad ADJ dii jai ดีใจ

glamorous ADJ mii sà-nèh มีเสน่ห์

glance V lùeap mawng เหลือบมอง

glass N (for drinking) kâew แก้ว, (material – as in a window or the windscreen of a car. It is also the Thai word for 'mirror') krà-jòk กระจก

glasses, spectacles N wâen taa แว่นตา

glide V lûehn lǎi ลื่นไหล

globe N lôhk โลก

glorious ADJ sà-ngàa-ngaam สง่างาม

glory N kìat-tì-yôt เกียรติยศ

glossy ADJ man waow มันวาว

glove N thùng mueh ถุงมือ

glow V plèhng plàng เปล่งปลั่ง

glue/paste N kaaw กาว

glutinous ADJ (or sticky) rice khâaw nǐao ข้าวเหนียว

go V pai ไป – a common greeting in Thai is 'Where are you going?' pai nǎi (literally, 'go'-'where') ไปไหน. To ask 'where have you been?' is

pai nǎi maa (literally, 'go'- 'where'-'come') ไปไหนมา

go along, join in V pai dûai ไปด้วย

go around, visit V pai yîam ไปเยี่ยม

go back/return V klàp pai กลับไป, or simply klàp กลับ

go for a walk V pai doehn lên ไปเดินเล่น

go home V klàp bâan กลับ บ้าน

go out, exit V àwk pai ออกไป

go out V (for fun) (pai) thîao (ไป)เที่ยว (NOTE: the word thîao is another quintessential Thai term and used in various ways – e.g. to go to a friend's house (for fun) is thîao bâan phûean เที่ยวบ้านเพื่อน; to go to the beach (for fun) is thîao chaai hàat เที่ยวชายหาด; to go to a bar (for fun) is thîao baa เที่ยวบาร์; (for men) to go out and fool around with loose women is thîao phûu-yǐng เที่ยวผู้หญิง; and someone (invariably male) who is habitually interested in going out on the town at

night is a nák thîao นักเที่ยว)

go out (fire, candle, electricity – as in a blackout) dàp ดับ (also slang meaning 'to die')

go to bed v pai nawn ไปนอน

goal N (objective) pâo mǎai เป้าหมาย, (in football/soccer) prà-tuu ประตู (Note: the same word for 'door' or 'gate')

goat N phǎe แพะ

God N phrá phûu pen jâo พระผู้เป็นเจ้า, or simply phrá jâo พระเจ้า

goddess N jâo mâeh เจ้าแม่

gold N (precious metal) thawng kham ทองคำ, or simply thawng ทอง; the Golden Triangle (the area in northern Thailand where the borders of Burma, Laos, and Thailand meet) sǎam lìam thawng kham สามเหลี่ยมทองคำ

gold ADJ (color) sǐi thawng สีทอง

golf N (from English) káwp กอล์ฟ; to play golf lên káwp เล่นกอล์ฟ

gone ADJ (no longer available; used up) mòt láew หมดแล้ว

gonorrhea N (VD) rôhk nǎwng nai (literally, 'disease'-'pus'-'in') โรคหนองใน

good ADJ dii ดี; very good dii mâak ดีมาก

goodbye INTERJ (from English) báai baai บ๊ายบาย, (FORMAL) laa kàwn ลาก่อน, (MORE COLLOQUIALLY) pai kàwn ná ไปก่อนนะ

good-looking ADJ duu dii ดูดี

good luck! N chôhk dii โชคดี

goodness (me)! INTERJ ôh hoh โอ๊โฮ

goods N sǐn kháa สินค้า

goose N hàan ห่าน

gossip N súp síp ninthaa ซุบซิบนินทา, or simply (to talk behind one's back) ninthaa นินทา

govern v pòk khrawng ปกครอง

government N rát-thà-baan รัฐบาล

gown N sûea khlum เสื้อคลุม

GPO (General Post Office, i.e. the main post office or, following the Thai, the central post office) prai-sànii klaang

71

ไปรษณีย์กลาง (klaang glaang means 'central/middle')

GPS (navigation system – from English; pronounced very similar to the English 'GPS') จีพีเอส

grab/snatch v yâeng แย่ง

grace N khwaam sà-ngàa-ngaam ความสง่างาม

graceful ADJ sà-ngàa-ngaam สง่างาม

gradually, bit by bit ADV thii lá nít ทีละนิด

graduate v rian jòp เรียนจบ

grain N than-yá-púeht ธัญพืช

gram N (weight) (from English) kram กรัม

grand, great ADJ yîng yài ยิ่งใหญ่, yài toh ใหญ่โต

grandchild N lǎan หลาน

granddaughter N lǎan sǎow หลานสาว

grandfather N (maternal) taa ตา, (paternal) pùu ปู่

grandmother N (maternal) yaai ยาย, (paternal) yâa ย่า

grandparents N pùu yâa taa yaai ปู่ย่าตายาย

grandson N lǎan chaai หลานชาย

grant v yin yawm ยินยอม

grant N (public fund to finance educational study) thun kaan-sùek-sǎa ทุนการศึกษา

grapes N à-ngùn องุ่น

graph N (from English) kráap กราฟ

grasp v khwáa คว้า

grass N yâa หญ้า

grasshopper N ták-kà-taen ตั๊กแตน

grateful ADJ khàwp-khun ขอบคุณ

grave N lǔm sòp หลุมศพ

gray, grey ADJ sǐi thao สีเทา

grease N (as used in cars/trucks etc.) jaa-rá-bii จารบี

greasy ADJ See *oily*

great (COLLOQUIAL – as in 'that's great/fantastic'/'tops!') sùt yâwt สุดยอด

Greater vehicle of Buddhism – the Mahayana doctrine lát-thí máhǎa-yaan ลัทธิมหายาน

greed N lôhp โลภ, lá-môhp ละโมบ

green ADJ (color) sǐi khǐao สีเขียว

green beans N thùa fàk

yaow ถั่วฝักยาว

green light N fai-khǐaw ไฟ
เขียว, phàan ผ่าน

greens N (green vegetables)
phàk sǐi khǐaw ผักสีเขียว, or
simply phàk khǐaw ผักเขียว

greet/welcome V thák thaai
ทักทาย, or tâwn ráp ต้อนรับ

greetings N kaan thák thaai
การทักทาย

grenade N lûuk rá-bùeat ลูก
ระเบิด

grief N khwaam sâo ความ
เศร้า

grill/toast N pîng ปิ้ง, or yâang
ย่าง

grind V bòt bud

grocery N khǎwng cham
ของชำ

grocery store N ráan khǎai
khǎwng cham ร้านขาย
ของชำ

ground, earth, soil, dirt
N din ดิน; ground, earth
phúehn din พื้นดิน

group N klùm กลุ่ม, phùak
พวก, (COLLOQUIAL) group
of friends/mates/buddies/
entourage phák phùak พรรค
พวก

grow, plant V plùuk ปลูก

grow up V toh โต

grow larger V toh khûen
โตขึ้น

grown ADJ pen phûu yài เป็น
ผู้ใหญ่

grumpy ADJ ngùt-ngìt
หงุดหงิด

guarantee V (insure) prà-kan
ประกัน, also làk prà-kan
หลักประกัน

guard V fâo yaam เฝ้ายาม;
a guard (night watchman)
yaam ยาม

guess V dao เดา

guest N (visitor in one's home,
hotel guest) khàehk แขก
(NOTE: this word is also used
to refer to swarthy people
with darker complexions such
as Indians, Pakistanis, and
Arabs in general)

guesthouse N ruean ráp-
rawng khàehk เรือนรับรอง
แขก (NOTE: the English word
'guesthouse' is commonly
used in Thai, pronounced
something like 'guest-how')

guest of honor N khàehk
phûu mii kìat แขกผู้มีเกียรติ

guide/lead N nam นำ

guidebook N năngsŭeh nam thîao หนังสือนำเที่ยว

guilty (of a crime), **to be wrong** ADJ phìt ผิด

guilty, to feel V rúu-sùek phìt รู้สึกผิด

guitar N kii-tâa กีตาร์

gulf N àow อ่าว

gum N (chewing gum) măak-fá-ràng หมากฝรั่ง, (the tissue that surrounds the bases of the teeth) ngŭeak เหงือก

gun N (general term) peuhn ปืน; pistol/handgun peuhn phók ปืนพก; rifle peuhn yaow ปืนยาว (literally, 'gun'-'long'); shotgun peuhn lûuk săwng ปืนลูกซอง; machine gun peuhn kon ปืนกล; gunman/hitman/hired killer mueh-peuhn (literally, 'hand'-'gun') มือปืน

gut N (intestine) lam-sâi ลำไส้, (guts (courage)) khwaam-klâa ความกล้า

guy N (fellow) phûean เพื่อน, guys túk khon ทุกคน

gym N (from English) yim ยิม; (COLLOQUIAL) to work out in the gym/go to the gym lên yim

(literally, 'play'-'gym') เล่นยิม

gypsy N (from English) yíp-sii ยิปซี

H

habit N (habitual behavior, often used to refer to a person's character – what sort of person they happen to be) ní-săi นิสัย

hacker N (i.e. computer hacker – from English) háek-kôeh แฮกเกอร์

hail N (hailstones) lûuk hép ลูกเห็บ

hair N (on the head – humans) phŏm ผม, (hair on rest of the human body apart from the head; also for animals, i.e. fur) khŏn ขน

half N khrûeng ครึ่ง Also see 'Eurasian'

hall N (or large room) hâwng thŏhng ห้องโถง

ham N muu haem หมูแฮม

hammer N kháwn ค้อน

hammock N pleh yuan เปล ยวน, (COLLOQUIAL) pleh yuan

hand N mueh มือ

handcuffs N kun-jaeh mueh (literally, 'key'-'hand') กุญแจมือ

handicap/handicapped/ disabled N phí-kaan พิการ

handicraft N ngaan fīi-mueh งานฝีมือ, or (FORMAL) hàt-thà-kam หัตถกรรม

handle N (of an object, e.g. a knife) dâam ด้าม

handle V (to deal with) jàt kaan จัดการ

hand out, distribute V jàehk แจก

hand over V mâwp hâi มอบให้

handsome ADJ làw หล่อ; (COLLOQUIAL) a good-looking, handsome man rûup làw รูปหล่อ

handwriting N laai mueh ลายมือ

handy ADJ sà-dùak สะดวก

hang V (a painting) khwǎehn แขวน; to hang down/dangle (e.g. fruit hanging down from a tree) hôi ห้อย

hang out V (meet up and chill out) joeh kan เจอกัน, (spend time in a certain place) pai thîaw ไปเที่ยว

hangover N mao kháang เมาค้าง

happen/occur V kòeht khûen เกิดขึ้น

happened V (as in 'what happened?') kòeht àrai khûen เกิดอะไรขึ้น

happiness N khwaam sùk ความสุข

happy ADJ mii khwaam sùk มีความสุข

happy birthday! EXP sùksǎn wan kòeht สุขสันต์วันเกิด (or simply the expression 'happy birthday' pronounced in the Thai way – something like 'háeppîi bértday')

happy new year! EXP sà-wàt-dii pii-mài สวัสดีปีใหม่

harbor, pier, port N thâa ruea ท่าเรือ

hard ADJ (to be difficult) yâak ยาก, (solid, stiff) khǎeng แข็ง

hard disk N (from English) háad-dís ฮาร์ดดิสก์; (from English) hard drive háad-drái ฮาร์ดไดร์ว

hardly ADV (e.g. able to do

something, any left, etc.)
thâehp jà mâi… แทบจะไม่
hardship N (difficult
circumstances) khwaam
lambàak ความลำบาก, or
simply lambàak ลำบาก
**hardworking, industrious,
diligent** ADJ khà-yăn ขยัน
harm N an-tà-raai อันตราย
harmonious ADJ (e.g. relations
with others) khâo kan dâi
เข้ากันได้
harsh ADJ run raeng รุนแรง
harvest V (gathering crops)
kèp kìaw เก็บเกี่ยว
harvest N (yield, output) phŏn
phá-lìt ผลผลิต
haste V rêhng rîip เร่งรีบ
hat, cap N mùak หมวก; *also
see entry under 'helmet'*
hate V klìat เกลียด
hatred N khwaam klìat ความ
เกลียด
haunted ADJ lăwn หลอน
have… V mii… มี (the Thai
word is used in various ways,
e.g. to have available, to own,
there is…)
have been somewhere
khoei pai เคยไป: e.g. If

someone asks you 'have you
ever been to Chiang Mai?' –
in Thai the question is khun
khoei pai chiang mài măi
คุณเคยไปเชียงใหม่ไหม. If
you have, the answer 'yes' is
khoei pai เคยไป, or simply
just khoei เคย. To answer in
the negative 'I've never been'
is mâi khoei pai, or simply
mâi khoei ไม่เคย
have done something khoei
tham เคยทำ: e.g. If some
asks you 'have you ever
ridden a horse?' – in Thai the
question is khun khoei khìi
máa măi คุณเคยขี่ม้าไหม. If
you have, the answer 'yes' is
khoei khìi เคยขี่, or simply
just khoei เคย. To answer in
the negative see the previous
entry.
have to, must V tâwng ต้อง
haven N thâa ruea ท่าเรือ
hawk N yìaw เหยี่ยว
hay N faang ฟาง
hazard, danger N an-tà-raai
อันตราย
haze N màwk หมอก
he, him PRON (also she, her

76

and the third person plural pronoun 'they') khǎo เขา

head N (COLLOQUIAL) hǔa หัว, (the more formal medical term is) sǐi-sà ศีรษะ, (the boss, person in charge) hǔa nâa หัวหน้า

head for, toward PREP mûng pai มุ่งไป

headdress N khrûeang prà-dàp sǐi-sà เครื่องประดับศีรษะ

heal V rák-sǎa รักษา

health N sùk-khà-phâap สุขภาพ

healthy ADJ sǒmbuun สมบูรณ์, to be healthy sùk-khà-phâap dii สุขภาพดี, or khǎeng raehng แข็งแรง (which normally would be translated as 'strong', but also means 'healthy and well')

hear V dâi-yin ได้ยิน; listen to (the radio) fang ฟัง

heart N hǔa jai หัวใจ (NOTE: in a more metaphorical sense i.e. 'my heart is not in it' just the word jai ใจ is used. In Thai there are numerous compound words that

incorporate jai ใจ: e.g. to 'feel sorry' as in 'feeling sorry on hearing bad news' is sǐa jai (literally, 'spoiled'-'heart') เสียใจ

heart attack N hǔa jai waai หัวใจวาย

heartbreak N òk-hàk อกหัก

heartwarming ADJ òp-ùn-jai อบอุ่นใจ

heat V tham hâi ráwn ทำให้ร้อน

heat N khwaam ráwn ความร้อน

heaven/paradise N sà wǎn สวรรค์

heavy ADJ nàk หนัก; also see 'weight'

heel N (of the foot) sôn tháo ส้นเท้า

height N khwaam sǔung ความสูง

hell N ná-rók นรก

hello, hi INTERJ (greeting used at any time of the day) sàwàt dii สวัสดี

hello! INTERJ (answering the phone, from English) han-lǒh ฮัลโหล

helmet N (i.e. crash helmet/

help motorcycle helmet) mùak kan nók หมวกกันน็อก

help v chûai ช่วย or chûai lŭea ช่วยเหลือ

help! INTERJ ('Please help!') chûai dûai ช่วยด้วย

helper, assistance N phûu chûai ผู้ช่วย

hen N mâe kài แม่ไก่

hence, therefore ADV dang nán ดังนั้น

hepatitis N rôhk tàp àk-sèhp (literally, 'disease/illness'-'liver'-'inflamed') โรคตับอักเสบ

her, his, their PRON khăwng kháo ของเขา; hers, his, theirs khăwng khăo ของเขา

herb N sà-mŭn-phrai สมุนไพร

herd N fŭung ฝูง

herd v tâwn ต้อน

herdman, herder N khon líang sàt คนเลี้ยงสัตว์

here ADV thîi níi ที่นี่

hereditary N kammá-phan (pronounced 'gum-àpun') กรรมพันธุ์

heritage N maw-rá-dòk มรดก

hero N phrá-èk (e.g. in a film – 'leading man') พระเอก;

wii-rá bù-rùt (e.g. in a war, in a disaster saving lives) วีรบุรุษ, hii-rôh (from English) ฮีโร่; heroine naang-èk (e.g. in a film – 'leading woman') นางเอก, wii-rá-sà-trii (e.g. in a conflict etc.) วีรสตรี

heroin N (narcotic) (from English) heroh-iin เฮโรอีน, (COLLOQUIAL) phŏng khăow (literally, 'powder'-'white') ผงขาว

herpes (STD) N rôhk roem โรคเริม

hiccup N sà-ùek สะอึก

hidden ADJ sâwn yùu ซ่อนอยู่

hide v (from someone) (do something hyourself) àehp แอบ; to hide something/ to be hidden sâwn wái ซ่อนไว้

hide-and-seek N lên sawn hăa เล่นซ่อนหา

hierarchy N lam-dàp-chán ลำดับชั้น

higgle v tàw rawng ต่อรอง

higgledy-piggledy ADJ yûng yŏehng ยุ่งเหยิง

high ADJ (in or at a lofty position, level, or degree,

78

i.e. mountain, prices etc.)
sŭung สูง

high-five v tii-moeh ตีมือ

highland N thîi râap sŭung
ที่ราบสูง

highlight v tham hâi dèhn
ทำให้เด่น

high-voltage ADJ fai-fáa
raeng sŭung ไฟฟ้าแรงสูง

highway N thaang lǔang
ทางหลวง

hijack v jîi khrûeang bin จี้
เครื่องบิน

hike v, **hiking** N doehn pàa
เดินป่า

hilarious ADJ tà-lòk ตลก

hill N noehn khǎo เนินเขา, or
simply noehn เนิน

hill tribe N chaow khǎo
(literally, 'people'-'mountain')
ชาวเขา

hinder/obstruct v kìit
khwǎang กีดขวาง

hindrance N sìng kìit
khwǎang สิ่งกีดขวาง

hint N bàwk bâi บอกใบ้

hip N sà-phôhk สะโพก

hippy N (from English) híp-
pîi ฮิปปี้

hire/rent v châo เช่า (NOTE: to

hire/rent a car is châo rót
เช่ารถ, while a rental car is
rót châo รถเช่า)

his PRON (or 'hers' or 'their(s)')
khǎwng khǎo ของเขา

history prà-wàt-ti-sàat
ประวัติศาสตร์; one's own
personal history prà-wàt
sùan tua ประวัติส่วนตัว

hit, strike, beat v (for a
person to hit, strike, or beat
another person or object)
tii ดี; to hit or collide with....
chon ชน

hit-and-run ADJ chon láew nǐi
ชนแล้วหนี

HIV N (also see 'AIDS' – from
English) etch-ai-wii เอชไอวี

hive N rang phûeng รังผึ้ง

hoarse ADJ sǐang hàep เสียง
แหบ

hobby/pastime N ngaan
à-dì-rèhk งานอดิเรก

hockey N (from English)
hawk-kîi ฮ็อกกี้

hoe N jàwp จอบ

hoist v yók khûen ยกขึ้น

hold, grasp v thǔeh ถือ or
jàp จับ

hold back v yùt wái หยุดไว้

hole N (but not of the 'hole in the ground' variety) ruu รู; hole in the ground lŭm หลุม

holiday N (festival) wan yùt thêht-sà-kaan วันหยุด เทศกาล, (vacation) wan yùt phák phàwn วันหยุดพักผ่อน, (public) wan yùt râatchá-kaan วันหยุดราชการ, or simply wan yùt วันหยุด

holy, sacred ADJ sàksìt ศักดิ์สิทธิ์

home, house N bâan บ้าน

homework N (from school, college) kaan bâan การบ้าน; housework ngaan bâan งา นบ้าน

homicide N kaan khâa khon การฆ่าคน

homosexual See 'gay'

honest ADJ sûeh-sàt ซื่อสัตย์

honey N náam phûeng (literally, 'water'-'bee') น้ำผึ้ง

honeymoon N (from English) han-nii-muun ฮันนีมูน

Hong Kong N hâwng kong ฮ่องกง

honk V biip trae บีบแตร

honor N kìat-tì-yót เกียรติยศ

honor V hâi kìat ให้เกียรติ

hoodlum/tough guy/thug N anthá-phaan อันธพาล, or (MORE COLLOQUIALLY) nák-leng นักเลง

hooker, whore N (prostitute) (POLITE) sŏh-pheh-nii โสเภณี, (COLLOQUIAL) phûu-yĭng hăa kin (literally, 'woman'-'look for'-'eat') ผู้หญิงหากิน, phûu-yĭng hăa ngoehn (literally, 'woman'-'look for'-'money') ผู้หญิงหาเงิน

hop V krà-dòht กระโดด

hope V wăng หวัง, or 'to hope that...' wăng wâa...หวังว่า

hope N khwaam wăng ความ หวัง

hopeful ADJ mii khwaam wăng มีความหวัง

hopefully ADV dûai khwaam wăng ด้วยความหวัง

horizon N khàwp-fáa ขอบฟ้า

hormone N (from English) haw-mohn ฮอร์โมน

horny ADJ (desirous of sex) (SLANG, RUDE) ngîan เงี่ยน; also yàak อยาก (which, in general usage, means 'want')

horrible, horrific ADJ (frightening) nâa klua น่ากลัว

horrify v tham hâi klua ทำให้กลัว

hors d'oeuvre(s), entrée, starter N khǎwng wâang ของว่าง

horse N máa ม้า

horseman N thá-hǎan-máa ทหารม้า

hospital N rohng phá-yaa-baan โรงพยาบาล

host N jâo phâap เจ้าภาพ

hostage N tua prá-kan ตัวประกัน

hostel N thîi-phák ที่พัก, (from English) hóhs-tehl โฮสเทล

hostess N (in an entertainment establishment) phûu-yǐng bawrí-kaan (literally, 'woman'-'service') ผู้หญิงบริการ

hostile N sàt-truu ศัตรู

hot ADJ (spicy) phèt เผ็ด, (temperature) ráwn ร้อน, (as in 'sexy' – from English) háwt ฮอท (NOTE: the word 'sexy' is also commonly used in Thai sék-sîi เซ็กซี่)

hotheaded ADJ jai ráwn ใจร้อน

hotel N rohng-raehm โรงแรม

(NOTE: in Thailand there are many 'short-time' hotels with 'canvas curtains' so a car can be parked discreetly. These are known as rohng-raehm mâan rûut (literally, 'hotel'-'curtain'-'zip') โรงแรมม่านรูด)

hot spring N náam phú ráwn น้ำพุร้อน

hour N chûa-mohng ชั่วโมง

house N See 'home'

houseboat N See 'raft'

housekeeper N (servant), maid (in hotel) mâeh bâan (literally, 'mother'-'house'-'home') แม่บ้าน

how? ADV yàang-rai อย่างไร, or yang-ngai ยังไง: e.g. 'how do you do it?' tham yàang-rai ทำอย่างไร, or (in colloquial speech like this) tham yang ngai ทำยังไง (NOTE: in contrast to the English form this question tag comes at the end of the sentence)

how are you? sa-baai dii rǒeh? (NOTE: the word rǒeh here, although spelled with an 'r', is commonly pronounced lǒeh) สบายดี

81

หรือ, also sa-baai dii măi
สบายดีไหม

however ADV yàang-rai kâw
taam อย่างไรก็ตาม

**how long (does it take)?/for
how long?** naan thâorài
นานเท่าไร (the word naan
means 'a long time' so the
question – naan thâorài –
has the following pattern
'long time' – 'how much?')

how long? (length) yaaw
thâorài ยาวเท่าไร (the word
yaaw means 'long' with
the question yaaw thâorài
having the following pattern
'long' – 'how much?')

how many...? kìi… กี่

how much? thâorài เท่าไร
– to say 'how much is it?',
'what's the price?', or 'what
does it cost?' (the word for
price/cost is raa-khaa ราคา)
the pattern is raa-khaa ราคา
thâorài i.e. 'price/cost' –
'how much?' ราคาเท่าไร

how old? aa-yú thâorài อายุ
เท่าไร (the word for 'age'
is aa-yú อายุ – again the
pattern is the same as above

hug V kàwt กอด

huge ADJ yài ใหญ่

human/human being N
má-nút มนุษย์

humane ADJ mii náam jai มี
น้ำใจ

humble ADJ thàwm tua ถ่อม
ตัว

humid ADJ chúehn ขึ้น

humiliate V khăi nâa ขาย
หน้า, sĭa nâa เสียหน้า

humorous, funny, amusing
ADJ khòp khăn ขบขัน, or
tà-lòk ตลก

hundred NUM rói ร้อย

hundred thousand NUM
săehn แสน

hungry ADJ hǐu หิว: the
common expression for
'I'm hungry' is hǐu khâaw
(literally, 'hungry'-'rice/food')
หิวข้าว; for 'I'm thirsty' the
expression is hǐu náam
(literally, 'hungry'-'water')
หิวน้ำ

hunt V lâa ล่า

hurricane N phaa-yú hoeh-rí-
khehn พายุเฮอริริเคน

hurry up! V rew-rew เร็วๆ

hurt (injured), sore ADJ jèp เจ็บ

hurt v (cause pain) tham hâi jèp ทำให้เจ็บ

husband N (POLITE) sǎa-mii สามี, (SLANG) phǔa ผัว (in more educated circles considered rude, generally seen as low class language – referring to the sexual partner of a woman, the couple not being formally married)

husk N plùehk เปลือก

hut, shack, shed N krà-thâwm กระท่อม, or krà-táwp กระต๊อบ

hybrid car N ('hybrid' from English) rót-yon hai-brìd รถยนต์ไฮบริด

hydrate v toehm náam เติมน้ำ

hydration N chum chûehn ชุ่มชื้น

hygiene/cleanliness N khwaam sà-àat ความสะอาด

I

I, me PRON (NOTE: there are numerous first person pronouns, i.e. the words for

'I' and 'me', and other ways to refer to oneself in Thai. This issue is too complex to be discussed here. For our purposes the following common polite terms will suffice: for males phǒm (the same word as 'hair on the head') ผม; for females dìchǎn ดิฉัน, or simply chǎn ฉัน)

ice N náam khǎeng น้ำแข็ง (literally, 'water'-'hard')

ice cream N (from English) ai-sà-khriim ไอสกรีม

ice pack N thǔng náam khǎeng ถุงน้ำแข็ง

icon N (from English) ai-khâwn ไอคอน

ICU (from the English abbreviation of the term 'Intensive Care Unit' – in common usage in Thai hospitals and used by the general public) ai-sii-yuu ไอซียู

ID (in this entry referring to 'Identity card' which all Thai citizens possess) bàt prà-chaachon (literally, 'card'-

'people/populace') บัตร
ประชาชน

idea N khwaam khít ความคิด

ideal N ù-dom-khá-tì อุดมคติ

identical, alike, the same as ADJ mǔean-kan เหมือนกัน, or simply mǔean เหมือน

identification card N bàt-prá-chaa-chon บัตร
ประชาชน

identity N (as in 'national identity/characteristics') èkkàlák เอกลักษณ์, Thai identity èkkàlák thai
เอกลักษณ์ไทย

ideologist N nák khít นักคิด

ideology N naew khít แนวคิด

idiom N (figure of speech) sǎm-nuan สำนวน

idiot N (a fool) khon ngô (literally, 'person'-'stupid')
คนโง่

idol N (from English) ai-dâwl
ไอดอล

if CONJ (used in much the same way as English) thâa ถ้า

ignite V jùt fai จุดไฟ

ignorant ADJ (to be unaware of something, not to know what's going on) (COLLOQUIAL)
mâi rúu rûeang ไม่รู้เรื่อง;
ignorant ('unschooled' or 'uneducated') khàat kaan sùek-sǎa (literally, 'missing/ without'-'education') ขาดการ
ศึกษา or mâi mii kaan sùek-sǎa (literally, 'no'-'have'-'education') ไม่มีการศึกษา

ignore V lá loei ละเลย, or mâi sǒn-jai (literally, 'no'-'interest') ไม่สนใจ

ill/sick ADJ pùai ป่วย, or simply mâi-sàbaai ไม่สบาย

ill will N mâi jing jai ไม่จริงใจ

illegal/illicit ADJ phìt kòt-mǎai ผิดกฎหมาย

illiterate ADJ (VERY INFORMAL)
mâi rúu nǎng-sǔeh
ไม่รู้หนังสือ, (MORE FORMAL)
mâi mii kan sùek-sǎa ไม่มี
การศึกษา

illness N khwaam jèp pùai
ความเจ็บป่วย

illude, deceive V làwk luang
หลอกลวง

illuminate V tham-hâi sà-wàang ทำให้สว่าง

illusion N phâap luang taa
ภาพลวงตา

illustration N phâap prà-kàwp ภาพประกอบ

image N phâap ภาพ, or rûup phâap รูปภาพ

imagination N jin-tà-naa-kaan (NOTE: the first syllable jin is pronounced like the English word 'gin') จินตนาการ

imagine V (visualize an image) néuk phâap นึกภาพ, (in the sense 'imagine/suppose that....?') sŏm-mút wâa สม-มุติว่า

imbalance N mâi sŏm-dun ไม่สมดุล

imitate V lian bàep เลียนแบบ

imitation N kaan lian bàep การเลียนแบบ

immature ADJ yang dèk ยัง เด็ก

immediately ADV than thii ทันที

immense ADJ jam nuan maâak จำนวนมาก

immigrant N phûu òp-phá-yóp ผู้อพยพ

immigration N (as in the Immigration Bureau where visas are extended, etc.) sam nák ngaan trùat

khon khâo mueang สำนักงานตรวจคนเข้าเมือง, (colloquially referred to by the abbreviation tǎw maw [pronounced like the words trùat ตรวจ – 'check/inspect' and mueang เมือง – 'country'] ตรวจ)ตม

immoral ADJ phìt sǐin ผิดศีล

immortal ADJ (FORMAL) am-má-tà อมตะ, mâi taai ไม่ตาย

immune ADJ mii phuum tâan thaan มีภูมิต้านทาน

impart V hâi khwaam rúu ให้ความรู้

impartial, fair ADJ yú-tì-tham ยุติธรรม

impatient ADJ jai ráwn (literally, 'heart'-'hot') ใจร้อน

impeach V fáwng ráwng ฟ้องร้อง

implicate V kìaw khâwng เกี่ยวข้อง

implicit ADJ chat jehn ชัดเจน

implore, beg for V khǎw ráwng ขอร้อง

imply V bàwk thǔeng บอกถึง

impolite, rude ADJ mâi sù-phâap ไม่สุภาพ

import N (imported goods) sǐn-

85

kháa nam khâo สินค้านำเข้า

import v nam khâo นำเข้า

importance N khwaam sămkhan ความสำคัญ

important ADJ sămkhan สำคัญ

impossible ADJ pen pai mâi dâi เป็นไปไม่ได้

impotent ADJ mâi mii raeng ไม่มีแรง

impress v tham-hâi prà-tháp jai ทำให้ประทับใจ

impression N khwaam prà-tháp jai ความประทับใจ

impressive ADJ nâa-prà-tháp jai น่าประทับใจ

improve v pràp-prung ปรับปรุง

improvement N kaan pràp-prung การปรับปรุง

impudence N mâi mii maa-rá-yâat ไม่มีมารยาท

impure ADJ mâi baw-rí-sùt ไม่บริสุทธิ์

in PREP (inside) nai ใน, (a period of time) phaai nai ภายใน

inaccurate ADJ mâi thùuk tâwng ไม่ถูกต้อง

inadequate ADJ mâi phaw ไม่พอ

incense N (joss sticks) thûup ธูป

inch ADJ níw นิ้ว

incident N hèht kaan เหตุการณ์

incite, provoke v yûa-yú ยั่วยุ

incline v (to have a certain tendency) mii naew nôhm มีแนวโน้ม, (to slope) iang เอียง

include v ruam รวม; including... ruam tháng... รวมทั้ง

income, wages, salary N raai dâi รายได้, (MORE COLLOQUIAL) ngoen duean เงินเดือน

incomparable ADJ thîap kan mâi dâi เทียบกันไม่ได้

incompatible ADJ (e.g. two people who do not get on) khâo kan mâi dâi เข้ากันไม่ได้

inconvenient ADJ mâi sà-dùak ไม่สะดวก

increase v phôehm เพิ่ม, or phôehm khûen เพิ่มขึ้น

incredible ADJ (as in 'amazing!', 'unbelivable!') mâi nâa chûea ไม่น่าเชื่อ

indeed! INTERJ (to emphasize something as in 'really, it's true!') jing-jing จริงๆ

independent ADJ (to be free, not to be controlled by others) ìtsàrà อิสระ

index N (in a printed work) dàt-chá-nii ดัชนี, (finger) níw chíi นิ้วชี้

India N prà-thêht in-dia ประเทศอินเดีย, **Indian** N khon in-dia คนอินเดีย

indifferent/blasé ADJ chŏei-chŏei เฉยๆ (NOTE: a very commonly used expression in Thai)

indigenous ADJ (person) chaow phúehn mueang ชาวพื้นเมือง; for something that is indigenous to a particular place simply – phúehn mueang พื้นเมือง

indigo N sĭi khraam สีคราม

indirect ADJ thaang âwm ทางอ้อม

Indonesia N (the country) indohnii-sia อินโดนีเซีย (in colloquial speech Indonesia is often referred to simply as indo อินโด)

Indonesian N chaow indohnii-sia ชาวอินโดนีเซีย, or khon indohnii-sia คนอินโดนีเซีย; Indonesian (language) phaa-săa indohnii-sia ภาษาอินโดนีเซีย

induct V náe nam แนะนำ

industry N (factories etc.) ùt-săahà-kam อุตสาหกรรม

inequality N mâi thâo kan ไม่เท่ากัน

inexpensive ADJ mâi phaehng ไม่แพง

inexperience N mâi mii prà-sòp-kaan ไม่มีประสบการณ์

infamous ADJ sĭa chûeh เสียชื่อ

infant N thaa rók ทารก

infect N tìt chúea ติดเชื้อ, or tìt rôhk ติดโรค

infection N kaan tìt chúea การติดเชื้อ, kaan tìt rôhk การติดโรค

influence N ìt-thí-phon อิทธิพล

influence V (to have influence – in Thai this generally means to have 'connections' enabling one to engage in 'extra legal' activities) mii ìt-thí-phon มีอิทธิพล (There is also the expression ìt-thí-phon mûehd อิทธิพลมืด which means 'dark influence(s)' or, more correctly in English, 'dark force(s)' which is used to refer to well-placed individuals involved behind the scenes in political intrigue, extortion, bribery, murder)

influenza N (the flu) khâi wàt yài ไข้หวัดใหญ่

inform V (e.g. the police about a problem) jâehng แจ้ง; inform (tell) bàwk บอก

informal ADJ mâi pen thaang kaan ไม่เป็นทางการ

information, data N khâw-muun ข้อมูล; knowledge khwaam rúu ความรู้

information booth/ hotel reception N (where information about various things is available)/public relations prà-chaa sǎmphan ประชาสัมพันธ์

ingredient(s) N (in a recipe) sùan prà-kàwp ส่วนประกอบ

inhabit/live V yùu aa-sǎi

อยู่อาศัย, or simply yùu อยู่

inhabitant N phûu yùu aa-sǎi ผู้อยู่อาศัย

inhale V sùut สูด

inhibit V hâam ห้าม

inhumane ADJ hòht rái โหดร้าย

initial ADJ rôehm tôn เริ่มต้น

initiate V rí-rôehm ริเริ่ม

inject V chìit ฉีด; an injection of medicine/vaccine/drug chìit yaa ฉีดยา

injured ADJ dâi ráp bàat jèp (literally, 'receive/get'-'injury') ได้รับบาดเจ็บ

injury N bàat jèp บาดเจ็บ

injustice N mâi yú-tì-tham ไม่ยุติธรรม

ink N mùek หมึก

innocent ADJ bawrí-sùt บริสุทธิ์ (NOTE: the English word 'innocent' – in-noh-sén อินโนเซนท์ – is also used in Thai. Additionally, the Thai term bawrí-sùt is also used to refer to a virgin)

innovation N ná-wát tà-kam นวัตกรรม

in order that, so that CONJ phûea thîi เพื่อที่

inquire v sàwp thăam สอบถาม

insane ADJ rôhk jìt โรคจิต; (or simply the word for) mad/ crazy bâa บ้า – a simple slang expression to express the same thing is to refer to such a person as mâi tem (literally, 'not'-'full') ไม่เต็ม

insect N (general term for insects) má-laehng แมลง

insecure ADJ mâi mân khong ไม่มั่นคง

insert v sâek แทรก

inside PREP khâang nai ข้างใน

insignificant ADJ mâi sǎm khan ไม่สำคัญ

insist v yuehn kraan ยืนกราน

inspect v trùat ตรวจ

inspector N phûu trùat sàwp ผู้ตรวจสอบ

inspire v ban-daan jai บันดาลใจ; **inspiration** N raeng ban-daan jai แรงบันดาลใจ

install v tìt tang ติดตั้ง

installment N phàwn jàai ผ่อนจ่าย

instance N tua yàang ตัวอย่าง

instant ADJ than thii ทันที

instead of PREP thaen thîi

แทนที่, or simply thaen แทน

institute N sà-thǎa-ban สถาบัน

instruct (to give advice) v hâi kham náe-nam ให้คำแนะนำ

instrument/tool N khrûeang mueh เครื่องมือ

insufficient ADJ mâi phaw ไม่พอ

insult/look down (someone) v duu thùuk ดูถูก

insure v prà-kan ประกัน; **insurance** N prà-kan phai ประกันภัย

integrate v phà-sǒm phá-sǎan ผสมผสาน

intellect N pan yaa ปัญญา, or sàtì-pan yaa สติปัญญา

intelligent ADJ mii sàtì-pan yaa มีสติปัญญา, (MORE COLLOQUIAL) chà-làat ฉลาด

intend v tâng-jai ตั้งใจ

intended for ADJ sǎm-ràp สำหรับ

intense ADJ khêhm khôn เข้มข้น

intention N khwaam tâng-jai ความตั้งใจ

interest N (a charge for a loan) dàwk bîa ดอกเบี้ย, (or collo-

89

quially, simply) dàwk ดอก

interest N (personal) khwaam sǒn-jai ความสนใจ

interested ADJ sǒn-jai สนใจ

interesting ADJ nâa sǒn-jai น่าสนใจ

interior ADJ phaai nai ภายใน

international ADJ naa-naa châat นานาชาติ

Internet N (from English) inthoehnèt อินเทอร์เน็ต, (COLLOQUIAL) nèt เน็ต

interpret/translate v plaeh แปล (NOTE: one common way to ask 'what does this/that mean?' is plaeh wâa àrai แปลว่าอะไร)

interpreter N lâam ล่าม

interrogate v sàwp sǔan สอบสวน

interrupt v khàt-jang-wà ขัดจังหวะ

intersection N (i.e. four-way intersection) sìi yâehk สี่ แยก (the word yâehk แยก means 'to separate'); a five-way intersection hâa yâehk ห้าแยก

intervene v sâek saeng แทรกแซง

interview v sǎm-phâat สัมภาษณ์

intimate ADJ (to be close to, a close friend) sà-nìt สนิท; also see 'friend'

intimidate v khùu ขู่

into PREP (to the inside) khâo pai khâang-nai (literally, 'enter'-'go'-'inside') เข้า ไปข้างใน

intolerant ADJ òt-thon อดทน

introduce v náe-nam tua แนะนำตัว

intrude, invade v bùk rúk บุกรุก

invent v prà-dìt ประดิษฐ์

invest v (in a business etc.) long thun ลงทุน

investigate v sùep สืบ

invisible ADJ mawng mâi hěn มองไม่เห็น

invitation N kham choehn คำเชิญ

invite v (COLLOQUIAL) chuan ชวน, (FORMAL) choehn เชิญ

invoice, receipt N bai kèp ngoehn ใบเก็บเงิน, (COLLOQUIAL) bai sèht ใบเสร็จ

involve v kìao khâwng เกี่ยวข้อง

iron N (steel) lèk เหล็ก, (an appliance) tao rîit เตารีด

iron V (clothes) rîit phâa รีดผ้า

ironic ADJ prà-chót ประชด

irregular ADJ mâi pòk-kà-tì ไม่ปกติ

irrelevant ADJ mâi kìaw khâwng ไม่เกี่ยวข้อง

irritate V kuan jai กวนใจ

Islam N (the religion of Islam) sàat-sà-nǎa ìt-sàlaam ศาสนาอิสลาม

island N kàw (pronounced very short like 'oh!' in 'Oh! Ooh' with a 'g' sound in front) เกาะ

isolate V yâek tua แยกตัว

issue N pan hǎa ปัญหา

it PRON man (the an pronounced like 'un' in 'unlucky') มัน (used for things, animals, an event, an issue, etc. – NOTE: when used to refer to a person it is extremely rude; at times some Thai people may use this to refer to foreigners which reflects a contemptuous attitude)

itch N khan คัน

itchy ADJ mii aa-kaan khan มีอาการคัน

item, individual thing N sìng สิ่ง

itinerary N phǎen kaan doehn thaang แผนการเดินทาง

itself PRON tua-ehng ตัวเอง

ivory N ngaa cháang งาช้าง

J

jabber V phûut rua พูดรัว

jacket N (from English) jáekkêt แจ็คเก็ต

jade N yòk หยก

jail/gaol N khúk คุก; to be in jail/gaol/incarcerated tìt khúk ติดคุก

jam N (from English, e.g. 'strawberry jam') yaehm แยม

January N má-ká raa-khom มกราคม

Japan N yîipùn ญี่ปุ่น

Japanese N chaow yîipùn ชาวญี่ปุ่น, or khon yîipùn คนญี่ปุ่น

jar N (i.e. a large water jar) òhng โอ่ง; a (very) small jar (e.g. containing face powder/ ointment etc.) krà-pùk กระปุก

jaw N kraam กราม

jealous/envious ADJ ìt-chǎa อิจฉา; jealous (a jealous boy-friend, wife etc.) hǔeng หึง; someone who is extremely jealous khîi hǔeng ขี้หึง

jealousy N khwaam ìt-chǎa ความอิจฉา

jeans N (from English) kaang keng yiin กางเกงยีน

jelly N wún วุ้น, (from English) yen lîi เยลลี่

jellyfish N maehng-kà-phrun แมงกะพรุน

jet ski N (from English) jét sà-kii เจ็ตสกี

jewel N phét phloi เพชรพลอย

jewelry N khrûeang phét phloi เครื่องเพชรพลอย

jinx N tua chôhk ráai ตัวโชค ร้าย, (COLLOQUIAL) tua suai ตัวซวย

job, work N ngaan งาน (NOTE: the same word also means 'a party' or 'a festive occasion')

jockey N nák khìi máa นักขี่ม้า

jogging N wing cháa cháa วิ่งช้าๆ

join, go along V pai dûai ไปด้วย

join together/participate V khâo ruam เข้าร่วม

joint N (in the body) khâw ข้อ

joke V (with someone) phûut lên พูดเล่น

jot down V jòt yâw yâw จดย่อๆ

journal N (periodical) waa-rá-sǎan วารสาร, (personal record) ban-thúek บันทึก

journalist N nák khàaw นัก ข่าว

journey N kaan doehn thaang การเดินทาง

joy N khwaam sà-nùk ความ สนุก

joyful ADJ sà-nùk สนุก

judge N See 'magistrate'

judge/decide V tàt-sǐn ตัดสิน

jug (of beer), pitcher N yùeak เหยือก

juice N (i.e. fruit juice) náam phǒnlá-mái น้ำผลไม้

July N kà-rákàdaakhom กรกฎาคม

jump V krà-dòht กระโดด

junction N thaang yâek ทาง แยก

June mí-thù-naayon มิถุนายน

92

jungle N pàa ป่า

junior N rûn náwng รุ่นน้อง

junk food N aa-hǎan khà-yà อาหารขยะ

junta N rát-thá-baan thá-hǎan รัฐบาลทหาร

juristic ADJ kòt-mǎai กฎหมาย

jury N khá-ná lûuk khǔn คณะ ลูกขุน

just, only ADV thâonán เท่านั้น; 'only/just ten baht' sìp bàat thâonán สิบบาทเท่านั้น (NOTE: a very useful and common expression meaning 'just this/that amount' is khâe níi (this) แค่นี้, or khâe nán (that) แค่นั้น. And for the sentence 'I just want this much' you say '(I' is understood) – ao khâe níi (literally, 'want'-'just'-'this') เอาแค่นี้)

just/fair ADJ yút-tì-tham ยุติธรรม

justice N khwaam yút-tì-tham ความยุติธรรม

justify V phí-sùut พิสูจน์

just now ADV dǐao níi ehng เดี๋ยวนี้เอง, or phaw dii พอดี

juvenile ADJ (FORMAL) yao-wá-chon เยาวชน, (COLLOQUIAL) wai-rûn วัยรุ่น

K

kale N khá-náa คะน้า

kangaroo N jing-jôh จิงโจ้

karaoke N khaa-raa oh-kè คาราโอเกะ

Karen N (ethnic group living in different areas along the Thai-Burmese/Myanmar border) kà-rìang กะเหรี่ยง

karma N kam (pronounced like 'gum' as in 'chewing gum') กรรม

keen ADJ mii wǎi phríp มี ไหวพริบ

keep V kèp เก็บ, also kèp wái เก็บไว้ (NOTE: wái ไว้ is an important word in Thai. In conjunction with other words it serves a number of functions. In a broader sense it means to 'preserve/conserve/uphold' and to 'place/leave/replace, restore/wear') See Thai-English section.

keeper N (phûu duu-lae) ผู้ดูแล

kettle N (hot water jug) (kaa náam) กาน้ำ

key N (to a room) (kunjaeh) กุญแจ

key ADJ (săm-khan) สำคัญ

keyboard N (of computer – from English) (khii-bàwt) คีย์บอร์ด

Khmer N See 'Cambodia'

kick V (tèh) เตะ

kickboxing N (i.e. Thai boxing) (muai thai) มวยไทย

kickoff N (rôehm tôn) เริ่มต้น

kid N (child) (dèk) เด็ก

kidnap/abduct V (lák phaa) ลักพา

kidney(s) N (tai) ไต

kidney beans N (thùa daehng) (literally, 'beans'-'red') ถั่วแดง

kill/murder V (khâa) ฆ่า

killer N (khâat-tà-kawn) ฆาตกร

kilogram N (kì-loh kram) กิโลกรัม, or simply (kì-loh) กิโล

kilometer N (kì-loh mêht) กิโลเมตร, or simply (kì-loh) กิโล

kind, good ADJ (of persons) (jai dii) ใจดี

kind N (type) (prà-phêht) ประเภท

kindergarten N (rohng rian à-nú-baan) โรงเรียนอนุบาล

king N (phrá-má-hăa kà-sàt) พระมหากษัตริย์ (NOTE: in everyday speech the Thai monarch is referred to as (nai lŭang) ในหลวง)

kingdom N (aà-naa-jàk) อาณาจักร

kinship N (khrâwp khrua) ครอบครัว

kiss V (jùup) (pronounced 'joop') จูบ

kitchen N (hâwng khrua) ห้องครัว, or simply (khrua) ครัว

kite N (wâow) ว่าว

kitten N (lûuk maew) ลูกแมว

knee N (hŭa khào) หัวเข่า or simply (khào) เข่า

kneel V (khúk khào) คุกเข่า

knife N (mîit) มีด; to be cut by a knife (i.e. wound inflicted by knife) (mîit bàat) มีดบาด; similarly 'cut by a piece of glass' (kâew bàat) แก้วบาด

knight N (àt-sà-win) อัศวิน

knit V (thàk) ถัก

knock V (on a door) (kháw)

L

(pronounced with a very short vowel – similar to the first part of the exclamation 'oh! ooh' preceded by a 'k' sound) เคาะ; knock on the door kháw prà-tuu เคาะประตู

know v rúu รู้ (somewhat more formal, and in certain contexts more polite, is the word sâap ทราบ)

know, be acquainted with v rúu-jàk รู้จัก

knowledge n khwaam rúu ความรู้

koala n (bear) khoh-aa-lâa โคอาล่า

Korea (North) kao-lǐi nǔea เกาหลีเหนือ

Korea (South) kao-lǐi tâi เกาหลีใต้

Korean (person) khon kao-lǐi คนเกาหลี

kungfu n muai jiin (literally, 'boxing'-'Chinese') มวยจีน

label n pâai ป้าย, or khrûeang mǎai เครื่องหมาย

labor, labour chái raeng ngaan ใช้แรงงาน

laborer, labourer n (construction worker) kam-má-kawn กรรมกร

lack v khàat khlaehn ขาดแคลน; lacking ADJ khàat ขาด

ladder n bandai บันได

ladle, dipper n krà-buai กระบวย

lady n sù-phâap sà-trii สุภาพ สตรี

lake n thá-leh sàap ทะเลสาบ

lamb n (mutton) núea kàe เนื้อแกะ

lamp n (lattern) tà-kiang ตะเกียง, (an electric lamp) kohm-fai โคมไฟ

land, plot, lot, property n thîi din ที่ดิน

land/go down v (plane) long ลง

landlord n jâo khǎwng bâan châo (literally, 'owner'-'house'-'rent') เจ้าของบ้านเช่า

lane N (of a highway – from English) lehn เลน, (anywhere in size from a small lane to what many would consider a significant road) soi ซอย

language N phaa-săa ภาษา; sign language phaa-săa bâi ภาษาใบ้

Laos N (country) prà-thêht lao ประเทศลาว, (COLLOQUIAL) lao ลาว

Laotian N khon lao คนลาว

laptop/notebook computer N *See* 'computer'

large, big ADJ yài ใหญ่

laser N săeng leh-sôeh แสง เลเซอร์

last ADJ (e.g. last piece of cake; to be last in a race) sùt tháai สุดท้าย

last name, surname N naam sà-kun นามสกุล

last night N mûea khuehn níi เมื่อคืนนี้

last week N aa thít thîi láew อาทิตย์ที่แล้ว

last year N pii thîi láew ปีที่แล้ว

late ADV (after the expected time) sǎai สาย, ADJ (delayed) cháa ช้า

late at night ADV dùek ดึก

lately/recently ADV mûea rew-rew níi เมื่อเร็วๆ นี้

later ADV thii lǎng ที่หลัง

laugh V hǔa ráw หัวเราะ

laugh at V hǔa ráw yáw หัวเราะเยาะ

launch N plòi ปล่อย

laundry N sák phâa ซักผ้า

lavatory/toilet N hâwng náam (literally, 'room'-'water') ห้องน้ำ

lavish ADJ fûm-fueay ฟุ่มเฟือย

lawn, oval, playing fields N sà-nǎam yáa สนามหญ้า

law, legislation N kòtmǎai กฎหมาย

lawyer N thá-naai-khwaam ทนายความ, (COLLOQUIAL) thá-naai ทนาย

lay V (to put something down i.e. 'to put a book on the table') waang วาง, (as in 'lay down on the bed') nawn long นอนลง; to lay/sleep on one's stomach nawn khwâm นอนคว่ำ; to lay/sleep on one's back nawn ngǎai นอน หงาย; to lay/sleep on one's side nawn tà-khaehng นอน ตะแคง

lay or set the table v (i.e. before dinner) jàt tó จัดโต๊ะ

layer, floor in a building N (e.g. on the tenth floor) chán ชั้น

layoff N lôehk jâang เลิกจ้าง

layout N phǎen-ngaan แผนงาน

lazy ADJ khîi kìat ขี้เกียจ

lead N (metal) tà kùa ตะกั่ว

lead v (or take someone somewhere) nam นำ, or phaa พา, (to guide someone somewhere) nam pai นำไป

leader N phûu nam ผู้นำ

leaf N bai mái ใบไม้

leak v rûa รั่ว, N (a crack or hole) roi-rûa รอยรั่ว

lean v ehn เอน

leap, jump v krá-dòht กระโดด

learn/study v rian เรียน

lease v (a property) hâi châo ให้เช่า

least ADJ (smallest amount) nói thîi sùt น้อยที่สุด

least ADV (at least) yàang nói อย่างน้อย

leather N nǎng หนัง

leave, depart (for) v àwk pai ออกไป

leave behind by accident v (i.e. forget) luehm ลืม

leave behind on purpose v thíng wái ทิ้งไว้

leave behind for safe-keeping v (deposit, store, leave something somewhere to be picked up later) fàak ฝาก

lecture v kaan banyaai การบรรยาย

leech N pling ปลิง

left (opposite of 'right') sáai ซ้าย; on the left khâang sáai ข้างซ้าย; left-hand side sáai mueh ซ้ายมือ; to be left-handed thà-nàt mueh sáai ถนัดมือซ้าย

left, remaining ADJ thîi lǔea ที่เหลือ

leg(s) N khǎa ขา

legal ADJ taam kòtmǎai ตามกฎหมาย

legend N tam naan ตำนาน

leisure N (free time) wehlaa wâang เวลาว่าง

lemon N (citrus) má-naaw มะนาว

lemongrass N tà-khrái ตะไคร้

lend v hâi yuehm ให้ยืม

97

length N khwaam yaow ความยาว

lens N (i.e. a camera lens – from English) len เลนส์

lesbian N (SLANG/COLLOQUIAL) feminine lesbian – from the English word 'lady') dîi ดี้, (butch lesbian – from the English word 'tom') tawm ทอม

less ADJ (a lesser amount) nói kwàa น้อยกว่า

lessen, reduce V lót long ลดลง, or simply lót ลด (as in 'reduce the price') lót raa-khaa ลดราคา

Lesser vehicle of Buddhism, Hinayana N latthí hĭnnáyaan ลัทธิ หินยาน

lesson N (at school; also used in the sense as a 'lesson' learned through experience) bòt rian บทเรียน

let, allow, permit V à-nú-yâat อนุญาต, let (someone do something etc.) hâi ให้ (NOTE: this is an important word in Thai used in a variety of ways – see the Thai-English section)

let someone know V (i.e to tell someone) bàwk บอก

letter N (as in a 'letter in the mail') jòt măai จดหมาย, (in the alphabet) àk-săwn อักษร, tua àk-săwn ตัวอักษร, or tua năng-sŭeh ตัวหนังสือ

lettuce N phàk salàt (literally, 'vegetable'-'salad') ผักสลัด

level N (even, flat) rîap เรียบ, or râap ราบ, (storey in a tall building) chán ชั้น, (position or rank on a scale) rá-dàp ระดับ

lewd ADJ (crude, obscene) laa-mók ลามก

liable ADJ ráp phìt châwp รับ ผิดชอบ

liberty N ìt-sà-rà-phâap อิสรภาพ

library N hâwng sà-mùt ห้อง สมุด

license N (i.e. driver's license) bai khàp khìi ใบขับขี่, **permit** N bai à-nú-yâat ใบ อนุญาต

lick V lia เลีย

lid N (of a jar etc.) făa ฝา

lie, tell a falsehood V koh-hòk โกหก, (COLLOQUIAL/SLANG) taw-lǎeh ตอแหล; a liar khon koh-hòk คนโกหก

lie down v nawn นอน

life N chii-wít ชีวิต, (as in 'this life', 'this incarnation') châat níi ชาตินี้

lifejacket N sûea chuuchîip เสื้อชูชีพ

lifetime N & ADJ (throughout one's life) tà-làwt chii-wít ตลอดชีวิต

lift, elevator N (from English) líp ลิฟท์

lift v (to give someone a lift in a car) pai sòng ไปส่ง, (to raise) yók ยก

light v (light a match) jùt จุด; (light a fire) jùt fai จุดไฟ

light ADJ (not heavy) bao เบา, (bright) sà-wàang สว่าง

light N (lamp) fai ไฟ

light bulb N làwt fai หลอดไฟ

lighter N (cigarette lighter) fai cháek ไฟแช็ค

lightning N fáa phàa ฟ้าผ่า

like ADJ (to be the same) mǔean เหมือน

like v (to be pleased by) châwp ชอบ

like this ADV (COLLOQUIAL) (i.e.

in this way/in this manner) bàehp níi แบบนี้ 'do it like this' (e.g. holding chopsticks) tham bàehp níi ทำแบบนี้

likely N pen pai dâi เป็นไปได้

like-minded ADJ (having the same ideas/tastes) mii jai trong kan ถูกใจกัน (literally, 'have'-'heart/mind'-'straight/direct'-'together') มีใจตรงกัน

likewise ADV mǔean kan เหมือนกัน

lime/lemon N má naaw มะนาว

limited/restricted ADJ (in time, space) jam-kàt จำกัด

line N (mark) sên เส้น, (queue – from English) khiu คิว

line up v (queue up) khâo khiu เข้าคิว

lineage N (ancestry) trà-kuun ตระกูล

link v chûeam เชื่อม

lion N sǐng-toh สิงโต, or simply sǐng สิงห์

lip(s) N rim fǐi pàak ริมฝีปาก

liquor, alcohol N lâo เหล้า

list N raai kaan รายการ

listen to v fang ฟัง

listening v (to someone talking, the radio) fang yùu ฟังอยู่

literate ADJ mii kaan sùek-săa มีการศึกษา

literature N wanná-khá-dii วรรณคดี

little ADJ (not much) nói น้อย; a little bit nít nòi นิดหน่อย, (small) lék เล็ก

livable ADJ nâa yùu น่าอยู่

live ADJ (alive) mii chii-wít yùu มีชีวิตอยู่

live, to be located V (stay in a place) yùu อยู่

lively/full of life ADJ chii-wít chii-waa ชีวิตชีวา

liver N tàp ตับ

load, burden N (i.e. responsibility) phaa-rá ภาระ

load V (up/pack a suitcase) banjù บรรจุ

loan V hâi yuehm ให้ยืม

loan N (of money) ngoehn kûu เงินกู้; go and get a loan (from a bank/money lender) kûu ngoehn กู้เงิน

loathe/dislike/despise V rang kìat รังเกียจ

lobster N kûng mangkawn (literally, 'prawn/shrimp'-'dragon') กุ้งมังกร

local ADJ thâwng thin ท้องถิ่น

located ADJ tâng yùu ตั้งอยู่, or simply yùu อยู่

location/site N (e.g. a good/ bad location for a home, business, etc.) tham-leh ทำเล

lock N mâeh kunjaeh (literally, 'mother'-'key') แม่กุญแจ (NOTE: colloquially the word for 'key' kunjaeh กุญแจ is also used to refer to a lock)

lock V (from English) láwk ล็อก

locked ADJ láwk láew ล็อก แล้ว

lodge, bungalow N (from English) bang-kà-loh บังกะโล

logic N hèht phŏn เหตุผล

logical ADJ mii hèt-phŏn (literally, 'have'-'reason') มี เหตุผล

loincloth N phâa khăaw máa ผ้าขาวม้า

lonely ADJ ngăo เหงา

long ADJ (length) yaow ยาว, (distance) klai ไกล, (time) naan นาน

look! EXCLAM (look at that!) duu sí ดูซิ

look after v (e.g. children) duulaeh ดูแล

look at v duu ดู

look for/search/look up v (find in book) hǎa หา

look(s) like v duu mǔean ดู เหมือน

look out! EXP (be careful) rá wang ระวัง

loose ADJ (not tight) lǔam หลวม

lose v (fail to win) pháeh แพ้, (mislay) tham hǎai ทำหาย, (unable to keep alive) sǐa chii-wít เสียชีวิต

lose money v (on a business venture) (COLLOQUIAL) khàat thun; lose money on (something and get nothing in return) sǐa ngoehn frii (literally, 'waste'-'money'-'free') เสียเงินฟรี

lost ADJ (vanished) hǎai หาย (i.e. lost property is khǎwng hǎai ของหาย), (can't find way) lǒng (thaang) หลง (ทาง)

lot, lots N (COLLOQUIAL) yóe yáe (both words pronounced very short) เยอะแยะ, or yóe mâak เยอะมาก

lottery N (from English) láwt toeh rîi ล็อตเตอรี่, (COLLOQUIAL) hǔai หวย; (COLLOQUIAL) to win the lottery thùuk hǔai ถูกหวย

loud ADJ dang ดัง (also colloquial term for 'famous')

lounge room/living room N hâwng ráp khàehk (literally, 'room'-'receive'-'guest[s]') ห้องรับแขก, or hâwng nâng lên (literally, 'room'-'sit'-'play') ห้องนั่งเล่น

love N khwaam rák ความรัก

love v rák รัก

lovely/adorable ADJ (of a person/cute behavior) nâa rák น่ารัก, (beautiful) sǔai-ngaam สวยงาม

low ADJ (opposite of 'high') tàm ต่ำ

loyal ADJ sûe-sàt ซื่อสัตย์

lubricate v tham-hâi lûen ทำให้ลื่น

luck N chôhk โชค

lucky ADJ chôhk dii โชคดี

luggage/bag/suitcase N krà pǎo กระเป๋า

luminous ADJ sà-wàang สว่าง

lump N (e.g. of rock; also a

lump/growth on the body) kâwn ก้อน

lunch N aa-hǎan klaang wan อาหารกลางวัน (i.e. eating lunch is thaan khâow thîang ทานข้าวเที่ยง, or MORE COLLOQUIAL kin khâaw thîang กินข้าวเที่ยง)

lung(s) N pàwt ปอด

lure V lâw jai ล่อใจ

lust/desire N tanhǎa ตัณหา

luxury N khwaam rǔu rǎa ความหรูหรา; luxurious rǔu rǎa หรูหรา

lychee N (fruit) lín-jìi ลิ้นจี่

lyric N núea phleng เนื้อเพลง

M

machine N khrûeang jàk เครื่องจักร

mad ADJ See 'crazy/insane'

madam, ma'am N (term of address) maà-daam มาดาม, mâem แหม่ม

made-to-order ADJ taam sàng ตามสั่ง

Mafia N maafia มาเฟีย (NOTE: this term is commonly used

in Thailand to refer to local criminal organizations or foreign gangs operating in Thailand)

magazine N nít-tà-yá-sǎan นิตยสาร

magic N (with spells, incantations – not stage magic) khaa-thǎa aa-khom คาถาอาคม

magistrate/judge N phûu-phí phâak-sǎa ผู้พิพากษา

magnet N mâeh lèk (literally, 'mother'-'iron/steel') แม่เหล็ก

mahout N (elephant keeper/ handler) khwaan cháang ควาญช้าง

maid N (female servant in a private residence) sǎow chái (literally, 'woman'-'use') สาว ใช้; room maid (in a hotel/ private residence) mâeh bâan แม่บ้าน

mail, post N (from English) mehl เมล์

mail V sòng ส่ง

mailman/postman N bùrùt praisànii บุรุษไปรษณีย์

main ADJ (most important) sǎmkhan สำคัญ

mainly ADV, **majority** N sùan

yài sùan yài, or **sùan mâak** ส่วนใหญ่

maintain v khong wái คงไว้

major/big ADJ (something important/significant) **yài** ใหญ่

make/do v **tham** ทำ

make up v (to apply cosmetics) **tàeng nâa** แต่งหน้า

makeup N (cosmetics) **khrûeang sǎmaang** เครื่อง สำอาง

Malaysia N **maalehsia** มาเลเซีย

Malaysian N (people) **chaow maàlehsia** ชาวมาเลเซีย

male N (human being) **chaai** ชาย; male (animal) **tua phûu** ตัวผู้

mama-san N (brothel keeper, female bar keeper) **mâe láo** แม่เล้า (NOTE: the word 'mama-san' is also commonly used)

man/men N **phûu chaai** ผู้ชาย

manage/organize v **jàt-kaan** จัดการ

manager N **phûu jàt-kaan** ผู้จัดการ

Mandarin N (official language of China) **phaa-sǎa jiin klaang** ภาษาจีนกลาง

mandate N **kham sang** คำสั่ง

mango N **má-mûang** มะม่วง

mangosteen N (fruit) **mang-khút** มังคุด

manhood N **khwaam klâa hǎan** ความกล้าหาญ

maniac ADJ See 'crazy/insane'

manicure N **tham lép** ทำเล็บ

manifest ADJ **chát jehn** ชัดเจน

manikin N **khon khráe** คน แคระ

manipulate v **ját kaan** จัดการ

mankind/humans/humanity N **má-nút** มนุษย์

manners N (etiquette/ behavior) **maa-rá-yâat** มารยาท

manual ADJ (to work with one's hands) (literally, 'do'-'by/with'-'hand') **tham dûai mueh** ทำด้วยมือ

manual N (instructional book, e.g. instructions on how to operate a DVD player) **khûu mueh** คู่มือ

manufacture v **phà-lìt** ผลิต

many, massive, much ADJ **mâak** มาก (COMMON

103

COLLOQUIAL) yóe (pronounced something like 'yer!' very short with a high tone) เยอะ

map N phǎen thîi แผนที่

March N mii-naakhom มีนาคม

margin N khàwp ขอบ

marijuana/marihuana N kan-chaa (pronounced 'gun-jar') กัญชา (NOTE: common slang for marijuana is núea [the normal word for 'meat/beef/flesh'] เนื้อ

mark N (symbol, sign) khrûeang-mǎai เครื่องหมาย, marks (score in a test or examination) khá-naen คะแนน

market N tà-làat ตลาด (NOTE: in Thailand there are markets that move from one location to another in the same town. For example on a Monday the market may be in one place, the next day somewhere else, and so on. Markets of this variety are referred to as tà-làat nát ตลาดนัด. The word nát นัด means 'appointment', 'to arrange to meet', 'to set a date')

married ADJ tàeng-ngaan láew แต่งงานแล้ว

marry/get married V tàeng-ngaan แต่งงาน

mask V nâa kàak หน้ากาก

massage V nûat นวด, such as Thai traditional massage nûat thai นวดไทย, or nûat phǎehn bohraan นวดแผน โบราณ

massage parlor N (these establishments, while generally offering normal straight massages, are primarily geared towards providing customers with sexual services) àab òb nûat อาบอบนวด

master N hǔa-nâa หัวหน้า

masturbate V (COLLOQUIAL/SLANG) for men chák wâow (literally, 'to pull/draw'-'kite') ชักว่าว; the equivalent for women tòk bèt ตกเบ็ด (which normally means 'to go fishing')

mat N (e.g. a woven floor mat) sùea เสื่อ

match/game N (from English) kehm เกม

matches N (COLLOQUIAL) mái-khìit ไม้ขีด, (or more fully) mái-khìit-fai ไม้ขีดไฟ

matchmaker N mâe-sùeh แม่สื่อ

mate N phûean เพื่อน

material N (e.g. building material) wát-thù วัตถุ (NOTE: the syllable thù here is pronounced very short), or wàtsà-dù วัสดุ

mathematics N khá-nít-sàat คณิตศาสตร์

matter (of) N (a subject of concern) rûeang เรื่อง, (as in 'It doesn't matter') i.e. when someone apologizes to you, you can say 'mâi pen rai' ไม่เป็นไร

mattress N thîi nawn ที่นอน

maximum/the most N mâak thîi sùt มากที่สุด

May N (month) phrúet-sà-phaa-khom พฤษภาคม

may AUX V àat jà อาจจะ: e.g. I may go chǎn/phǒm àat jà pai ฉัน/ผมอาจจะไป

maybe, perhaps ADV àat jà อาจจะ, also baang thii บางที (which may also be translated as 'sometimes')

me See the entry under 'I'

meal N múeh มื้อ

mean ADJ (stingy) (COLLOQUIAL) khîi nǐao (literally, 'feces/ shit'-'sticky'), i.e. someone who is so tight they want to keep their own excrement) ขี้ เหนียว, (unkind, cruel) jai-ráai ใจร้าย

mean V (intend) mii jehttà-naa มีเจตนา, (denote) khwaam hǎi khwaam หมายความ (NOTE: the expression 'What does it/ this/do you mean?' is mǎi khwaam wâa àrai หมาย ความว่าอะไร) Also see 'interpret/translate'

meaning N (the 'meaning' of something) khwaam mǎi ความหมาย

meanwhile ADV (in the meantime/at the same time) nai wehlaa diao kan ในเวลา เดียวกัน

measure V wát วัด

meat/flesh N núea เนื้อ

meatball N (which, in fact, may either be beef, pork, or fish) lûuk chín ลูกชิ้น

mechanic N (the general term for a skilled tradesman is châang ช่าง followed by the particular area of expertise: note motor vehicle = rót รถ; engine = khrûeang เครื่อง). The full word for a motor mechanic is either châang rót ช่างรถ, or châang khrûeang ช่างเครื่อง).

meddle V (interfere in someone else's affairs) yûng ยุ่ง

media N (mass media, radio, television, Internet etc.) sùeh muanchon สื่อมวลชน, (COLLOQUIAL) sùeh สื่อ

medical ADJ thaang kaan phâeht ทางการแพทย์

medicine/drug N yaa ยา

meditate V tham sà-maa-thí ทำสมาธิ

meditation N kaan tham sà-maa-thí การทำสมาธิ

medium N (size – neither big nor small) khà-nàat klaang ขนาดกลาง

meet V phóp พบ

meeting N (e.g. a conference) pràchum ประชุม

melodious ADJ (pleasing to the ear, a beautiful sound) phai-ráw ไพเราะ, (or simply and more commonly) phrá-w เพราะ

melon N (i.e. fruit/vegetables in the melon family) taeng แตง: e.g. watermelon taeng moh แตงโม; cucumber taeng kwaa แตงกวา

melt V lá-laai ละลาย (the same word also means 'dissolve')

member N (e.g. of a club) sà-maa-chík สมาชิก

memory N (one's memory) khwaam song jam ความทรงจำ

mend/fix/repair V sâwm ซ่อม

menstruate V (a woman's period) mii prà-jam duean มีประจำเดือน, (COLLOQUIAL) pen men เป็นเมนส์

mentally retarded ADJ panyaa àwn (literally, 'intellect'-'weak/tender/soft') ปัญญาอ่อน

mention V klàaw thǔeng กล่าวถึง

menu N (from English) mehnuu เมนู, or raai-kaan aa-hǎan รายการอาหาร

merchandise N (commercial products, goods) sĭn-kháa สินค้า

merchant N khon khăai คนขาย

merely/only ADV phiang เพียง

merge V ruam รวม

mess N, **messy** ADJ rók รก (i.e. a messy house bâan rók บ้านรก)

message N khâw khwaam ข้อความ; SMS message (from English) es-em-es เอส เอ็มเอส

metal N (COLLOQUIAL) lèk เหล็ก (NOTE: this term actually means 'iron' or 'steel'; the proper word for 'metal' is loh-hà โลหะ)

meter/metre N (length – from English) méht เมตร

method N (of doing something) wí-thii วิธี

microwave N (oven) (COLLOQUIAL – from English) wéhf (pronounced similar to 'wave') เวฟ

midday N thîang wan เที่ยงวัน

middle/center N sŭun klaang ศูนย์กลาง

middle ADJ klaang กลาง (i.e. the middle of a road is 'klaang thà-nŏn กลางถนน)

midnight N thîang khuehn เที่ยงคืน

migrate V òp-phá-yóp อพยพ; **a migrant** N phûu òp-phá-yóp ผู้อพยพ

mild ADJ (not spicy) mâi phèt ไม่เผ็ด, (not severe – as in a storm, a protest, etc.) mâi run raehng ไม่รุนแรง, (gentle) àwn yohn อ่อนโยน

mile N (distance – from English) mai ไมล์

militant ADJ bùk-rúk บุกรุก

military N thá-hăan ทหาร

milk N nom นม (also the common word for a woman's breasts)

milkshake N nom-pàn นมปั่น

million NUM láan ล้าน

millionaire N (or a wealthy person) sèht-thĭi เศรษฐี

mince V (meat/pork etc.) sàp สับ

mind N (remembrance; memory) khwaam jam ความจำ, (manner of feeling or thought) jìt-jai จิตใจ, or simply jai ใจ

mind, care, to be concerned (about) rang kìat รังเกียจ, (COLLOQUIAL) tǔeh ถือ

mine N (i.e. diamond mine) mǔeang เหมือง, or mǔeang râeh เหมืองแร่

mineral N râeh แร่

minibus/van N rót tûn รถตู้

ministry N (as in a government ministry) krà-suang กระทรวง

minor ADJ (not important) mâi sǎmkhan ไม่สำคัญ

minority N (group) chon klùm nói ชนกลุ่มน้อย

minus N (−) lóp ลบ

minute N naa thii นาที

miracle N sìng àt-sà-jan สิ่ง อัศจรรย์

mirror krà-jòk กระจก

miscellaneous ADJ (misc) bèt tà-lèt เบ็ดเตล็ด

miser/skinflint/tightwad N khon khîi nǐao คนขี้เหนียว

misery N khwaam thúk ความ ทุกข์

misfortune, bad luck N chôhk rái โชคร้าย

miss v (too late for, i.e. a bus, a flight) phlâat พลาด, (think

of somebody) khít thǔeng คิดถึง

Miss N (title for an unmarried woman) naang sǎow นางสาว

missing ADJ (absent) hǎai หาย, or hǎai pai หายไป

mist, fog N màwk หมอก

mistake N khwaam phìt ความผิด

mistaken ADJ (incorrect in understanding) phìt phlâat ผิดพลาด

mistress/minor wife N (a complex and significant area of Thai social life) mia nói เมียน้อย (NOTE: a man's 'major wife' is known colloquially as a mia lǔang เมียหลวง) Also see entry under 'wife'

misunderstand v, **misunderstanding** N khâojai phìt เข้าใจผิด

mix/blend v phà-sǒm ผสม

moan N sǐang khraang เสียง คราง

mobile/cell phone N (also see 'telephone') thoh-rá-sàp mueh tǔeh โทรศัพท์มือถือ, (COLLOQUIAL) mueh tǔeh มือถือ

smartphone (from English)
sà-márt fohn สมาร์ทโฟน

mock/make fun of v yáw
yóei เยาะเย้ย

model N (a design of an item)
bàep แบบ, (one who models
clothes or cosmetics) naang
bàep นางแบบ

moderate ADJ paan klaang
ปานกลาง

modern ADJ than sà-mǎi ทัน
สมัย

modest, simple, ordinary
ADJ tham-má-daa ธรรมดา

modify v kâe khǎi แก้ไข

molar N fan-kraam ฟันกราม

mold/mould N raa รา

moment N (the present time,
i.e. at the moment) tawn
níi ตอนนี้, (a short period
of time, i.e. in a moment)
dǐao (COLLOQUIAL) เดี๋ยว (in a
more formal environment
– e.g. office/surgery etc.
a receptionist would say
'please wait a moment') raw
sák khrûu รอสักครู่)

moment ago ADV (i.e. just a
moment/second/minute ago)
mûea kîi níi เมื่อกี้นี้

Monday N wan jan วันจันทร์

monarch N kà-sàt กษัตริย์

money N ngoehn เงิน (this
word also means 'silver'),
(MORE COLLOQUIAL) tang ตังค์
(shortened from another
old Thai term for 'money'
sà-taang สตางค์: 100 sàtaang
= one baht), to have no
money/to be broke (SLANG)
mâi mii tang ไม่มีตังค์,
or thǎng tàehk (literally,
'bucket'-'broken') ถังแตก

monitor N (of computer),
screen N jaw (pronounced
like the English word 'jaw')
จอ

monk N (a Buddhist monk)
phrá พระ

monkey N ling ลิง

monotonous ADJ nâa bùea
น่าเบื่อ

month N duean เดือน

monument N ànù-sǎa-wárii
อนุสาวรีย์

mood N See 'passion' (NOTE:
'to be in a bad mood' aa rom
sǐa อารมณ์เสีย)

moody/irritable ADJ ngùt-ngìt
หงุดหงิด

moon N duang jan ดวงจันทร์

moonlight N săeng jan แสงจันทร์

mop V thŭu phúen ถูพื้น

morality N sĭin-lá-tham ศีล ธรรม

more ADJ (comparative) kwàa กว่า: e.g. better dii kwàa (literally, 'good'-'more') ดีกว่า

more of N (things) /**more than** ADV mâak kwàa มากกว่า

more or less IDIOM mâi mâak kâw nói ไม่มากก็น้อย

moreover ADV nâwk jàak nán นอกจากนั้น

morning N (time), cháo เช้า, or tawn cháo ตอนเช้า

moron/stupid person N khon ngôh คนโง่

mortgage N jam nawng จำนอง

mosque N sù-rào สุเหร่า

mosquito N yung ยุง

most ADJ (superlative) thîi sùt ที่สุด: e.g. the most expensive phaeng thîi sùt แพงที่สุด, (the most) mâak thîi sùt มากที่สุด

mostly, for the most part ADV sùan yài ส่วนใหญ่

mother N (COMMON/COLLOQUIAL) mâeh แม่, (MORE FORMAL) maan daa มารดา; **stepmother** mâeh líang แม่เลี้ยง

mother-in-law N (wife's mother) mâeh yaai แม่ยาย; (husband's mother) mâeh sǎa-mii แม่สามี

motor/engine N khrûeang yon เครื่องยนต์, or simply khrûeang เครื่อง

motorcycle N maw-toeh-sai มอเตอร์ไซค์, (MORE COLLOQUIAL) rót khrûeang รถเครื่อง (also see 'taxi' for 'motorcycle taxi')

motor vehicle N (specifically 'a car') rót yon รถยนต์

mountain N phuu khǎo ภูเขา

mouse N (rat) nǔu หนู, (computer) máo เมาส์ (from English)

mouth N pàak ปาก

mouthwash N (i.e. Listerine) náam yaa bûan pàak น้ำ ยาบ้วนปาก

move V khlûean thîi เคลื่อนที่, (from one place to another e.g. to move house) yáai ย้าย

movement, motion N
khwaam khlûean wǎi ความ
เคลื่อนไหว

movie N nǎng หนัง

movie house/cinema N
rohng nǎng โรงหนัง

mow, cut V (the lawn/grass)
tàt ตัด

Mr N (title) naai นาย

Mrs N (title) naang นาง

MSG/msg N (flavor enhancer)
phǒng chuu rót (literally,
'powder'-'boost/lift/elevate'-
'taste') ผงชูรส

mug N yùeak เหยือก

multiple ADJ lǎai หลาย

municipality N têht-sà-baan
เทศบาล

muscle N klâam núea กล้าม
เนื้อ

museum N phíphít-tháphan
พิพิธภัณฑ์

mushroom(s) N hèt เห็ด

music N dontrii ดนตรี

musician N nák don trii นัก
ดนตรี

Muslim N mút-sà-lim มุสลิม

must AUX V tâwng ต้อง; e.g. (I)
must go (chǎn) tâwng pai
ต้องไป

mustache/moustache N
nùat หนวด

mute ADJ (unable to speak) bâi
ใบ้; to be mute pen bâi เป็น
ใบ้ See 'language' (for 'sign
language')

my, mine PRON (male speaking)
khǎwng phǒm ของผม;
(female) khǎwng dìchǎn/
chǎn ของดิฉัน/ฉัน

Myanmar N See 'Burma'

N

nail N (finger, toe, claws of
an animal) lép เล็บ, (used in
carpentry/building) tà-puu
ตะปู

naive ADJ sûeh ซื่อ

naked ADJ plueai เปลือย; a
naked body/to be in the nude
(FORMAL) plueai kaai เปลือย
กาย, or (SIMPLE COLLOQUIAL)
póh โป๊

name N chûeh ชื่อ; 'what's your
name?' khun chûeh àrai
(literally, 'you'-'name'-'what'?)
คุณชื่ออะไร

nap N ngîip งีบ

narcotic(s) N yaa sèp tìt (literally, 'drug'-'consume'-'stuck/addicted') ยาเสพติด

narrow ADJ khâehp แคบ; to be narrow-minded/petty jai khâehp (literally, 'narrow'-'heart') ใจแคบ

nation, country N châat ชาติ

national ADJ hàeng châat แห่งชาติ

national anthem N phlehng châat เพลงชาติ

national park N ùt-thá-yaan hàeng châat อุทยานแห่งชาติ

nationality N sănchâat สัญชาติ: e.g. Thai nationality sănchâat thai สัญชาติไทย

native ADJ (indigenous) phúen mueang พื้นเมือง

natural ADJ pen thammá-châat เป็นธรรมชาติ

nature N thammá-châat ธรรมชาติ

naughty ADJ son (pronounced like the English word 'on' with 's' in front) ซน

nauseous ADJ khlûehn sâi คลื่นไส้

navel N (belly button) sà dueh สะดือ

navy N kawng tháp ruea กองทัพเรือ

navy blue/dark blue/royal blue N sĭi náam-ngoehn สีน้ำเงิน

navigate V nam-thaang นำทาง

near, nearby ADJ klâi ใกล้ (NOTE: the Thai words 'near' klâi ใกล้ and 'far' klai ไกล are perhaps the most significant examples of the importance of getting the tones correct as they convey the completely opposite meaning. Hint: the word for 'near' has a falling tone and when said, is shorter than the mid-tone word for 'far' klai ไกล. To say 'very near' simply repeat the word twice klâi-klâi ใกล้ๆ)

nearly ADV kùeap เกือบ

neat, orderly, well-behaved ADJ rîap rói เรียบร้อย – This term is widely used and conveys the notion of ideal behavior and deportment. (NOTE: this term is also commonly used to express the idea that a job/task has been successfully completed, something like 'done!')

necessary ADJ jam-pen (jam จำ is pronounced like 'jum' in the English word 'jump') จำเป็น

neck N khaw คอ

necklace N sôi khaw สร้อยคอ

necktie N (from English) nékthai เน็คไท

need N khwaam jam-pen ความจำเป็น

need v jam-pen-tâwng จำเป็นต้อง

needle N khěm เข็ม

neglect v mâi sŏn jai ไม่สนใจ

negotiate v tàw rawng ต่อรอง

neighbor N phûean bâan เพื่อนบ้าน

nephew N lǎan chaai หลานชาย

nerve N sên prà-sàat เส้นประสาท

nervous/anxious ADJ kang-won jai กังวลใจ

nest N (e.g. bird's nest) rang รัง; bird's nest rang nók รังนก

net N taa-khàai ตาข่าย,

(mosquito net) múng มุ้ง

network N khruea khàai เครือข่าย; social network khruea khàai sǎngkhom เครือข่ายสังคม

neutral ADJ (impartial) pen klaang เป็นกลาง

never ADV mâi khoei ไม่เคย (NOTE: for a fuller description of how the word khoei เคย is used see 'have')

never mind! IDIOM mâi pen rai ไม่เป็นไร

nevertheless ADV (FORMAL) yàang-rai kâw taam อย่างไรก็ตาม, or (COLLOQUIAL) yang-ngai kâw taam ยังไงก็ตาม

new ADJ mài ใหม่

news N khàow ข่าว

newspaper N nǎng sǔeh phim หนังสือพิมพ์

new year N pii mài ปีใหม่, (the expression) 'Happy New Year' sàwàt dii pii mài สวัสดีปีใหม่ (NOTE: the traditional Thai new year [13–15 April] is called sǒng-kraan สงกรานต์)

New Zealand N niu sii-laehn นิวซีแลนด์

113

next ADJ (in line, sequence) tàw pai ต่อไป

next to PREP thàt pai ถัดไป

next week N aa-thít nâa อาทิตย์หน้า

next year N pii nâa ปีหน้า

nice/good ADJ dii ดี

nickname N (NOTE: most Thai people have both a first name and a nickname – frequently a shortened version of their first name — or something else, invariably short, altogether) chûeh lên (literally, 'name'-'play') ชื่อเล่น

niece N lǎan sǎow หลานสาว

night N klaang khuehn กลาง คืน

nightclothes/nightdress/ pajamas N chút nawn ชุด นอน

nightclub N (from English) nái-khláp ไนท์คลับ

nightly ADJ thúk khuehn ทุกคืน

nine NUM kâo เก้า

nineteen NUM sìp kâo สิบเก้า

nipple N hǔa nom หัวนม

ninety NUM kâo sìp เก้าสิบ

no, not DET mâi mii ไม่มี (used

with nouns. NOTE: there are many ways of expressing 'no' – this being dependent on the form of the question asked), e.g. 'to have no friends' mâi mii phûean ไม่มีเพื่อน

no, not ADV mâi ไม่ (used with verbs and adjectives), e.g. 'it's not hot' mâi ráwn ไม่ร้อน (NOTE: 'not' may be expressed in other ways depending on the form of question asked, or nature of statement being made)

nobody N (as in 'there is nobody here') mâi mii khrai ไม่มีใคร

noise, a sound N sǐang เสียง

noisy, loud noise ADJ sǐang dang เสียงดัง

nominate V tàeng tang แต่งตั้ง

none PRON mâi mii ไม่มี

nonsense N (to be meaning-less) rái sǎa rá ไร้สาระ, or lěow-lǎi เหลวไหล

nonstop ADJ mâi yùt ไม่หยุด

noodles N (rice noodles) kǔai tǐao ก๋วยเตี๋ยว, or (egg noodles) bà-mìi บะหมี่

noon N tawn thîang ตอนเที่ยง

114

normal ADJ pà-kà-tì ปกติ

normally ADV dohy pà-kà-tì โดยปกติ

north N nŭea เหนือ

north-east N tàwan àwk chǐang nŭea ตะวันออก เฉียงเหนือ (NOTE: in Thailand the north-east region of the country is referred to as iisǎan – this is written in English in various ways: Isarn/Isan/Isaan – อีสาน)

north-west N tà-wan tòk chǐang nŭea ตะวันตกเฉียง เหนือ

nose N jà-mùuk จมูก; (COLLOQUIAL) 'mucous' khîi mûuk (literally, 'excrement' - shortened word for 'nose') ขี้มูก

nostril N ruu jà-mùuk รูจมูก

notable ADJ dèhn เด่น

note N (i.e. banknote) (COLLOQUIAL) (from the English 'bank') báeng แบงค์

notebook N sà-mùt สมุด

note down V jòt nóht จดโน้ต, or (MORE COLLOQUIALLY – the equivalent to) 'jot it down' jòt wái จดไว้

nothing N (as in 'nothing is going on') mâi mii arai ไม่มีอะไร (NOTE: in certain instances, e.g. in response to the question 'What did you say?' to answer 'Nothing!' the word plàaw เปล่า [which also means 'empty/vacant/plain/ bare'] is commonly used)

notice V (to notice something) sǎngkèht สังเกต

notify V (the police) jâehng khwaam แจ้งความ

notorious ADJ sǐa chûeh เสียชื่อ

novel N ná-wá ní-yaai นวนิยาย, or simply ní-yaai นิยาย

November N phrúet-sà-jì-kaa-yon พฤศจิกายน

noun N (part of speech) kham-naam (pronounced 'narm') คำ นาม, or simply naam นาม

nourish V bam-rung บำรุง

now ADV dǐao níi เดี๋ยวนี้, or tawn níi ตอนนี้

nowadays/these days ADV sà-mǎi níi สมัยนี้

no way! INTERJ (COLLOQUIAL) (e.g. there is 'no way' to get there, or 'Can I go with you?' – 'No way!') mâi mii thaang ไม่มี ทาง

nowhere ADV (as in a sentence such as 'there is nowhere like home') mâi mii thîi nǎi ไม่มี ที่ไหน (literally, 'no'-'have'-'where'?')

nude ADJ plueai เปลือย, or 'naked body/nude' plueai kaai เปลือยกาย, or (SIMPLE COLLOQUIAL) póh โป๊

nuisance N tham-hâi ram-khaan ทำให้รำคาญ

numb ADJ chaa ชา

number N (from English; most commonly used when asking for a telephone number) boeh เบอร์, (general term for 'number' is) mǎai lêhk หมายเลข

numerous ADJ mâak-maai มากมาย

nurse N phá-yaa-baan พยาบาล

nut N (food, i.e. nuts in general) thùa ถั่ว, (a crazy person) khon bâa คนบ้า

nutrient N sǎan aa-hǎan สาร อาหาร

nutrition N phoh-chá-naa-kaan โภชนาการ

nylon N (from English) nai lâwn ไนลอน

O

oar/paddle N mái phaai ไม้พาย

oat N khâao óht ข้าวโอ๊ต

oath N kham sǎa baan คำ สาบาน

obese ADJ See 'fat'

obey V **obedient** ADJ chûea fang เชื่อฟัง

object, thing N sìng khǎwng สิ่งของ

object V (to oppose) khát kháan คัดค้าน

oblige V bang kháp บังคับ

obscure ADJ múeht มืด

observe V sang kèht สังเกต

obsess V khrâwp khrawng ครอบครอง

obstacle N ùp-pà-sàk อุปสรรค

obstinate/stubborn ADJ dûeh ดื้อ

obstruct/block V khàt

116

khwǎang ขัดขวาง

obtain/get v dâi ráp ได้รับ, or simply dâi ได้

obvious ADJ chát jehn ชัดเจน

occasion/opportunity N oh-kàat โอกาส

occasionally ADV pen khráng khraow เป็นครั้งคราว; once in a while (COLLOQUIAL) naan-naan thii นานๆ ที

occupation N (profession – term often, but not always, used to refer to someone with professional qualifications) aa-chîip อาชีพ; (colloquially the word for 'work' – ngaan งาน – is used): 'What (work) do you do?' (khun) tham ngaan àrai ทำงานอะไร

occupy v yúet khrawng ยึด ครอง

occur v (for something to happen) kòeht khêun เกิดขึ้น

ocean N má-hǎa sà-mùt มหาสมุทร (*also see* 'sea')

o'clock ADV naa lí kaa นาฬิกา (Note: this word is used in the 24 hour system of telling the time such as in official Thai news broadcasts and more

generally at sea/by aircraft/ the military etc.: e.g. 13 naa lí kaa = 1 p.m.). The everyday Thai system of telling the time is somewhat more complex and cannot be outlined here.

October N tù-laa-khom ตุลาคม

odd ADJ plàek แปลก

odor N (i.e. to smell not so good) mii klìn มีกลิ่น

of course IDIOM nâeh nawn แน่นอน

off ADV (no longer functioning or operating) pìt ปิด (i.e. turned off the light pìt fai ปิดไฟ)

off ADJ (absent or away from work) yùt-ngaan หยุดงาน; off to (going to somewhere) àwk pai ออกไป

offend v (break the law) tham phìt ทำผิด, (to displease someone/to be offensive) tham hâi mâi phaw jai ทำให้ไม่พอใจ

offer v yùt-nǒeh เสนอ; suggest náe nam แนะนำ

office N thîi tham ngaan ที่ ทำงาน, (also commonly – from English) áwp-fít ออฟฟิศ

official(s) N (i.e. government servants, bureaucrats) khâa râat-chá-kaan ข้าราชการ, or jâo nâa thîi เจ้าหน้าที่

official ADJ (having a formal character) pen thaang kaan เป็นทางการ

often ADV bòi บ่อย; very often bòi-bòi บ่อยๆ

oil N (general term for 'oil', and common word for petrol/gasoline) náam-man น้ำมัน

oily/greasy ADJ (food) lîan เลี่ยน; e.g. greasy food aa-hǎan lîan อาหารเลี่ยน

ointment N (from English 'cream') kriim ครีม

okay ADJ ADV N tòk-long ตกลง (the English word OK is also widely used oh-keh โอเค)

old ADJ (of people) kàeh แก่; an old person khon kàeh คนแก่; (of things) kào เก่า

old times N (i.e. 'in the past....') sà-mǎi kàwn สมัย ก่อน

older brother N (or sister) phîi พี่ (NOTE: an important word in Thai with a far broader meaning than simply 'older brother/older sister'; it is used by a junior or younger person to mean 'you' when speaking to an older or higher status person in various, mainly less formal, contexts. In addition the term is also commonly used to mean 'he/she' when talking about another older or higher status individual)

olive N má-gkàwk มะกอก

omit V tàt-àwk ตัดออก

omniscient ADJ râwp rúu รอบรู้

on PREP (i.e. on top) bon บน; (a particular date) wan thîi วันที่

on ADJ (operating or in use) pòeht เปิด

on board IDIOM (on a ship, train, or plane) yùu bon... อยู่บน

on fire IDIOM fai mâi ไฟไหม้

on foot ADV (walking, using the feet) doehn เดิน

on the whole/generally ADV dohy thûa pai โดยทั่วไป

on time, punctual ADJ trong weh laa ตรงเวลา

once ADV (at one time in the

118

past) khráng nùeng ครั้งหนึ่ง; a single time khráng diao ครั้งเดียว; once in a while – see 'occasionally'

one NUM nùeng หนึ่ง

one-way ticket N tŭa thîao diao (literally, 'ticket'-'trip'-'single') ตั๋วเที่ยวเดียว

one who, the one who (did something etc.) khon thîi… คนที่

oneself PRON tua-ehng ตัวเอง

ongoing ADJ tàw nûeang ต่อเนื่อง

onion N hăwm yài หอมใหญ่

only ADJ & ADV thâo-nán เท่านั้น

open V pòeht เปิด (same word as 'turn on')

open air N klaang jâeng กลางแจ้ง

operate V tham-ngaan ทำงาน

operation N kaan phàa-tàt การผ่าตัด

opinion N khwaam hĕn ความเห็น

opium N fìn ฝิ่น

opportunity/chance N oh-kàat โอกาส

oppose V, **opposed** ADJ tàw tâan ต่อต้าน

opposite PREP (across from) trong khâam ตรงข้าม

opposite ADJ (contrary) khàt yáeng ขัดแย้ง

opposition N (opposed to the government) fàai kháan ฝ่ายค้าน

oppress V bang kháp บังคับ

opt V lûeak เลือก

optimal ADJ màw thîi-sùt เหมาะสมที่สุด

optimistic ADJ mawng lôhk ngâe dii มองโลกแง่ดี

option/alternative N thaang lûeak ทางเลือก

optional ADJ lûeak dâi เลือกได้

or CONJ rŭeh (commonly pronounced [incorrectly] with an 'l' sound – lŭeh) หรือ

oral ADJ dûai pàak (literally, 'with'-'mouth') ด้วยปาก, or oral sex chái pàak ใช้ปาก (NOTE: for such delicate subject matter the terms given are the least crude and offensive of the possibilities) (fellatio – sucking) om อม, (cunninglis – licking) lia เลีย

orange N (fruit) sôm ส้ม;

119

(color) sǐi sôm สีส้ม

orchard N sǔan สวน

orchid N klûai mái กล้วยไม้

order v (give a command) sàng สั่ง

order N (a command) kham sàng คำสั่ง; (a written form for food, goods, medicine, etc.) bai sàng ใบสั่ง; (sequence) taam lam dàp ตามลำดับ

orderly/well-arranged ADJ pen rá-bìap เป็นระเบียบ

ordinary tham-má-daa ธรรมดา: e.g. 'ordinary person' khon tham-má-daa คนธรรมดา (NOTE: ordinary folk/householders – both in the city and rural areas – are colloquiallly known by the term chaow bâan ชาวบ้าน)

organ N à-wai-yá-wá อวัยวะ

organization N ong-kaan (pronounced 'ong-garn') องค์การ, or ong-kawn องค์กร

organize/arrange v jàt kaan จัดการ

oriental ADJ tá-wan-àwk ตะวันออก

origin N jùt rôehm tôn จุดเริ่มต้น; source (the source of

something, e.g. bootlegged DVDs) làeng แหล่ง

original N (the first and genuine form of something) tua jing ตัวจริง, or khǎwng jing ของจริง; the original of a document is tôn chà-bàp ต้นฉบับ

originate, come from v maa jàak มาจาก: e.g. 'what country do you come from?' khun maa jàak prà-thêht àrai คุณมาจากประเทศอะไร

ornament N (for the home) khrûeang prà-dàp เครื่องประดับ

orphan N dèk kam-phráa เด็กกำพร้า

orphanage N bâan dèk kam-phráa บ้านเด็กกำพร้า

ostrich N nók krà-jàwk-thêht นกกระจอกเทศ

other ADJ ùehn อื่น: e.g. 'other person' khon ùehn คนอื่น

otherwise ADV mí-chà-nán มิฉะนั้น

ought to, should AUX v khuan ควร

our(s) PRON khǎwng rao ของเรา: e.g. our house bâan

khǎwng rao บ้านของเรา, (colloquial and even simpler) bâan rao บ้านเรา (NOTE: This is a very common idiomatic way in which Thai people refer to their own country or hometown – i.e. 'our home')

oust v lâi àwk ไล่ออก

out ADV (i.e. take something out – 'a plate out of the cupboard') àwk ออก; to take out/withdraw thǎwn ถอน: e.g. take out a tooth/pull a tooth out thǎwn fan ถอนฟัน

outage N (power failure) fai dàp ไฟดับ

out-of-date/outdated/old-fashioned ADJ láa sà-mǎi ล้าสมัย, (colloquial) choei เชย

outfit (matching set of clothing) chút ชุด

outgoing, friendly ADJ khâo kàp khon ngâai เข้ากับคนง่าย

outing N (to go out for fun/pleasure) (pai) thîao (ไป) เที่ยว (NOTE: an important Thai word – thîao – is used in a wide range of ways to refer to a pleasant/enjoyable visit somewhere – to a friend's

house, the beach, a disco, bar, another country, etc.)

outlook N mum-mawng มุมมอง

output N phǒn-phà-lìt ผลผลิต

outrageous ADJ hòht ráai โหดร้าย

outright ADJ tem thîi เต็มที่

outside PREP khâang nâwk ข้างนอก

outsider N khon nâwk คนนอก

outstanding ADJ dòht dèhn โดดเด่น

oval N (shape) rûup khài รูปไข่

oven N tao òp เตาอบ

over, finished, completed ADJ sèt เสร็จ

over ADV (from an upward position to an inverted position) klàp กลับ (i.e. to turn something over klàp dâan กลับด้าน)

overall ADJ dohy ruam โดยรวม

overcast, cloudy mii mêhk มีเมฆ

overcome v ao-chá-ná เอาชนะ

overdose N (of a drug) yaa

121

koen khà-nàat ยาเกินขนาด

overlook v (not to notice) mawng khâam มองข้าม

overpass N (a pedestrian overpass) sà-phaan loi (literally, 'bridge'-'float') สะพานลอย

overseas N tàang prà-thêht ต่างประเทศ

overtake/pass v (another vehicle) saeng แซง

over there ADV thîi nôhn ที่ โน้น

overturn/capsize v (turn over) lôm ล่ม, khwâm คว่ำ

overturned ADJ (vehicle following an accident – on its roof) ngǎai tháwng หงาย ท้อง

owe v pen nîi เป็นหนี้

owl N nók hûuk นกฮูก

own, on one's IDIOM (by oneself or alone) khon diao คนเดียว; to come alone/on one's own maa khon diao มาคนเดียว

own, personal ADJ (belonging to oneself) khǎwng sùan tua ของส่วนตัว

own v (owner) pen jâo

khǎwng เป็นเจ้าของ

oxygen N (from English) áwk-sì-jên (jên pronounced like 'gen' in the English word) ออกซิเจน

oyster N (general term) hǎwy หอย; a large succulent type of oyster hǎwy naang rom หอยนางรม (NOTE: the word hǎwy is also a common slang term for a woman's vagina)

P

pace N jang-wà จังหวะ

pack v (luggage) kèp khǎwng เก็บของ

package, parcel N hàw khǎwng ห่อของ, or simply hàw ห่อ, or (sent by post) hàw phát-sà-dù ห่อพัสดุ

packet N hàw lék (literally, 'package'-'small') ห่อเล็ก (a small packet, or sachet, is also referred to as a sawng ซอง)

paddy N khâow plùeak ข้าว เปลือก

paddy field N naa นา

padlock N mâe kun-jae แม่กุญแจ

page N (in a book) nâa หน้า

pagoda/stupa N (spire shaped solid structure with no interior space, not a temple though located in temple grounds) jeh-dii เจดีย์

paid ADJ jàai láew จ่ายแล้ว

pain N /**painful** ADJ jèp เจ็บ; very painful jèp mâak เจ็บ มาก

painkiller N yaa kâeh pùat ยา แก้ปวด

paint N sǐi สี (NOTE: sǐi สี is also the word for 'color')

paint V (house, furniture) thaa sǐi ทาสี

painting N phâap wâat ภาพ วาด

pair N khûu คู่ (i.e. a pair of shoes is rawng tháo nùeng khûu รองเท้าหนึ่งคู่)

pair V (to form pairs or a pair) jàp khûu จับคู่

pajamas/pyjamas N chút nawn ชุดนอน

palace N (royal) wang วัง, or (more formally) phrá-râat-chá-wang พระราชวัง

pale ADJ (as in a pale face of someone unwell or in a state of shock) sǐit ซีด: e.g. a pale face nâa sǐit หน้าซีด

palm (of hand) See 'sole'

pan N (frying pan/wok) krà-thá กระทะ (NOTE: both syllables are very short)

pancake N phaen-khéhk แพนเค้ก (from English; the word 'pancake' is widely understood)

panda N (animal) mǐi phaen-dâ (literally, 'bear'-'panda') หมีแพนด้า

panic ADJ tòk jai ตกใจ

panorama N phâap kwâang (literally, 'picture'-'wide') ภาพ กว้าง

panties N (underpants for women) kaang-kehng nai กางเกงใน

pants/trousers N kaang-kehng กางเกง

papaya N má-lá-kaw มะละกอ

paper N krà-dàat กระดาษ; sandpaper krà-dàat saai (literally, 'paper'-'sand') กระดาษทราย

paper currency, banknote

N (FORMAL) thá-ná-bàt ธนบัตร, or simply use báeng แบงค์ (from English)

parade/procession N khà-buan hàeh ขบวนแห่ (NOTE: a common event as part of cultural life, especially in rural Thailand)

paradise/heaven N sà-wǎn สวรรค์

paragraph N yâw nâa ย่อหน้า

parallel ADJ khà-nǎan ขนาน

paralytic/paralyzed N, ADJ am-má-phâat อัมพาต

paraphrase V yâw khwaam ย่อความ

parasite N phá-yâat พยาธิ

pardon me? INTERJ, what did you say? (a most useful expression) àrai ná อะไรนะ

parents N phâw mâeh (literally, 'father'-'mother') พ่อแม่

park N (a public park/garden) sǔan sǎa-thaa rá-ná สวนสาธารณะ

park V (car) jàwt rót จอดรถ

parliament N rát-thà-sà-phaa รัฐสภา

parrot N nók kâew นกแก้ว;

parrot fish (common in southern Thailand) plaa nók kâew ปลานกแก้ว

part N (of something/not the whole) sùan ส่วน; for the most part/the majority sùan mâak ส่วนมาก; a part/one part (of something) sùan nùeng ส่วนหนึ่ง, (spare part of car/machine) à-lài อะไหล่

participate V mii sùan rûam มีส่วนร่วม

particular ADJ **particularly** ADV **especially** ADV dohy cha pháw โดยเฉพาะ

partition N (a lightweight wall dividing one room) phà-nǎng-kân ผนังกั้น

partner N (in business) hûn sùan หุ้นส่วน; (spouse) khûu sǒmrót คู่สมรส

party N (birthday party etc.) ngaan งาน (NOTE: the same word also means the opposite – 'work'); (political party i.e. political party) phák พรรค (i.e. political party phák kaan mueang พรรคการเมือง)

pass V (of time) phàan ผ่าน, (undergo an exam) sàwp

124

phàan สอบผ่าน (NOTE: to fail an exam is sàwp tòk สอบตก)

pass away, die v taai ตาย

pass out, black out v sà-lòp สลบ

passenger N phûu dohy săan ผู้โดยสาร

passion/mood N (with feeling – this term can be used in either a positive or negative sense. NOTE: it also has 'sexual' overtones) aa-rom อารมณ์; passionate mii aa-rom mâak มีอารมณ์มาก

passionfruit N (not particularly common in Thailand) săo-wá-rót เสาวรส

passport N năngsŭeh doehn thaang (literally, 'book'-'travel') หนังสือเดินทาง, (colloquial) (from English) páat-sà-pàwt พาสปอร์ต

password/pin number N rá-hàt รหัส

past, former ADJ à-dìit อดีต; in the past bai à-dìit ในอดีต

pastime/hobby N ngaan à-dìrèhk งานอดิเรก

pat, tap v tàe แตะ

path N thaang doehn ทางเดิน

pathetic ADJ nâa song săan น่าสงสาร

patient ADJ (the ability to wait/ endure)/to have patience òt thon อดทน

patient N (sick person in hospital) khon khâi คนไข้

patron N (client/customer) lûuk kháa ลูกค้า

pattern, design, style N bàehp แบบ

patterned ADJ (i.e. to have a pattern – material, etc.) mii laai มีลาย

pause v yùt phák หยุดพัก

pavilion N (common in Thailand – an airy, open structure where one can sit and relax) săa-laa ศาลา

pawn v jam-nam (pronounced 'jum' as in 'jumble', and 'num' as in 'number') จำนำ; a pawnshop rohng jam-nam โรงจำนำ

pay v jàai จ่าย; to pay a bill jàai bin จ่ายบิล (NOTE: the word bin บิล is from English as is the word chék เช็ค given below). In higher class restaurants to ask to 'pay

125

the bill' it is usual to say chék bin เช็คบิล. On the other hand when paying for a meal at a street stall, or at an ordinary cheap restaurant it is usual to say kèp tang dûai เก็บตังค์ด้วย

pay attention to/concentrate v (on something) ao jai sài (literally, 'take'-'heart/mind'-'put') เอาใจใส่, tâng-jai ตั้งใจ

pay off v (a debt) chái nîi ใช้หนี้

payment N jàai ngoehn จ่ายเงิน

peace N (not war) săntì-phâap สันติภาพ

peaceful ADJ sà-ngòp สงบ

peacock N nók yuung นกยูง

peak, summit N yâwt ยอด (Note: common colloquial usage – the word yâwt is used when checking the balance of credit on one's mobile/cell phone. The expression for 'the balance' in such a case is yâwt ngoen ยอดเงิน)

peanut N thùa lí-sŏng ถั่วลิสง

pearl N khài múk ไข่มุก

pea(s) N thùa ถั่ว

peasant N (peasant farmer/rice farmer) chaow naa ชาวนา

pedestrian crossing N thaang máa laai ทางม้าลาย (Note: máa laai ม้าลาย means 'zebra')

pee/piss/urinate N & V (COLLOQUIAL) yîao เยี่ยว, or chìi ฉี่

peel v (a piece of fruit) pàwk ปอก

pen N pàak-kaa ปากกา

penalize v long thôht ลงโทษ

pencil N din-sŏw ดินสอ

penis N (COLLOQUIAL; extremely vulgar – equivalent of the English 'cock/dick/prick') khuai ควย, (COLLOQUIAL; but significantly less vulgar – the equivalent of something like 'willy') jŭn จู๋ (pronounced similar to the word 'Jew' but with a rising tone)

pension N (government payment to retired workers) bîa bam-naan เบี้ยบำนาญ, or simply bam-naan บำนาญ

people/person N khon คน, (more broadly as in) 'the

people/public' prà-chaa-chon ประชาชน

pepper N (i.e. black pepper) phrík thai พริกไทย, (chili pepper) phrík พริก

peppermint N sà-rá-nàe สะระแหน่

perceive v khâo jai เข้าใจ

percent/percentage N (from English) poeh-sen เปอร์เซ็นต์

perfect ADJ sŏm-buun สมบูรณ์, or dii lôeht ดีเลิศ

perform v (work/do work) (FORMAL) pàtìbàt ngaan ปฏิบัติงาน (NOTE: the word 'do' tham is colloquially used – e.g. 'perform work/do work/work' tham ngaan ทำงาน), (present a dramatic or musical work) sà-daeng แสดง

performance N (work) kaan tham ngaan การทำงาน, (dramatic production) kaan sà-daeng การแสดง

perfume N náam hŏwm (literally, 'water'-'fragrant') น้ำหอม

perhaps, maybe ADV àat jà อาจจะ, (a common alternative is) baang thii บางที

period N (a full stop) jòp จบ, (menstrual) prá-jam duean ประจำเดือน, (COLLOQUIAL) (from English – menstruation) men เมนส์; to be having one's period pen men เป็นเมนส์, (of time) ráya wehlaa ระยะ เวลา

permanent ADJ thăa-wawn ถาวร

permit, license N bai à-nú-yâat ใบอนุญาต

permit/allow v à-nú-yâat อนุญาต

person N khon คน

personality N bùk-khá-lík บุคลิก, or simply ní-săi นิสัย

perspective N khwaam khít ความคิด

perspire/sweat v ngùea àwk เหงื่อออก

persuade v chuan ชวน

pet N (animal) sàt líang สัตว์เลี้ยง

petrol/gasoline N náam man น้ำมัน

petrol station N See 'gasoline/gas'

pharmacy, drugstore, chemist N ráan khăai yaa

ร้านขายยา

phase N (stage) rá-yá ระยะ

phenomenon N praa-kòt-kaan ปรากฏการณ์

Philippines N fí líp-pin ฟิลิปปินส์

philosophy N pràt-yaa ปรัชญา

phlegm N (mucus) sĕm-hà เสมหะ

phobia N khwaam klua ความกลัว

phone N See 'telephone'

photocopy N săm-nao สำเนา

photocopy V thăai săm-nao ถ่ายสำเนา

photograph N rûup thàai รูปถ่าย, or simply rûup รูป

photograph V thàai rûup ถ่ายรูป

pick, choose V lûeak เลือก

pick up V (e.g. to pick someone up from the airport) ráp รับ

pickpocket N khà-mohy lúang krà-pǎo ขโมยล้วงกระเป๋า

pickpocket V lúang krà-pǎo ล้วงกระเป๋า

picky ADJ See 'fussy'

picture N (general term used for both photographic and non-photographic images) rûup phâap รูปภาพ, (movie) nǎng หนัง

piece, portion, section N tawn ตอน (NOTE: commonly used in 'time expressions': e.g. tawn cháo ตอนเช้า '[in] the morning', tawn yen ตอนเย็น '[in] the evening')

piece N (a piece or item) chín ชิ้น

pierce, penetrate V jàw เจาะ

pig N mǔu หมู

pigeon N nók phí-râap นกพิราบ

pigtail N (hairstyle) hǎng pia หางเปีย; ponytail hǎng máa (literally, 'tail'-'horse') หางม้า

pile N (e.g. a pile of rubbish) kawng กอง

pill(s) N yaa mét (literally, 'pill'-'medicine/drug') ยาเม็ด

pillar N sǎo เสา

pillion ADV (seated behind the rider on a motorcycle) (COLLOQUIAL) sáwn tháai ซ้อนท้าย

pillow/cushion N mǎwn หมอน

pimp, procurer N (SLANG) maehng-daa แมงดา

pimple(s) N See 'acne'

pin number/PIN N See 'password'

pinch V (e.g. to pinch someone on the arm) yìk หยิก

pineapple N sap-pà-rót สับปะรด

pink N sǐi chomphuu สีชมพู

pipe N thâw ท่อ

pistol N puen phók ปืนพก

pit N lǔum หลุม

pitcher, jug N yùeak เหยือก

pity V (to feel pity/sympathy) song sǎan สงสาร

pitiful ADJ nâa song sǎan น่าสงสาร

place N thîi ที่ (used in conjunction with the name of a particular place, e.g.) at home thîi bâan ที่บ้าน; at a/ the store thîi ráan ที่ร้าน. (Or it can be used as follows: 'He has a place' [this could refer to a home/a piece of land, etc.] khǎo mii thîi เขามีที่)

place/put (on) V waang วาง

placid ADJ ngîap เงียบ

plain ADJ (not complicated or not fancy) rîap รียบ, (flat) thîi râap ที่ราบ

plan N (from English) phǎehn แผน

plan V waang phǎehn วางแผน

plane N khrûeang bin เครื่องบิน

planet N daow khráw ดาวเคราะห์

plant N (general term covering everything from a small plant to a large tree) tôn mái ต้นไม้

plant V plùuk ปลูก

plastic N (from English; pronounced either) pláat-sàtìk or pláastìk พลาสติก

plastic or cosmetic surgery N sǎn-lá-yá-kam ศัลยกรรม (in colloquial speech often pronounced sǎn-yá-kam)

plate N jaan (pronounced 'jarn') จาน

plateau N thîi râap ที่ราบ

platform N (at a bus/railway station) chaan chaa laa ชานชาลา

play V lên เล่น

playful ADJ khîi lên ขี้เล่น

plead v (beg) âwn wawn อ้อนวอน, (advocate (a case) in a court of law) hâi kaan ให้การ

pleasant ADJ (in the sense of a 'pleasant atmosphere' – somewhere where one feels 'relaxed and comfortable') sà-baai jai สบายใจ

please v (go ahead – 'come in', 'sit down' etc.) choehn (pronounced similar to the word 'churn') เชิญ, (request for help) chûai ช่วย, (request for something) khǎw ขอ

please v (to please someone/ attend to someone's needs/ wishes) ao jai sài (literally 'take'-'heart'-'put') เอาใจใส่, or simply ao jai เอาใจ

pleased ADJ dii jai ดีใจ

pleasing ADJ (to hit the spot) thùuk jai ถูกใจ; (COLLOQUIAL; to be pleasing in the sense of) meeting all one's 'requirements', or 'specifications' thùuk sà-pék ถูกสเป็ก (NOTE: the word here sà-pék สเป็ก is from English)

pleasure N khwaam sùk ความสุข

plenty N (a lot) mâak maai มากมาย

plow/plough v thǎi ไถ

plug N (bath) plák ปลั๊ก, (electric) plák fai ปลั๊กไฟ

plus CONJ (as in '2 plus 2', or 'the price of the ticket, plus the hotel, plus the rental car') bùak บวก

pocket N (also the word for 'bag' as in 'suitcase' or 'overnight travel bag', etc.) krà-pǎo กระเป๋า

poem N klawn กลอน

poet N kà-wii กวี

point/dot N jùt จุด

point (out) v chíi ชี้

point of view N khwaam hěhn ความเห็น

poison N yaa phít ยาพิษ

poisonous ADJ mii phít มีพิษ; a poisonous snake nguu mii phít งูมีพิษ

pole N sǎo เสา

police N tam-rùat ตำรวจ, (SLANG) chà-lǎam bòk (literally, 'shark'-'land' or 'land shark') ฉลามบก

police station N sà-thǎa-nii tamrùat สถานีตำรวจ,

(COLLOQUIAL) rohng phák
โรงพัก

policy N (i.e. government
policy, the policy of a
company) ná-yoh-baai
นโยบาย

polish V khàt ngao ขัดเงา, or
simply khàt ขัด (pronounced
like the English word 'cut',
but with a low tone)

politics N kaan mueang
การเมือง; to be involved in
politics lên kaan mueang
(literally, 'play'-'politics')
เล่นการเมือง; a politician nák
kaan mueang นักการเมือง

polite ADJ sù-phâap สุภาพ

pollution N mon-lá-phaa-wá
มลภาวะ

pool N sà สระ (i.e. swimmimg
pool is sà wâai náam สระ
ว่ายน้ำ)

poor ADJ jon จน

ponytail N (hairstyle) See
'pigtail'

popular ADJ pen thîi ní yom
เป็นที่นิยม

population N (i.e. 'what is the
population of Thailand?') prà-
chaakawn ประชากร

porch/verandah N rá-biang
ระเบียง

pork N núea mǔu เนื้อหมู or
simply mǔu หมู

pornographic ADJ /porno/
porn N (abbreviated from
English; colloquial) póh โป๊;
a pornographic film/DVD
etc. nǎng póh หนังโป๊; a
pornographic magazine/
book, etc. nǎngsǔeh póh
หนังสือโป๊ (NOTE: the word
póh is also commonly used
to describe someone who is
scantily dressed or revealing
more skin/flesh than
appropriate in public)

port/wharf/harbor N thâa
ruea ท่าเรือ

portable ADJ phók phaa ngâai
พกพาง่าย

portion, serve N thîi ที่; (e.g.
in a restaurant when ordering)
two cups of coffee kaa-faeh
sǎwng thîi กาแฟสองที่

pose V (to pose for the
camera/strike a pose) waang
thâa วางท่า

position N (in an organization)
tam-nàeng ตำแหน่ง;

131

(position/posture – e.g. yoga posture) thâa ท่า

possess v pen jâo khǎwng เป็นเจ้าของ

possessions N sǒmbàt สมบัติ, (COLLOQUIAL) khâw khǎwng (literally, 'rice'-'thing(s)') ข้าวของ, or sìng khǎwng สิ่งของ

possible ADJ pen pai dâi เป็นไปได้ (NOTE: 'impossible' is pen pai mâi dâi เป็นไปไม่ได้)

possibly ADV See 'perhaps/maybe'

post, pole, column N sǎo เสา

post, mail N jòt-mǎai จดหมาย

postcard N prai-sà-nii-yá-bàt ไปรษณียบัตร, or (from English) póht-sà-kâat โปสการ์ด

post office N prai-sà-nii ไปรษณีย์

postpone v lûean เลื่อน

postponed, delayed ADJ lûean weh-laa เลื่อนเวลา

posture N See 'position'

pot N (for cooking) mâw หม้อ (NOTE: also used as a slang

term for 'vagina')

potato N man fàràng มันฝรั่ง, or simply man มัน

poultry N (i.e. chicken) kài ไก่

pour v (a drink) rin ริน; to pour water or some other liquid over something râat ราด (Note: this word is used, for example, when food, such as curry, is served over/on top of rice – so, rather than having two dishes – one of rice and one of curry/or a stir-fry – there is but one dish [often translated in a menu] as râat khâw ราดข้าว)

poverty N (also see 'hardship') khwaam yâak jon ความยากจน

powder N (as certain cosmetics) pâeng แป้ง, (tiny loose particles) phǒng ผง

power, authority N am-nâat อำนาจ

powerful ADJ mii am-nâat มีอำนาจ

practice v fùek hàt ฝึกหัด, or simply just fùek ฝึก

praise v (COLLOQUIAL) chom ชม (the same word is also

translated as 'admire'), or (formal) yók yâwng ยกย่อง

pram/stroller N (for a baby/ young child) rót kěn dèk rót รถ เข็นเด็ก

prawn/shrimp N kûng กุ้ง

pray v (Buddhist style) sùat mon สวดมนต์, (Christian style) à-thít-thǎan อธิษฐาน

prayer N bòt sùat mon บท สวดมนต์

precious/valuable ADJ mii khâa (literally, 'have'-'value') มีค่า

precise ADJ thùuk tâwng ถูก ต้อง

predict v See 'forecast'

prefer v châwp mâak kwàa (literally, 'like'-'more than') ชอบมากกว่า

pregnant ADJ tháwng ท้อง (Note: same word as 'stomach')

prejudice N à-khá-tì อคติ, (COLLOQUIAL) 'to look down on someone' duu thùuk ดูถูก

prepare, make ready v triam เตรียม

prepared/ready ADJ (to do something) phráwm พร้อม

prescription N (from a doctor) bai sàng yaa ใบสั่งยา

present N (gift) khǎwng khwǎn ของขวัญ

present v (a formal request, ideas – in a formal context) sà-něeh เสนอ

present, at the moment ADJ tawn-ní ตอนนี้

presently, nowadays ADV (FORMAL – for COLLOQUIAL see 'now') pàt-jù-ban-ní ปัจจุบันนี้

preserve v à-nú-rák อนุรักษ์

president N (of a republic) prà-thaa-na thíp-baw-dii ประธานาธิบดี

press v kòt กด

pressure N khwaam kòt dan ความกดดัน Also see 'blood pressure'

prestige N chûeh sǐang ชื่อ เสียง

pretend v klâehng แกล้ง (Note: this is an interesting Thai word that also means 'to do something to someone else out of spite or malice', 'to annoy or tease')

pretty ADJ (beautiful) sǔai สวย, (cute) nâa rák น่ารัก

133

prevent, protect v pâwng kan ป้องกัน

previous/before ADV kàwn ก่อน: e.g. to come/arrive before someone else maa kàwn มาก่อน; previously tàeh kàwn แต่ก่อน

prey N yùea เหยื่อ

price N raakhaa ราคา

pride/dignity N sàk-sĭi ศักดิ์ศรี

priest N (Christian) bàat lŭang บาทหลวง

primary school N rohng rian prà-thŏm โรงเรียนประถม; primary (school) education pràthŏm sèuk-sǎa ประถม ศึกษา

prime minister N naayók rát-thà-montrii นายกรัฐมนตรี

prince N jâo chaai เจ้าชาย

princess N jâo yĭng เจ้าหญิง

principal ADJ sǎm-khan สำคัญ

principle N kòt กฎ

print v phim พิมพ์ (NOTE: the English word 'print' is now widely used – e.g. print a document/photograph etc.) prín ปริ๊นท์

prison N (COLLOQUIAL) khúk

คุก; to be imprisoned/jailed tìt khúk (literally, 'stuck'-'prison') ติดคุก

prisoner N nák thôht นักโทษ

private ADJ (not public) sùan tua ส่วนตัว

privilege N à-phí-sìt อภิสิทธิ์

prize/reward N raang-wan รางวัล

probably ADV See 'perhaps'

problem N pan-hǎa ปัญหา, (COLLOQUIAL) 'no problem(s)/ no worries' mâi mii pan-hǎa ไม่มีปัญหา

procedure, process N khán tawn ขั้นตอน

procession N See 'parade'

proclaim v prá-kàat ประกาศ

procrastinate v phlàt wan ผลัดวัน

produce/manufacture v phà-lìt ผลิต

product N phà-lìt-tà-phan ผลิตภัณฑ์

profession, occupation N aa-chîip อาชีพ; a professional mueh aa-chîip มืออาชีพ

professor N sàat-traa-jaan ศาสตราจารย์

134

profile N prà-wàt ประวัติ

profit N (financial gain from business) kam-rai กำไร

profound ADJ (to have a deep meaning) léuk-séung ลึกซึ้ง, or (more colloquially simply) séung ซึ้ง

program N (e.g. television program, list of items – *also see* 'menu') raai-kaan รายการ

prohibit v *See* 'forbid', 'forbidden'

project N khrohng-kaan โครงการ

promise v & N sǎnyaa สัญญา (NOTE: as a noun this word means a 'contract')

promote v sòng-sǒehm ส่งเสริม

pronounce v àwk sǐang ออกเสียง

proof/evidence N làk-thǎan หลักฐาน

propaganda v *See* 'advertise'

proper, appropriate ADJ màw-sǒm เหมาะสม

property N sáp-sǐn ทรัพย์สิน *Also see* 'possessions'

propose v (offer for consideration) sà-nǒeh เสนอ, (ask someone to marry) khǎw tàeng-ngaan ขอแต่งงาน

prosper v (develop) jà-roehn เจริญ; progress (in the sense of development to more complex, advanced society) khwaam jà-roehn ความเจริญ; (to do well) râm-ruai (râm pronounced like the English word 'rum') ร่ำรวย

prostitute N sǒh-pheh-nii โสเภณี; *also see* 'hooker'

protest v prà-thúang (NOTE: the syllable prà is very short) ประท้วง; a 'protest march' is doehn prà-thúang (literally, 'walk'-'protest') เดินประท้วง

proud ADJ phuum-jai ภูมิใจ

prove v phí-sùut พิสูจน์

proverb N sù-phaa-sìt สุภาษิต

provide v (afford) hâi ให้

province N (administrative unit; there are presently 76 provinces in Thailand outside the Bangkok area) jang-wàt จังหวัด

prude N prudish ADJ – a 'fuddy-duddy' (i.e. to be opposed to liberal social

135

ideas/behavior) châo rá-bìap เจ้าระเบียบ

psychiatrist N jìt-tà-phâet (literally, 'mind/spirit'-'doctor') จิตแพทย์

pub N (from English) phàp (pronounced similar to the English word 'pup') ผับ

pubic hair/pubes N (VULGAR) mŏi หมอย

public ADJ sǎa-thaa rá-ná สาธารณะ; a public place thîi sǎa-thaa rá-ná ที่สาธารณะ

public relations N prà-chaa sǎm-phan ประชาสัมพันธ์ (NOTE: the same term is used for both an 'information booth/tourist information' and 'reception' in a hotel)

publish V tii-phim ตีพิมพ์

puke, vomit V aa-jian อาเจียน, or (COLLOQUIAL) ûak อ้วก

pull V dueng ดึง

pump V sùup สูบ; a pump N khrûeang sùup เครื่องสูบ (NOTE: the word sùup is also used to mean 'smoke' as in 'smoke a cigarette' sùup bùrìi สูบบุหรี่)

pumpkin N fák thawng ฟักทอง

punch V (as in to 'punch' someone) tòi ต่อย, or chók ชก

punctual/on time ADJ trong weh-laa ตรงเวลา

punish V long thôht ลงโทษ

pupil/student N nák rian นักเรียน

puppet N hùn krà-bàwk หุ่น ระบอก

puppy N lûuk mǎa ลูกหมา

purchase, buy V súeh ซื้อ

pure/inocent ADJ bawrí-sùt บริสุทธิ์

purple N sǐi mûang สีม่วง

purpose N (i.e. 'the purpose is to increase literacy') jùt mûng mǎai จุดมุ่งหมาย

purse N (for money) krà-pǎo ngoehn กระเป๋าเงิน

pus N (in a wound) nǎwng หนอง

push V phlàk ผลัก, or dan (pronounced like the word 'done') ดัน

put, place V (i.e. put the books on the table) waang วาง

put off, delay, postpone V lûean เลื่อน

put on (clothes) v sài ใส่
puzzled/confused ADJ
ngong งง

Q

quake v sàn สั่น
qualification N khun-ná-
sŏmbàt คุณสมบัติ
quality N (as in 'good quality
merchandise') khun-ná-
phâap คุณภาพ: e.g. good
quality khun-ná-phâap dii
คุณภาพดี
quantity N jam-nuan จำนวน
quarrel v See 'argue'
quarter N (¼) sèht nùeng sùan
sìi เศษหนึ่งส่วนสี่
queen N prá raa-chí-nii พระ
ราชินี, or simply raa chí-nii
ราชินี
queer N (gay/homosexual)
keh เกย์ (from English), ADJ
(brightly colored) sòt-săi
สดใส
question N, v kham thăam
คำถาม
queue N (from English) khiu
คิว; to line up in a queue

khâo khiu (literally, 'enter'-
'queue') เข้าคิว

quick ADJ **quickly** ADV rew เร็ว
quicken v rêhng เร่ง
quiet ADJ ngîap เงียบ
quit v (resign) laa àwk ลา
ออก; (discontinue, i.e 'quit
smoking') lôehk เลิก
quite ADV (really) thii diao ที
เดียว (COLLOQUIAL); (rather)
khâwn khâang ค่อนข้าง
quiz v, N thòt sàwp ทดสอบ

R

rabbit N krà-tàai กระต่าย
race N (i.e. race of people
– Caucasian, Asian, etc.)
chúeah châat เชื้อชาติ;
(competition) kaan khàeng
khăn การแข่งขัน
racism N lát-thí yìat phĭu
(literally, 'ism/doctrine'-
'despise'-'skin') ลัทธิเหยียด
ผิว
radiation N rang sĭi รังสี
radio N wít-thá-yú วิทยุ
raft N (also 'houseboat') phaeh
แพ

rail N (i.e. travelled by rail/train) dohy rótfai โดยรถไฟ

railroad, railway N thaang rótfai ทางรถไฟ

rain N fŏn ฝน

rain V fŏn tòk ฝนตก

raincoat N sûea kan fŏn เสื้อกันฝน

raise, lift V yók ยก

raise V (bring up children) líang เลี้ยง, (increase in amount, e.g. wages) khûen ขึ้น

rambutan N ngáw เงาะ

rancid ADJ (foul smelling) měhn hǔehn เหม็นหืน

random ADJ sùm สุ่ม

Rangoon (largest city in Burma) N yâang kûng ย่างกุ้ง

rank N (an official position, e.g. military, police) yót ยศ

rape V khòm khǔen ข่มขืน

rapid ADJ (very quick) rûat rew รวดเร็ว or simply rew เร็ว

rare ADJ (uncommon) hǎa yâak หายาก; (uncooked) dìp ดิบ

rarely, seldom, not often ADV mâi bòi ไม่บ่อย

rash N (skin eruption) phùen ผื่น (NOTE: 'to have a rash' is

rat/mouse N nǔu หนู

rate of exchange N (for foreign currency) àt-traa lâehk plian อัตราแลกเปลี่ยน

rather ADV (i.e. 'rather big', 'rather expensive') khâwn khâang... ค่อนข้างฯ

rational ADJ (scientific; reason as opposed to superstition) mii hèht mii phŏn มีเหตุมีผล, or simply mii hèht phŏn มีเหตุผล

rattan N (i.e. rattan furniture) wǎai หวาย

raven N plôn ปล้น

raw, uncooked ADJ dìp ดิบ

razor N (for shaving) mîit kohn มีดโกน (kohn pronounced like 'own' with a 'g' in front); a razor blade bai mîit kohn ใบมีดโกน

reach/arrive V thǔeng ถึง

react V (to react to something) mii pàti-kì-rí-yaa มีปฏิกิริยา; reaction, response pàti-kì-rí-yaa ปฏิกิริยา

read V àan อ่าน

ready ADJ phráwm พร้อม, to get ready triam tua เตรียม

ตัว, to make ready tham hâi phráwm ทำให้พร้อม

realize, become aware of v rúu tua รู้ตัว

real ADJ (to be genuine, not an imitation) tháeh แท้; real (not imaginary) khǎwng jing ของจริง

reality N khwaam pen jing ความเป็นจริง

really ADV (in fact) thîi jing ที่จริง

really! (it's true) jing-jing จริงๆ

really? INTERJ (is that so?) jing rǔeh จริงหรือ

rear ADJ (of the bus/plane/shop, etc.) khâang lǎng ข้างหลัง, or dâan lǎng ด้านหลัง

reason N (as in a reason for doing something) hèht phǒn เหตุผล

reasonable/fair ADJ (price) phaw sǒm khuan พอสมควร, appropriate máw-sǒm เหมาะสม

recall v (an incident that occurred/where some missing object may be found) núek àwk นึกออก

receipt N bai sèt ใบเสร็จ

receive v ráp รับ

recent ADJ **recently** ADV mûea rew-rew níi เมื่อเร็วๆ นี้

recess N phák pák พัก

recipe N sùt aà-hǎan สูตรอาหาร; recipe or cookbook tam-raa aà-hǎan ตำราอาหาร

recite v thâwng jam ท่องจำ

reckless ADJ sà-phráo สะเพร่า

recognize/remember v jam dâi จำได้

recommend v náenam แนะนำ

reconcile v prawng dawng ปรองดอง

record N ban-thúek บันทึก

record v àt-sĭang อัดเสียง

recover v (to recover something) ao klàp kheun เอากลับคืน

recovered ADJ (to be cured) hǎai láew (literally, 'disappear'–'already') หายแล้ว

red N sĭi daeng สีแดง

Red Cross, the (humanitarian organization) sà-phaa kaa-châat สภากาชาด

reduce v (speed, weight, etc.) lót ลด

redundant ADJ (superfluous) mâak koehn pai มากเกินไป, (overlapping) sám-sáwn ซ้ำซ้อน

reef N hǐn pà-kaa-rang หินปะการัง

refer V âang-thǔeng อ้างถึง

refill V toehm เติม

reflect V (e.g. for light to reflect off the water) sà-tháwn สะท้อน

reform V pràp-prung ปรับปรุง

refreshment N (i.e. a drink) khrûeang dùehm เครื่องดื่ม

refrigerator N tûu yen (literally, 'cupboard'-'cold') ตู้เย็น

refugee N phûu líi-phai ผู้ลี้ภัย

refuse/reject/deny V pàtì-sèht ปฏิเสธ; refusal kaan pàtì-sèht การปฏิเสธ

regarding/concerning PREP kìao kàp เกี่ยวกับ

region N (of a country – general geographic term) phuumí-phâak ภูมิภาค (NOTE: Thailand has four major regions – the center, the north, the north-east, and the south.) The word used

to refer to 'region' is phâak ภาค, more commonly for the Central Region phâak klaang ภาคกลาง and the Northern Region phâak nǔea ภาคเหนือ. The Northeast Region is commonly referred to as ii-sǎan อีสาน, while Southern Thailand is pàk tâi (literally, 'part'-'south') ปักษ์ใต้.

register V (a marriage etc.) jòt thá-bian จดทะเบียน

registered post N (i.e. registered letter) jòtmǎai long thá-bian จดหมายลงทะเบียน

regret V (to feel sorry) sǐa jai เสียใจ, or sǐa daai เสียดาย

regrettably ADV (what a pity!) nâa sǐa daai น่าเสียดาย

regular, normal ADJ pàkàtì ปกติ

relatives N (family) yâat ญาติ

relax/rest V phák phàwn พักผ่อน

release V (let go/set free) plòi ปล่อย

reliable ADJ (trustworthy) wái waang-jai ไว้วางใจ

religion N sàat-sà-nǎa ศาสนา

140

remainder N (that which is left over) thîi lǔea ที่เหลือ

remarkable ADJ dòht-dèhn โดดเด่น

remedy N wí-thii rák-sǎa (literally, 'method'-'treat') วิธี รักษา

remember V jam (pronounce like 'jum' in 'jumble') จำ

remind V tuean เตือน (also the word for 'to warn')

remove V (take something out of...) aw àwk (literally, 'take'-'out') เอาออก

rent V châo เช่า, rent out V hâi châo ให้เช่า

repair V (a car, etc.) sâwm ซ่อม

repeat V tham sám (sám pronounced similar to the English word 'sum') ทำซ้ำ; **repeatedly** ADV sám-sám ซ้ำๆ

replace, substitute V See 'instead'

reply/answer V tàwp ตอบ

reply V (in writing) khǐan tàwp เขียนตอบ

report N, V raai ngaan รายงาน

reporter N See 'journalist'

represent V tham thaen ทำ แทน

representative N tua thaen ตัวแทน

request V (in the sense of imploring someone to do something etc.) khǎw ráwng ขอร้อง; (to ask for, as in 'May I....?') khǎw ขอ

require/want V (FORMAL) tâwng kaan ต้องการ, (COLLOQUIAL) yàak อยาก (i.e. want to eat yàak kin อยากกิน)

rescue/help V chûai lǔea ช่วยเหลือ

research N ngaan-wí-jai งานวิจัย

research V tham wí-jai ทำวิจัย

resemble, similar ADJ (COLLO-QUIAL) duu khláai ดูคล้าย, also duu mǔean ดูเหมือน

reserve V (a room in a hotel) jawng จอง

resident, inhabitant N phûu aa-sǎi ผู้อาศัย

resign V See 'quit'

resist V tàw-tâan ต่อต้าน, or simply tâan ต้าน

resolve V (a problem) kâeh pan hǎa แก้ปัญหา

respect N khwaam khao-róp ความเคารพ

141

respect v (somebody) khao-róp เคารพ, or náp-thǔeh นับถือ

respond v (FORMAL) tàwp sà-nǎwng ตอบสนอง

response N kham tàwp คำตอบ

responsible ADJ ráp phìt châwp รับผิดชอบ; **responsibility** N khwaam ráp phìt châwp ความรับผิดชอบ

rest N (i.e. remainder/what's left over) thîi lǔeah ที่เหลือ

rest/relax v phák phàwn พักผ่อน

restaurant N ráan aa-hǎan ร้านอาหาร

restless/agitated ADJ (COLLOQUIAL) yùu mâi sùk อยู่ไม่สุข

restrain v dueng ao wái ดึงเอาไว้

restrict v (limit availability/to be limited – time, etc.) jam-kàt จำกัด

restroom N (bathroom) hâwng náam ห้องน้ำ

result N (e.g. of a test, etc.) phǒn ผล

resulting from, as a result

retail ADJ (the sale of goods in small quantities) khǎai plìik ขายปลีก

retarded ADJ (to be mentally retarded) panyaa àwn (literally, 'intellect'-'weak/soft') ปัญญาอ่อน

retired ADJ kà-sǐan-aa-yú เกษียณอายุ, or (MORE COLLOQUIALLY) kà-sǐan เกษียณ

return v (go back) klàp กลับ (e.g. return home is klàp bâan กลับบ้าน); (give back) khuehn คืน

return ticket N (round trip ticket) tǔa pai klàp (literally, 'ticket'-'go'-'return') ตั๋วไปกลับ

reveal v (make known/to be open – not keeping secrets) pòeht phǒei เปิดเผย

reverse, back up v thǒi lǎng ถอยหลัง, or simply thǒi ถอย

reversed, backwards, inside out v klàp khâang กลับข้าง

review v thóp thuan ทบทวน

revise v trùat kâe ตรวจแก้

conj pen phǒn maa jàak... เป็นผลมาจาก

142

revolt/rebellion/coup d'état N pàtìwát ปฏิวัติ

revolting/disgusting ADJ nâa rang-kìat น่ารังเกียจ, or khà-yà khà-yǎehng ขยะแขยง

reward/prize N raang-wan รางวัล

rhythm N See 'tempo'

rice N (cooked) khâow sǔai ข้าวสวย; (uncooked) khâow sǎan ข้าวสาร; (food) khâow ข้าว

rice fields N (irrigated) naa นา

rich/wealthy ADJ ruai รวย

rid: get rid of/eliminate v (pests, termites etc.) kamjàt กำจัด

ride N (in car) nâng rót นั่งรถ

ride v (on a bicycle, an animal) khìi ขี่

ridiculous ADJ (meaningless) rái sǎará ไร้สาระ

right/correct ADJ thùuk ถูก, or thùuk tâwng ถูกต้อง

right N (right-hand side) khwǎa ขวา; to be right-handed thànàt mueh khwǎa ถนัดมือขวา

rights N sìt-thí สิทธิ (often pronounced as simply sìt สิทธิ)

right now ADV dǐao níi เดี๋ยวนี้

rind/peel N (i.e. orange peel) plùek เปลือก, (also the general word for) bark on a tree, e.g. plùek mái เปลือกไม้

ring N (jewelry) wǎehn แหวน; (boxing ring) weh-thii เวที (also means 'stage for performances')

ring v (to ring someone on the phone) thoh pai โทรไป; (to sound a doorbell) kòt krìng กดกริ่ง

rinse/wash v (plates, hands, etc.) láang ล้าง: e.g. wash your face láang nâa ล้างหน้า

riot N jà-laajon จลาจล

rip/tear v chìik ฉีก

ripe ADJ (of fruit) sùk สุก

rise v (ascend) khûen ขึ้น; (increase) phôehm khûen เพิ่มขึ้น

risk/risky ADJ sìang เสี่ยง

ritual/ceremony N phí-thii พิธี

rival N khûu khàeng คู่แข่ง

river N mâeh náam (literally, 'mother'-'water') แม่น้ำ

road/street N (major thoroughfare) thà-nǒn ถนน

143

roar v kham raam คำราม

roast v (cook in an oven) òp อบ, (grill, BBQ) yâang ย่าง; (toast) pîng ปิ้ง

rob v (a bank) plôn ปล้น; to rob (a person/to hold someone up) jîi จี้

robot N hùn yon หุ่นยนต์

rock N hǐn หิน

rocket N jà-rùat จรวด

role N (a role in a movie, the role of the press, etc.) bòt bàat บทบาท

roll v (to roll over) klîng กลิ้ง

roll N (as in a roll of toilet paper) múan ม้วน; to roll/make a cigarette muan bùrìi มวนบุหรี่

roof N lǎng khaa หลังคา

room N (in house/hotel, etc.) hâwng ห้อง; (to have some free/extra space) thîi wâang ที่ว่าง

root N (of plant or a tooth) râak ราก

rope/string N chûeak เชือก

rose N (flower) kù-làap กุหลาบ

rotate v mǔn wian หมุน เวียน

rotten ADJ nâo เน่า

rough ADJ (as in a rough road/ an unshaven face) khrù khrà ขรุขระ

roughly, approximately ADV prà-maan ประมาณ

round ADJ (shape) klom กลม

round, around, surrounding ADV râwp-râwp รอบๆ

routine N ngaan prà-jam (literally, 'work'-'regular') งาน ประจำ

rub v (also 'scrub') thǔn ถู

rubber N yaang ยาง

rubber band N (COLLOQUIAL) nǎng yaang หนังยาง

rubbish N khà-yà ขยะ; rubbish bin thǎng khà-yà ถังขยะ

ruby N tháp-thim ทับทิม (the word also means 'pomegranate'). NOTE: mét tháp-thim เม็ดทับทิม is slang for 'clitoris' (literally, 'seed'-'ruby')

rude/crude/coarse ADJ (speech/behavior) yàap khaai หยาบคาย, also mâi sù-phâap ไม่สุภาพ

rules N kòt กฎ

rumor N khàaw lueh ข่าวลือ

run v wîng วิ่ง

run away v (i.e. to flee) wîng nǐi วิ่งหนี

rural ADJ (the countryside) chon-nabòt ชนบท, (COLLOQUIAL) bâan nâwk บ้าน นอก

rush v rîip รีบ

rust N sà-nǐm สนิม; **rust** v sà-nǐm khûen สนิมขึ้น

ruthless ADJ thaa run ทารุณ

S

sabotage v tham laai ทำลาย

sack v (to dismiss an employee) See 'fire'

sack N (bag – e.g. sack of rice) krà-sàwp กระสอบ

sacred/sacrosanct ADJ sàk-sìt ศักดิ์สิทธิ์

sacrifice v sǐa sàlà เสียสละ; sacrifice kaan sǐa sàlà การ เสียสละ

sad ADJ sôo เศร้า

safe ADJ plàwt-phai ปลอดภัย; safety khwaam plàwt-phai ความปลอดภัย

safe N (for keeping valuables – from English) tûu sép ตู้เซฟ

sago N (food) sǎa-khuu สาคู

sail v (a yacht) lâen ruea แล่นเรือ

salad N (from English) sà-làt สลัด; also see 'lettuce'

salary, wage N ngoehn duean เงินเดือน

sale (for) IDIOM (available to customers) khǎai ขาย (also 'sell')

sale (on) IDIOM (reduced prices) lót raa-khaa ลดราคา

sales assistant N phá-nák-ngaan khǎai พนักงานขาย

saline N náam kluea น้ำเกลือ

saliva N (spittle) náam laai น้ำลาย

salt N kluea เกลือ

salt-water N (sea water) náam khem น้ำเค็ม

salty ADJ (taste) khem เค็ม

same PRON (i.e. the same) mǔean เหมือน

sample/example N tua yàang ตัวอย่าง

sand N saai ทราย

sandals N rawng tháo tàe รองเท้าแตะ

sanitation N khwaam sà-àat ความสะอาด

145

satay N (grilled/BBQ meat/ chicken, etc. on a wooden skewer) sà-téh สะเต๊ะ; satay stick(s) mái sà-téh ไม้สะเต๊ะ

satellite N daow thiam ดาวเทียม

satire N sìat sǐi เสียดสี

satisfied ADJ pen thîi phaw jai เป็นที่พอใจ, or simply phaw jai พอใจ; to satisfy someone tham hâi phaw jai ทำให้พอใจ

Saturday N wan sǎo วันเสาร์

sauce N (from English) sáwt ซอส; (dipping sauce – spicy, sweet/sour, etc.) nám jîm น้ำจิ้ม

savor ADJ (flavor) rót รส, (smell) klin กลิ่น

saw N (tool) lûeai เลื่อย

say V phûut พูด; say that… phûut wâa… พูดว่า…

scales N taa châng ตาชั่ง

scandal N rûeang êuh chǎow เรื่องอื้อฉาว

scanner N (from English) khrûeang sà-kaen เครื่อง สแกน

scar N phlǎeh pen แผลเป็น

scare V (to scare someone) tham hâi tòk-jai ทำให้ตกใจ

scarce ADV mâi khôi mii ไม่ค่อยมี, or hǎa yâak (literally, 'find'-'difficult') หา ยาก

scared/scary ADJ nâa klua น่ากลัว

scarf N phâa phan khaw (literally, 'cloth'-'wrap around'- 'neck') ผ้าพันคอ

scatter V krà-jaai กระจาย

scenery, view N (from English) wiu วิว

scent N kliin hǎwm กลิ่นหอม

sceptical ADJ song-sǎi สงสัย

schedule N kam-nòt กำหนด

scholar N nák wí-chaa-kaan นักวิชาการ

scholarship N (INFORMAL) thun lâo rian ทุนเล่าเรียน, or thun kaan sèuk-sǎa ทุนการศึกษา, (COLLOQUIAL) thun ทุน

school N rohng-rian โรงเรียน

schoolchild N dèk nák-rian เด็กนักเรียน

science N wít-thá-yaa-sàat วิทยาศาสตร์

146

วิทยาศาสตร์
scissors N kan-krai กรรไกร
scold/berate v wâa ว่า
scope N khàwp khèt ขอบเขต
score N khá-naen คะแนน
scorn v duu thùuk ดูถูก
Scotland N sà-káwt-laehn
สก็อตแลนด์
Scottish, Scots N chaow
sà-káwt ชาวสก็อต
scrap N (scrap of food, scrap
of paper, something left over,
etc.) sèht เศษ: e.g. scrap of
food sèht aa-hǎan เศษอาหาร
scrape v (e.g. scrape paint off
something) khùut ขูด
scratch v (scratch an itch)
kao เกา, also (aggressively
scratched – by someone with
long fingernails, a cat etc.)
khùan ขวน; a scratch (e.g.
on a car) roi khùut รอยขูด
scream v ráwng kríit ร้อง
กรี๊ด
screen N (of computer or
television) jaw (pronounced
like the English word 'jaw')
จอ
screw N (COLLOQUIAL – used
with a screwdriver) náwt

(pronounced very similar to
the word 'not') นอต
screwdriver N khǎi khuang
ไขควง
scrub v thǔu ถู, or khàt ขัด
sculpt v pân ปั้น
sculpture N rûup pân รูปปั้น
sea, beach N thá-leh ทะเล
seafood N aa-hǎan thá-leh
อาหารทะเล
search for/look for/seek
v hǎa หา; to ask 'what are
you looking for?' khun hǎa
àrai (literally, 'you'-'look for'-
'what') คุณหาอะไร
season N rúe-duu ฤดู, or
(MORE COLLOQUIALLY) nâa หน้า
(NOTE: the same word as
'face', 'page of a book', etc.);
summer/hot season nâa
ráwn (literally, 'season'-'hot')
หน้าร้อน (In Thailand the
'high season', in terms of
tourist arrivals [Nov-Feb], is
colloquially referred to as nâa
hai หน้าไฮ)
seat N thîi nâng ที่นั่ง
second N (measure of time)
wí-naa-thii วินาที
second ADJ (as in second

place) thîi săwng ที่สอง

secondhand ADJ (e.g. a used car) mueh săwng มือสอง; a used car rót mueh săwng (literally, 'car/vehicle'-'hand'-'two') รถมือสอง

secret N khwaam láp ความลับ (i.e. to keep a secret khwaam láp rák·săa khwaam láp รักษาความลับ)

secretary N lêh-khăa nú-kaan เลขานุการ, or (COLLOQUIALLY SIMPLY) leh-khăa เลขา

section/segment N (of something) tawn ตอน

secure/stable ADJ mân-khong มั่นคง

seduce v lâw-jai ล่อใจ

see v hĕn เห็น

seed N má-lét เม็ด (although commonly pronounced mét)

seek v See 'search'

seem v (e.g. it might rain) duu mŭean ดูเหมือน

see you later! INTERJ phóp kan mài พบกันใหม่

seize v yúet ยึด

seldom ADV (or 'not often') mâi bòi ไม่บ่อย

select/choose v lûeak เลือก

self N ehng เอง, or tua ehng ตัวเอง

self-assured ADJ mân-jai tua ehng มั่นใจตัวเอง

selfish ADJ hĕn kàe tua เห็นแก่ตัว

sell v khăai ขาย

semen/sperm N (medical term) náam à-sù-ji น้ำอสุจิ, also náam kaam น้ำกาม

send v sòng ส่ง

senior ADJ aa-wú-soh อาวุโส

sensible/reasonable ADJ mii hèht phŏn มีเหตุผล

sensitive ADJ (tender feeling – physical) rúu-sùek wai รู้สึกไว

sentence N (in written language) prà-yòhk ประโยค

sentence v (a final judgment in a criminal case) tàt-sĭn ตัดสิน

separate v yâehk แยก

September N kan-yaa-yon กันยายน

sequence/order N taam lam-dàp ตามลำดับ

serious ADJ (i.e. not joking) ao jing เอาจริง; (severe) ráai raeng ร้ายแรง

servant N khon chái คนใช้

serve V (INFORMAL) ráp chái รับ
ใช้, (FORMAL) hâi baw-rí-kaan
บริการ

service N bawrí-kaan บริการ

sesame seeds N ngaa งา;
sesame oil náam-man ngaa
น้ำมันงา

set N (i.e. a set of something
– clothes, crockery, etc.)
chút ชุด

settle V (resolve) kâe pan-hǎa
แก้ปัญหา

settle down V tâng rók-râak
ตั้งรกราก

set up V (equipment) tìt-tâng
ติดตั้ง; (establish) kàw-tâng
ก่อตั้ง

seven NUM jèt เจ็ด

seventeen NUM sìp jèt สิบเจ็ด

seventy NUM jèt sìp เจ็ดสิบ

several/many ADJ lǎai หลาย

severe/violent ADJ run
raehng รุนแรง

sew, stitch V yép เย็บ

sex, gender N phêht เพศ

sex, sexual activity N
(POLITE) rûam phêht ร่วมเพศ;
(COLLOQUIAL) 'to have sex' ao
kan เอากัน; 'sleep together'

nawn dûai kan (literally,
'lie down'-'together') นอน
ด้วยกัน; (slang – vulgar and
extremely rude) 'to fuck' yét
เย็ด (Note: the English word
'sex' is widely known and
pronounced sék เซ็กส์)

sexy ADJ See 'hot'

shack N krà-thâwm กระท่อม

shade N (the shade of a tree)
rôm ร่ม

shadow N ngao เงา

shake V (move something up
and down) khà-yào เขย่า; (to
cause vibration) sàn สั่น

shake hands (in greeting) jàp
mueh kan จับมือกัน

shall, will AUX V (indicator of
future tense/action) jà จะ:
e.g. will/shall go jà pai จะไป

shallow ADJ (opposite of
'deep') tûehn ตื้น

shame N khwaam lá-aai jai
ความละอายใจ

shame ADJ (as in 'what a shame!')
nâa khǎai nâa น่าขายหน้า

shampoo N (hair shampoo)
yaa sà phǒm ยาสระผม, or
chaem-phuu แชมพู (from
English)

149

shape N (the shape of something) rûup รูป

shapely ADJ (i.e. to have a good figure) hùn dii หุ่นดี

shark N plaa chà-lăam ปลาฉลาม, or simply chà-lăam ฉลาม

sharp ADJ khom คม

sharp-tongued ADJ (vitriolic) (COLLOQUIAL) pàak jàt ปากจัด

shave V kohn โกน

she/her PRON khǎo เขา (NOTE: the same term is also used for 'he/him' and 'they')

sheep N kàe แกะ

sheet N (of paper) phàen krà-dàat แผ่นกระดาษ; (for bed, i.e. bedsheet) phâa puu thîi nawn ผ้าปูที่นอน

shelf/shelves N (for books) chán năng-sǔeh ชั้นหนังสือ

shell N plùeak hǒi เปลือกหอย, (COLLOQUIAL SIMPLY) hǒi หอย

shift N (as in a 'shift at work'/'night shift', etc.) wehn เวร: e.g. the night shift wehn klaang kheun เวรกลางคืน, or (MORE COLLOQUIALLY) a shift (either day or night) kà กะ

shingles N (medical condition) rôhk nguu sà-wàt โรคงูสวัด

shiny ADJ (skin/shoes, etc.) pen man เป็นมัน

ship N ruea เรือ

shirt N sûea chóeht (chóeht from English 'shirt') เสื้อเชิ้ต

shit N See 'excrement'

shiver N tua sàn ตัวสั่น

shock ADJ (to be in a 'state of shock') tòk tàleung ตกตะลึง, aa-kaan cháwk (cháwk from English 'shock') อาการช็อก

shoe(s) N rawng tháo รองเท้า

shoot V (with a gun) ying ยิง

shop/store N ráan ร้าน

shop, go shopping V pai súeh khǒrng ไปซื้อ ของ – also very common, particularly with reference to going to a supermarket/ department store/mall (from English) cháwp ชอป, or cháwp-pîng ชอปปิ้ง

shopkeeper N jâo khǎwng ráan เจ้าของร้าน

short ADJ (dress/piece of writing, etc.) sân สั้น

short ADJ (not tall) tîa เตี้ย

shortcut N (get somewhere

150

by shortest route) thaang lát
ทางลัด

shorts N (short trousers)
kaang-kehng khǎa
สั้น กางเกงขาสั้น; (i.e.
underpants/boxer shorts)
kaang-kehng nai กางเกงใน

shoulder N bàa บ่า

shout V tà-kohn ตะโกน

show V (e.g. one's feeling; to
perform in a film/play/live
performance etc.) sà-daehng
แสดง

show V (live performance)
kaan sà-daehng sòt การ
แสดงสด

shower V (or bath) àap náam
อาบน้ำ

showerhead N (in the
bathroom) fàk bua ฝักบัว

shrimp/prawn N kûng กุ้ง

shrimp (prawn) paste N
kàpì กะปิ

shrine N sǎan jâo ศาลเจ้า

shut/close; closed V pìt ปิด

shut up! V (SLANG) hùp pàak
หุบปาก, or ngîap เงียบ

shy/bashful ADJ aai อาย; a
very shy person khon khîi
aai คนขี้อาย

sibling N (older) phîi พี่ Also
see 'older brother/sister';
(younger) náwng น้อง

sick, ill ADJ pùai ป่วย, or
simply mâi sàbaai ไม่สบาย

side ADJ khâang ข้าง, also
(commonly used) dâan ด้าน

side effect(s) N (of medicine/a
drug) phǒn khâang khiang
ผลข้างเคียง

sightseeing N pai thát-sá-
naa-jawn ไปทัศนาจร, or
simply pai thîao ไปเที่ยว

sign/poster/placard N
(ranging from small to very
large) pâai ป้าย

sign V sen เซ็น; to sign your
name sen chûeh เซ็นชื่อ

signal N (radio signal, etc.)
sǎn-yaan สัญญาณ

signature N laai sen ลายเซ็น

significant/important ADJ
sǎm-khan สำคัญ

silent ADJ ngîap เงียบ

silk N mǎi ไหม; silk cloth phâa
mǎi ผ้าไหม

silly ADJ (difficult to readily
convey in Thai the sense this
word is commonly used in
English – arguably, the Thai

for 'without reason/irrational'
is acceptable, although
somewhat formal; the word
for 'stupid' would be simply
too strong): rái hèht-phŏn
ไร้เหตุผล

silver N (metal) ngoehn เงิน
(NOTE: the same word as
'money'); silver (the color) sĭi
ngoehn สีเงิน

similar ADJ khláai คล้าย, or
mŭean เหมือน

simple/easy ADJ ngâai ง่าย

since PREP tâng-tàeh ตั้งแต่

sincere ADJ jing-jai (literally,
'real/true'-'heart/mind') จริงใจ

sing V ráwng phlehng
(literally, 'sing'-'song') ร้อง
เพลง

singer N nák ráwng นักร้อง

Singapore N sĭngkhá-poh
สิงคโปร์

single ADJ (not married) sòht
โสด

single N (i.e. one person) khon
diao คนเดียว; just the one/
single (thing) yàang diao
อย่างเดียว

singlet/undershirt N See
'vest'

sink/sunk V (also 'drown')
jom จม

sink N (for washing up), also
'bathtub') àang náam อ่างน้ำ

sir N (a polite form of address
to, or talking about a higher
status person – 'you', 'he/
she') thâan ท่าน

sister N (older) phîi sǎow พี่
สาว; (younger) náwng sǎow
น้องสาว

sister-in-law N (older) phîi
sà-phái พี่สะใภ้; (younger)
náwng sà-phái น้องสะใภ้

sit V nâng นั่ง; sit down/have a
seat nâng long นั่งลง

situated ADJ tâng yùu ตั้งอยู่

situation N (e.g. political
situation, etc.) sà-thǎan-
nákaan สถานการณ์

six NUM hòk หก

sixteen NUM sìp hòk สิบหก

sixty NUM hòk sìp หกสิบ

size N khà-nàat ขนาด (NOTE:
the English word 'size' is also
used in Thai: sái ไซส์)

skewer N mái sìap ไม้เสียบ

ski N (from English – noun/
verb) sà-khii สกี; water ski
sà-khii náam สกีน้ำ; jet ski

152

jet sà-khii เจ็ดสกี

skilful ADJ mii tháksà มีทักษะ, (COLLOQUIAL) the word for 'clever/adept' – kèng เก่ง

skill N (COLLOQUIAL) fĭi mueh ฝีมือ

skin N phǐu-nǎng ผิวหนัง, or simply phǐu ผิว

skirt N krà-prohng กระโปรง

skull N hǔa kà-lòhk หัว กะโหลก

sky N fáa ฟ้า

slang N phaa-sǎa tà-làat (literally, 'language'–'market') ภาษาตลาด (the English word 'slang' is also used sà-laeng สแลง)

slap V tòp ตบ

slash V fan ฟัน

slave N thâat ทาส

sleep V nawn làp นอนหลับ

sleepy ADJ ngûang-nawn ง่วง นอน, or simply ngûang ง่วง

sleeve N khǎen sûea แขนเสื้อ

slender ADJ (but shapely) sà-òht sà-ong สะโอดสะอง

slice N (slice/piece of cake, etc.) chín ชิ้น

slide V (slide the door) lûean เลื่อน

slightly, a little bit ADV nít nòi นิดหน่อย

slim/thin ADJ phǎwm ผอม

slip; slippery V, ADJ (surface) lûehn ลื่น

slip N (petticoat, underskirt – from English) sà-líp สลิป

slippers/flip flops/thongs N rawng tháo tàe รองเท้าแตะ

slope N lâat khǎo ลาดเขา

sloppy/slovenly ADJ (work) sà-phrâo สะเพร่า

slow ADJ cháa ช้า; (to speak/drive) slowly cháa cháa ช้าๆ

slum N chum-chon aeh-àt ชุมชนแออัด, (also from English – pronounced similar to the English but with two syllables) sà-lam สลัม

small ADJ (in size) lék เล็ก

smart ADJ chà-làat ฉลาด (NOTE: sometimes used, somewhat ironically, to refer to someone else's 'cleverness' to further their own interests)

smartphone N See 'mobile/cell phone'

smell, to have a bad odor V (also see 'stink') mii klìn มีกลิ่น

smell/sniff v (something) dom ดม

smelling salts N yaa dom (literally, 'medicine/drug'-'smell') ยาดม

smile v yím ยิ้ม

smoke N khwan ควัน

smoke v (tobacco) sùup สูบ (NOTE: the English work 'smoke' pronounced sà-móke สะโม้ก is sometimes used to refer to oral sex [i.e. fellatio])

smooth ADJ (to go smoothly) râap rûehn ราบรื่น; (of surfaces) rîap เรียบ

SMS/sms N (texting) (from English) es-em-es เอสเอ็มเอส

smuggle v lák lâwp ลักลอบ

snail N thâak ทาก

snack N khà-nŏm ขนม

snake N nguu u งู

snatch v See 'grab'

sneaker N rawng-tháo kii-laa รองเท้ากีฬา

sneeze v jaam จาม

sniff/snort v (a substance) nát นัด

snore v kron กรน

snow N hì-má หิมะ; **snow** v

snowpeas N thùa lan-tao ถั่วลันเตา

snuggle v khlaw-khlia คลอเคลีย

so, therefore CONJ dang nán ดังนั้น

soak v jùm จุ่ม, or châeh แช่

soap N sà-bùu สบู่

sober v mâi mao ไม่เมา

soccer N (from English) fút bawn ฟุตบอล, (COLLOQUIAL) bawn บอล

society N sǎng-khom สังคม; sociable châwp sǎng-khom ชอบสังคม

socket N (electric)/powerpoint thîi sìap plák ที่เสียบปลั๊ก

socks N thǔng tháo ถุงเท้า

sofa, couch N (from English) soh-faa โซฟา

soft ADJ (to the touch): (for skin) nîm นิ่ม; (for cloth, etc.) nûm นุ่ม

soft drink N (a fizzy drink, soda pop) náam àt lom น้ำอัดลม

sold ADJ khǎai láew (literally, 'sell'-'already') ขายแล้ว

soldier N thá-hǎn ทหาร

154

sold out ADJ khǎai mòt láew
ขายหมดแล้ว

sole N (of the foot) fàa tháo
ฝ่าเท้า (NOTE: palm (of hand) is
fàa mueh ฝ่ามือ)

solid N khǎwng khǎeng
ของแข็ง

solution N thaang àwk
ทางออก (this translation can
be used to mean 'an exit')

solve V (a problem) kâeh
panhǎa แก้ปัญหา

some, partly ADJ bâang บ้าง

somebody, someone PRON
baang khon บางคน

something PRON baang yàang
บางอย่าง

sometimes ADV baang thii
บางที

somewhere (some
unspecified place) ADV baang
hàeng บางแห่ง, or
bang-thîi บางที่ (literally
means 'some-places')

son N lûuk chaai ลูกชาย

son-in-law N lûuk khǒei
ลูกเขย

song N phlehng เพลง

soon ADV nai mâi cháa
ในไม่ช้า

sore/painful ADJ jèp เจ็บ

sorrow/sad ADJ sâo เศร้า

sorry, regretful ADJ sǐa jai
เสียใจ

sorry! INTERJ khǎw thôht
ขอโทษ

sort, type N chá-nít ชนิด

sort out, deal with, arrange
V jàt kaan จัดการ

sound/noise N sǐang เสียง

soul/spirit N win-yaan
วิญญาณ

soup N (from English) súp ซุป,
(clear soup) náam súp น้ำซุป

sour ADJ (taste) prîao เปรี้ยว
(As a slang, this word is
also used to describe young
women who dress and act
with little trace of modesty)

source/cause/reason N (e.g.
of/for a problem) sǎahèht
สาเหตุ

south N (direction) tâi ใต้

south-east N tà-wan àwk
chǐang tâi ตะวันออกเฉียงใต้

Southeast Asia N eh-chia
aa-khá-neh เอเชียอาคเนย์

south-west N tà-wan tòk
chǐang tâi ตะวันตกเฉียงใต้

souvenir N khǎwng thîi

155

rálúek ของที่ระลึก

soybean(s) N thùa lŭeang ถั่ว
เหลือง, or (more commonly
– e.g. when referring to tofu)
tâo hûu เต้าหู้; soyabean milk
náam tâo hûu น้ำเต้าหู้

soy sauce N (salty) sii-íu
ซีอิ๊ว; (sweet) sii-íu wǎan
ซีอิ๊วหวาน

space N (a physical space or
gap) châwng wâang ช่องว่าง;
(outer) à-wá-kâat อวกาศ

spacious ADJ thîi kwâang ที่
กว้าง

spade/shovel N phlûa พลั่ว

sparrow N (ubiquitous small
bird) nók krà-jàwk นก
กระจอก (NOTE: the word
krà-jàwk กระจอก which, by
itself, means 'small/petty' is
also used as a slang term to
mean 'crappy/lousy/shitty' to
describe something of very
poor quality)

speak V phûut พูด

special ADJ phí-sèht พิเศษ

specific/in particular ADJ
dohy chà pháw โดยเฉพาะ

specimen/example N tua
yàang ตัวอย่าง

spectacles/glasses N wâen
taa แว่นตา

speech N kham praa-sǎi คำ
ปราศรัย

speed N khwaam rew ความเร็ว

speedboat N ruea rew เรือ
เร็ว, (from English) sà-pìit
bóht สปีดโบ๊ท

spell V (a word) sà-kòt สะกด

spell N (magical incantation)
khaa-thǎa คาถา

spend V (as in 'spend money/
time') chái ใช้; e.g. spend
money chái ngoehn ใช้เงิน

sperm N See 'semen'

spew V See 'vomit'

spices N khrûeang thêht
เครื่องเทศ

spicy ADJ phèt เผ็ด

spider N maehng mum
แมงมุม; spider web yai
maehng mum ใยแมงมุม

spill V (to spill a glass of water)
tham hòk ทำหก

spin V (e.g. used in making
a 'milkshake', 'pedalling
a bicycle' etc.) pàn ปั่น;
a milkshake/fruit shake/a
'smoothie' náam pàn น้ำปั่น,
mǔn (more general term for

'spin'; also means 'dial' for old style telephones mǔn หมุน

spinach N phàk khǒhm ผักโขม

spine N krà-dùuk sǎn lǎng กระดูกสันหลัง

spirit N See 'soul'

spirit house N (found everywhere in Thailand – to propitiate the local spirits) sǎan phrá-phuum ศาลพระภูมิ

spirits, hard liquor N lâo เหล้า

splendid ADJ yâwt yîam ยอดเยี่ยม

spoiled ADJ (of food) sǐa เสีย

spokesman/spokeswoman/ spokesperson N khoh-sòk โฆษก

sponge N fawng náam ฟองน้ำ

spoon N cháwn ช้อน

sport(s) N kii-laa กีฬา

spot N (small mark) jùt จุด

spotted ADJ (pattern) laai jùt ลายจุด

spouse N (husband or wife) khûu sǒm-rót (literally, 'pair'- 'marriage') คู่สมรส

spray N (i.e. to spray something) e.g. mosquito repellent: sà-preh สเปรย์, (from English) chìit sà-preh ฉีดสเปรย์

spread V krá-jaai กระจาย

spring N (metal part) (from English) sà-pring สปริง

spy N nák sùep นักสืบ

squad N klùm กลุ่ม (or tiim ทีม from 'team' in English)

square N (shape) sìi lìam สี่เหลี่ยม; (as in Tiananmen Square) jà-tùràt จัตุรัส

squeeze V (press) bìip บีบ, (extracting liquid, e.g. squeeze an orange) khán คั้น

squid N plaa mùek ปลาหมึก

squirrel N krà-râwk กระรอก

stab V thaeng แทง

stable/secure ADJ mân-khong มั่นคง

staff N (member in a store) phá-nák-ngaan พนักงาน

stage N (for performances, also 'boxing ring') weh-thii เวที

stagger V (e.g. stagger along drunk) doehn soh-seh เดินโซเซ

157

stain N roi pûean รอยเปื้อน

stairs N ban-dai บันได

stalk v àep-taam แอบตาม

stall N (of vendor) phǣehng khǎi khǒng แผงขายของ

stamp N (ink) traa pám ตราปั๊ม; (postage – from English) sà-taehm แสตมป์

stand v yuehn ยืน

stand up v lúk khûen ลุกขึ้น

standard N (i.e. commercial/ legal standard) mâat-trà-thǎan มาตรฐาน

stapler N (for stapling pieces of paper) (COLLOQUIAL) máek แม็ก

star N (in the heavens) daow ดาว (NOTE: also used in the English sense of a famous person or celebrity)

stare v (to stare at someone) mawng jawng มอง, or jâwng จ้อง

start/begin v rôehm เริ่ม

startle v sà-dûng สะดุ้ง

starve v hǐw mâak หิวมาก

state N rát รัฐ

state v phûut พูด

stationery khrûeang khǐan เครื่องเขียน

statistics N sà-thì-tì สถิติ

statue N rûup pân รูปปั้น

status N (financial status) thǎa-ná ฐานะ

stay v (somewhere) yùu อยู่, or phák yùu พักอยู่ (NOTE: 'Where are you staying?' ('you' understood) is phák yùu thîi nǎi พักอยู่ที่ไหน)

stay/remain v yùu kàp thîi อยู่กับที่

stay overnight v kháang khuehn ค้างคืน

steal v khà-mohy ขโมย (NOTE: the same word is also a noun meaning 'a thief/thieves')

steam N ai náam ไอน้ำ

steam v steamed ADJ (e.g. rice) nûeng นึ่ง

steel N lèk เหล็ก

steep ADJ (e.g. a steep hill) chan ชัน

steer v mǔn phuang maa-lai หมุนพวงมาลัย

steering wheel N phuang maa-lai พวงมาลัย

step N (when walking) kâow ก้าว

step v (on something) yìap เหยียบ

steps, stairs N bandai บันได

stepfather N phâw líang พ่อ

เลี้ยง; stepmother mâeh líang แม่เลี้ยง

sterile v (unable to have children) pen măn เป็นหมัน

stick v tìt kàp ติดกับ

stick, branch of tree N gìng mái กิ่งไม้; a walking stick mái tháo ไม้เท้า

stick out v yûehn àwk maa ยื่นออกมา

sticky ADJ nĭao เหนียว

sticky rice N khâow nĭao ข้าว เหนียว

stiff ADJ (as in 'hard'/opposite of 'flexible') khăeng แข็ง

still, even now ADV yang ยัง: e.g. (he's) 'still in Thailand' yang yùu mueang thai (literally, 'still'-'stay/be located'-'Thailand') ยังอยู่เมืองไทย

sting v (burning/stinging sensation) sàep แสบ

stink v měn เหม็น

stir v (a liquid/when cooking etc.) khon คน, or kuan กวน

stock market N tà-làat hûn (literally, 'market'-'share(s)') ตลาดหุ้น

stomach N tháwng ท้อง (NOTE: also the word for 'pregnant')

stone N (material) hĭn หิน; a stone/rock kâwn hĭn ก้อนหิน

stool N See 'excrement'

stop N (i.e. a bus stop) pâai rót-meh ป้ายรถเมล์

stop v (to halt) yùt หยุด; (cease doing something) lôehk เลิก

stop by, pay a visit (pop in and see someone) wáe แวะ

stop it! INTERJ yùt ná หยุดนะ

store v (to collect – e.g. collect stamps) sà-sŏm สะสม

storm N phaa-yú พายุ

story, storey N (of a building) chán ชั้น

story N (tale) rûeang เรื่อง

stout ADJ (plump) ôuan อ้วน, (COLLOQUIAL playful) pûm pûi ปุ้มปุ้ย

stove/charcoal cooker N tao เตา

straight ADJ (not crooked) trong ตรง

straight ahead ADJ trong pai (khâang nâa) ตรงไป(ข้าง หน้า)

strait(s) N (geographical feature, e.g. Straits of Hormuz) châwng khâehp ช่องแคบ

strange/unusual/weird ADJ plàehk แปลก

stranger N khon plàehk nâa (literally, 'person'-'strange'-'face') คนแปลกหน้า

straw N (for drinking) làwt หลอด

stream N (water course) lam-thaan ลำธาร

street/road N thà-nǒn ถนน

strength, power N kamlang กำลัง

stress N **stressful** ADJ khwaam khrîat ความเครียด, or simply khrîat เครียด

stretch V yûeht ยืด

strict ADJ khrêng khrát เคร่งครัด

strike/protest V prà-thúang ประท้วง

strike, hit V tii ตี

string/rope N chûeak เชือก

strip V (take clothes off) kâeh phâa แก้ผ้า

striped ADJ mii laai มีลาย (more generally, this also means 'to have a pattern/design' on material/surface)

strong ADJ khǎeng raehng แข็งแรง

structure N (e.g. the structure of a building/of society) khrohng sâang โครงสร้าง

stubborn ADJ dûeh ดื้อ

stuck ADJ (i.e. won't move) tìt ติด

student N nák-rian นักเรียน

study/learn V rian เรียน

stuffy ADJ (hot, airless atmosphere) òb âow อบอ้าว

stumble V sà-dùt สะดุด, or lóm ล้ม

stupid ADJ ngôh โง่

style/design N bàehp แบบ (the English word 'style' is also used in various ways – e.g. for clothing and behavior etc. – but pronounced in the Thai way sà-tai สไตล์)

stylish/fashionable/modern ADJ than sà-mǎi ทันสมัย

subject N hǔa khâw หัวข้อ

subject matter N nûea hǎa เนื้อหา

submarine N ruea dam náam เรือดำน้ำ

succeed V sǎmrèt สำเร็จ

success N khwaam sǎmrèt ความสำเร็จ

such as, for example... IDIOM chên... เช่น

suck v dùut ดูด, also om อม
(NOTE: this word is also a slang term used to describe female on male oral sex [i.e. fellatio])

sudden ADJ **suddenly** ADV than thii ทันที

sue v (to sue someone; also to 'accuse') fáwng ฟ้อง

suffer v thúk-jai ทุกข์ใจ

suffering ADJ mii-khwaam-thúk มีความทุกข์

sufficient/enough ADJ phaw-phiang พอเพียง, or simply phaw พอ

sugar N náam-taan น้ำตาล

sugarcane N ôi อ้อย

suggest v náenam แนะนำ

suggestion N kham náenam คำแนะนำ

suicide v (to commit suicide) khâa tua taai ฆ่าตัวตาย

suit N (clothes) (from English) sùut สูท

suitable, fitting, appropriate ADJ màw-sŏm เหมาะสม

suitcase N krà-pǎo sûea phâa กระเป๋าเสื้อผ้า

summary N **summarize** v sà-rùp สรุป

summer N nâa ráwn หน้าร้อน

summit N (mountain peak) yâwt ยอด

sun N phrá aathít พระอาทิตย์

sunbathe v àap-dèet อาบแดด

Sunday N wan aa-thít วันอาทิตย์

sunglasses N wâen kan dàeht แว่นกันแดด

sunlight N sǎehng dàeht แสงแดด, or simply dàeht แดด

sunny ADJ dàeht àwk แดดออก

sunrise N phrá aa-thít khûen พระอาทิตย์ขึ้น

sunset N phrá aa-thít tòk din พระอาทิตย์ตกดิน

superficial ADJ (not deep – used figuratively) phǐu phǒen ผิวเผิน

superior/better ADJ dii kwàa ดีกว่า

supermarket N (from English) suu-pôeh-maa-kèt ซูเปอร์มาเก็ต

superstitious ADJ (believing in ghosts, omens, etc.) (COLLOQUIAL) thǔeh phǐi ถือผี

supervise/oversee/control v (work) khûap khum

161

ควบคุม; supervise/look over (e.g. children) duu-laeh ดูแล

supply v (goods/provisions, etc.) jàt hǎa จัดหา

support v (to provide support) sà-nàp sà-nǔn สนับสนุน, also ùt-nǔn อุดหนุน

suppose v sǒm-mút สมมุติ

suppress v (illegal activity) pràap praam ปราบปราม

supreme ADJ sǔung sùt สูงสุด

sure ADJ nâeh jai แน่ใจ

surf v (on a surfboard) lên tôh khlûehn เล่นโต้คลื่น

surface N phǐu phúehn ผิวพื้น

surface mail/ordinary mail N prai-sà-nii tham-má-daa ไปรษณีย์ธรรมดา

surfboard N krà-daan tôh khlûehn กระดานโต้คลื่น

surgery N (medical operation) phàa tàt ผ่าตัด; (operating room) hâwng phàa tàt ห้องผ่าตัด

surname N naam sà-kun นามสกุล

surprised ADJ plàehk jai แปลกใจ

surprising ADJ nâa plàehk jai น่าแปลกใจ

surroundings N sìng wâeht láwm สิ่งแวดล้อม (also the word for the 'environment')

survey v sǎm-rùat สำรวจ

survive v rôwt chii-wít รอด ชีวิต, (common idiom) to save one's own skin ao tua rôwt เอาตัวรอด

suspect v sǒng-sǎi สงสัย

suspicion N khwaam sǒngsǎi ความสงสัย

swallow N kluehn กลืน

swamp/waterhole N bueng บึง

swear v (as in 'I swear it wasn't me') sǎa-baan สาบาน; to swear at someone dàa ด่า

sweat N ngùea เหงื่อ

sweat v ngùea àwk เหงื่อออก

sweep v kwàat กวาด; a broom mái kwàat ไม้กวาด

sweet ADJ wǎan หวาน

sweet/dessert N khǎwng wǎan ของหวาน, also khànǒm-wǎan ขนมหวาน (literally means 'sweet-treat')

sweet and sour ADJ prîao wǎan เปรี้ยวหวาน

sweetheart/darling N thîi rák ที่รัก

sweets/candy N khà-nŏm ขนม; a sweet you suck on lûuk om ลูกอม

swim V wâai náam ว่ายน้ำ

swimming costume, swimsuit N chút wâai náam ชุดว่ายน้ำ

swimming pool N sà wâai náam สระว่ายน้ำ

swing V kwàeng แกว่ง

switch N (from English) sà-wít สวิตช์

switch V (change) plìan เปลี่ยน

switch on, turn on V pòeht เปิด

swollen ADJ buam บวม

swoon V See 'faint'

sword N dàap ดาบ

symbol N sănyálák สัญลักษณ์

sympathy N **sympathetic** ADJ hĕn òk hĕn jai (literally, 'see'-'chest'-'see'-'heart') เห็นอกเห็นใจ

symptom N aa-kaan อาการ

synthetic ADJ săng-khráw สังเคราะห์

syringe N khĕm chìit yaa (literally, 'needle'-'inject'-'medicine/drug') เข็มฉีดยา

syrup N (cordial/sweet concentrate) náam chûeam น้ำเชื่อม, also (from English) sai-ráp ไซรัป

system N (e.g. of government/ of running a business etc.) rá-bòp ระบบ

T

table N tó โต๊ะ (NOTE: at times this word is also used colloquially to refer to chairs)

tablecloth N phâa puu tó ผ้าปูโต๊ะ

tablet(s) N yaa mét ยาเม็ด

tablet PC N (computer) (from English) tháeb-lét phii sii แท็บเล็ตพีซี

tail N (of an animal) hăng หาง

take V ao เอา (NOTE: used in conjunction with other words to express various distinct meanings – e.g. take the book away ao năngsŭeh pai เอาหนังสือไป; bring the book here ao năng-sŭeh maa เอาหนังสือมา)

take care of V duu laeh ดูแล

163

take off v (clothes/shoes) thàwt ถอด

tale N ní-thaan นิทาน

talk v phûut พูด

talk about v phûut rûeang… พูดเรื่อง

tall ADJ sǔung สูง

tame ADJ (of an animal) chûeang เชื่อง

tampon N ('sanitary napkin') phâa à-naa-mai ผ้าอนามัย

tank N thǎng ถัง (same word used for 'bucket'): e.g. petrol tank thǎng náam-man ถัง น้ำมัน; (military vehicle) rót thǎng รถถัง

tap N (i.e. turn on the tap) kók náam ก๊อกน้ำ

tape N (sticky) théhp เทป (from English)

target N (used for shooting practice) pâo เป้า (SLANG/ COLLOQUIAL – also refer to the groin region of males)

task N ngaan งาน

taste N rót รส, or (more fully) rót châat รสชาติ

taste v (e.g. sample food) chim ชิม

tasty ADJ àròi อร่อย, or mii rót

châat (literally, 'have'-'taste') มีรสชาติ

tattoo N sàk สัก

tax N phaa-sǐi ภาษี (NOTE: to pay tax(es) is sǐa phaa-sǐi เสียภาษี. Also see 'VAT')

taxi N tháek-sǐi แท็กซี่; motorcycle taxi (very common in most areas of Bangkok) maw-toeh-sai ráp jâang มอเตอร์ไซค์รับจ้าง (NOTE: a motorcycle taxi rank is known colloquially as a win วิน)

tea N chaa ชา, or náam chaa น้ำชา (NOTE: some types of tea – usually very sweet – commonly sold in Thailand are as follows: hot tea chaa ráwn ชาร้อน; iced tea chaa yen ชาเย็น; iced black tea chaa dam yen ชาดำเย็น)

teach v sǎwn สอน

teacher N (from the Sanskrit derived term 'guru') khruu ครู

teak/teakwood N mái sàk ไม้สัก

team N (from English – pronounced very similar to the original) thiim ทีม; group khána, คณะ

tear/rip v chìik ฉีก

tears N náam-taa (literally, 'water'-'eye{s}') น้ำตา

tease v yâeh แหย่

teaspoon N cháwn chaa (literally, 'spoon'-'tea') ช้อนชา

technician/tradesperson N châang ช่าง (general term)

teenager(s) N wai rûn วัยรุ่น

teeshirt/T-shirt N sûea yûeht เสื้อยืด

teeth/tooth N fan ฟัน

telephone N thoh-rá-sàp โทรศัพท์ (also see 'mobile/cell phone')

telephone number N boeh thoh-rá-sàp เบอร์โทรศัพท์

television N thii wii ทีวี (COLLOQUIAL), also (more formally) thoh-rá-thát โทรทัศน์

tell v lâo เล่า (a story); to tell someone bàwk บอก

temperature N ùn-hà-phuum อุณหภูมิ

temple N wát วัด (Buddhist); an ancient temple wát bohraan วัดโบราณ; (Chinese) săan jâo ศาลเจ้า

tempo/rhythm N jang-wà จังหวะ

temporary ADJ chûa khraaw ชั่วคราว

ten N sìp สิบ

tender ADJ nûm นุ่ม

tendon N en เอ็น

tennis N then-nít เทนนิส (from English) (pronounced 'ten'-'nit')

tens of, multiples of ten ADJ lăai sìp หลายสิบ

tense ADJ tueng ตึง (as in 'a tense or strained muscle')

tent N tén เต็นท์ (from English)

ten thousand NUM mùehn หมื่น

terminal N sà-thăa-nii สถานี

terminate v jòp จบ

terrible, to be ADJ yâeh แย่

terrify v tham-hâi klua ทำให้กลัว

territory N khèht เขต

terrorist N phûu kàw kaan ráai ผู้ก่อการร้าย

test v trùat sàwp ตรวจสอบ (investigation); (test for its quality) thót sàwp ทดสอบ; (test someone's knowledge) sàwp sàwp สอบ

testicles N lûuk an-thá ลูกอัณฑะ (medical term), (COLLOQUIAL)

khài ไข่ (not particularly
vulgar, but better left unsaid
– the word used here means
'egg(s)', the equivalent of the
English 'balls/nuts')

Thai N thai ไทย; Thai language
phaa-săa thai ภาษาไทย

Thailand N (COLLOQUIAL)
mueang thai เมืองไทย,
or (FORMAL) prà-thêht thai
ประเทศไทย

than PREP kwàa: e.g.
more than... mâak kwàa...
มากกว่า; better than... dii
kwàa... ดีกว่า

thank V **thank you** INTERJ
khàwp khun ขอบคุณ

that PRON nán นั่น นั้น; those lào
nán เหล่านั้น

that, which, the one who
CONJ thîi ... ที่

theater N (drama) rohng
lá-khawn โรงละคร

their/theirs ADJ khăwng khăo
ของเขา

then CONJ (used as a connecting word when relating
a series of events – e.g. 'she
went to the beach and then
to see her friends in town and

then....') láew แล้ว

there ADV thîi nân ที่นั่น

therefore CONJ dang nán ดังนั้น

there is, there are PRON (also
'to have') mii มี

they, them PRON khăo เขา,
or (something like 'that
group') phûak khăo พวกเขา

thick ADJ (of liquids) khôn ข้น;
(not thin) năa หนา

thief N khà-mohy ขโมย (also
see 'steal')

thigh N khăa àwn ขาอ่อน

thin ADJ (skinny) phăwm ผอม,
(of things) baang บาง

thing N khăwng ของ, or sìng
สิ่ง; things sìng khăwng สิ่งของ

think V (ponder) trài trawng
ไตร่ตรอง khít คิด, also
commonly néuk นึก: e.g. 'I
can't think of it' néuk mâi
àwk นึกไม่ออก; or 'I've
thought of it/I've got it' néuk
àwk láew นึกออกแล้ว

third N (⅓) sèht nùeng sùan
săam เศษหนึ่งส่วนสาม

third... ADJ (the third brother,
in third place, etc.) ...thîi
săam ที่สาม

thirsty ADJ hĭu náam หิวน้ำ

thirteen NUM sìp săam สิบสาม

thirty NUM săam sìp สามสิบ

this PRON níi นี้ **these** lâo níi เหล่านี้

though, even though CONJ máeh wâa แม้ว่า

thought(s) N khwaam khít ความคิด

thousand NUM phan พัน

thread N dâai ด้าย

threaten V khùu ขู่

three NUM săam สาม

thrill/thrilling/exciting ADJ tùen-tên ตื่นเต้น (NOTE: a word that means 'a thrill' (as in an adrenaline 'rush') is sĭao เสียว. This term is also used, for example, when hearing the sound of someone scratching their nails on a blackboard, or when getting a thrill from doing something dangerous (e.g. bungee jumping). In addition sĭao also refers to the pleasurable tingling sensation when sexually aroused.)

throat N lam khaw ลำคอ, or simply khaw คอ

through PREP (pass through/

pass by) phàan ผ่าน

throw V khwâang ขว้าง

throw away, throw out V khwâang thíng ขว้างทิ้ง, or simply thíng ทิ้ง

thunder N fáa ráwng ฟ้าร้อง

Thursday N (full form) wan phá-rúe-hàt sà-baw-dii วันพฤหัสบดี, (normal colloquial term) wan phá-rúe-hàt วันพฤหัส

thus, so CONJ dang nán ดังนั้น, (MORE COLLOQUIAL) kâw-loei ก็เลย

ticket N (for transport/ entertainment, etc.) tŭa ตั๋ว (NOTE: tickets for entertainment/sport, etc. are also referred to as bàt บัตร – pronounced like the word 'but') a fine bai sàng ใบสั่ง

tickle V jîi จี้ (NOTE: also slang, meaning 'to rob someone with a weapon')

ticklish ADJ ják-kà jîi จั๊กจี้

tidy/neat/well behaved ADJ (in dress/speech/behavior) rîap rói เรียบร้อย

tie, necktie N (from English) nék-thai เน็คไท

tie v phùuk ผูก

tiger N sŭea เสือ

tight ADJ nâen แน่น (NOTE: the English word 'fit' is commonly used to refer to tight-fitting clothing, fít ฟิต)

till/until PREP jon kwàa จนกว่า, or kwàa jà กว่าจะ

timber/wood N mái ไม้

time N wehlaa เวลา; 'what's the time?' weh-laa thâo rài เวลาเท่าไร, or (more commonly) kìi mohng láew (literally, 'how many'-'hour'-'already') กี่โมงแล้ว

times N (i.e. 4 × 4 = 16) khuun คูณ

timetable N taa-raang wehlaa ตารางเวลา

tin N (e.g. a tin of beans) krà-pǎwng กระป๋อง

tiny ADJ lék mâak เล็กมาก

tip N (the end of something, e.g. end of one's nose, etc.) plaai ปลาย; (to give someone a tip for their service) (from English) thíp ทิป

tire/tyre N (on a car) yaang rót ยางรถ (NOTE: a flat tire/tyre is yaang baehn ยางแบน)

tired ADJ (sleepy) ngûang ง่วง; (worn out) nùeai เหนื่อย

tissue N (paper) (from English) krà-dàat thít-chûu กระดาษทิชชู

title N (to a piece of land) chànòht thîi din โฉนดที่ดิน

to, toward(s) PREP (a place) pai yang… ไปยัง

tobacco N yaa sùup ยาสูบ, or yaa sên ยาเส้น

today N wan níi วันนี้

toe N níu tháo นิ้วเท้า; toe nail lép tháo เล็บเท้า

tofu/soyabean N tâo hûu เต้าหู้

together N dûai kan ด้วยกัน

toilet N (i.e. bathroom) hâwng náam ห้องน้ำ

toilet paper N krà-dàat cham-rá กระดาษชำระ, (COLLOQUIAL) krà-dàat chét kôn (literally, 'paper'-'wipe'-'bottom') กระดาษเช็ดก้น

tolerate v òt-thon อดทน

tomato N ma-khŭea thêht มะเขือเทศ

tomorrow ADV, N phrûng níi พรุ่งนี้

tongue N lín ลิ้น

tonight ADV, N khuehn níi คืนนี้

too ADV (also) dûai ด้วย; (excessive) koehn pai เกินไป: too expensive phaehng koehn pai แพงเกินไป, (MORE COLLOQUIAL) phaehng pai แพงไป

too much ADV mâak koehn pai มากเกินไป

tool, utensil, instrument N khrûeang mueh เครื่องมือ

tooth N fan ฟัน (fan pronounced like the English word 'fun')

toothbrush N praehng sǐi fan แปรงสีฟัน

toothpaste N yaa sǐi fan ยาสีฟัน

toothpick N mái jîm fan ไม้จิ้มฟัน

top ADJ (on top) khâang bon ข้างบน; top/peak (of hill, mountain) yâwt ยอด

topic N (topic in essay, etc.) hǔa khâw หัวข้อ

top secret N khwaam láp sùt yâwt ความลับสุดยอด

torch, flashlight N fai chǎai ไฟฉาย

torn/ripped ADJ (e.g. torn jeans – also refers to worn

out clothes etc.) khàat ขาด

torture V thaw-rá-maan ทรมาน

total N, ADJ (the whole lot) tháng mòt ทั้งหมด

touch V tàe แตะ

tough ADJ (chewy – a tough piece of meat) nǐao เหนียว; (as in strong physically) khǎeng raehng แข็งแรง; tough (as in mentally tough) jai khǎeng ใจแข็ง

tourism N kaan thâwng thîao การท่องเที่ยว

tourist N nák thâwng thîao นักท่องเที่ยว

tow V (i.e. to tow a caravan) lâak ลาก

towel N phâa chét tua ผ้าเช็ดตัว, also (MORE COLLOQUIALLY) phâa khǒn nũn ผ้าขนหนู

tower N hǎw khoi หอคอย

town N mueang เมือง (also used in certain cases to refer to a country e.g. Thailand mueang thai เมืองไทย, China mueang jiin เมืองจีน)

toxic ADJ (poisonous) pen phít เป็นพิษ

toy N khǎwng lên ของเล่น

trace N râwng-roi ร่องรอย

track V tìt-taam ติดตาม

trade N kaan kháa การค้า

trade V **exchange** lâehk plìan แลกเปลี่ยน

traditional ADJ dâng doehm ดั้งเดิม

traffic N kaan jà-raa-jawn การจราจร

traffic jam N rót tìt รถติด

train V (someone) fùek ฝึก

train N rót fai รถไฟ

train station N sà-thǎa-nii rót fai สถานีรถไฟ

transfer V (remove from one place to another) yáai ย้าย; (send data/money from one form to another) ohn โอน

transform V plìan เปลี่ยน

translate V plaeh แปล (Note the following useful expression: 'what does it/that mean?' plaeh wâa àrai แปลว่าอะไร)

transparent ADJ (used both in the usual sense of 'clear' and referring to the operations of a company/government etc. – 'transparency') pròhng sǎi โปร่งใส

transport V khǒn sòng ขนส่ง

(NOTE: this term is used colloquially to refer to a bus station serving inter-province travel)

transexual ADJ plaeng phêht แปลงเพศ

transvestite N (ladyboy) kà-thoei กะเทย

trap N kàp-dàk กับดัก

trash N khà-yà ขยะ

travel V doehn thaang เดินทาง

travel agency N (COLLOQUIAL) baw-rí-isàt thâwng thîao บริษัทท่องเที่ยว

traveler N nák doehn thaang นักเดินทาง, or khon doehn thaang คนเดินทาง

tray N thàat ถาด

tread V (walk on) yìap เหยียบ

treasure/wealth N sàp sǒmbàt ทรัพย์สมบัติ

treat V (someone to dinner) líang เลี้ยง; (behave towards) tham tàw ทำต่อ; (give medical aid) rák-sǎa รักษา

tree N tôn mái ต้นไม้

tremble/shake V (with fear) sàn สั่น, or tua sàn ตัวสั่น

trendy ADJ (i.e. the latest something) than sá-mǎi ทัน

สมัย (Note: than pronounced similar to the English word 'ton'; the English word 'trend' has also found its way into Thai – tren เทรนด์)

trespass v (on someone's property) rúk lám รุกล้ำ; (on someone's property, i.e. inappropriate touching) lûang koen ล่วงเกิน

triangle N sǎam lìam สามเหลี่ยม (Note: the tri-border area [Thailand, Burma, Laos] the 'Golden Triangle' – sǎam lìam thawng kham สามเหลี่ยมทองคำ)

tribe N phào เผ่า; hill tribe chaow khǎo ชาวเขา

tricky ADJ (as in a tricky person trying to pull the wool over someone's eyes) mii lêh lìam มีเล่ห์เหลี่ยม

trim v lem เล็ม

trip/journey N kaan doehn thaang การเดินทาง

tripe/offal N (COLLOQUIAL) phâa khîi ríu ผ้าขี้ริ้ว (Note: this term phâa khîi ríu also means 'rag' [for wiping things up])

troops, army N kawng tháp กองทัพ

trouble N (as in 'hardship') khwaam lam-bàak ความลำบาก

troublemaker N khon kàw kuan คนก่อกวน

troublesome ADJ (e.g. for life to be troublesome/difficult) lam-bàak ลำบาก

trousers/pants N kaang-kehng กางเกง

truck N rót ban-thúk รถบรรทุก

true ADJ jing จริง

truly ADV jing-jing จริงๆ

trust v wái jai ไว้ใจ

truth N khwaam jing ความจริง; to speak the truth phûut khwaam jing พูดความจริง

try v phá-yaa-yaam พยายาม

try on v (clothes) lawng sài ลองใส่

try out v (to try something out) lawng ลอง

Tuesday N wan ang-khaan วันอังคาร

tub N àang อ่าง

tube N thâw ท่อ

tuktuk taxi N rót túk túk รถ

ตุ๊กตุ๊ก, or simply túk túk
ตุ๊กตุ๊ก

tunnel N ù-mohng อุโมงค์

turkey N (fowl) kài nguang
ไก่งวง

turn V (change the direction,
e.g. turn the car) lîao เลี้ยว

turn around V lîao klàp เลี้ยว
กลับ

turn off V pìt ปิด

turn on V pòeht เปิด

turtle/tortoise N tào เต่า

tutor N khruu-săwn-phí-sèht
(literally, 'teacher'-'special')
ครูสอนพิเศษ

TV N (from English) thii wii ทีวี

tweezers N khiim nìip คีมหนีบ

twelve NUM sìp săwng สิบสอง

twenty NUM yîi sìp ยี่สิบ

twice ADV săwng khráng สอง
ครั้ง

twin N (as in 'twin bed') pen
khûu เป็นคู่

twins N (children/people) făa
fàet ฝาแฝด (often just the
word fàet แฝด is used)

twist V (e.g. as in a 'twisted
leg') bìt บิด

two N săwng สอง

type, sort N chá-nít ชนิด

type/print V phim พิมพ์

typhoon N tâi-fùn ไต้ฝุ่น

typical ADJ pen tham-má-daa
เป็นธรรมดา

tyre N See 'tire'

U

ugly ADJ (physically ugly) nâa
klìat น่าเกลียด (NOTE: in Thai
this is commonly expressed
as 'not pretty/beautiful' – mâi
sŭai ไม่สวย. Furthermore,
it should be noted that the
term nâa klìat น่าเกลียด is
also commonly used to refer
to 'unsightly/inappropriate
behavior')

umbrella N rôm ร่ม (NOTE: this
word also means 'shade')

unable ADJ (not capable of
doing something/do not have
ability to do something) mâi
săa-mâat ไม่สามารถ; (MORE
COLLOQUIAL) cannot do (something) tham mâi dâi (literally,
'do'-'no'-'can') ทำไม่ได้

unaware ADJ mâi rúu tua
ไม่รู้ตัว

unbearable ADJ (to be intolerable - as in 'I can't handle it') thon mâi dâi ทนไม่ได้, or thon mâi wǎi ทนไม่ไหว

uncertainty N khwaam mâi nâeh nawn ความไม่แน่นอน

uncle N (general term - *also see* 'aunt') lung ลุง (NOTE: this word is pronounced with a very short 'u' - and it does not sound like the English word 'lung'. It is a word that is often used to an unrelated elder male meaning 'you/he')

uncomfortable ADJ (e.g. an uncomfortable place) mâi sà-dùak sà-baai ไม่สะดวกสบาย; uncomfortable (in the sense of feeling uncomfortable about something) mâi sà-baai jai ไม่สบายใจ

unconscious ADJ mâi dâi sà-tì ไม่ได้สติ

uncover/reveal V (e.g. the truth) pòeht phǒei เปิดเผย

under PREP tâi ใต้

undergo/experience V prà-sòp ประสบ, (MORE COLLOQUIAL) joeh-kàp เจอกับ

underpants N kaang-kehng nai กางเกงใน

undershirt N sûea chán nai เสื้อชั้นใน

understand V khâo jai เข้าใจ; **misunderstand** V khâo jai phìt เข้าใจผิด

underwear N chút chán nai ชุดชั้นใน

undress/to get undressed V kâeh phâa แก้ผ้า

unemployed ADJ wâang ngaan ว่างงาน

unequal ADJ mâi thâokan ไม่เท่ากัน

unfaithful ADJ (in matters of the heart) nâwk jai (literally, 'outside'-'heart') นอกใจ; for a married person to have a lover mii chúu มีชู้

unfortunate ADJ **unfortunately** ADV chôhk ráai โชคร้าย

unhappy ADJ mâi mii khwaam sùk (literally, 'no'-'have'-'happiness') ไม่มีความสุข

uniform N (clothing - police/military uniform etc.)

173

khrûeang bàehp เครื่องแบบ

uninteresting ADJ See 'boring'

United Kingdom N (FORMAL TERM) sà-hà ràat-chá aa-naa-jàk สหราชอาณาจักร, or simply (UK) yuu kheh ยูเค

United States N (FORMAL TERM) sà-hà-rát à-meh-rí-kaa สหรัฐอเมริกา, or simply à-meh-rí-kaa อเมริกา, or sà-hà-rát สหรัฐฯ

universal ADJ (i.e. occidental – of the 'modern' Western world) săa-kon สากล; in general thûa pai ทั่วไป

university N má-hăawít-thá-yaa-lai มหาวิทยาลัย, (COLLOQUIAL) má-hăalai มหาลัย

unlawful ADJ phìt kòt măai ผิดกฎหมาย

unless CONJ nâwk jàak... นอกจาก

unlimited ADJ mâi jam-kàt ไม่จำกัด

unlock V khăi kun jae ไขกุญแจ, or pòeht-láwk เปิดล็อค (literally means 'open'-'lock')

unlucky ADJ chôhk ráai โชคร้าย

unnecessary ADJ mâi jam-pen ไม่จำเป็น

unripe ADJ mâi sùk ไม่สุก (it can be used to refer to uncooked food)

unsatisfactory ADJ mâi phaw jai ไม่พอใจ, or mâi dii phaw ไม่ดีพอ, or (not as good as it should be) mâi dii thâo thîi khuan ไม่ดีเท่าที่ควร

until PREP jon krà-thâng จนกระทั่ง, also (MORE COLLOQUIALLY) jon kwàa... จนกว่า, or simply kwàa กว่า

unwrap V kâeh àwk แก้ออก

up, upward ADV khûen ขึ้น

update V, N (from English, with essentially the same meaning and pronunciation) àp dèht อัพเดท

upgrade V yók-rá-dàp ยกระดับ

uphold V yók-khûen ยกขึ้น

upset, unhappy ADJ mâi sà-baai jai ไม่สบายใจ

upside down ADV (e.g. a car on its roof) ngăai tháwng หงายท้อง

upstairs ADJ, ADV khâang bon ข้างบน

urban N nai mueang ในเมือง
urge, to push for V (e.g. equal rights) rîak ráwng เรียกร้อง
urgent ADJ rêng dùan เร่งด่วน, or simply dùan ด่วน
urinate V (medical/formal term) pàt-săa-wá ปัสสาวะ, (COLLOQUIAL – whereas in English one might say 'piss' – in Thai this is not a vulgar word) chìi ฉี่, or (mildly vulgar) yîao เยี่ยว
use, utilize V chái ใช้
used to ADJ (to be used to) chin ชิน, to be accustomed to... khún khoei kàp... คุ้นเคยกับ; (do something) khoei เคย (NOTE: for fuller description of how the word khoei เคย is used – see 'have')
useful ADJ mii prà-yòht มีประโยชน์
useless ADJ mâi mii prà-yòht ไม่มีประโยชน์, (COLLOQUIAL – as in a 'useless person') mâi dâi rûeang ไม่ได้เรื่อง
usual ADJ pà-kà-tì ปกติ
usually ADV taam pà-kà-tì

taam pà-kà-tì, or (MORE SIMPLY COLLOQUIAL) pà-kà-tì ปกติ
uterus/womb N mót lûuk มดลูก
utmost ADJ thîi-sùt ที่สุด

V

vacant ADJ wâang ว่าง: e.g. (at a hotel) 'do you have any vacant rooms?' mii hâwng wâang măi (literally, 'have'-'room'-'vacant'-'question marker') มีห้องว่างไหม
vacation/holiday N wan yùt phák phàwn (literally, 'day'-'stop'-'rest') วันหยุดพักผ่อน
vaccination N chìit wák-siin ฉีดวัคซีน
vacuum N sŭn-yaa-kàat สุญญากาศ
vagabond/vagrant/ homeless person N (FORMAL) khon phá-neh-jawn คนพเนจร, or (COLLOQUIAL) khon rêh-rôn คนเร่ร่อน
vagina N (colloquial – not too vulgar) jǐm จิ๋ม, also (VERY COLLOQUIAL) pí ปี๋, (colloquial

175

and extremely vulgar, the
equivalent of the English
word 'cunt') hĭi หี

vague ADJ khlum khruea
คลุมเครือ

vain ADJ (self-important) thŭeh
tua ถือตัว, or yĭng หยิง

valid/usable ADJ chái dâi
ใช้ได้

valley N hùp khăo หุบเขา

valuable ADJ mii khun khâa
มีคุณค่า

value N (cost/price) raa-khaa
ราคา

value V (to estimate a price) tii
khâa ตีค่า

van N (vehicle) rót tûu รถตู้

vanish V hăi pai หายไป

various ADJ lăai หลาย

varnish V khlûeap เคลือบ

vase N jaeh-kan แจกัน

vast ADJ yài-toh ใหญ่โต

VAT N (value added tax –
Thailand does have one)
phaa-sĭi mun-lá-khâa
pôehm ภาษีมูลค่าเพิ่ม

venereal disease/VD N
(general term for STDs)
kaam-má-rôhk กามโรค

vegetable(s) N phàk ผัก

vegetarian N mang-sà-wí-rát
มังสวิรัติ

vegetarian ADJ kin jeh กินเจ

vehicle N (general term for
wheeled vehicles) rót รถ

vein N (in the body) sên lûeat
เส้นเลือด

verandah N See 'porch'

**vernacular/colloquial/
spoken language** N phaa-
săa phûut ภาษาพูด

very, extremely ADV mâak มาก

vest, waistcoat N sûea kák
เสื้อกั๊ก

vet N (animial doctor) sàt-tà-
wá-phaet สัตวแพทย์

via PREP phàan ผ่าน

vibrant/lively/full of life ADJ
mii chii-wít chii-waa มีชีวิต
ชีวา, or râa roehng ร่าเริง

Vientiane N (the capital of
Laos) wiang-jan เวียงจันทน์
(pronounced something like
wiang-jahn)

Vietnam N wîat-naam
เวียดนาม

Vietnamese N (people) chaow
wîat-naam ชาวเวียดนาม

view, panorama N (from
English) wiu วิว

view, look at v chom wiu ชมวิว

village N mùu bâan หมู่บ้าน

villager N (also more generally 'ordinary folk' – both in the country and the city) chaow bâan ชาวบ้าน

vinegar N náam sôm น้ำส้ม (Thai vinegar is not quite the same as 'western vinegar'. It is something which one adds to such things as noodle soup, etc. to enhance the flavor)

violent ADJ run raehng รุนแรง; violence khwaam run raehng ความรุนแรง

virus N (from English) chúea wai-rát เชื้อไวรัส, or simply wai-rát ไวรัส

visa N (from English) wii-sâa วีซ่า

visit v yîam เยี่ยม; make a visit pai yîam ไปเยี่ยม

visitor N (guest in one's home) khàehk แขก

vitamin(s) N (from English) wí-taa-min วิตามิน

vivid ADJ sòt-sǎi สดใส

vocabulary N (words) sàp ศัพท์ (pronounced very similar to the English word 'sup' – from 'supper')

voice/sound N sǐang เสียง (also the colloquial word for 'a vote' in an election)

voicemail N (from English) wois-mehl วอยซ์เมล์

volcano N phuu khǎo fai ภูเขาไฟ

volume N (quantity) pà-rí-maan ปริมาณ; volume (sound level) rá-dàp sǐang ระดับเสียง

volunteer v aa-sǎa อาสา, N (a person who performs voluntary service) aa-sǎa-sà-màk อาสาสมัคร

vomit v (POLITE) aa-jian อาเจียน, (colloquial – though less polite) spew/chuck/throw up ûak อ้วก

voodoo, black magic N sǎi-yá-sàat ไสยศาสตร์

vote N (from English) wòht โหวต, also àwk sǐang ออกเสียง, or long khá-naehn ลงคะแนน

vulgar/crude/coarse ADJ yàap khaai หยาบคาย

177

W

wages N khâa jâang ค่าจ้าง
Also see 'salary'

waist N (of the body) eho เอว

wait (for) v raw รอ

waiter/waitress N (COLLOQUIAL) dèk sòehp เด็กเสิร์ฟ

wake someone up v plùk ปลุก

wake up v tùehn ตื่น

walk v doehn เดิน

walking distance N (within) doehn pai dâi เดินไปได้

wall N (i.e. a stone/solid wall) kam-phaehng กำแพง; wall (internal wall of a house) phà-năng ผนัง

wallet N krà-pǎo sà-taang กระเป๋าสตางค์, or (MORE COLLOQUIALLY) krà-pǎo tang กระเป๋าตังค์

want v (FORMAL) with the sense of 'need' tâwng kaan ต้องการ, or (COLLOQUIAL) more like the sense of 'wanting' something yàak อยาก

war N sǒng-khraam สงคราม

war, to make v tham sǒng-khraam ทำสงคราม

wardrobe N tûu sûea phâa ตู้เสื้อผ้า

warehouse N koh-dang โกดัง

warm ADJ ùn อุ่น (also for something [e.g. food] to be warm)

warmth N (the feeling of 'warmth') òp ùn อบอุ่น

warn v tuean เตือน

warning N kham tuean คำเตือน

warranty N ráp-prà-kan รับประกัน

wash v (objects – e.g. car, windows, etc. but also to wash the face, hands, feet) láang ล้าง

wash the dishes v láang jaan ล้างจาน; to wash clothes sák phâa ซักผ้า; to wash hair sà phǒm สระผม

wart N hùut หูด

waste N khǎwng sǐa ของเสีย

wasteful ADJ plueang เปลือง

watch N (wristwatch; also 'clock') naa-lí-kaa นาฬิกา

watch v (show, movie) duu ดู, **stare** v mawng มอง

watch over, guard v fâo เฝ้า

water N náam น้ำ

178

water buffalo N khwaai ควาย

waterfall N náam tòk น้ำตก

watermelon N taeng moh แตงโม

waterproof ADJ kan náam กันน้ำ

water-ski N sà-kii náam สกีน้ำ

wave N (in the sea) khlûehn คลื่น

wave V (hand) bòhk mueh โบกมือ

wax N khîi phûeng ขี้ผึ้ง; ear wax khîi hŭu ขี้หู

way N (i.e. the way to get somewhere) thaang ทาง; 'which way do you go?' pai thaang năi (literally, 'go'-'way'-'which') ไปทางไหน; (method of doing something) wí-thii วิธี; (by way of, e.g. bus/train etc.) dohy โดย

way in N thaang khâo ทางเข้า

way out/exit N thaang àwk ทางออก

we, us PRON rao เรา

weak ADJ (lacking physical strength) àwn aeh อ่อนแอ

wealthy ADJ mâng khâng มั่งคั่ง, or simply 'rich' ruai รวย

weapon N aa-wút อาวุธ

wear V sài ใส่

weary ADJ nùeai เหนื่อย

weather N aa-kàat อากาศ

weave V (cloth etc.) thaw (pronounced 'tore') ทอ

weaving N kaan thaw การทอ

website N (from English) wép sái เว็บไซต์

wedding N ngaan tàeng-ngaan งานแต่งงาน

Wednesday N wan phút วันพุธ

weed N (i.e. a weed in the garden) wát-chá-phûet วัชพืช

week N (FORMAL) sàp-daa สัปดาห์, (more commonly) aa-thít อาทิตย์

weekend N wan sùt sàp-daa วันสุดสัปดาห์, (COLLOQUIAL) săo aa-thít เสาร์อาทิตย์

weekly ADV thúk aa-thít ทุกอาทิตย์

weep/cry V ráwng hâi ร้องไห้

weigh V châng ชั่ง; to weigh yourself/for someone to weigh themselves châng náam-nàk ชั่งน้ำหนัก

weight N náam-nàk น้ำหนัก

weight, to gain v náam-nàk khûen น้ำหนักขึ้น, (COLLOQUIAL) ûan khûen (literally, 'fat'-'increase/go up') อ้วนขึ้น

weight, to lose v lót náam-nàk ลดน้ำหนัก

welcome! INTERJ yin-dii tâwn ráp ยินดีต้อนรับ

welcome v (to welcome someone) tâwn ráp ต้อนรับ

well ADJ (as in 'do something well') dii ดี

well N (for water) bàw náam baa-daan บ่อน้ำบาดาล, or simply bàw náam บ่อน้ำ

well-behaved ADJ tham tua dii ทำตัวดี

well-cooked/well-done ADJ sùk สุก

well done! ADJ dii mâak ดีมาก

well-mannered ADJ maa-rá-yâat dii มารยาทดี

well off/wealthy ADJ ruai รวย

west N (direction) tà-wan tòk ตะวันตก

Westerner N chaow tàwan tòk ชาวตะวันตก

wet ADJ pìak เปียก

whale N plaa waan ปลาวาฬ

what? PRON (or which?) àrai อะไร (NOTE: unlike English, 'what?' in Thai comes at the end of a sentence. For example — 'what's your name' khun chûeh àrai (literally, 'you'-'name'-'what?') คุณชื่ออะไร; 'what color is it?' sǐi àrai (literally, 'color'-'what?') สีอะไร, or 'what's your telephone number?' thoh-rá-sàp boeh àrai (literally, 'telephone'-'number'-'what?') โทรศัพท์เบอร์อะไร

what are you doing? khun tham àrai คุณทำอะไร

what for? phûea àrai เพื่ออะไร

what is going on?/what's up? (COLLOQUIAL) wâa-ngai ว่าไง

what kind of? chá-nít nǎi ชนิดไหน, (MORE COLLOQUIAL) bàehp nǎi แบบไหน

what time is it? kìi mohng láew กี่โมงแล้ว

wheel N láw ล้อ

when? PRON ADV mûea-rài เมื่อไร (usually used at the end of a sentence): e.g.

180

'when are you going?' khun jà pai mûea-rài (literally, 'you'-'will'-'go'-'when') คุณจะไปเมื่อไร

whenever ADV (as in the expression: 'whenever you like' or, 'any time at all') mûea-rài kâw dâi เมื่อไรก็ได้

where? ADV thîi năi ที่ไหน (usually used at the end of a sentence): e.g. 'where is she?' khăo yùu thîi năi เขาอยู่ที่ไหน

where to? pai thîi năi ไปที่ไหน

which? PRON năi năi (usually used at the end of a sentence): e.g. 'which person?' khon năi คนไหน

while/during CONJ nai khà-nà thîi… ในขณะที่

whisper V krà-síp กระซิบ

whistle V phìu pàak ผิวปาก

white N sĭi khăaw สีขาว

who? PRON khrai ใคร

whole, all of N tháng mòt ทั้งหมด

whole ADJ (e.g. a set to be whole/complete) khróp ครบ

wholesale N (price) khăai sòng ขายส่ง (NOTE: retail price is khăai plìik ขายปลีก)

why? ADV tham-mai ทำไม (generally used, in contrast to English, at the end of a sentence)

wicked/evil ADJ ráai ร้าย

wide ADJ kwâang กว้าง

width N khwaam kwâang ความกว้าง

widow N mâeh mâai แม่ม่าย

widowed ADJ pen mâai เป็นม่าย

widower N phâw mâai พ่อม่าย

wife N (FORMAL/POLITE) phan-rá-yaa ภรรยา, (COMMON COLLOQUIAL) mia เมีย

Wifi/wifi N (from English) wai-fai วายฟาย

wig N (from English) wík วิก

wild ADJ (of animals) pàa ป่า: e.g. wildcat maew pàa แมวป่า

will/shall AUX V (common marker of future tense) jà จะ

win V chá-ná ชนะ; (a/the) winner N phûu chá-ná ผู้ชนะ

wind N (a breeze and stronger) lom ลม

181

window N (in house) nâa tàang หน้าต่าง

wine N (from English) waai ไวน์

wing N (of a bird) pìik ปีก

wink V kà-phríp taa กะพริบตา

winter N (in Thailand the 'cool season' – Nov-Jan) nâa nǎow หน้าหนาว

wipe V chét เช็ด

wire N lûat ลวด; an electrical wire sǎi fai สายไฟ

wise ADJ chà-làat ฉลาด

wish/hope N wǎng หวัง; to wish or hope for... wǎng wâa... หวังว่า

witch N mâeh mót แม่มด

with PREP kàp กับ

withdraw/take out V (money from a bank/a tooth etc.) thǎwn ถอน

with pleasure IDIOM dûai khwaam yin-dii ด้วยความ ยินดี

within reason/limits IDIOM phaai nai khâw jamkàt (pronounced 'jum-gut') ภาย ในข้อจำกัด

without PREP pràat-sà-jàak ปราศจาก, or dohy mâi mii โดยไม่มี

witness N phá-yaan พยาน; to witness hěn pen phá-yaan เห็นเป็นพยาน

wobble V (as in 'to walk with a wobble') sòh seh โซเซ

woman N phûu yíng ผู้หญิง

womanizer N (philanderer, cassanova) jâo chúu เจ้าชู้

wonderful ADJ nâa prà-làat jai น่าประหลาดใจ

wood/timber N mái ไม้

wooden ADJ (i.e. made from wood) tham dûai mái ทำด้วยไม้, or tham jàak mái ทำจากไม้

wool N (from a sheep) khǒn kàe ขนแกะ

word N kham คำ

work/occupation N aa-chîip อาชีพ, (MORE COLLOQUIAL) ngaan งาน

work V tham ngaan ทำงาน

work (e.g. for a piece of machinery, etc. to function) tham ngaan ทำงาน (NOTE: the English word 'work' is also commonly used in this sense but with a slightly 'Thai-ified' pronunciation)

worker on a ship N lôukruea เรือลูก

world N lôhk โลก

worm N (general term for 'worm-like' creatures) nǎwn หนอน; earthworm sâi duean ไส้เดือน

worn out, tired ADJ nùeai เหนื่อย; (COLLOQUIAL) to have 'no more energy' mòt raehng หมดแรง

worn out/torn ADJ (clothes etc.) khàat ขาด (NOTE: this term is also used to refer to something that is 'lacking' or 'missing' – from a dish of food/a part from a machine, etc.)

worn out/broken/ unrepairable ADJ (machine) phang (similar in sound to 'pung' with the 'ung' sound pronounced as in 'bungle') พัง

worry V (about someone) pen hùang เป็นห่วง; to feel worried, be anxious kang-won กังวล

worse ADJ (e.g. a medical condition) yâeh long แย่ลง

worship V buu-chaa บูชา

worst ADJ yâeh thîi sùt แย่ที่สุด

worth, to have N mii khâa มีค่า

worthless ADJ rái khâa ไร้ค่า

worthwhile/to be worth it ADJ (i.e. value for money) khúm khâa คุ้มค่า, or simply khúm คุ้ม

would like/may I have? khǎw ขอ

wound N bàat phlǎeh บาดแผล, or simply phlǎeh แผล

wrap V hàw ห่อ

wreck V See 'destroy'

wrist N khâw mueh ข้อมือ

write V khǐan เขียน

writer N nák khǐan นักเขียน

wrong ADJ (incorrect) phìt ผิด; (mistaken) khâojai phìt เข้าใจผิด; (morally) tham phìt ทำผิด

X

x-ray N (from English) ék-sà-reh เอ็กซเรย์

183

Y

yatch/sailboat N ruea bai
เรือใบ

yank/pull violently/snatch
v (as in to have your bag
'snatched') krà-châak
กระชาก

yard N (open space) laan ลาน

yawn v hăw หาว

yeah ADV (English colloquial
form of 'yes') châi ใช่, (MORE
COLLOQUIAL) jâ จ้ะ

year N **years old** ADJ (e.g. 16
years old) pii ปี

yell/shout v tà-kohn ตะโกน

yellow N sĭi lŭeang สีเหลือง

yes INTERJ châi ใช่ (NOTE: there
are a number of other ways
to say 'yes' in Thai depending
on the form of the question
asked. But this is the general
form used to respond to
many simple questions in
the affirmative. The opposite
to châi ใช่ is mâi châi ไม่ใช่
which means 'no' – again,
this being dependent on the
form of the question asked.
Also see 'no', 'not')

yesterday N, ADV mûea waan
níi เมื่อวานนี้

yet ADV (as in 'not yet') yang ยัง
(Note: the word yang is part
of the question form 'have
you/he/they (verb) yet?' rúe
yang หรือยัง: e.g. 'have you
eaten yet?' khun kin khâaw
rúe yang คุณกินข้าวหรือ
ยัง. If you haven't eaten yet
you would normally answer
yang (not yet). If, on the other
hand, you had eaten you
could answer – kin láew 'I've
eaten' กินแล้ว. For another
important meaning of yang
see 'still')

you PRON (general polite term)
khun คุณ; you (INTIMATE) thoeh
เธอ (NOTE: the corresponding
'intimate' Thai word for 'I'
that thoeh is paired with is
chǎn ฉัน. These terms for
'I' and 'you' are found in the
vast majority of Thai popular
songs. Try listening for them)

you're welcome! INTERJ mâi
pen rai ไม่เป็นไร

young ADJ (in years) aa-yú nói
อายุน้อย

younger brother or sister
N (or more generally meaning
'you' when addressing a
junior person in a store/
restaurant etc.) náwng น้อง

your PRON khǎwng khun
ของคุณ

youth, youths N (young
people) yao-wá-chon
เยาวชน, (INFORMAL) nùm sǎow
(literally, 'young men'-'young
women') หนุ่มสาว

Z

zebra N máa laai (literally,
'horse'-'stripe/striped') ม้า
ลาย

zero N sǔun ศูนย์

zip/zipper N (from English)
síp ซิป

zone/area N khèht เขต

zoo N sǔan sàt (literally,
'garden/park'-'animal')
สวนสัตว์

185

Thai–English

A

aa N อา aunt or uncle (i.e. a younger sister or brother of one's father)

aa-chìip N อาชีพ occupation, profession, career

aa-hǎan N อาหาร food

aa-hǎan cháo N อาหารเช้า breakfast, morning meal

aa-hǎan jeh (pronounced similar to 'jay') N อาหารเจ Chinese vegetarian food, vegan food

aa-hǎan klaang wan/tìang N อาหารกลางวัน/อาหารเที่ยง lunch, midday meal

aa-hǎan tháleh N อาหารทะเล seafood

aa-hǎan wâang N อาหารว่าง an entrée/starter/hors d'oeuvres

aa-hǎan yen N อาหารเย็น dinner, evening meal

aai (long vowel) ADJ อาย to be shy, embarrassed

aa-jaan N อาจารย์ teacher (usually with degree), university lecturer

aa-jian N อาเจียน (POLITE) to vomit; (COLLOQUIAL) ûak อ้วก throw up/puke/spew

aa-kaan N อาการ (physical) condition/symptom

aa-kàat N อากาศ weather, air

àan v อ่าน to read

àan lên v อ่านเล่น to read for pleasure

àan mâi àwk ADJ อ่านไม่ออก illegible

àan nǎng sǔe v อ่านหนังสือ to read

àang àap náam N อ่างอาบน้ำ a bath(tub)

àang láang nâa N อ่างล้างหน้า wash basin

àao N อ่าว a bay, gulf (as in the 'Gulf of Thailand' **àao thai** อ่าวไทย)

âao อ้าว (COLLOQUIAL) an exclamation meaning something like 'Oh!', 'huh!', 'eh!'

àap náam v อาบน้ำ to bathe, take a bath, take a shower, to have a wash

àap náam fàk bua v อาบน้ำ ฝักบัว to have a shower

aarom N อารมณ์ emotion, mood, temper

aa-rom-khǎn N อารมณ์ขัน humor

àat AUX V อาจ may, might

àat jà AUX V อาจจะ could, might, may ADV perhaps, maybe, possibly

àat (jà) pen pai dâi PHR อาจ(จะเป็นไปได้) (that) could well be possible

aa-thít N อาทิตย์ a week

aa-thít-nâa N อาทิตย์หน้า next week

aa-thít-níi N อาทิตย์นี้ this week

aa-thít thîi-láew N อาทิตย์ที่ แล้ว last week

àat-yaa-kawn N อาชญากร (FORMAL) criminal, (COLLOQUIAL) **phûu ráai** ผู้ร้าย 'evil doer'/'baddie'

aa-wút N อาวุธ a weapon (general term), arms

aa-yú N อายุ age

aa-yú mâak/sǔung aa-yú ADJ อายุมาก/สูงอายุ aged, to be (very) old

aa-yú nói ADJ อายุน้อย young (in age)

aa-yú thâo rài PHR อายุเท่าไร how old (are you/is she/it)? (NOTE: the pronoun – 'you/ she/he' etc. – comes before the question tag)

à-dìit ADJ อดีต (the) past, former (e.g. prime minister/husband)

ae N (pronounced like 'air') แอร์ air (conditioning)

àep v แอบ to hide

áeppôen N (from English) แอปเปิล apple

ai (short vowel) v ไอ to cough

âi N ไอ้ a derogatory title used with first names of men and also for insult

ai náam N ไอน้ำ steam

ai-oh-diin N ไอโอดีน iodine

ai-sà-kriim N (commonly pronounced something like 'ai-tim' – from English) ไอศกรีม ice cream

ai-sǐa N ไอเสีย exhaust fumes

à-kà-tanyuu N อกตัญญู to be ungrateful, thankless

à-khá-tì N อคติ bias, prejudice

àk-sǎwn N อักษร letter (in alphabet)

àk-sèp VT อักเสบ become inflamed; a response of body tissues to infection

à-lài N อะไหล่ spare part (of machine), replacement part(s)

am V อำ to hide, conceal

à-mátà ADJ อมตะ to be immortal (NOTE: also commonly used in the sense of something being 'classic' – as in a 'classic song' etc.)

à-meh-rí-kaa N อเมริกา America

à-meh-rí-kan N อเมริกัน an American; from America

amnâat N, V อำนาจ authority, to have power

amphoeh N (pronounced similar to 'am-pur') อำเภอ an administrative district (often written in English as 'amphoe')

an N (pronounced like 'un') อัน universal classifier (i.e. counting word) for things when the specific classifier for the item is unknown – e.g. may be used in the case of such things as hamburgers, spectacles, etc.

à-naa-jaan ADJ อนาจาร lewd/ immoral (act or conduct)

à-na-khót N อนาคต the future

an-dàp N อันดับ series, order, rank

à-naa-mai N อนามัย hygiene

ang-krìt N อังกฤษ England, English

ang-khaan N อังคาร Tuesday

à-ngùn N องุ่น grapes

àn nǎi อันไหน which one?

an-tàraai N, ADJ อันตราย danger; to be dangerous; peril, harm; dangerous

à-nú-baan N อนุบาล kindergarten

à-númát V (FORMAL) อนุมัติ to approve/consent, e.g. of a building, or a tender (for a project) etc.

à-núrák V อนุรักษ์ to preserve/

189

conserve, e.g. an old building or historical site etc.

ànú-sǎa-wárii N อนุสาวรีย์ a monument

à-nú-sǎ-wárii chai N อนุสาวรีย์ชัยฯ (COLLOQUIAL – slightly shortened version of the formal full name) the Victory monument in Bangkok, commemorating the Thai armed forces and temporary gains of territory in WW II

à-nú-sǎ-wárii prà-chaa-thíp-pàtai N อนุสาวรีย์ประชาธิปไตย the Democracy Monument in Bangkok commemorating the establishment of a representative form of politics after the overthrow of the Absolute Monarchy in 1932

à-nú-yâat V อนุญาต to let, allow, permit

àn-yá-má-nii N อัญมณี precious stones

ao V เอา to take, receive or accept (something from someone)

ao àwk V เอาออก to take out, remove

ao cháná เอาชนะ to defeat/ beat (someone/something)

ao iik láew เอา อีกแล้ว Not again!/Here we go again/(they're) at it again

ao jai V เอาใจ to please someone, make (someone) happy, to go along with (someone)

ao jai sài V เอาใจใส่ to pay attention (to), take an interest (in), be conscientious, put one's mind to something

ao jing ADJ (COLLOQUIAL) เอาจริง serious (i.e. to do something seriously/not kidding around)

ao kan V (COLLOQUIAL/SLANG) เอากัน to have sex/to mate/ to screw

ao lá (COLLOQUIAL) เอาละ OK then, now then

ao loei (COLLOQUIAL) เอาเลย go for it!

ao maa V เอามา to bring

ao mǎi (colloquial question

form used for offering something to someone) เอา ไหม Do you want it?

ao pai v เอาไป to take (away)

ao prìap v เอาเปรียบ to take advantage of (someone else), to exploit (someone)

ao tàeh jai tua ehng ADJ, V เอาแต่ใจตัวเอง to be self-centered/self-indulgent; think of one's own interests rather than anyone else's

ao tua râwt IDIOM (COLLOQUIAL) เอาตัวรอด to save one's own skin, to get out of a predicament

àp ADJ อับ stale, musty

àp-aai ADJ อับอาย shameful

à-páatméhn N (from English) อพาร์ตเมนต์ apartment

à-phai v อภัย to pardon/forgive (When used in speech as in to 'forgive' someone you say **hâi à-phai** ให้อภัย)

àrai อะไร (question word generally used at the end of a sentence) what?

àrai iik อะไรอีก (is there) anything else?

àrai kan (COLLOQUIAL) อะไร กัน 'what's going on?', 'what's up?'

àrai kâw dâi (COLLOQUIAL) อะไรก็ได้ anything at all/anything is OK, e.g. in response to the question 'what would you like to eat?' – 'anything at all/anything would be OK'

àrai ná (COLLOQUIAL) อะไร นะ pardon me? what did you say?

àròi ADJ อร่อย to be delicious, tasty

à-sù-jì N อสุจิ sperm, semen

àt v อัด to compress, pack tight, press

àt-chàriya N อัจฉริยะ a genius, prodigy, master (of some art or skill)

àt dii wii dii v อัดดีวีดี to record a DVD

àt sĭang v อัดเสียง to record (music/a voice/a sound)

àthí-baai v อธิบาย to explain

à-thí-kaan-baw-dii N อธิการบดี president (for college)

àt-traa N อัตรา rate

àt-traa lâeh plian N อัตรา แลกเปลี่ยน rate of exchange for foreign currency

à-wá-kâat N อวกาศ space (i.e. outer space)

à-wai-yá-wá N อวัยวะ organ (of the body)

àwk PREP ออก out

àwk jàak V ออกจาก to leave, depart

àwk kamlang kaai V (pronounced something like 'ork gum-lung guy') ออกกำลังกาย to exercise

àwk pai V ออกไป to go out, leave, exit; also used when someone (in a room/house) is angry and orders/commands another person to 'get out!'

àwk sǐang V ออกเสียง to pronounce (a word), also – to vote (in an election)

âwm V อ้อม to go around, make a detour

àwn ADJ อ่อน soft, tender, mild (not strong), weak, feeble

àwn aeh ADJ อ่อนแอ to be weak/to feel weak

âwn wawn V อ้อนวอน to plead/beg

âwn yohn ADJ, ADV อ่อนโยน to be gentle (behavior)/graceful; gracefully

áwp-fít N (from English) ออฟ ฟิศ office

áwt-sà-treh-lia N ออสเตรเลีย Australia

B

bàa N บ่า shoulder

bâa ADJ บ้า to be insane, crazy: (COLLOQUIAL) **âi bâa** ไอ้บ้า 'You must be mad/out of your mind', 'You jerk/dickhead'

bâa-bâa baw-baw ADJ (COLLOQUIAL) บ้าๆบอๆ odd, crazy

baa N (from English) บาร์ a bar (serving drinks)

baa bii khiu N (from English) บาร์บีคิว barbeque

baa daan N บาดาล underground region

bâa kaam V บ้ากาม to crave sex

bàai N ป่าย afternoon, from midday until 4 p.m. – generally referred to as **tawn bàai** ตอนบ่าย

bàai bìang V ป่ายเบี่ยง to be evasive, equivocate, dodge (e.g. answering a question)

baan V บาน to bloom

baan N บาน classifier for doors, windows, mirrors

bâan N บ้าน home, house: (COLLOQUIAL) **klàp bâan** กลับบ้าน to go home/ return home; **phûean bâan** (literally, 'friend'-'house') เพื่อนบ้าน neighbor

bâan nâwk N (COLLOQUIAL) บ้านนอก the country, rural, up-country, the sticks

bâang ADJ, ADV บ้าง some, partly, somewhat: e.g. **phŏm khǎw bâang** ผม ขอบ้าง can I (male speaking) have some?

baang ADJ บาง some: e.g. **baang khon** บางคน some people; **baang khráng** บาง ครั้ง some time(s); **baang hàeng** บางแห่ง some places;

baang yàang บางอย่าง some things

baang ADJ บาง to be thin (of objects)

bàap N บาป sin, moral wrongdoing

bàat N บาท Baht (Thai currency) IDIOM (COLLO-QUIAL) **mâi tem bàat** ไม่เต็มบาท to be mad/not the full quid (Baht)/a few screws loose

bàat V บาด to cut/slice/ wound; **bàat jèp** บาดเจ็บ to be injured/wounded; **bàat jai** บาดใจ to be hurt, for one's feelings to be hurt; **bàat phlǎeh** บาดแผล a wound/cut/laceration (NOTE: a very loud or deafening noise, e.g. deafening music is **bàat hǔu** บาดหู; also to be intolerable/offensive to the eyes/dazzling **bàat taa** บาดตา)

bàat N บาตร the alms or begging bowl of a Buddhist monk (NOTE: to make an offering of food to a monk by placing food

in his bowl is to **tàk bàat**
ตักบาตร)

bàat lŭang N บาทหลวง a
priest (from any one of the
Christian denominations),

báat-sakèht-bawn N (from
English) บาสเก็ตบอล
basketball

bàat-thá-yák N บาดทะยัก
tetanus

baehn ADJ แบน to be flat
(e.g. a flat tire/tyre)

baehn V, N (from English)
แบน to ban; a ban

bàehp N แบบ design/style/
kind/pattern (for tailoring)
(NOTE: a female model is
nang bàehp นางแบบ while
a male model is **naai bàehp**
นายแบบ)

bàehp fawm N (from English
'form') แบบฟอร์ม a form (a
document with blanks for
filling in with information)

bàehp fùek hàt N แบบฝึกหัด
exercise (school work)

bàehp níi ADV แบบนี้
(COLLOQUIAL) (do it) like
this (NOTE: to elicit the
response 'like this' – you

could ask the following
question 'how do you do
it?' **bàehp năi** แบบไหน)

bàeng V แบ่ง to divide/share/
separate

báeng N (taken from 'bank'
in English) แบงค์ banknote

bàet-toeh-rîi N (from
English) แบตเตอรี่ battery
(NOTE: in colloquial speech
this is commonly just **bàet**
แบต)

bàet min tán N (from
English) แบดมินตัน
badminton

bai N (from English) ไบ
bisexual

bai N ใบ classifier for round
and hollow objects, e.g.
fruit, eggs

bâi N ใบ้ dumb (unable to
speak)

bai à-nú-yâat N ใบอนุญาต
a permit/form giving
approval (e.g. to build a
house)/a licence

bai khàp khìi N ใบขับขี่ a
driver's licence (for a car,
truck, or motorbike)

bai mái N ใบไม้ a leaf, leaves

194

bai pliu N ใบปลิว leaflet

bai koēht N ใบเกิด birth certificate

bai sà-màk N ใบสมัคร application form

bai sàng N ใบสั่ง order (placed for food, goods); a ticket (fine)/police summons

bai sàng yaa N ใบสั่งยา a prescription

bai sèt N ใบเสร็จ a receipt

bai yàa N ใบหย่า divorce certificate

bam-bàt V (pronounced 'bum-but') บำบัด to treat/cure/alleviate/relieve (a condition) (NOTE: physiotheraphy is kaai-yá-phâap bam-bàt กายภาพบำบัด)

bà-mìi N บะหมี่ egg noodles

bam-naan N (pronounced 'bum-narn') บำนาญ a pension

bam nèt N บำเหน็จ reward, remuneration

bam rung V บำรุง to improve, maintain

banchii N บัญชี an account

(e.g. a bank account) (NOTE: to open a bank account is **pòeht banchii** เปิดบัญชี)

bandai N บันได steps, stairs, a ladder

bandai lûean N บันไดเลื่อน an escalator

ban dìt N บัณฑิต university graduate, scholar

bang V บัง to block the view

bâng fai N บั้งไฟ skyrocket (commonly fired during certain festivals in NE Thailand)

bang-kà-loh N (from English) บังกะโล lodge, bungalow (guest house)

bangkháp V บังคับ to force, compel

bang-oehn ADV บังเอิญ accidentally, by accident, by chance, unexpectedly (e.g. to meet someone by accident)

banjù V บรรจุ to load (up), pack (a suitcase)

banphá-burùt N บรรพบุรุษ ancestor(s)

ban-thoehng ADJ บันเทิง joyful, entertained

banthúek N, V บันทึก a note/memorandum; to note, record (e.g. minutes of a meeting, etc.)

banthúek khàaw prajam wan N บันทึกประจำวัน diary, journal

banyaai V บรรยาย to lecture, describe

ban-yaa-kàat N บรรยากาศ climate, atmosphere, ambience

bao ADJ เบา to be light (not heavy) (NOTE: to do something gently/softly – e.g. a massage/to speak – is **bao-bao** เบาๆ)

bâo taa N เบ้าตา eye-socket

bao wǎan N เบาหวาน diabetes

bàt N (pronounced like the word 'but') บัตร a card/ticket/coupon (NOTE: an identity card – held by all adult Thai citizens – is **bàt prà-chaachon** บัตรประชาชน; also widely used in Thailand – name card/business card **naam bàt** นามบัตร)

bàt eh-thii-em N บัตรเอทีเอ็ม ATM card

bàt choehn N บัตรเชิญ invitation card

bàt khreh dìt N บัตรเครดิต credit card

bèhng VT เบ่ง to swell, expand

bàw N เบาะ cushion/padded seat (in car etc.)

bàw náam baa-daan N บ่อน้ำบาดาล a well (for water)

bàwk V บอก to tell; let someone know

bàwk khàwp khun บอกขอบคุณ to say thank you

bàwk láew V (COLLOQUIAL) บอกแล้ว (I) told you already, (I) told you so

bàwk mâi thùuk (COLLOQUIAL) บอกไม่ถูก (I) can't say, (I) can't put my finger on it

bàwk sǐa jai V บอกเสียใจ to say sorry

baw-khǎw-sǎw N บ.ข.ส. bus terminal

bàwp bang ADJ บอบบาง frail, thin, breakable, fragile

bawm N (from English) บอมบ์

bomb (also commonly used following the troubles in the three southernmost provinces on Thailand's east coast: **khaa bawm** คาร์บอมบ์ car bomb)

bawn N (from English) บอล a ball, (COLLOQUIAL) the game of football (soccer)

bàwn N บ่อน place for gambling (the full expression for 'a gambling den' is **bàwn kaan phá-nan** บ่อนการพนัน)

bâwng kanchaa N บ้องกัญชา a bong (water pipe) for smoking marihuana

bawrí-jàak V บริจาค to donate, give to charity

bawrí-kaan N, V บริการ service; to give service

bawrí-sàt N บริษัท company, firm

bawrí-sùt ADJ บริสุทธิ์ to be pure, innocent – also used to refer to a virgin

bawrí-wehn N บริเวณ vicinity, area

bàwt ADJ บอด to be blind; **khon taa bàwt** (literally

'person'-'eye[s]'-'blind') คนตาบอด a blind person

bàwt sǐi ADJ บอดสี to be color blind (literally, 'blind'-'color')

bèt N เบ็ด a fish hook

beung N บึง a swamp/marsh

bêung ADJ บึ้ง serious, solemn

bia N (from English) เบียร์ beer

bìat V เบียด to squeeze in

biang V เบี่ยง to turn, turn aside

bîao ADJ เบี้ยว crooked, deformed

bì-daa N บิดา (FORMAL) father

bìip V บีบ to squeeze, compress

bìip trae V บีบแตร to honk

bìip khaw V บีบคอ to strangle

bin N (from English) บิล (the) bill

bin V บิน to fly

bin-thá-bàat V บิณฑบาต to go about with an alms bowl to receive food

bìt V บิด to twist, N บิด dysentery

bláek-meh V (from English)

แบล็กเมล์ to blackmail

boeh N (from the English word 'number' and pronounced 'ber') เบอร์ (most commonly used to refer to telephone numbers and sometimes numbers of lottery tickets; also used when selecting a particular young woman in a massage parlor or a dancer in a go-go bar – these women generally wear 'numbers' when working)

bòehk V เบิก to withdraw (money), requisition (funds)

boh N โบว์ bow (ribbon)

bòhk mueh V โบกมือ to wave a hand/hands

boh-lîng N โบลิ่ง bowling

boh-nút N (from English) โบนัส a bonus

bohraan ADJ โบราณ ancient, antique, old-fashioned

bòht N โบสถ์ a place of worship but of a non-Buddhist variety: e.g. a Christian church

bòht fàràng โบสถ์ฝรั่ง; a synagogue **bòht yiu** โบสถ์ยิว

bòi ADV, ADJ บ่อย often; frequent

bòk N บก land (as opposed to sea), terrestrial

bon PREP บน on, at

bòn V บ่น to complain

bòt V บด to grind

bòt bàat N บทบาท a role (e.g. in a movie/in real life)

bòt khwaam N บทความ an article (e.g. in a newspaper)

bòt rian N บทเรียน a lesson (i.e. in a classroom/in real life)

bòt sŏnthá-naa N (FORMAL) บทสนทนา conversation

bòt sùat mon N บทสวดมนต์ a prayer

bráwkkhohlîi N (from English) บรอกโคลี่ broccoli

brèhk N, V (from English) เบรก a brake (in a car); to brake (while driving) (NOTE: the same word is also used for the English word 'break' as in to 'have a break' [while working])

bua N บัว lotus (flower), water lily

bùak PREP, V บวก plus; to add

buam ADJ บวม to be swollen

bûan V บ้วน to spit out; **náam yaa bûan pàak** น้ำยาบ้วน ปาก mouthwash (e.g. Listerine)

bùat V บวช to be ordained, enter the (Buddhist) monkhood (the full expression being **bùat phrá** บวชพระ)

bùea V เบื่อ to be bored, be tired of, fed up (with), cannot stand (someone or something)

bûeang tôn ADJ เบื้องต้น introductory/ elementary/ primary (e.g. level of learning); initially/at the outset

bùkkhá-lík N บุคลิก character/personality

bùp V บุบ to pound lightly

bun N บุญ Buddhist concept of merit (for the afterlife)

bun khun N บุญคุณ a favor, kindness, sense of indebtedness to someone else for their kindness or support. A very significant aspect of Thai culture.

burìi N บุหรี่ cigarette

bù-rùt-prai-sà-nii N บุรุษ ไปรษณีย์ postman

bùt N บุตร (pronounced similar to 'put' but with a 'b' rather than a 'p', and a low tone) child/children/ offspring (NOTE: an adopted child is **bùt bun-tham** บุตร บุญธรรม)

buu-chaa V บูชา to worship/ revere/venerate

buum N บูม boom

bùut ADJ บูด to be rancid/ sour/spoiled (of food) (NOTE: to be sullen-looking/ sour-faced is **nâa bùut** หน้าบูด)

CH

NOTE: all the entries here begin with 'ch'—this being a sound found both in English and Thai. As for the single English letter 'c' (pronounced as 'see') – this is represented by other letters and in other ways with the system of romanization used in this dictionary

chaa N ชา tea; ADJ also to be numb, without sensation

cháa ADJ ช้า to be slow; **cháa-cháa** ADV ช้าๆ (e.g. drive/speak) slowly

chǎi V ฉาย to shine a light (NOTE: **chǎi nǎng** ฉายหนัง is to screen/show a movie/ film)

chaai ADJ, N ชาย male, masculine (general term and only for humans); N edge, rim, border

chaai daehn N ชายแดน border (between countries)

chaai hàat N ชายหาด beach

chaai thá leh N ชายทะเล seashore

chaam N ชาม a bowl

cháang N ช้าง an elephant

châang N ช่าง a tradesperson, skilled person (a few examples are included in the following entries)

châang prá-paa N ช่างประปา

plumber

châang fai-fáa N ช่างไฟฟ้า an electrician (NOTE: the word **fai-fáa** ไฟฟ้า means 'electricity/electrical')

châang khrûeang N ช่าง เครื่อง mechanic

châang mái N ช่างไม้ carpenter (NOTE: the word **mái** ไม้ means 'wood')

cháang náam N ช้างน้ำ hippopotamus (nowadays the abbreviated English form 'hippo' is commonly used in Thailand: **híppo** ฮิปโป)

châang phâap N ช่างภาพ photographer, cameraman

châang tàt phǒm N ช่าง ตัดผม barber

chaan mueang N ชานเมือง outskirts, environs of a city

châat N ชาติ nation, country

chá-baa N ชบา hibiscus

chà-bàp N ฉบับ classifier for counting newspapers, letters, and documents

chàe ADJ แฉะ swampy, wet

chǎeh V แฉ to reveal, disclose, expose

chaem pehn N (from English) แชมเปญ champagne

châeng V แช่ง to curse

châeh khǎeng V แช่แข็ง to freeze; to be frozen

chá-nii N ชะนี gibbon

chái V ใช้ to use, utilize

châi ใช่ yes (NOTE: one of numerous ways 'yes' is expressed in Thai)

chái dâi (COLLOQUIAL) ใช้ได้ It's usable/it works; also valid

chái jàai V ใช้จ่าย to spend money, to expend

chái mâi dâi ADJ (COLLOQUIAL) ใช้ไม่ได้ no good, unusable, out of order

chái mòt V ใช้หมด to use up

chái nîi V ใช้หนี้ to pay off a debt, repay

chái weh-laa V ใช้เวลา to spend time

chai yoh PHR ไชโย hooray, cheers!

chák V ชัก to have convulsions, pull, jerk

chák cháa V ชักช้า to hesitate

ADV, ADJ slowly, sluggish

chák chuan V ชักชวน to invite, persuade, induce (someone to do something)

chák wâaw V ชักว่าว to fly a kite; (SLANG) to masturbate, jerk off

chà-làak N ฉลาก label, lot (as a ticket in a lottery)

chà-lǎam N ฉลาม shark

chà-làat ADJ ฉลาด astute, bright, smart, intelligent

chà-láwng V ฉลอง to celebrate (e.g. on passing an exam)

chà-lìa V เฉลี่ย to average (numbers), divide equally

chà-lěoi V เฉลย to solve (a problem or puzzle), give an answer

chà-lǒem V เฉลิม to celebrate (e.g. the King's birthday)

chá-law V ชลอ to slow down

chàm ADJ ฉ่ำ juicy, wet, damp, moist, humid

chám ADJ ช้ำ to be bruised

chamnaan V ชำนาญ to be highly skilled at something, have expertise

chamrút ADJ ชำรุด to be damaged

chan ADJ ชัน to be steep (e.g. a hill)

chán N ชั้น a layer, level, story (of a building); class, category

chán bon N ชั้นบน upstairs, upper story, upper layer, upper shelf

chán lâang N ชั้นล่าง downstairs, lower story, lower layer, lower shelf

chán mát-thá-yom N ชั้นมัธยม secondary grades, junior/high school

chán nam ADJ ชั้นนำ leading, outstanding

chán prà-thŏm N ชั้นประถม elementary grades, grade school level

chăn PRON (INFORMAL/ INTIMATE) ฉัน I, me V to eat (only for monk)

chá-ná V ชนะ to win, beat, defeat, be victorious

chang V ชัง to hate, detest

châng V ชั่ง to weigh (something)

châng man PHR (COLLOQUIAL)

202

ช่างมัน 'Who cares!', 'Forget it!', 'To hell with it!'

chá-nít N ชนิด type, sort

chánít nǎi ชนิดไหน, (or more commonly) **bàehp nǎi** แบบไหน what kind of?

chà-nòht N โฉนด land titles, property

châo V เช่า to hire, rent

châo V เฉา to wilt, wither, shrivel up

cháo N เช้า morning

cháo mûehd N เช้ามืด dusk

cháo trùu N เช้าตรู่ dawn, very early in the morning

chaow bâan N ชาวบ้าน villager(s) (also general term for 'common people' whether in cities, towns, or villages)

chaow prá-mong N ชาวประมง fisherman

chaow indohnii-sia N ชาวอินโดนีเซีย Indonesian person/people

chaow khǎméhn N ชาวเขมร Cambodian person/people

chaow khǎo N ชาวเขา hill tribe(s)

chaow maa-lehsia N ชาว
มาเลเซีย Malaysian person/
people

chaow naa N ชาวนา a
farmer, someone who
works the land (rice
growers etc.)

chaow phà-mâa N ชาวพม่า
Burmese person/people

chaow phúehn mueang
N ชาวพื้นเมือง indigenous
person/people

chaow phút N ชาวพุทธ
Buddhist(s)

chaow râi N ชาวไร่
intercropping farmer

chaow sǔan N ชาวสวน
gardener

chaow thai N ชาวไทย Thai
person/people

chaow tàang prathêht N
ชาวต่างประเทศ a foreigner/
foreigners

chaow ta-wan tòk N ชาว
ตะวันตก a westerner

chaow wîat-naam N ชาว
เวียดนาม Vietnamese
person/people

chaow yîipùn N ชาวญี่ปุ่น
Japanese person/people

chà-pháw ADV เฉพาะ only,
exclusively for

chá-raa ADJ (FORMAL) ชรา
old, aged (of people)

chát ADJ, ADV ชัด clear;
clearly (e.g. the image on a
television screen; to speak
clearly or fluently)

chát jehn ADJ ชัดเจน to
be distinct (a view, the
meaning of what is said,
the way someone speaks),
very clear

cháw N ช่อ cluster, bunch
(fruit, flowers)

cháw dàwk mái N ช่อดอกไม้
bouquet

cháwk N ชอล์ก chalk

cháwk ADJ ช็อค shocked

cháwk-koh-láet N (from
English) ช็อกโกแลต
chocolate

cháwn N ช้อน spoon

cháwn chaa N ช้อนชา
teaspoon

cháwn tó N ช้อนโต๊ะ
tablespoon

châwng N ช่อง hole,
aperture, slot, space, gap
(also used when referring

to a television channel –
e.g. Channel 7 is **châwng
jèt** ช่องเจ็ด

châwng khâehp N ช่อง
แคบ strait (i.e. Straits of
Gibraltar), narrow channel

châwng khlâwt N (polite
medical term) ช่องคลอด
vagina

châwng tháwng N ช่องท้อง
abdomen

châwng wâang N ช่องว่าง a
gap, a vacant space

châwp V ชอบ to be fond of;
like, be pleased by

châwp jai ADJ ชอบใจ pleased
with, happy, amused

cháwp-pîng N, V (from
English) ช้อปปิ้ง shopping;
to shop

châwp mâak kwàa V ชอบ
มากกว่า to prefer

chék N, V เช็ค a (bank/
travellers') cheque/
check (also used in the
English sense of 'to check
something to see if it is
OK/functioning' etc.)

chên ADV เช่น for example
…, such as

chên khoei เช่นเคย as usual,
as before (e.g. he's doing it
again, as usual)

chên nán เช่นนั้น like that, in
that way/manner

chét V เช็ด to wipe

chia V เชียร์ (from English)
to cheer

chîang ADJ เฉียง oblique,
aslant, deflected, inclined,
diagonal

chîao V เฉียว to swoop down
upon, snatch, snatch away
suddenly, pass swiftly

chîao ADJ เชี่ยว strong, swift,
rapid (of current of water)

chîao chaan ADJ เชี่ยวชาญ
to be skilled, experienced,
expert

chiat V เฉียด to pass too
close, very close, just miss,
almost graze

chíi V ชี้ to point (at, to)

chìi V (COLLOQUIAL) ฉี่ to
urinate, pee

chíi tua V ชี้ตัว to identify,
point at (a person)

chíi jaeng V ชี้แจง to explain

chíi níu V ชี้นิ้ว to give orders
(i.e. point the finger

204

ordering someone to do this, that and the other)

chìik v ฉีก to tear, rip

chìit v ฉีด to inject: **chìit yaa** ฉีดยา to give an injection of liquid medicine

chìit sà-preh v ฉีดสเปรย์ to spray

chìit wák-siin v ฉีดวัคซีน to vaccinate, perform a vaccination

chii-wá-wít-thá-yaa N ชีววิทยา biology

chii-wít N ชีวิต life

chii-wít chii-waa ADJ (COLLOQUIAL) ชีวิตชีวา to be lively, vibrant, full of life

chim v ชิม to taste or sample something

chin ADJ ชิน to be accustomed (to)/used to/familiar (with)

chín N ชิ้น piece, section, morsel, slice

chìng N ฉิ่ง cymbal

ching cháa N ชิงช้า swing

chít ADJ ชิด close, near, nearby

chòk v ฉก to snatch, grab, strike (as a snake)

choehn v (pronounced like 'churn') เชิญ to invite (formally); please (go ahead)

chóeht N (from English) เชิ้ต shirt with collar

choei ADJ (COLLOQUIAL) เชย to be outdated, old fashioned, not with it

chŏei ADJ เฉย to be impartial, indifferent, uninterested in; (commonly reduplicated when spoken: **chŏei–chŏei** เฉยๆ)

choeh-rîi N เชอร์รี่ cherry

chohey v โชย to blow gently (wind)

chôhk ADJ โชก soaking wet

chôhk N โชค luck

chôhk dii โชคดี good luck! To be lucky

chôhk dii thîi… ADV โชคดีที่ fortunately

chôhk ráai ADV โชคร้าย unluck(il)y, unfortunately

chók v ชก to punch, strike

chók muay N ชกมวย boxing (Western style), fighting

chom v ชม to admire, compliment, praise

205

chom wiu v ชมวิว to view, look at

chomphuu N ชมพู pink (color) (for a list of the most common colors see the entry under **sǐi** สี which means 'color')

chomphûu N ชมพู่ rose apple (fruit)

chom-rom N ชมรม gathering, meeting club

chon v ชน to collide with/bump into, crash into

chong v ชง to infuse, steep in

chong chaa v ชงชา to make (a cup/pot of) tea

chon klùm nói N ชนกลุ่มน้อย ethnic group, minority group

chonná-bòt N (FORMAL) ชนบท (COLLOQUIAL) **bâan nâwk** N บ้านนอก countryside, rural area

chót chái v ชดใช้ to reimburse, repay, compensate

chót choei v ชดเชย to compensate (for damage to property, etc.), indemnify

chûa ADJ ชั่ว bad, vile, wicked

chûa khànà N ชั่วขณะ a moment, an instant

chûa khraow ADJ ชั่วคราว to be temporary

chûa mohng N ชั่วโมง an hour; classifier for counting hours

chûai v ช่วย to assist, help; please (request for help: e.g. 'can you please give me that glass')

chûai chii wít v ช่วยชีวิต to rescue

chûai dûai ช่วยด้วย help! (there's a fire/there's been an accident)

chûai lǔea v ช่วยเหลือ to rescue

chûai oh kàat v ฉวยโอกาส to seize the opportunity

chûai tua ehng v ช่วยตัวเอง to help oneself, masturbate

chuan v ชวน to invite (ask along)

chûea v เชื่อ to believe

chûea fang v เชื่อฟัง to obey

chûea jai v เชื่อใจ to trust

chúea raa N เชื้อรา fungus, mould/mold

206

chúea rôhk N เชื้อโรค germs, infection (often simply **chúea** เชื้อ)

chûeak N เชือก rope, string, cord

chûea mân V เชื่อมั่น to believe firmly

chûeang ADJ เชื่อง to be tame (animal)

chûea th̆ue V เชื่อถือ to have trust

chùeay ADJ, ADV เฉื่อย slow; steadily but gently, lazily (of a breeze blowing)

chûeh N ชื่อ name

chûeh dang ADJ ชื่อดัง famous

chûeh jing N ชื่อจริง first name, personal name

chûeh lên N ชื่อเล่น nickname

chúehn ADJ ชื้น damp, humid

chûeh s̆iang N ชื่อเสียง fame, reputation

chûi ADJ (COLLOQUIAL) ชุ่ย crappy, lousy; done in a careless, slipshod way

chùk chŏehn N ฉุกเฉิน emergency

chum chon N ชุมชน N assemblage of people, community

chum num V ชุมนุม to gather together, congregate

chŭn ADJ ฉุน to be pungent (odor); to be angry

chúp V ชุบ to soak; to plate (metal)

chút N ชุด set (of clothes, furniture, etc.)

chút chán nai N ชุดชั้นใน underwear (more typically used to refer to female underwear)

chút nawn N ชุดนอน nightclothes, pajamas

chút wâai náam N ชุดว่ายน้ำ swimming costume, swimsuit

chúu N ชู้ adulterer, lover (usually refer to extramarital relations)

D

dàa V ด่า to curse, scold or berate; to tell someone off; to swear at

dâai N ด้าย thread (e.g.

207

cotton thread)

dâam N ด้าม handle; classifier for pens

dâan N ด้าน side (e.g. the back side of a house, the other side of an object, etc.), direction

dâan ADJ ด้าน to be hard/calloused, rough to the touch; also matte finish, dull, not shiny (NOTE: **nâa dâan** หน้าด้าน is thick skinned, shameless, brazen)

dâan khwǎa N ด้านขวา on the right side

dâan nâa N ด้านหน้า front, in the front

dâan nâwk N ด้านนอก outside

dâan sáai N ด้านซ้าย on the left side

dàan trùat khâo mueang N ด่านตรวจเข้าเมือง immigration office

dàap N ดาบ sword

daa-raa N ดารา movie/TV star

dàat fáa N ดาดฟ้า deck

daehng N แดง red (for a list of the most common colors

see the entry under **sǐi** สี which means 'color')

dàeht N แดด sunlight, sunshine (NOTE: **àab dàeht** v อาบแดด is to sunbake, sunbathe)

dàeht àwk ADJ แดดออก to be sunny

dâi v ได้ to obtain, get, be able to, can; get to, gain (**dâi** is an important 'function' word in Thai. For example, 'can you?' (**dâi mái**) questions are formed in this way: 'name of activity' + 'can you?' – **ao rót maa dâi mái** เอารถมาได้ไหม 'Can you bring the car?' To simply answer yes is **dâi** ได้; to answer no is **mâi dâi** ไม่ได้.)

dâi prìap v ได้เปรียบ to have an advantage

dâi dii v ได้ดี to make good, do well

dâi kam-rai v ได้กำไร to profit

dâi phǒn v ได้ผล to be effective, get results

dâi ráp v ได้รับ to get,

receive

dâi ráp à-nú-yâat v ได้รับ อนุญาต to be allowed to, be given permission

dâi ráp bàat jèp v ได้รับบาด เจ็บ to be injured

dâi thîi v ได้ที่ to get the upper hand, not excessive or extreme

dâi yin v ได้ยิน to hear

dam N ดำ black, a dark hue (for a list of the most common colors see the entry under **sǐi** สี which means 'color')

dam náam v ดำน้ำ to dive

dan v (pronounced like 'dun') ดัน to push, shove

dang ADJ (pronounced like 'dung') ดัง to be loud (sound); also to be famous

dâng doehm ADJ ดั้งเดิม traditional, original

dâng jà-mùuk N ดั้งจมูก bridge of the nose

dang nán CONJ (FORMAL) ดัง นั้น so, therefore

dao v เดา to guess, speculate

daow N ดาว star

daow hǎang N ดาวหาง comet

daow thiam N ดาวเทียม satellite

daow tòk N ดาวตก shooting star, meteor

dàp v ดับ to go out (fire, candle), extinguish; (SLANG) to die/be killed

dàp fai v ดับไฟ to put out a fire

dàt v (pronounced like 'dut') ดัด to bend; to shape; to straighten out

dàt phǒm v ดัดผม to perm hair

dàwk N ดอก classifier for flowers, incense, arrows

dàwk bîa N ดอกเบี้ย interest (money)

dàwk bua N ดอกบัว lotus, water lily

dàwk kà-làm N ดอกกะหล่ำ cauliflower

dàwk mái N ดอกไม้ flower

dàwk mái fai N ดอกไม้ไฟ fireworks

dáwktoeh N (from English) ด็อกเตอร์ Doctor (PhD)

dawn N (pronounced like 'don') (COLLOQUIAL) ดอล dollar

dawn-lâa N (from English) ดอลลาร์ dollar

dawng ADJ (pronounced like 'dong') ดอง pickled, preserved (fruit, vegetables)

dèk N เด็ก child (young person; also commonly used to refer to adults who are in very junior, or lowly, positions in an organization)

dèk àwn N เด็กอ่อน infant, baby, a small child

dèk chaai N เด็กชาย boy

dék kamphráa N เด็กกำพร้า an orphan

dèk nák-rian N เด็กนักเรียน schoolchild(ren)

dèk phûu-yǐng N เด็กผู้หญิง girl

dèk wát N เด็กวัด temple boy

dèn ADJ เด่น prominent, conspicuous

dèt ADJ เด็ด decisive, resolute, bold ADV really, quite

dèt khàat ADV เด็ดขาด absolutely, strictly, definitely

dǐao ADV เดี๋ยว for a moment, just a moment

diao ADJ เดียว single, one, only (NOTE: **khon diao** N คนเดียว is 'alone', 'by oneself'; 'single person')

diao kan เดียวกัน the same – as in **khon diao kan** คนเดียวกัน 'the same person'

dǐao níi ADV เดี๋ยวนี้ right now, now

dǐao níi ehng ADV เดี๋ยวนี้เอง just now

dichǎn PRON, FEM (FORMAL) ดิฉัน I

dîi N (COLLOQUIAL) ดี้ (feminine) lesbian (from the English word 'lady')

dii ADJ ดี fine (okay), good, nice, well

dii jai ADJ ดีใจ glad, happy

dii khûen V ดีขึ้น to improve, get better

dii kwàa ADV, ADJ ดีกว่า better, better than

dii mâak ADJ ดีมาก well done! very good

dii thîi sùt ADJ ดีที่สุด (the) best

dii wii dii N (from English) ดีวีดี DVD

diit v ดีด to flick, pluck, flip

dík N (COLLOQUIAL – from English 'dictionary') ดิค dictionary

din N ดิน earth, soil, ground

din phǎo N ดินเผา porcelain, china

dîn ron v ดิ้นรน to struggle

din-sǎw N ดินสอ pencil

ding ADJ ดิ่ง vertical, righteous

dip ADJ ดิบ raw, uncooked, unripe, rare (as with a steak)

doehm ADJ เดิม former, previous, old, original

doehn v เดิน to walk

doehn lên v เดินเล่น to go for a stroll; to walk for leisure

doehn maa ADV เดินมา on foot (coming); **doehn pai** ADV เดินไป on foot (going)

doehn-pàa v เดินป่า to hike

doehn pai dâi v เดินไปได้ (within) walking distance

doehn ruea v เดินเรือ to operate/sail a vessel/ship/boat

doehn thaang v เดินทาง to travel, take a trip

doehn thaang dohy plàwt phai ná (POLITE EXPRESSION) เดินทางโดยปลอดภัยนะ Have a safe trip

dohn v, PASSIVE (pronounced as in 'Methad*one*') โดน e.g. **dohn rót chon** โดนรถ ชน to be hit by a car, to be punished, to get it in the neck (NOTE: **dohn dii** v (COLLOQUIAL) โดนดี to cop it, to get what one is asking for)

dòht v โดด to jump, leap, spring, bound

dohy PREP โดย by (author, artist); by way of; by means of

dohy bang-oehn ADV โดย บังเอิญ accidentally, by chance

dohy chà-phá-w ADV โดย เฉพาะ particularly, especially

dohy mâi mii ADV โดยไม่มี without

dohy mâi tâng-jai ADV โดย ไม่ตั้งใจ by chance, not intentionally

dohy pà-kà-tì ADV โดยปกติ

normally, usually

dohy rótfai โดยรถไฟ (to go/be transported) by rail, by train

dohy ṣĭn choehng ADV โดยสิ้นเชิง completely (thoroughly)

dohy thûa pai ADV โดยทั่วไป in general, generally

dohy trong ADV โดยตรง directly

doi N ดอย hill, mountain, peak (used in the North of Thailand)

dòk ADJ ดก abundant, plentiful

dom V ดม to smell, inhale, sniff

don-trii N ดนตรี music

dù ADJ ดุ fierce, vicious (e.g. a vicious dog) V to blame, find fault with, censure

dù ráai ADJ ดุร้าย ferocious, pugnacious, wild

dûai PREP ด้วย as well, with, by, too, also

dûai kan ADV ด้วยกัน together

dûai khwaam praat-thànǎa dii (FORMAL) ด้วยความ ปรารถนาดี best wishes

dûai khwaam sĭa jai (FORMAL) ด้วยความเสียใจ with regret(s), regrettably

dûai khwaam wǎng (FORMAL) ด้วยความหวัง hopefully

dûai khwaam yindii (FORMAL) ด้วยความยินดี with pleasure

dûai mueh PREP ด้วยมือ by hand

dûai tua-ehng ADV ด้วยตัวเอง by oneself

dûai wí-thii (FORMAL) ด้วย วิธี...by means of, using the method of

dùan ADJ ด่วน to be urgent, pressing, express (e.g. as in express bus)

dûan V ด้วน to cut, cut off, cut cut off, amputated, cut short

duang N ดวง fortune, luck

duang aa-thít N ดวงอาทิตย์ sun

duang jan N ดวงจันทร์ (the) moon

duean N เดือน month

duean nâa N เดือนหน้า next month

duean níi N เดือนนี้ this month

duean thîi láew N เดือนที่แล้ว last month

dùeat V เดือด to reach the boiling point, rage at

dùeat ráwn ADJ เดือดร้อน to be in trouble, in a fix, distressed

dûeh ADJ ดื้อ stubborn, obstinate, headstrong

dùehm V ดื่ม to drink

dùek ADV ดึก late at night

dueng V ดึง to pull

dueng ao wái V ดึงเอาไว้ (pull up) to restrain; to tighten (a rope etc.) up

dueng dùut V ดึงดูด to attract

duu V ดู to look at, see, watch (TV, movie)

duu àwk V ดูออก to be able to see through (someone or something), to understand, to be able to tell

duu duang V ดูดวง to look at one's horoscope N fortune telling

duu laeh V ดูแล to take care of, look after

duu lên V ดูเล่น to look at

something for fun (to pass time)

duu măw V (COLLOQUIAL) (**măw** is pronounced 'more' with a rising tone) ดูหมอ to have your fortune told/ read, see a fortune teller

duu mŭean ดูเหมือน to seem (e.g. as if something was going to happen), look as if

duu mŭeankan ดูเหมือนกัน to look the same

duu sí (COLLOQUIAL) ดูซิ look!

duu thùuk V ดูถูก to look down on someone, insult, disparage

dùut ดูด to suck, absorb, soak up

E

eh-chia N เอเชีย Asia

eh-ds N เอดส์ AIDS (the fuller form is **rôhk eh-ds** (literally, 'disease' + 'AIDS') โรคเอดส์)

eh-yêhn N (from English) เอเย่นต์ agent, agency

213

èhk-kàchon ADJ เอกชน private (company/sector)

èhk-kà-phâap N เอกภาพ unity, solidarity

èhk-kà-râat ADJ เอกราช (of a state, nation) independent, free sovereign

èhk-kà-sǎan N เอกสาร document(s), printed material, records

éhk-sà-reh V, N (from English) เอ็กซเรย์ X-ray

ehn V เอน to lean, recline

ehng N เอง self (NOTE: tua ehng ตัวเอง is 'myself')

ehn lǎng V เอนหลัง to lean back

eh-o N เอว waist

en N เอ็น tendon, sinew, gut

en-duu V เอ็นดู to adore, like very much

èt V เอ็ด (COLLOQUIAL) to scold

F

fǎa N ฝา lid, cover, (internal) wall

fǎa chii N ฝาชี cover placed over a dish of food

fǎa fàet N ฝาแฝด twins

fàa V ฝ่า to go against, violate, disobey

fàa N ฝ่า palm (of the hand), sole (of the foot)

fàa tháo N ฝ่าเท้า sole (of the foot)

fâa ADJ ฝ้า clouded (like a cloudy film of the surface of something), scum, blemish; **pen fâa** เป็นฝ้า to have freckles

fáa N ฟ้า sky, light blue color (for a list of the most common colors see the entry under sǐi สี which means 'color')

fáa lâep N ฟ้าแลบ lightning

fáa phàa N ฟ้าผ่า lightning

fǎa phànǎng N ฝาผนัง wall (of a room or building)

fáa ráwng N ฟ้าร้อง thunder

fâai N ฝ้าย cotton

fàai N ฝ่าย side, group, party

214

fàai diaow N ฝ่ายเดียว one (party, side)

fàai trong khâam N ฝ่ายตรงข้าม opponent(s), (the) opposition (in politics etc.)

fàak V ฝาก to leave behind for safekeeping, deposit, entrust to someone, leave with

fàak krà-pǎo V ฝากกระเป๋า to leave luggage

fàak krà-pǎo dâi mái ฝากกระเป๋าได้ไหม May I leave my luggage?

fàak ngoehn V ฝากเงิน to deposit money (in the bank)

faam N (from English 'farm', pronounced similar to the English) ฟาร์ม farm

fǎan V ฝาน to slice, cut thin

faang N ฟาง straw

fàat ADJ ฝาด astringent (in taste)

fâat V ฟาด to strike, slap, hit hard

fae-chân N (from English) แฟชั่น fashion (i.e. the latest fashion, etc.)

fáek N (from English) แฟกซ์

fax (message or machine)

fâem N แฟ้ม file, folder

faen N แฟน boy/girlfriend, fan (admirer) (NOTE: also commonly used to refer to a husband or wife)

fǎeng V แฝง to hide, conceal

fàet ADJ แฝด twin, double, coupled, paired (NOTE: **fǎa fàet** N ฝาแฝด is 'twins')

fǎi N ไฝ mole, beauty spot

fai N ไฟ fire; light (lamp)

fai chǎai N ไฟฉาย flashlight, torch

fai cháek N ไฟแช็ค cigarette lighter

fai fáa ADJ, N ไฟฟ้า electric; electricity

fai mâi V ไฟไหม้ to be on fire

fai nâa N ไฟหน้า headlight

fai tháai N ไฟท้าย tail-light

fàk N ฝัก pod, hull, case, sheath, scabbard

fák V ฟัก to hatch

fàk bua N ฝักบัว shower (head)

fák thawng N (pronounced 'fuck tong') ฟักทอง pumpkin

fan N (pronounced like 'fun') ฟัน tooth, teeth

fǎn v, n (pronounced like 'fun' with a rising tone) ฝัน to dream; a dream

fǎn klaang wan n ฝันกลางวัน to daydream

fǎn ráai n ฝันร้าย a nightmare

fǎn thǔeng v ฝันถึง to dream about (somebody)

fang v ฟัง to listen, hear

fǎng v ฝัง to bury, implant

fàng n ฝั่ง bank (river), shore

fang phlehng v ฟังเพลง to listen to music

fang yùu v ฟังอยู่ (to be) listening (the use of **yùu** อยู่ after a verb indicates the present continuous tense – '...ing')

fâo v เฝ้า to watch over, tend, take care of, keep watch

fâo duu v เฝ้าดู to keep an eye on, keep watch (over, on)

fâo rá-wang v เฝ้าระวัง to guard against, be on the alert/lookout (for)

fàràng n ฝรั่ง caucasian, westerner; guava (fruit)

fàràngsèht n ฝรั่งเศส France, French

fàw v, adj ฝ่อ to wither, dry out; abortive

fawng n ฟอง foam, bubbles, froth, lather; a classifier for eggs

fáwng v ฟ้อง to sue, file legal proceedings, accuse, complain to someone about somebody else

fawng náam n ฟองน้ำ a sponge

fáwng ráwng v ฟ้องร้อง to sue, bring charges against

fǐi n ฝี boil, pustule, abscess (Note: **plùuk fǐi** ปลูกฝี is 'to vaccinate')

fǐi-dàat n ฝีดาษ smallpox

fǐi mueh n ฝีมือ workmanship, craftsmanship, handiwork, skill

fǐi pàak n ฝีปาก verbal skill/gift of the gab

fǐi thâo n ฝีเท้า speed of foot

filíppin n ฟิลิปปินส์ the Philippines

fim n ฟิล์ม film (for camera; or the tinted film on a car windscreen)

fin n ฝิ่น opium

fiu n (from English) ฟิวส์ fuse

216

fláet N (from English) แฟลต flat, apartment

fláet N (from English) แฟลช flash (camera)

flúk N (from English) ฟลุค fluke, a lucky chance

foeh-ní-jôeh N (from English – pronounced like 'fer-ni-jer') เฟอร์นิเจอร์ furniture

fǒi N ฝอย shreds, fibers, droplets, trivial details; v (COLLQUIAL) to brag

fók chám ADJ ฟกช้ำ bruised, swollen

fǒn N ฝน rain (NOTE: **nâa fǒn** หน้าฝน is the 'rainy season' – generally from late May/ early June to the end of October)

fǒn láeng N ฝนแล้ง drought

fǒn tòk v ฝนตก to rain, be raining, it is raining

frii ADJ (from English) ฟรี free

fùeak N เฟือก cast or split (e.g. for a broken arm/leg)

fueang N เฟือง gearwheel

fúehn v ฟื้น to recover, regain consciousness, come to (after fainting)

fǔehn v ฝืน to disobey, contrary to, do something against (the law, one's will, etc.)

fùeht ADJ ฝืด tight, stuck, difficult to move

fùek v ฝึก to practice, drill/train

fùek hàt/fùek sáwm v ฝึกหัด/ฝึกซ้อม to train

fuen N ฟืน firewood

fûm-fueay N, ADJ ฟุ่มเฟือย luxury; luxurious, extravagant, unnecessary

fùn N ฝุ่น dust

fút N ฟุต foot (length)

fút bawn N ฟุตบอล (COLLOQUIAL) **bawn** บอล soccer/football

fuu v ฟู (COLLOQUIAL) to become fluffy

fûuk N ฟูก mattress

fǔung N ฝูง a crowd, group, herd, flock, pack

fǔung nók N ฝูงนก a flock of birds

fǔung plaa N ฝูงปลา a school of fish

217

H

hâa NUM ห้า five

hàa N ห่า cholera demon/ spirit held responsible for plagues; (SLANG – rude) **âi hàa** ไอ้ห่า shit, damn, bastard

hǎa V หา to look for, look up (find in book), search for

hǎa kin V (COLLOQUIAL) หากิน to make a living

hǎa maa dâi V หามาได้ to earn

hǎa mâi joeh V (COLLOQUIAL) หาไม่เจอ cannot find (something)

hǎa ngoehn V (COLLOQUIAL) หาเงิน to make (some) money, to make a living

hǎa rûeang V (COLLOQUIAL) หาเรื่อง to look for trouble; be abrasive, provocative

hâa sip NUM ห้าสิบ fifty

hǎa wâa V หาว่า to accuse (someone of doing something)

hǎa yâak ADJ หายาก rare (scarce)

háad dis N (from English) ฮาร์ดดิสก์ hard disk

hǎai V หาย to be lost, to disappear ADJ to be missing

hǎai jai V หายใจ to breathe

hǎai jai àwk V หายใจออก to breathe out

hǎai jai khâo V หายใจเข้า to breathe in

hǎai pai V หายไป to disappear, vanish

hǎai wai wai หายไวๆ get well soon!

hǎam V หาม to carry, bear

hàam ADJ ห่าม almost ripe (fruit)

hâam V ห้าม to forbid, be forbidden

hàan N ห่าน goose

hǎan V หาร to divide

hǎan dûai V หารด้วย divided by (e.g. 4 hǎan dûai 4 = 1 (4 ÷ 4 = 1))

hǎang N หาง tail

hàang ADJ ห่าง to be apart/ distant from

hǎang-pia N หางเปีย pigtail

hâang sàp-phá-sǐnkháa N ห้างสรรพสินค้า (COLLOQUIAL) **hâang** ห้าง department store

hàap V หาบ to carry a pole across one's shoulder

218

hàat N หาด beach

hǎe N แห fishing net

haehm N (from English) แฮม ham

hâehng ADJ แห้ง to be dry

hâehng láehng ADJ, N แห้งแล้ง dry (weather), drought

hàeng N แห่ง of; classifier for places

hâi V ให้ to give; to, for; to allow, have something done (A very important 'functional' word in Thai. Here are a couple of examples [space limitations make it impossible to go into greater detail about the broad range of uses of **hâi** ให้]: To have something done: **hâi khǎo ao rót maa** ให้เขาเอารถมา – 'have him/ get him to bring the car (along)'; To do something for somebody: **khǎo súeh yean hâi faehn** เขาซื้อ ยีนให้แฟน 'he brought a pair of jeans for his girlfriend'. In the first

example the meaning of **hâi** ให้ is rendered by the word 'have'; in the second example it is the equivalent of the English word 'for'.)

hâi aa-hǎan V ให้อาหาร to feed (the dog)

hâi àphai V ให้อภัย to forgive

hâi châo V ให้เช่า to rent out

hâi kaan V ให้การ to plead (in court)

hâi khuehn V ให้คืน, (or simply) **khuehn** V คืน to return, give back

hâi thaan V ให้ทาน to give alms

hâi yuehm V ให้ยืม to lend

hàk ADJ หัก to break/fracture (e.g. of bones); also to deduct (money owed etc.)

hàk lǎng V (COLLOQUIAL) หัก หลัง to double-cross, betray

hǎm N (SLANG; Isaan dialect) หำ balls (gonads)

hàn V หั่น to cut up, slice

hǎn V หัน to turn

hǎn klàp V หันกลับ to turn back

hǎn lǎng V หันหลัง to turn around

hăn nâa v หันหน้า to face, turn one's head, turn the face toward a direction

hăn phuang-maa-lai v หัน พวงมาลัย to steer (to turn the steering wheel – 'steering wheel' is **phuang-maa-lai** พวงมาลัย)

hanlŏh (from the English greeting) ฮัลโหล hello! (used on the phone)

hào v เห่า to bark

hăo N เหา louse, lice

hăow v หาว to yawn

hàt N (pronounced 'hut' with a low tone) หัด measles

hàt v หัด to drill, practice

hàt yur rá man หัดเยอรมัน German measles

heh-lí-kháwp-tôeh N เฮลิคอปเตอร์ helicopter

hĕow N เหว gorge, chasm, abyss

heh-roh-iin N (from English) เฮโรอีน heroin

hàw v (pronounced 'hor') ห่อ to wrap (up a parcel, etc.)

hàw khăwng N ห่อของ package

hăw duu daaw N หอดูดาว observatory

hăw khoi N หอคอย tower

hăw phák N หอพัก dormitory, hostel

hăwm ADJ หอม to be sweet-smelling, fragrant, aromatic

hăwm v หอม to kiss (the old Thai way of kissing is more like nuzzling or sniffing of one another's cheeks, i.e. face cheeks)

hăwm yài N หอมใหญ่ onion (or **hŭa hăwm** หัวหอม)

hâwng N ห้อง room (in house, hotel)

hâwng khăai tŭa N ห้องขาย ตั๋ว ticket office

hâwng khăai tŭa yùu thîi năi ห้องขายตั๋วอยู่ที่ไหน Where is the ticket office?

hâwng kèp khăwng N ห้อง เก็บของ storeroom

hâwng khrua N ห้องครัว kitchen

hâwng kong N ฮ่องกง Hong Kong

hâwng náam N ห้องน้ำ toilet (bathroom), lavatory

220

hâwng nâng lên N ห้องนั่ง เล่น sitting room, living room, lounge (room)

hâwng nawn N ห้องนอน bedroom

hâwng ráp khàek N ห้อง รับแขก living room

hâwng rian N ห้องเรียน classroom

hâwng sà-mùt N ห้องสมุด library

hâwng tâi din N ห้องใต้ดิน basement

hâwng thŏhng N ห้องโถง hall (as in 'assembly hall')

hàwp V หอบ to pant, breathe heavily

hèht-kaan N เหตุการณ์ happening, incident, event

hèht phŏn N เหตุผล reason

hĕn V เห็น to see, regard, to think (used to give opinion in reporting speech, e.g. 'I think that')

hĕn dûai V เห็นด้วย to agree

hĕn jai V เห็นใจ to be sympathetic, understand someone else's position

hĕn kàeh tua ADJ เห็นแก่ตัว to be selfish

hĕn pen phá-yaan V เห็น เป็นพยาน to witness (something)

hèp N เห็บ tick, wood tick, hail

hèt N เห็ด mushroom(s)

hĭi N (COLLOQUIAL, EXTREMELY RUDE) หี vagina (or, more accurately, 'cunt')

hìip N หีบ chest (box)

hìmá N หิมะ snow

hìmá tòk V หิมะตก to snow, snowing

hĭn N หิน rock, stone

hin duu N ฮินดู Hindu

hĭn pà-kaa-rang N หิน ปะการัง coral (commonly simply **pà-kaa-rang** ปะการัง)

hĭn puun N หินปูน limestone, tartar

hĭu, hĭu-khâow ADJ หิว, หิว ข้าว to be hungry

hĭu V หิ้ว to carry

hĭu náam V หิวน้ำ to be thirsty

hòht, hòht-ráai ADJ โหด, โหด ร้าย cruel, wild, brutal, ruthless

hŏi N หอย mollusc/oyster/clam

hôi v ห้อย to hang, be suspended

hôi naang rom N หอยนางรม a type of large, fleshy oyster

hôi thâak N หอยทาก snail (or simply **thâak** ทาก)

hòk NUM หก six

hòk v หก to spill (liquid)

hòk lóm v หกล้ม to fall over, take a tumble, (or, more simply, **lóm** ล้ม)

hòk sìp NUM หกสิบ sixty

hŏng N หงส์ a swan

hòt v หด to shrink

hŭa N หัว head, top

hŭa boh-raan ADJ หัวโบราณ to be old-fashioned, conservative

hŭa-dûe ADJ หัวดื้อ stubborn

hŭa jai N หัวใจ heart

hŭa jai waai N หัวใจวาย a heart attack

hŭa kào ADJ หัวเก่า conservative, old-fashioned

hŭa khăeng ADJ หัวแข็ง obstinate, stubborn, headstrong

hŭa khào N หัวเข่า knee

hŭa khâw N หัวข้อ subject, topic, heading

hŭa láan ADJ หัวล้าน bald

hŭa mâe mueh N หัวแม่มือ thumb

hŭa nâa N หัวหน้า chief, leader, head, boss

hŭa nom N หัวนม nipple(s)

hŭa săi ADJ (COLLOQUIAL) หัวใส bright, shrewd

hùai ADJ (COLLOQUIAL/SLANG) ห่วย lousy, crappy, crummy, (SLANG) to suck

hŭai N หวย underground lottery

hûan v, ADJ ห้วน to be brusque; curt, uncouth (talk or speech)

hŭan v หวน to turn back

hŭang v, ADJ หวง to be jealous (of); possessive (of things), unwilling to part with something

hùang ADJ ห่วง to be anxious, concerned/worried (about)

hŭa ráw v หัวเราะ to laugh

hŭa ráw yáw v หัวเราะเยาะ to laugh at

hŭa sà-măwng N หัวสมอง brain concussion

222

hǔeng v หึง to be jealous (commonly of a sexual nature)

hùn N หุ่น dummy, mannequin, also the shape/appearance of someone's figure (NOTE: 'robot' is **hùn yon** หุ่นยนต์)

hûn N หุ้น share, stock (as traded on the stock market)

hûn sùan N หุ้นส่วน partner (in business)

hǔng v หุง to cook (rice)

hùp khǎo N หุบเขา valley

hùp pàak v หุบปาก to close the mouth, (COLLOQUIAL) shut up!

hǔu N หู ear(s)

hǔu fang N หูฟัง headset, headphone, earphone

hǔu nùak ADJ หูหนวก (to be) deaf

hǔu tueng ADJ หูตึง hard of hearing

hùut N หูด wart

I

iang v เอียง to bend, slant, incline

ii PRON อี (derogatory) title used with the first names of women, bound element in names of birds and animals

ii-kaa N อีกา crow

iik ADV ... อีก again

iik ADV อีก... another (different); else, more

iik an nùeng อีกอันหนึ่ง (Can I have) another one

iik khon nùeng (COLLOQUIAL) อีกคนหนึ่ง another person, one more person

iik khráng nùeng (COLLOQUIAL) อีกครั้งหนึ่ง again, one more time

iik mâi naan (COLLOQUIAL) อีกไม่นาน soon

iik sàk nòi (COLLOQUIAL) อีกสักหน่อย (Could I have) a little more

ii-sùk-ii-sǎi N อีสุกอีใส chicken pox

iik yàang nùeng IDIOM อีก

อย่างหนึ่ง by the way, another thing

ii-meh N (from English) อีเมล์ email (message)

ii-săan N อีสาน the north-eastern region of Thailand – commonly written in English as Isaan, Isarn

i-lék-thrawnik ADJ (from English) อิเล็กทรอนิก electronic

im V อิ่ม to be full, eaten one's fill, had enough

india N อินเดีย India

indohniisia N อินโดนีเซีย Indonesia (colloquially Indonesia is often referred to as **in-doh** อินโด)

ing V อิง to lean on/against

in-sii N อินทรี eagle ADJ อินทรีย์ organic

in-toeh-nét N (from English) อินเทอร์เน็ต Internet (or simply **nét** เน็ต)

it N อิฐ brick, a brick

i-taa-lii N อิตาลี Italy, Italian

itchăa N, V อิจฉา envy; to be jealous of

it-sà-laam N (alternative pronunciation 'islaam') อิสลาม Islam

ìt-sà-rà ADJ อิสระ to be free, independent

ìt-sà-rà-phâap N อิสรภาพ freedom

ìt-thí-phon N อิทธิพล influence

J

jà AUX V จะ shall, will; future indicator

jàa N จ่า leader, head, chief

jâa ADJ จ้า bright (light), intense, glaring

jàai V จ่าย to pay

jàai láew จ่ายแล้ว (for a bill that has been) paid

jàai tà-làat V จ่ายตลาด to buy the groceries, go to shop at the market

jàai yaa V จ่ายยา to give medicine

jàak PREP จาก of, from

jàak kan V จากกัน to separate (from one another)

jàak pai V จากไป to depart, go away from a place

jaam V จาม to sneeze

jaan N จาน a plate/dish

jaang V, ADJ จาง to fade; faded, dilute

jâang V จ้าง to hire

jàehk V แจก to hand out, distribute

jaeh-kan N แจกัน a vase (for flowers)

jâehng V แจ้ง to inform, notify

jâehng khwaam แจ้งความ to report (to the police)

jáekkêt N (from English) แจ็คเก็ต a jacket, coat

jà-tù-ràt N จตุรัส square

jai N ใจ heart, mind

jai àwn ADJ ใจอ่อน yielding, soft-hearted, easily influenced, easily touched

jai bàap ADJ ใจบาป sinful

jai bun ADJ ใจบุญ pious, charitable

jai chúen ADJ ใจชื้น relieved

jai dam ADJ ใจดำ merciless, mean

jai diao ADJ ใจเดียว faithful

jai dii ADJ ใจดี to be kind, good (of people)

jai hǎai ADJ ใจหาย shocked, stunned with fear

jai khǎeng ADJ ใจแข็ง unyielding

jai khâep ADJ ใจแคบ selfish, narrow-minded

jai klâa ADJ ใจกล้า brave, bold

jai kwâang ADJ ใจกว้าง to be generous, broad-minded, magnanimous

jai loi ADJ ใจลอย absent-minded

jai ngâai ADJ ใจง่าย cheap (women), easy to get

jai ráai ADJ ใจร้าย malicious

jai ráwn ADJ ใจร้อน impatient, impetuous, hasty

jai sàn ADJ ใจสั่น frightened

jai tàek ADJ ใจแตก spoiled, self-indulgent and unrestrained

jai yen ADJ ใจเย็น calm, cool-hearted, steady, imperturbable

jàk-kà-jàn N จั๊กจั่น cicada

ják-kà-jîi ADJ จักจี้ ticklish

jàk-krà-phát N จักรพรรดิ emperor

jàk-krà-waan N จักรวาล universe

jàk-krà-yaan N จักรยาน bicycle

225

jàk-krà-yaan-yon N (FORMAL) จักรยานยนต์ motorcycle, (COLLOQUIAL) **maw-toeh-sai** มอเตอร์ไซค์ (from English)

jàk yép phâa N จักรเย็บผ้า sewing machine

jam V (pronounced like 'jum' in 'jump') จำ to remember, retain

jam dâi V จำได้ to remember, recognize

jam jai V จำใจ to force/be forced to do something

jam jeh ADJ จำเจ tiresome, monotonous, repetitious

jam kàt V จำกัด to limit, define

jam lawng V จำลอง to imitate, copy, reproduce, model

jam leoy N จำเลย defendant

jam nam V จำนำ to pawn, mortgage

jam nawng V จำนอง to mortgage

jam-nuan N จำนวน amount

jam-pen ADJ จำเป็น to be necessary V to need

jà-mùuk N จมูก nose

jang ADV (COLLOQUIAL) จัง very (used as an intensifier, e.g. 'very beautiful' **sǔai jang** สวยจัง)

jang-wà N จังหวะ rhythm

jang-wàt N (pronounced something like 'jung-what') จังหวัด a province (regional administrative unit)

jâo N เจ้านาย master

jâo bàow N เจ้าบ่าว bridegroom/groom

jâo chaai N เจ้าชาย prince

jâo chúu N เจ้าชู้ philanderer

jâo khǎwng N เจ้าของ owner

jâo nâa thîi N เจ้าหน้าที่ official, bureaucrat, public servant, authority (person in charge)

jâo nîi N เจ้าหนี้ creditor

jâo phâap N เจ้าภาพ host (of a party, wedding, etc.)

jâo sǎow N เจ้าสาว bride

jâo ying N เจ้าหญิง princess

jàp V จับ to capture, arrest, catch, grab

jà-raa-jawn N จราจร traffic

jà-rùat N จรวด rocket

jàt V (pronounced like the

English word 'jut' as in 'to jut out') จัด to arrange (e.g. furniture); also used as an intensifier: e.g. extreme, intense – ráwn jàt ร้อนจัด intense/extreme heat

jàt hâi rîap rói v จัดให้เรียบ ร้อย to tidy up

jàt-kaan v จัดการ to manage, organize, sort out, deal with

jàt tó v จัดโต๊ะ to lay or set a table

jaw N (pronounced like the English word 'jaw') จอ screen, monitor (of television/computer)

jàw ruu v เจาะรู to make a hole

jawn-jàt N จรจัด homeless wanderer, vagebond

jawng v จอง to reserve, book (seats, tickets), i.e. **khǎw jawng tǔa paj...sǎwng thîi nâng** ขอจองตั๋วไป...สองที่ นั้น I'd like to reserve two seats to ...

jâwng v จ้อง to gaze at, stare

jawng hǎwng ADJ จองหอง unduly proud, haughty

jàwt v จอด to stop (a vehicle), i.e. **rót jàwt thî... mái?** รถจอดที่...ไหม Does this train/bus stop at...?; **jàwt thî...dâi mái?** จอดที่... ได้ไหม Could you please stop at...?

jàwt rót v จอดรถ to park a vehicle

jeh N (pronounced similar to 'jay') เจ vegetarian; **kin jeh** v กินเจ to eat vegetarian food

jéng ADJ (COLLOQUIAL) เจ๊ง (of an object – e.g. a mobile phone) to be broken, worn out, kaput; (for a business) to go broke/bankrupt

jěng (COLLOQUIAL) เจ๋ง 'that's cool, great, awesome'

jèp ADJ เจ็บ to be sore, hurt (injured)

jèp mâak ADJ เจ็บมาก to be very painful

jèt NUM เจ็ด seven

jèt sìp NUM เจ็ดสิบ seventy

jii v จี้ to poke, tickle, point at/out, prod, exhort

jîi N จี้ pendant of a necklace

jiin N (pronounced like the

227

English word 'jean(s)') จีน China, Chinese

jiin klaang N จีนกลาง Mainland China; also used to refer to Mandarin Chinese (language)

jiip v (pronounced like 'jeep' with a low tone) จีบ to flirt with someone, court, try to chat up someone

jìm v จิ้ม to dip in, pick

jìm N จิ๋ม (COLLOQUIAL) vagina

jing ADJ จริง to be true, real

jing jai ADJ จริงใจ sincere, honest

jing jang ADJ จริงจัง serious

jing-jing ADV จริงๆ really, truly, indeed!

jing-jôh N จิงโจ้ kangaroo

jîng-jòk N จิ้งจก house lizard

jîng-rìit N จิ้งหรีด cricket (insect)

jing rǔeh INTERJ จริงหรือ Really? Is that so? (used to express surprise)

jìp v จิบ to sip

joeh v (pronounced like 'jer' in 'jerk') เจอ to meet, find

jóhk N โจ๊ก joke; rice porridge

johm tii v โจมตี to attack (in a war)

john N โจร robber

john sà-làt N โจรสลัด pirate

jom v จม to sink or drown

jom náam v จมน้ำ to drown

jon ADJ จน to be poor

jon krà-thâng CONJ จนกระทั่ง until

jong jai v จงใจ to intend

jòp v จบ to end (finish)

jòt v จด to take note, jot down

jòt-mǎai N จดหมาย letter; mail

jòt-mǎai-long thàbian N จดหมายลงทะเบียน registered letter/mail

jàw v เจาะ to drill, make a hole

juan ADV จวน almost

juea jaang ADJ เจือจาง thin (of liquids)

jùeht ADJ จืด bland, tasteless

jueng CONJ จึง (FORMAL – more written than spoken language) consequently, therefore

jùk N จุก topknot, stopper (of bottle), cork

jùt N จุด point, dot

jùt fai V จุดไฟ to light a fire

jùt-jùt ADJ จุดๆ spotted (pattern)

jùt-măi plaai thaang N จุดหมายปลายทาง destination

jùt mûng măai N จุดมุ่งหมาย purpose

jùt rôehm tôn N จุดเริ่มต้น origin, starting point

jûu-jîi ADJ จู้จี้ fussy

jùu-johm V จู่โจม to attack, rush

juung V จูง to tow, drag

jùup V, N จูบ kiss

K

NOTE: This letter should not be confused with the English 'k' sound. In this case 'k' is pronounced like 'g' in 'gun', or like the 'k' in the word 'skin'

kà V กะ to estimate (the price), guess

kà N กะ a shift – as in a shift at work (i.e. the night shift)

kaa-faeh N (pronounced 'gar-fey') กาแฟ coffee

kaa kii ADJ กากี khaki (color)

kaai-yá-kam N กายกรรม gymnastics

kaam N กาม sexual desire

kâam N ก้าม claw, pincer (of crab)

kaam-má-rôhk N กามโรค venereal disease

kaam-má-thêhp N กามเทพ Cupid, Eros

kaan N การ the action/task/business of...

kaan bâan N การบ้าน homework

kaan bàat jèp N การบาดเจ็บ injury

kaan bin N การบิน flying, aviation

kaan chûay lŭea N การช่วยเหลือ aid, assistance

kaan doehn thaang N การเดินทาง trip, journey

kaan hâi àphai N การให้อภัย forgiveness, mercy

kaan kàw sâang N การก่อสร้าง building, construction

kaan khàeng khăn N การ

แข่งขัน competition, a race of game

kaan lûeak tâng N การเลือก ตั้ง election

kaan mueang N การเมือง politics

kaan ngoehn N การเงิน finance

kaan prá chum N การประชุม meeting, conference

kaan rák săa N การรักษา care, maintenance, remedy

kaan thûut N การทูต diplomacy

kaan pàtibàt ngaan N การ ปฏิบัติงาน performance (of work)

kaan pàtisèht N การปฏิเสธ refusal

kaan phát-thà-naa N การ พัฒนา development

kaan sà-daehng N การ แสดง a display, a show, a performance

kaan sĭa sàlà N การเสียสละ sacrifice

kaan sùek-săa N การศึกษา education

kaan tàwp sànăwng N การตอบสนอง reaction, response

kaan thák thaai N การทักทาย greetings

kaan tham aa-hăan N การทำ อาหาร cooking, cuisine

kaan thòk panhăa N กา รถกปัญหา discussion (of issues)

kaan thót sàwp N การ ทดสอบ test, examination

kaang V กาง to spread out, stretch out, hang out

kâang N ก้าง fishbone

kaang-kehng N กางเกง trousers, pants

kaang-kehng khăa sân N กางเกงขาสั้น shorts (short trousers)

kaangkehng nai N กางเกงใน underpants, panties

kaa-tuun N (from English) การ์ตูน cartoon

kà-bòt N กบฏ rebel, rebellion

kà-laa N กะลา hard shell coconut

kà-laa-sĭi N กะลาสี sailor, seaman

kà-lá-manng N กะละมัง enameled bowl or basin

kà-làm dàwk N กะหล่ำดอก cauliflower

kà-làm plii N กะหล่ำปลี cabbage

kà lòhk N กะโหลก skull, hard shell of the coconut

kà ràt N กะรัต carat

kà riang N กะเหรี่ยง Karen tribe

kà-rii N กะหรี่ (COLLOQUAIL) curry; female prostitute

kà-tan-yuu ADJ กตัญญู grateful

kà-tì-kaa N กติกา rule (in sports)

kà-rá kà-daa-khom N กรกฎาคม July

kà-sèht-trà-kam N เกษตรกรรม agriculture

kà-thí N กะทิ coconut cream/ milk

kà-wii N กวี poet

kà-thoey N กะเทย a trans-vestite, also referred to by the English term 'ladyboy'

kàe N แกะ sheep

kâe kháen V แก้แค้น to take revenge

kâe khǎi V แก้ไข to correct, mend, revise, resolve

kàe sàlàk V แกะสลัก to carve

kaeh PRON (COLLOQUIAL, INFORMAL) แก you, he, she, they

kàeh ADJ แก่ old (of persons), strong (coffee)

kâeh V แก้ to fix (repair); to loosen, untie; to amend, revise, correct

kàeh dàet ADJ, N (COLLOQUIAL) แก่แดด to be cheeky; a whipper snapper, smart arse kid

kâeh hâi thùuk V แก้ให้ถูก to correct

kàeh kwàa ADJ แก่กว่า to be older, elder

kâeh panhǎa V แก้ปัญหา to solve (a problem)

kâeh phâa V แก้ผ้า to get undressed, take off clothing, be naked

kàeh tua V แก่ตัว to get old, grow old

kâeh tua V แก้ตัว to make excuses, find an excuse/ make up for one's losses/ failures

kâehm N แก้ม cheek(s)

kaehng N แกง curry

kaehng jùet N แกงจืด mild soup/plain soup

kaehng phèt N แกงเผ็ด hot curry

káet N (from English) แก๊ส gas (e.g. cooking gas)

kâew N แก้ว glass (for drinking)

kâew hǔu N แก้วหู eardrum

kài N (pronounced similar to 'guy') ไก่ chicken

kái N (from English) ไกด์ a guide

kài nguang N ไก่งวง turkey

kài yâang N ไก่ย่าง BBQ or grilled chicken

kàk khǎng V กักขัง to confine, restrict, detain

kam N (pronounced like 'gum') กรรม karma

kam dao N กำเดา nosebleed

kam kuam ADJ กำกวม ambiguous

kam lai N กำไล bracelet, bangle

kamjàt V (pronounced 'gum-jut') กำจัด to rid, get rid of

kamlang AUX, V (pronounced 'gum-lung') กำลัง to be presently doing N strength, power, (armed) force

kamlang doehn thaang ADV กำลังเดินทาง on the way, in the process of travelling

kam-má-kaan N กรรมการ committee, judge (competition)

kam-má-phan ADJ (pronounced 'gummàpun') กรรมพันธุ์ hereditary, congenital, genetic

kam-má-thǎn N กำมะถัน sulfur

kam-má-yìi N กำมะหยี่ velvet

kam mueh V กำมือ to clench the fist

kamnan N (pronounced 'gum none') กำนัน sub-district headman, chief of sub-district (tambon)

kam-nòt N กำหนด schedule, program

kam-nòt-kaan N กำหนดการ schedule, program

kam pân N กำปั้น fist

kam-phaehng N กำแพง (stone or brick) wall (of a yard or town)

kam-phuu-chaa N กัมพูชา Cambodia

kamrai N กำไร profit

kan ADV กัน together, mutually v to prevent

kân v กั้น to cut off, shut off, bar

kan thòe กันเถอะ let's (e.g. go) (used at the end of a sentence to urge the other party to do something)

kan-chaa N (pronounced 'gun jar') กัญชา marihuana, hemp, grass, dope, pot, weed

kan chon N กันชน bumper

kan daan ADJ กันดาร barren, arid, lacking

kang hǎn N กังหัน windmill

kankrai N กรรไกร scissors

kang won N กังวล worry

kan-yaa-yon N กันยายน September

kao v เกา to scratch lightly

kào ADJ เก่า old (of things)

kâo NUM เก้า nine

kâo îi N เก้าอี้ chair

kâo sìp NUM เก้าสิบ ninety

kaolǐi nǔea N เกาหลีเหนือ North Korea

kaolǐi tâi N เกาหลีใต้ South Korea

kaow N กาว glue

kâow v ก้าว to step

kâow nâa v ก้าวหน้า to advance, go forward

kâow ráow ADJ ก้าวร้าว aggressive, disrespectful

kàp CONJ กับ and PREP with

kàp dàk N กับดัก trap, snare

kàp tan N กัปตัน captain

kàp khâow N (COLLOQUIAL) กับข้าว the food eaten with rice (e.g. curry/vegetables/soup, etc.)

kàp klâem N กับแกล้ม hors d'oeuvres, entrée, a light meal

kà-phrao N กะเพรา sweet basil

kà-phríp v กะพริบ to blink (flash on and off)

kà-phríp-taa กะพริบตา eyes blinking

kàpì N กะปิ fish paste

kàrú-naa กรุณา please ... (a very polite, formal means of asking for something); kindness, mercy

kàt v (pronounced like 'gut' with a low tone) กัด to bite

kàt fan N กัดฟัน to gnash

233

one's teeth

kàt kan v (COLLOQUIAL) กัดกัน to be at odds with another person, to snipe at

kàw N เกาะ island

kàw v เกาะ to cling to

kâw ADV (pronounced 'gor') ก็ also, too, either (used to add an agreeing thought)

kâw loei CONJ ก็เลย then, so

kàw sâang v ก่อสร้าง to construct

kàw tâng v ก่อตั้ง to establish, set up

káwf N (from English) กอล์ฟ golf

káwk N ก๊อก, **káwk náam** ก๊อก น้ำ tap, faucet

kàwn ADV ก่อน first, earlier, before

kâwn N ก้อน lump; classifier for lump-like objects, cube (e.g. sugar)

kàwn nii ADV ก่อนนี้ earlier, before this, previously

kawng N กอง troop, force, pile, heap

kawng tháp N กองทัพ troops, the military, the army (in particular)

kawng-tháp aa-kàat N กองทัพอากาศ air force

kawng-tháp-bòk N กองทัพ บก army, military land forces

kawng-tháp-ruea N กองทัพ เรือ navy, naval forces

kaw-rá-nii N กรณี a case (e.g. a legal case), a particular instance (NOTE: (COLLOQUIAL) **khûu kaw-rá-nii** คู่กรณี the other party in an accident/incident)

kàwt v กอด to embrace, hug

ké N เก๊ะ a drawer (in a table etc.)

kéh ADJ เก๊ fake

kêh ADJ เก๋ to be with it, stylish, chic

keh N (pronounced 'gay') (from English) เกย์ gay, homosexual

kehm N (from English) เกม match, game

kèng ADJ เก่ง clever, smart, good at something (also used colloquially to mean 'a lot': e.g. **kin kèng** กินเก่ง 'to eat a lot'; **nawn kèng** นอนเก่ง 'to sleep a lot')

kèp v เก็บ to save, collect, accumulate, keep, pick up

kèp khǎwng v เก็บของ to gather things together, pack (luggage)

kèp kòt v (COLLOQUIAL) เก็บ กด to suppress (one's true feelings)

kèp-ngoehn v เก็บเงิน to save money, check the bill

kèp tó v เก็บโต๊ะ to clear the table (e.g. after dinner)

kèp tua v เก็บตัว to avoid others, keep to oneself, shun society

kia N (from English) เกียร์ gear

kíao N เกี๊ยว small Chinese dumpling or wonton

kìao v เกี่ยว to cut (with sickle), harvest, reap, to pertain (to), be related (to) (often used in a negative sense/statement, e.g. 'It's got nothing to do with it/ He's got nothing to do with it', etc. **mâi kìao** ไม่เกี่ยว)

kìao kàp PREP เกี่ยวกับ about, regarding, concerning

kìao khâwng v เกี่ยวข้อง to involve, in connection with

kíao náam N เกี๊ยวน้ำ wonton soup

kìat N เกียรติ honor, dignity

kìat-tì-yót N เกียรติยศ honor, prestige

kìi... กี่ how many...?: **kìi chûa mohng** กี่ชั่วโมง how many hours (e.g. will it take to clean the house)?

kìi-laa กีฬา sport(s)

kìi mohng láew (EXP) กี่โมง แล้ว what's the time?

kìit khwǎang v กีดขวาง to hinder, obstruct

kìitâa N (from English) กีตาร์ guitar

ki-loh(kram) N (COLLOQUIAL – kiloh) กิโล(กรัม) kilogram

ki-loh(méht) N (COLLOQUIAL – kiloh) กิโล(เมตร) kilometer

kin v กิน to eat; (SLANG) to be corrupt, take bribes

kin aa-hǎan cháo v กินอา หารเช้า to eat breakfast

kin jeh v กินเจ to be vegetarian

kin jù v กินจุ to eat a lot (until you're stuffed)

kin khâow v กินข้าว to eat

235

(breakfast, lunch, dinner, a meal; the expression itself means literally, 'eat'-'rice')

kíp N กิ๊บ hairclip

kìng mái N (pronounced **ging** [low tone]-**mai** [high tone]) กิ่งไม้ the branch of a tree

kíng-kàa N กิ้งก่า tree lizard

kíng-kue N กิ้งกือ millipede

kìt-jà-kam N กิจกรรม activity

klâa hǎan ADJ กล้าหาญ to be brave, daring

klaai pen V กลายเป็น to become (e.g. friends)

klâam núea V กล้ามเนื้อ muscle(s)

klaang N กลาง in the middle, center

klaang khuehn N กลางคืน night

klaang mueang N กลางเมือง city/town center

klaang wan N กลางวัน day/daytime

klâehng V แกล้ง to pretend, tease someone (maliciously), annoy (deliberately, intentionally)

klai ADJ (with a mid tone and a longer sounding vowel than the word for 'near')

klâi ใกล้ ไกล to be far away, distant, a long way

klâi ADJ ใกล้ near, nearby, close to

klâi wehlaa ใกล้เวลา almost time (e.g. to go), to approach (in time)

klàn V กลั่น to distill, extract

klân V กลั้น to suppress, hold back, restrain, inhibit, refrain from

klàow hǎa V กล่าวหา to accuse

klàow kham praa-sǎi V (FORMAL) กล่าวคำปราศรัย to make (give) a speech

klàow thǔeng V (FORMAL) กล่าวถึง to mention

klàp V กลับ to return (e.g. home), turn over (e.g. a steak on a BBQ pit)

klàp bâan V กลับบ้าน to return home, go back home

klàp jai V กลับใจ to have a change of heart, turn over a new leaf, be reformed

klàp khâang ADJ กลับข้าง to be inside out, be on back to front

klàp maa V กลับมา to come

236

back (to where you began from)

klàp pai v กลับไป to return (to where you began from)

klèt N เกล็ด scale, flake, tuck, dart

klawn N กลอน bolt, latch; a kind of Thai verse form

klawng N กลอง a drum

klâwng N กล้อง, กล้องถ่ายรูป a camera; also pipe

klâwng sàwng thaang klai N กล้องส่องทางไกล binoculars

klàwng N กล่อง box

klàwng krà-dàat N กล่อง กระดาษ cardboard box

kliat v เกลียด to hate

klìn N กลิ่น odor, a smell

klîng v กลิ้ง to roll, slide

klom ADJ กลม round (shape)

klua v กลัว to be afraid, to fear

klua phǐi v กลัวผี to be afraid of ghosts

klua taai v กลัวตาย to be afraid of death/dying

klûai N กล้วย banana

klûai mái N กล้วยไม้ orchid(s)

klueah N เกลือ salt

kluehn v กลืน to swallow

klùm N กลุ่ม group

klûm jai ADJ กลุ้มใจ to be depressed, glum

koehn ADV เกิน to exceed, surpass

koehn pai ADV, ADJ เกินไป too... (e.g. expensive, small, big, etc.); excessive

kòeht v (pronounced like 'gurt/girt') เกิด to be born

kòeht àrai khûen (COLLOQUIAL) เกิดอะไรขึ้น what happened?

kòeht khûen v เกิดขึ้น to happen, occur, come about

koh-dang N โกดัง warehouse

koh-hòk v (pronounced 'go hok') โกหก to lie

koh-kôh N (from English) โก้ โก้ cocoa

kohn v โกน to shave

kohng v โกง to cheat

kôi N ก้อย the little finger, pinky

kôm v ก้ม to bend down, stoop, bow

kôn N ก้น bottom, buttocks

kongsŭn N, ADJ กงสุล consul; consular

kòp N กบ a frog

kòt N กฎ rule, regulation, law

kòt V กด to press

kòt krìng V กดกริ่ง to ring (door bell)

kòtmǎai N กฎหมาย laws, legislation

kraam N กราม jaw

kràap V กราบ to postrate oneself (as a sign of respect), (in some contexts this could be) to grovel

krà-buai N กระบวย ladle, dipper

krà-buan kaan N กระบวนการ a movement (e.g. for human rights), a process

krà-daan N กระดาน board, plank

krà-daan prà-kàat N กระดาน ประกาศ signboard, bulletin board

krà-dàat N กระดาษ paper

krà-dàat khǎeng N กระดาษ แข็ง cardboard (literally 'paper'-'hard/stiff')

krà-dàat thít-chûu (from English) กระดาษทิชชู่ tissue paper, toilet paper

krà-dàat saai N กระดาษทราย sandpaper

krà-dìng N กระดิ่ง bell, doorbell

krà-dòht V กระโดด to jump

krà-dum N กระดุม button

krà-dùuk N กระดูก bone(s)

krà-dùuk sǎn lǎng N กระดูก สันหลัง the spine/backbone

krà-jaai sǐang V กระจายเสียง to broadcast

krà-jàwk ADJ (SLANG) กระจอก piddling, petty, of no significance, crap

krà-jòk N กระจก glass (material), the windshield of a car, a mirror

krà-tìk N กระติก thermos bottle

krà-tùk V กระตุก to jerk

krà-tûn V กระตุ้น to encourage, stimulate

kram N กรัม gram

krà-pǎo N กระเป๋า a bag, a pocket in a garment

krà-pǎo doehn thaang N กระเป๋าเดินทาง (or **kra-pǎo sûea phâa** N กระเป๋าเสื้อผ้า) a suitcase

krà-pǎo ngoehn N กระเป๋า

เงิน, or (MORE COLLOQUIAL) **krà-pǎo tang** กระเป๋าตังค์ a purse/wallet

krà-pǎo thǔe N กระเป๋าถือ handbag

krà-pǎo tham ngaan N กระเป๋าทำงาน briefcase

krà-pǎwng N กระป๋อง a can, tin

krà-phǒm PRON, MASC (FORMAL) กระผม I, me

krà-pháw aa-hǎan N กระเพาะอาหาร stomach

krà-pháw pàt-sǎa-wá N กระเพาะปัสสาวะ urinary bladder

krà-prohng N กระโปรง a skirt

krà-pùk N กระปุก (a smallish) receptacle or box (e.g. for ointment, jewelry, etc.)

krà-râwk N กระรอก squirrel

krà-sǎe N กระแส current, flow, stream (of river, sea); a trend/vogue

krà-sǎeh fai-fáa N กระแส ไฟฟ้า electric current

krà-sǎeh náam N กระแสน้ำ current of water

krà-sàwp N กระสอบ sack, bag

krà-sìp V กระซิบ to whisper

krà-suang N กระทรวง (government) ministry

krà-sǔn N กระสุน a bullet

krà-tàai N กระต่าย rabbit

krà-thá N กระทะ a wok/ Chinese-style frying pan for making stir-fried dishes

krà-thǎang N กระถาง flowerpot

krà-thâwm N กระท่อม hut, shack, cottage

krà-thiam N กระเทียม garlic

krà-thong N กระทง basket, small banana leaf receptacle, an integral part of the Loi/Loy (which means 'float') Krathong Festival (**Loi kratong** ลอย กระทง) that marks the end of the rainy season

kràwk (baehp) fawm V กรอก(แบบ)ฟอร์ม to fill out a form

krawng V กรอง to filter, strain

kràwp ADJ กรอบ crisp, brittle

kràwp N กรอบ a frame,

(within the) confines/limit-ations (of)

kràwp rûup N กรอบรูป a (picture) frame

krehng-jai N, V เกรงใจ a key Thai concept which means something like a fear of imposing on someone else; to be thought of, in Thai culture, as considerate

kreng ADJ, V เกร็ง tense, stiffened; to flex a muscle

kròht V โกรธ to be upset/cross/angry

krom N กรม (a government) department, e.g. **krom tam-rùat** กรมตำรวจ the police department

kron V กรน to snore

krong N กรง cage

kròt N กรด acid (not LSD)

krùat N กรวด pebble

krung N กรุง city

krung-thêhp N กรุงเทพฯ Bangkok (literally 'City of Angels')

kǔai tǐao N ก๋วยเตี๋ยว noodles

kǔai tǐao náam N ก๋วยเตี๋ยวน้ำ noodle soup

kuan V กวน to bother, annoy,

disturb (someone)

kuan jai ADJ กวนใจ to bother, disturb, be irritating

kùeap ADV เกือบ almost, nearly

kùlàap N กุหลาบ a rose (bush/flower)

kum-phaaphan N กุมภาพันธ์ February

kûng N กุ้ง shrimp, prawn; **kûng mangkawn** (literally, 'prawn'-'dragon') กุ้งมัง lobster

kun-jaeh N กุญแจ key (to room)

kunjaeh mueh N กุญแจมือ handcuffs

kuu N กู (IMPOLITE) I, me

kûu V กู้ to borrow (money), take a loan

kwàa ADJ กว่า over, more, more than (NOTE: this word is used to make comparisons in Thai – **dii kwàa** ดีกว่า better; **yài kwàa** ใหญ่กว่า bigger; **phaehng kwàa** แพงกว่า more expensive [than...])

kwaang N กวาง deer; stag; doe

240

kwâang ADJ กว้าง broad, spacious, wide

kwàat V กวาด to sweep

kwàeng V แกว่ง to swing

KH

NOTE: like the English sound 'k'

khâ ค่ะ female polite particle (when answering a question or making a statement)

khá คะ female polite particle (when asking a question)

khá-ná-baw-dii N คณบดี Dean of Faculty

khàa N ข่า galangal (spice used in Thai cooking)

khăa N ขา leg(s)

khâa V ฆ่า to kill, murder

khăa àwn N ขาอ่อน thigh

khâa N ค่า value (cost)

khâa baw-rí-kaan N ค่าบริการ service fee/charge

khâa baw-rí-kaan e-thii-em thâo-rài ค่าบริการเอทีเอ็ม เท่าไร What is the fee for using the ATM machine?

khâa chái jàai N ค่าใช้จ่าย expenses

khâa dohy-săan N ค่า โดยสาร fare (for a bus, plane trip)

khâa jâang N ค่าจ้าง wage(s)

khâa prà-jam N ค่าประจำ a regular customer

khâa pràp N ค่าปรับ a fine (for infringement)

khâa râat-chákaan N ข้า ราชการ government official(s), bureaucrat(s), public servant(s)

khâa rót N ค่ารถ fare (for bus/taxi)

khâa tham-niam N ค่า ธรรมเนียม fee (for official service)

khâa tŭa N ค่าตั๋ว fare (for transportation ticket)

khâa-tŭa chán-nùeng/ chán-săwng thâo-rài ค่า ตั๋ว ชั้นหนึ่ง/ชั้นสอง เท่าไร How much is a first class/ second class train?

khâa-tŭa thîaw-diaw/pai-klàp thâo-rài ค่าตั๋ว เที่ยว เดียว/ไปกลับ เท่าไร How much is a single/return ticket?

khăai v ขาย for sale, to sell

khăai láew v ขายแล้ว to be sold

khăai mòt láew ADJ, V ขายหมดแล้ว sold out; to have sold the lot

khâam PREP, V ข้าม across; to cross, go over

khăam thà-nŏn v ข้ามถนน to cross the road

kháan v ค้าน to oppose, be opposed to

khâang N ข้าง side

khâang bon N, ADJ ข้างบน upstairs

khaang N คาง chin

khâang-khâang PREP ข้างๆ next to, beside

kháang khuehn v ค้างคืน to stay overnight

khâang lâang N, ADJ ข้างล่าง below, downstairs

khâang lăng PREP ข้างหลัง in the rear of, behind

khâang nâa N, ADJ ข้างหน้า front, in the front

khâang nai N, ADJ ข้างใน inside

khâang nâwk N, ADJ ข้างนอก outside

khâang tâi PREP, N, ADJ ข้างใต้ at the bottom (base), underneath

khàat v ขาด to lack; to break (e.g. a rope) N lack of ADJ to be lacking, be insufficient, be torn

khàat mòt ADJ ขาดหมด (completely) worn out (e.g. of clothes)

khàat pai ADJ ขาดไป to be missing (absent)

khàat thun v ขาดทุน to lose money (on an investment), take a loss

khâat wâa... v คาดว่า to expect that... (e.g. he'll arrive tomorrow)

khà-buan N ขบวน a procession

khâe ADV แค่ just, only, merely, e.g. (COLLOQUIAL) **khâe níi** แค่นี้ 'just this much'; **khâe năi** แค่ไหน 'to what degree' or 'how much' (e.g. do you love her?)

khàehk N แขก guest, a person of swarthy complexion – in Thailand

242

commonly used to refer to people from the Indian subcontinent and the Middle East

khàehk phûu mii kìat N แขก ผู้มีเกียรติ guest of honor

khàehn N แขน arm(s)

khaeh-na-daa N แคนาดา Canada

khâehp ADJ แคบ narrow

khaeh-ráwt N (from English) แครอต carrot

khàeng v แข่ง to compete in a race

khǎeng raehng ADJ แข็งแรง to be strong

kháep suun N (from English) แคปซูล capsule (medicine/vitamins)

khài N ไข่ egg

khâi N ไข้ fever

khài daehng N ไข่แดง egg yolk

khài dao N ไข่ดาว a fried egg

khài jiao N ไข่เจียว an omelette

khài khon N ไข่คน scrambled eggs

khài lùak N ไข่ลวก soft boiled egg

khâi lûeat àwk N ไข้เลือดออก dengue fever

khài man N ไข่มัน fat (body fat), grease

khài múk N ไข่มุก pearl(s)

khài múk thiam N ไข่มุก เทียม cultured pearl(s)

khài tôm N ไข่ต้ม hard boiled egg(s)

khâi wàt yài N ไข้หวัดใหญ่ flu, influenza

khǎm ADJ (pronounced like 'come' with a rising tone) ขำ to be funny, amusing

kham N คำ word(s)

kham choehn N คำเชิญ an invitation

kham dàa N คำด่า abuse, blame; a swear word

kham mueang N คำเมือง the dialect spoken in the northern part of Thailand

kham náe-nam N คำแนะนำ advice, suggestion

kham praa-sǎi N คำปราศรัย a speech

kham ráwng thúk N คำร้อง ทุกข์ a complaint

kham sàng N คำสั่ง order, command

243

kham sàp N คำศัพท์ vocabulary

kham tàwp N คำตอบ answer, response

kham thǎam N คำถาม question

kham tuean N คำเตือน warning

kham yók yâwng N คำยกย่อง (words of) praise

khàmĕhn N เขมร Cambodia

khamnuan V คำนวณ to calculate

khà-mohy V ขโมย to steal N a thief, thieves

khà-mùat khíu V ขมวดคิ้ว to frown

khà-mùk khà-mŭa ADJ ขมุกขมัว overcast (weather)

khan ADJ คัน to be itchy N classifier for counting vehicles, umbrellas, spoons and forks

khân N ขั้น stage, grade, step, rank

khǎn N ขัน dipping bowl (used when bathing in the old-style Thai manner)

khà-nà níi ADV ขณะนี้ at

present, at this moment

khà-nàat N ขนาด size

khànǒm N ขนม sweets, dessert, snacks

khànǒm khéhk N ขนมเค้ก cake

khànǒm-pang N (pang pronounced like 'pung') ขนมปัง bread

khànǒm-pang kràwp N ขนมปังกรอบ a cracker (biscuit)

khà-nŏm wǎan N ขนมหวาน confectionery, dessert

khà-nŭn N ขนุน jackfruit

khǎo N เขา mountain

khǎo PRON เขา she, her, he, him, they, them

khào N เข่า knee

khâo V เข้า to enter, go in

khâo hǎa V เข้าหา to approach

khâo in-ter-nèt V เข้าอินเตอร์เน็ต access to the Internet

khâo kan V เข้ากัน (COLLOQUIAL) to get on well together, get on (with)

khâo-jai V เข้าใจ to understand

khâo-jai phìt V เข้าใจผิด to misunderstand

244

khảo khâang v (COLLOQUIAL) เข้าข้าง to take sides (with someone)

khâo khiu v เข้าคิว to queue, line up (khiu คิว from English)

khâo maa v เข้ามา to come in, enter

khâo rûam v เข้าร่วม to join in, attend, participate

khàaw N ข่าว news, report

khảaw ADJ ขาว white (for a list of the most common colors see the entry under **sĭi** สี which means 'color')

khâaw N ข้าว rice

khâaw kaehng N ข้าว แกง rice and curry, (COLLOQUIAL) (Thai) food

khâaw klâwng N ข้าวกล้อง brown rice, unpolished rice

khâaw lǎam N ข้าวหลาม a Thai sweetmeat – glutinous rice with coconut milk roasted in a section of bamboo

khàaw lueh N ข่าวลือ a rumor

khâaw nĭao N ข้าวเหนียว sticky or glutinous rice

khâaw phàt N ข้าวผัด fried rice

khâaw phôht N ข้าวโพด corn

khâaw sǎa-lii N ข้าวสาลี wheat

khâaw sǎan N ข้าวสาร rice (uncooked)

khâaw sŭai N ข้าวสวย rice (cooked)

khàaw yài N ข่าวใหญ่ a big/ significant news story

kháp ADJ คับ to be tight (fitting)

khàp v ขับ to drive a vehicle

khát kháan v คัดค้าน to protest, object

khàt ngao v ขัดเงา to polish

khaw N คอ neck

kháw v เคาะ to knock

khǎw v ขอ to ask for, request (informally), apply for permission, request

khǎw..... ขอ...คะ/ครับ I'd like to.../May I … please?

khâw N (pronounced like 'khor' with a falling tone) ข้อ joint (in the body), articulation; also clause, section, provision, question/point(s) (as in 'there are a number of questions/points to be addressed')

khâw bòk-phrâwng n ข้อบกพร่อง defect

khaw hǒi n คอหอย throat

khâw khwaam n ข้อความ message

khâw mueh n ข้อมือ wrist

khâw muun n ข้อมูล information, data

khâw ráwng v ขอร้อง to request (formally)

khâw sà-daehng khwaam yin-dii dûai (FORMULAIC EXPRESSION) ขอแสดงความ ยินดีด้วย congratulations!

khâw sà-nǒeh n ข้อเสนอ a (FORMAL) proposal

khaw sǎw ABBREV ค.ศ. *anno domini* – the Christian Era

khâw sàwk n ข้อศอก elbow

khǎw thaang nòi ขอทาง หน่อย excuse me! (can I get past)

khâw tháo n ข้อเท้า ankle

khâw thét jing n ข้อเท็จ จริง fact

khǎw thôht v ขอโทษ to apologize; sorry!, excuse me!

khâw tòk-long n ข้อตกลง an agreement

khǎw yuehm v ขอยืม to borrow

khawm-phiu-tôeh n คอมพิวเตอร์, (COLLOQUIAL) khawm คอม computer

khá́wn n ค้อน hammer

khâwn-khâang ADV ค่อนข้าง rather, fairly

khǎwng n ของ thing(s), belongings

khǎwng v ของ to belong to; indicates the possessive – "of"

khǎwng chán PRON ของฉัน my, mine

khǎwng hǎai n ของหาย lost property

khǎwng kào n ของเก่า antiques

khǎwng khǎo PRON ของเขา his, hers, theirs

khǎwng khwǎn n ของขวัญ a present (gift)

khǎwng kin n ของกิน edibles, things to eat

khǎwng lên n ของเล่น toy(s)

khǎwng plawm n ของปลอม a copy, a fake, pirated merchandise

khǎwng rao PRON ของเรา our, ours

khǎwng sùan tua N ของ ส่วนตัว one's own personal possession(s)

khǎwng thiam ADJ ของเทียม synthetic, artificial

khǎwng thîi ra-lúek N ของที่ ระลึก souvenir

khǎwng wǎan N (COLLOQUIAL) ของหวาน a sweet, dessert

khàwp N ขอบ border, edge

khàwp khun ขอบคุณ to thank, thank you

khà-yà N ขยะ garbage, rubbish

khà-yǎn ADJ ขยัน to be hardworking, diligent

khà-yào V เขย่า to shake (something)

khem ADJ เค็ม salty (to the taste)

khêm ADJ เข้ม intense, strong, concentrated

khěm N เข็ม a needle

khěm khǎeng ADJ เข็ม แข็ง strong, unyielding; industrious, assiduous

khěm khàt N เข็มขัด belt

khêm khôn ADJ เข้มข้น concentrated (liquid), sharp (taste), flavorful

khèt N เขต boundary, frontier, zone, district

khèt V เข็ด (COLLOQUIAL) to have learned one's lesson, chastened, dare not do something again

khǐan V เขียน to write, draw

khîan V เฆี่ยน to whip

khǐan jòt-mǎai V เขียน จดหมาย to correspond (write letters)

khǐan tàwp V เขียนตอบ to reply (in writing)

khǐang N เขียง a chopping board

khǐao ADJ เขียว green (for a list of the most common colors see the entry under **sǐi** สี which means 'color')

khíao V เคี้ยว to chew

khìi V ขี่ to ride (a motorbike/ horse)

khìi jàk-krá-yaan V ขี่จักรยาน to ride a bike

khîi N ขี้ feces, excrement (shit – although the Thai word is in no way rude or

coarse as is the English term)

khîi aai ADJ ขี้อาย given to shyness (actually 'extremely shy')

khii-bawt N (from English) คีย์บอร์ด keyboard (of computer)

khîi kiat ADJ ขี้เกียจ to be lazy

khîi mao N, ADJ ขี้เมา a drunkard; alcoholic

khîi nĭao ADJ ขี้เหนียว to be stingy

khîi phûeng N ขี้ผึ้ง wax

khîi yaa N ขี้ยา a junkie, drug addict

khiim N คีม pliers

khĭng N ขิง ginger

khít V คิด to think, have an opinion

khít dàwk bîa V คิดดอกเบี้ย to charge interest (on a loan etc.), or simply **khít dàwk** คิดดอก

khít mâak ADJ (COLLOQUIAL) คิดมาก to be anxious/overly sensitive, to worry incessantly

khít mâi thŭeng ADJ, V คิด ไม่ถึง (to be) unexpected; to assume something wouldn't happen

khít tang V (COLLOQUIAL) คิด ตังค์ to ask for the bill in a downmarket restaurant or eatery on the street

khít thŭeng V คิดถึง to miss (e.g. a loved one)

khiu N (from English – although in practice the concept generally has little meaning in Thailand) คิว queue, line

khíu N คิ้ว eyebrow

khláai ADJ คล้าย to be similar, analogous

khlâwng ADJ คล่อง to be fluent (in a language), to do something physical well

khlawng N (often written in English as 'klong') คลอง canal, watercourse, channel

khlâwt lûuk V คลอดลูก to give birth (to a child)

khlohn N โคลน mud, slush

khlûean thîi V เคลื่อนที่ to move

khlûehn N คลื่น a wave (in the sea)

248

khlùi N ขลุ่ย flute

khlum v คลุม to cover

khlum khruea ADJ คลุมเครือ to be vague, ambiguous

khoei ADV เคย ever – used to ask questions in the form 'have you ever…?' To respond 'yes (I have)' the answer can simply be **khoei** เคย. As for a negative response ('I have never…') the answer is simply **mâi khoei** ไม่เคย

khŏei N เขย male in-law (son-in-law, brother-in-law)

khoei pai v เคยไป to have been to somewhere before

khoei tham v เคยทำ to have done something before

khoei tua v (COLLOQUIAL) เคยตัว to be habitual; used to doing something (e.g. going to bed very late etc.)

khohm fai N โคมไฟ lamp

khóhng ADJ โค้ง curved, convex

khóhng N โค้ง a curve, a bend in the road

khoi v คอย to wait for

khôi ADV ค่อย gradually, little by little

khôi yang chûa v ค่อยยัง ชั่ว to get better from an illness, to be on the mend

khŏm ADJ ขม bitter (taste)

khom ADJ คม to be sharp (of knives, razors, etc.)

khŏn N ขน body hair

khôn ADJ ข้น thick (of liquids), to be condensed (e.g. condensed milk)

khon N คน person, people; classifier for people

khon à-meh-rí-kan N คน อเมริกัน American (person)

khon áwt-sà-treh-lia N คน ออสเตรเลีย Australian (person)

khon bâa N คนบ้า a lunatic, mad person

khon chái N คนใช้ a servant

khon diao ADJ คนเดียว on one's own, alone; single (only one), sole

khon fâo ráan N คนเฝ้าร้าน shopkeeper

khon jiin N (pronounced 'jean') คนจีน Chinese (person)

khon jon N คนจน a poor person, someone who is poor

khon kao-lǐi N คนเกาหลี a Korean (person)

khon khâi N คนไข้ a patient, a sick person

khon khàp N คนขับ driver

khôn khîi kohng N คนขี้โกง a cheat, a dishonest/crooked person

khon lao N คนลาว a Laotian person

khón phóp V ค้นพบ to discover, find out

khon plàehk nâa N คนแปลกหน้า a stranger

khǒn sàt N ขนสัตว์ wool

khon sòehp N คนเสิร์ฟ waiter, waitress

khon thîi... คนที่ the one/ person who...

khong ADV คง probably, possibly

khóp V คบ to associate (with), socialize

khòp khǎn ADJ ขบขัน to be humorous

khrai PRON ใคร who? whom

khrai kâw dâi ใครก็ได้

anybody at all, anyone, e.g. in response to a question such as: 'who can go into the park?' (answer) **khrai kâw dâi** ใครก็ได้ anybody at all/anyone

khráng N ครั้ง time; classifier for times, occasions – e.g. to say 'five times' is the number 5 (**hâa**) followed by **khráng** ครั้ง

khráng kàwn ADV ครั้ง ก่อน (**kàwn** pronounced 'gorn' with a low tone) previously, before; the last time

khráng khraaw ADV ครั้งคราว occasionally, from time to time

khráng râek ADV ครั้งแรก the first time

khrao N (often pronounced by Thais very similar to the English word 'cow') เครา beard

khráp ครับ (often pronounced like 'cup' with a high tone) male polite particle

khráw ráai N เคราะห์ร้าย misfortune

khrâwp khrawng v ครอบ
ครอง to occupy, rule over,
possess

khrâwp khrua N ครอบครัว
family

khrêng khrát ADJ เคร่งครัด
strict, observant (of rules,
regulations, religious
teachings)

khriim N (from English) ครีม
cream

khrístian N คริสเตียน
Christian; **chaw khrít** N
ชาวคริสต์ a Christian

khrohng kaan N โครงการ
project, scheme, program
(e.g. as in some form of
development project etc.)

khrohng sâang N โครงสร้าง
structure (of a building, of
society)

khrók N (pronounced 'crock')
ครก mortar (for pulversing
and grinding spices/
ingredients for a meal)

khróp ADJ, ADV ครบ to be
complete/full (e.g. set of
items)

khróp thûan ADJ ครบถ้วน
in full

khrù khrà ADJ ขรุขระ rough,
uneven, bumpy (surfaces –
e.g. a road)

khrua N ครัว kitchen

khruea khàai N เครือข่าย
network

khrûeang N เครื่อง machine

khrûeang bin N เครื่องบิน an
aeroplane/airplane

**khrûeang bin àwk kii-
mohng** เครื่องบินออกกี่โมง
What is the departure time?

**khrûeang bin thŭeng kii-
mohng** เครื่องบินถึงกี่โมง
What is the arrival time?

**khrûeang bin pai... kii-
chûa-mohng** เครื่องบินไป...
กี่ชั่วโมง How long is the
flight to …?

khrûeang dùehm N เครื่องดื่ม
drink(s), refreshment(s)

khrûeang fai fáa N
เครื่องไฟฟ้า electrical
appliance(s), electrical
goods

khrûeang jàk N เครื่องจักร
machine(ry)

khrûeang khĭan N เครื่อง
เขียน stationery

khrûeang khít lêhk N เครื่อง

คิดเลข calculator

khrûeang mueh N เครื่องมือ tool, utensil, instrument

khrûeang nawn N เครื่องนอน bedding, bedclothes

khrûeang phét phloi N เครื่องเพชรพลอย jewelry

khrûeang prà-dàp kaai N เครื่องประดับกาย bodily ornaments, accessories in fashion contexts

khrûeang ráp thoh-rá-sàp N เครื่องรับโทรศัพท์ an answering machine

khrûeang thêht N เครื่องเทศ spice(s)

khrûeang yon N เครื่องยนต์ an engine, a machine

khrûeng ADJ ครึ่ง half

khruu N ครู teacher

khruu yài N ครูใหญ่ headmaster

khuai N ควย (EXTREMELY RUDE SLANG) penis (or, more accurately – dick/prick/cock)

khuan AUX V ควร should, ought to

khùan V ขวน to scratch (as in a cat scratching

something with its paws), scrape

khùap N ขวบ year – when used to refer to child's age, used for up to approximately ten years old

khùat N ขวด bottle

khùean N เขื่อน a dam

khuehn V คืน to give back, return

khuehn N คืน night

khuehn níi N คืนนี้ tonight

khûen V ขึ้น to rise, ascend, go up; to increase; to board/get on (e.g. a bus/plane)

khûen chàai N ขึ้นฉ่าย Chinese celery

khûen krûeang-bin prà-tou à-rai ขึ้นเครื่องบินประตูไร What is the boarding gate?

khûen rót thîi chaan-chaa-laa nǎi ขึ้นรถที่ชานชาลาไหน At which platform/terminal can I get on the bus/train?

khûen sǎay nǎi pai... ขึ้นสายไหนไป... Which number/line does it go to?

khûen yùu kàp ขึ้นอยู่กับ

252

(COLLOQUIAL) it depends on…

khui v คุย to chat

khúk N คุก jail, prison, the slammer

khúkkîi N (from English) คุกกี้ cookie, sweet biscuit

khun pron คุณ you (respectful form of address)

khún khoei คุ้นเคย to be used to, accustomed to (also the more colloquial term **chin** ชิน)

khún khoei kàp... คุ้นเคย กับ... to be acquainted/ familiar with...

khun naai คุณนาย sir/ madam (term of address – NOTE: this would only ever be used by a Thai person as it is integral to the very hierarchial nature of Thai society. For a non-Thai to address someone like this would be very odd)

khun-ná-sŏmbàt N คุณสมบัติ (educational) qualification, characteristic

khun pâa pron คุณป้า aunt

(respectful address to an older lady)

khùu v ขู่ to threaten

khûu N คู่ a pair

khûu khàeng N คู่แข่ง rival, competitor

khûu mân N คู่หมั้น fiancé, fiancée

khûu mueh N คู่มือ manual, handbook (e.g. instruction booklet for appliance etc.)

khûu nawn N คู่นอน lover, sexual partner (or, to use that dreadful expression 'fuck buddy')

khûu sŏmrót N (FORMAL) คู่สมรส partner, spouse

khuun v คูณ to multiply

khwǎa ADJ ขวา right (i.e. on the right)

khwǎa mueh ADJ ขวามือ right-hand side

khwaai N ควาย a water buffalo

khwaam N ความ the sense, the substance, the gist (of a matter, an account), also **khwaam...** ความ ...ness, commonly used by being placed in front of

253

adjectives/verbs to form abstract nouns expressing a state or quality: e.g. '...ness' as in **khwaam dii** ความดี goodness, virtue (see other examples in the following entries)

khwaam chûai lǔea N ความช่วยเหลือ help, assistance

khwaam chûea N ความเชื่อ belief, faith

khwaam hěn N ความเห็น opinion

khwaam ìtchǎa N ความอิจฉา jealousy

khwaam jam-pen N ความจำเป็น need, necessity

khwaam jàroehn N ความเจริญ progress

khwaam jèp pùai N ความเจ็บป่วย illness

khwaam jing N ความจริง truth, the truth

khwaam khao-róp N ความเคารพ respect

khwaam khít N ความคิด idea, thoughts

khwaam khlǔean wǎi N ความเคลื่อนไหว movement, motion

khwaam khrîat N ความเครียด tension, stress (COLLOQUIAL) **khrîat** เครียด to be stressed out

khwaam klìat N ความเกลียด hatred

khwaam klua N ความกลัว fear

khwaam kòt dan N ความกดดัน pressure

khwaam kròht N ความโกรธ anger

khwaam kwâang N ความกว้าง width

khwaam lambàak N ความลำบาก hardship

khwaam láp N ความลับ secret, confidentiality

khwaam lóm lěhw N ความล้มเหลว failure, bankruptcy

khwaam mǎai N ความหมาย meaning (i.e. the 'meaning' of something)

khwaam mâi sà-ngòp N ความไม่สงบ a disturbance, turmoil, absence of peace

khwaam mân-khong N ความมั่นคง security

khwaam mân-jai N ความมั่นใจ confidence

khwaam òp-ùn N ความอบอุ่น warmth

khwaam phá-yaa-yaam N ความพยายาม attempt, effort

khwaam phìt N ความผิด fault, mistake, error

khwaam plàwt phai N ความปลอดภัย safety

khwaam rák N ความรัก love, affection

khwaam ráp phìt châwp N ความรับผิดชอบ responsibility

khwaam ráp rúu N ความรับรู้ awareness

khwaam rew N ความเร็ว speed

khwaam rúu N ความรู้ knowledge

khwaam rúu-sùek N ความรู้สึก feeling, emotion

khwaam sà-àat N ความสะอาด cleanliness

khwaam sǎa-mâat N ความสามารถ ability, capacity (to fulfill a task)

khwaam sǎmkhan N ความสำคัญ importance

khwaam sǎmrèt N ความสำเร็จ success

khwaam song jam N (jam pronounced 'jum' as in 'jumble') ความทรงจำ memory (i.e. one's memory)

khwaam sǒngsǎi N ความสงสัย suspicion, curiosity

khwaam sǒn-jai N ความสนใจ interest (in something)

khwaam sǔung N ความสูง height

khwaam taai N ความตาย death

khwaam tàehk tàang N ความแตกต่าง difference (between this and that)

khwaam tâng-jai N ความตั้งใจ intention

khwaam thâo thiam N ความเท่าเทียม equality

khwaam yâak jon N ความยากจน poverty

khwaam yaow N ความยาว length

khwaan N ควาญ mahout/elephant keeper/driver

khwâang V ขว้าง to throw, hurl

khwǎang V ขวาง to impede, obstruct, thwart

khwǎang thaang v ขวางทาง to bar/block the way

khwǎang thíng v ขว้างทิ้ง to throw away, throw out

khwǎehn v แขวน to hang (e.g. a picture on the wall)

khwan N ควัน smoke (e.g. from a fire)

L

lá ละ per, each one: e.g. **pii lá khráng** ปีละครั้ง once a year

lâ ล่ะ a particle used at the end of an utterance to ask the following sort of question: 'and what about…?'

lâa v ล่า to hunt

láa ADJ ล้า lag, be tired

lá-aai v ละอาย to feel ashamed

laa àwk v ลาออก to resign, quit (a job)

lâa cháa ADJ ล่าช้า late/tardy

laa kàwn v ลาก่อน to say goodbye, farewell

laa-mók ADJ ลามก obscene, lewd, smutty

laa phák v ลาพัก to take leave (from work)

laa pùai v ลาป่วย to take sick leave

lâa sùt ADV ล่าสุด the latest; also – at the latest

lǎai ADJ หลาย many, various, several

laai N, ADJ ลาย design/pattern (e.g. on a T-shirt/piece of material); patterned, striped

laai mue N ลายมือ handwriting, fingerprint

laai sen N ลายเซ็น signature

lǎai sìp ADJ หลายสิบ tens of, multiples of ten, many

lâam N ล่าม (an) interpreter

láan NUM ล้าน million

lǎan N หลาน grandchild, niece, nephew

laan N ลาน open space, ground

lǎan chaai N หลานชาย grandson, nephew

laan jàwt rót N ลานจอดรถ a parking lot

lǎan khǒei N หลานเขย the husband of one's niece or granddaughter

256

lǎan sǎow N หลานสาว granddaughter, niece

lǎan sà-phái N หลานสะใภ้ the wife of one's nephew or grandson

lâat yaang V ลาดยาง paved with asphalt

laang N ลาง omen, portent, sign

lâang ADV ล่าง below, beneath

láang V ล้าง to wash/rinse/ cleanse (e.g. dishes, a car, one's face, etc., not clothes)

laang dii N ลางดี good omen, favorable sign

láang jaan V ล้างจาน to wash the dishes

laang ráai N ลางร้าย bad/ evil omen

láe CONJ (pronounced something like **léh!**) และ and

lâehk chék V แลกเซ็ค to cash a check/cheque

lâehk ngoehn V (COLLOQUIAL) แลกเงิน to change money

lâehk ngoehn dâi thîi nǎi แลกเงินได้ที่ไหน Where can I exchange money?; **khǎw**

lâehk-ngoehn...dawn-lâa ขอ แลกเงิน...ดอลลาร์ I'd like to exchange...dollars.

lâehk plîan V แลกเปลี่ยน to trade, exchange

lǎehm ADJ แหลม pointed, jagged; sharp (as in bright/ clever)

lâen ruea V แล่นเรือ to sail a boat

láew ADV แล้ว already – a word which indicates completion/past tense: go already = gone **pai láew** ไปแล้ว; **láew** แล้ว is also commonly used in conversation to 'connect' statements, meaning, for example, either 'then (so and so happened)', or 'and then (that happened)'

láew jà thammai (COLLOQUIAL) แล้วจะทำไม So what!

láew tàeh IDIOM (COLLOQUIAL) แล้วแต่ it depends, as you like, (that's) up to (so and so)

lǎi V ไหล to flow

lá-iat ADJ ละเอียด fine,

257

delicate, to be pulverized
(into powder/small pieces),
meticulous/careful
(craftsmanship)

lâi àwk v ไล่ออก to fire
someone

lâi pai v ไล่ไป to chase away,
chase out

lâi taam v ไล่ตาม to chase
after

lák láwp v ลักลอบ to
smuggle (e.g. drugs, etc.)

lák yím N ลักยิ้ม dimple

làk mueang N หลักเมือง Lak
Muang, the city pillar

lá-khawn N (pronounced
'làcorn') ละคร play,
theatrical production

lá-khawn thii wii N ละครทีวี
television soap opera

láksànà N ลักษณะ
characteristic(s), (the)
nature or appearance (of
something)

làk-thǎan N หลักฐาน
evidence

lambàak ADJ (**lam** pronounced
like 'lum' in 'lumber',
bàak like 'bark') ลำบาก
troublesome, tough (life)

lam iang ADJ ลำเอียง partial

lam-yai N ลำไย longan (fruit)

lǎng N, ADV หลัง back (part of
body); back, rear

lǎng jàak CONJ หลังจาก after

lǎng jàak nán ADV หลังจากนั้น
afterwards, then

lǎng-khaa N หลังคา roof

lang mái N ลังไม้ wooden
box, crate

lâo N เหล้า spirits, liquor,
alcohol

lâo v เล่า to tell a story, relate

laow N ลาว Laos (the
country), Lao (people/
language)

làp v หลับ to sleep, nap; **làp
taa** v หลับตา to close/shut
one's eyes

làp nai v หลับใน to daydream

látthí N ลัทธิ sect, doctrine,
creed

látthí hǐnná-yaan N ลัทธิ
หินยาน Lesser vehicle of
Buddhism, Hinayana

látthí khaa-thawlìk N
ลัทธิคาทอลิก Roman
Catholicism

látthí khǒng júeh N ลัทธิ
ขงจื๊อ Confucianism

látthí má-hǎa-yaan N ลัทธิ มหายาน Greater vehicle of Buddhism, Mahayana

làw ADJ (pronounced 'lor' with a low tone) หล่อ to be handsome

láw N (pronounced 'lor' with a high tone) ล้อ wheel; **sǎam láw** สามล้อ a trishaw (and common word for 'tuk-tuk' – a motorized 'trishaw')

láwk V (from English – and pronounced much like the English word) ล็อก to lock

láwk láew ADJ ล็อกแล้ว to be locked

làwk luang V (làwk pronounced like 'lork') หลอกลวง to deceive (in colloquial speech commonly just **làwk** หลอก)

lawng V ลอง to try, to try out, attempt (to do something), experiment (in the sense of trying something)

lawng sài V ลองใส่ to try on (clothes)

làwt N หลอด tube, (drinking) straw

láwt-toeh-rîi N (from English) ล็อตเตอรี่ lottery

lêhk N เลข number, numeral

lêhk khîi N เลขคี่ (an) odd number

lêhk khûu N เลขคู่ (an) even number

lêhkhǎa N เลขา secretary

lehn N (from English) เลน lane (of a highway)

lehw ADJ เลว bad (of a person)

lěhw ADJ เหลว the opposite of solid, e.g. liquid-like

lék ADJ เล็ก little, small, diminutive

lèk N เหล็ก iron, metal

lèk klâa N เหล็กกล้า steel

lék nói ADJ เล็กน้อย small, not much, a tiny bit

lêm N เล่ม classifier used when counting or referring to numbers of books, candles, knives

len N เลนส์ (from English) lens (of a camera)

lên V เล่น to play

lên don-trii V เล่นดนตรี to play musical instruments

lên pai thûa V เล่นไปทั่ว to

259

play around
lên tôh khlûehn v
เล่นโต้คลื่น to surf/ride a
surfboard
lép N เล็บ nail(s) – as in
fingernail(s), toenail(s), also
– for animals – 'claws'
lép mueh N เล็บมือ
fingernail
lép tháo N เล็บเท้า toenail
lia v เลีย to lick
lian v เลียน to imitate, copy,
mimic; (also, more fully)
lian bàehp v เลียนแบบ to
copy (e.g. someone else's
style of dressing etc.)
lîan ADJ เลี่ยน greasy, oily,
fatty (food)
líang v เลี้ยง to bring up,
raise (children or animals);
to treat (someone/a friend/
acquaintance, e.g. by
taking them out for drinks
or dinner – food or drinks)
líao v เลี้ยว to turn, make
a turn
líao klàp v เลี้ยวกลับ to turn
around
lín N ลิ้น tongue
lín-chák N ลิ้นชัก drawer

ling N ลิง monkey
lín-jìi N ลิ้นจี่ lychee (fruit)
lip N (from English) ลิฟต์ lift,
elevator
lít N (from English) ลิตร liter
lôehk v เลิก to cease/stop/
give up (e.g. smoking
cigarettes)
lôehk kan v เลิกกัน to break
off a relationship
loei เลย a word used
in a number of senses
such as: 'therefore, so,
beyond'; also used to
intensify adjective, often in
conjunction with 'no/not' –
in this sense meaning '... at
all'. For example: 'no good
at all' **mâi dii loei** ไม่ดีเลย,
or 'not expensive at all' **mâi
phaehng loei** ไม่แพงเลย
lôh N โหล dozen
lôhk N โลก the earth, world
loi v ลอย to float
loi náam v ลอยน้ำ to float in
the water
lom N ลม wind, breeze
lôm ADJ ล่ม capsized/
overturned (boat)
lóm v ล้ม to topple, fall over,

260

collapse; to overthrow (a government)

lom bâa mǔu N ลมบ้าหมู epilepsy

lom hǎai jai N, V ลมหายใจ breath; to breathe

lom jàp V (COLLOQUIAL) ลมจับ about to faint, about to have a fainting spell; (also, more commonly) **pen lom** เป็นลม to faint/pass out

lóm lá-laai V ล้มละลาย to go bankrupt, be wiped out financially

lom phát ADJ, V ลมพัด windy; (the wind) is blowing

lǒng V หลง to be infatuated (with), to be crazy about (someone or something)

long V ลง to go downwards; to land (plane), get off (transport): **khǎw long thîi…** ของลงที่… I'd like to get off at …

lǒng (thaang) V หลง (ทาง) to get lost, lose one's way (literally and metaphorically)

long kha-naehn sĭang V ลงคะแนนเสียง to vote

long maa V ลงมา to come down

long phung V (COLLOQUIAL) ลงพุง to get paunchy, develop a gut

long tha-bian V ลงทะเบียน to register

long thun V ลงทุน to invest (e.g. in a business)

lóp V ลบ to subtract, deduct, minus (in doing mathematical calculations); to erase (e.g. the writing on a blackboard)

lòp V หลบ to avoid, evade, duck, shy away from

lót V ลด to reduce, decrease, lower

lót long V ลดลง to decrease, lessen, reduce

lót náam-nàk V ลดน้ำหนัก to lose weight, diet (the English word 'diet' has also found its way into Thai and pronounced in a similar way)

lót raa-khaa V ลดราคา to discount or reduce the price

lŭam ADJ หลวม loose (the opposite of 'tight')

lúan ADV ล้วน all/the whole lot, completely

lǔang ADJ หลวง great, (owned by the) state, royal: **thànǒn lǔang** N ถนนหลวง public road/thoroughfare; **mueang lǔang** N เมืองหลวง capital city; (COLLOQUIAL) **nai lǔang** ในหลวง His Majesty the King

lúang V ล่วง to go beyond/exceed (rules, the law); to trespass (against someone), violate, infringe

lúang krà-pǎo V ล้วงกระเป๋า to pickpocket

lûat N ลวด wire

lûat nǎam N ลวดหนาม barbed wire

lǔea V เหลือ to be left over

lûeai N เลื่อย a saw

lûeai V เลื้อย to crawl, slither (as a snake)

lûeak V เลือก to pick, choose, select

lûeak dâi V เลือกได้ to be optional, to have the choice

lûean V เลื่อน to put off, delay

lûean àwk pai V เลื่อนออกไป

to postpone, delay

lǔeang เหลือง yellow (for a list of the most common colors see the entry under **sǐi** สี which means 'color')

lûeat N เลือด blood

luehm V ลืม to forget

luehm taa V ลืมตา to open one's eyes

luehm tua V ลืมตัว to forget oneself, lose one's self-control

lûehn V, ADJ ลื่น to slip, to be slippery

lúek ADJ ลึก deep (e.g. water), profound

lúek láp ADJ ลึกลับ to be mysterious

lúk V ลุก to stand, get up, rise

lúk khûen V ลุกขึ้น to get up (from bed)

lǔm sòp N หลุมศพ grave

lún V (COLLOQUIAL) ลุ้น to back/support/cheer (e.g. a team); to win (a prize in a competition)

lung N, PRON ลุง uncle – either parent's older brother; also used as a pronoun (i.e. 'you' or 'he') to refer to an

262

older unrelated male in a
friendly way

lûuk N ลูก child (offspring);
classifier for small round
objects, e.g. fruit, and
'ball-like' things

lûuk anthá N ลูกอัณฑะ
(medical term) testicle(s)

lûuk chaai N ลูกชาย son

lûuk chín N ลูกชิ้น meat/pork/
fish ball(s), one of the main
ingredients in noodle soup

lûuk fàet N ลูกแฝด twins

lûuk kháa N ลูกค้า customer,
client

lûuk khŏei N ลูกเขย son-
in-law

lûuk khrûeng N ลูกครึ่ง
person of mixed race
(e.g. European+Asian =
'Eurasian')

lûuk lăan N ลูกหลาน
descendant(s)

lûuk măa N ลูกหมา puppy/
puppies

lûuk maew N ลูกแมว
kitten(s)

lûuk náwng N ลูกน้อง
employee(s)

lûuk phîi lûuk náwng N ลูกพี่

lûuk náwng cousin

lûuk phûu chaai N, ADJ ลูก
ผู้ชาย man; (to be) manly

lûuk săow N ลูกสาว daughter

lûuk-sà-phái N ลูกสะใภ้
daughter-in-law

lûuk taa N (commonly pronounced **lûuk-kàtaa** ลูกกะ
ตา) ลูกตา eyeball(s)

lûuk thûng N ลูกทุ่ง country/
hillbilly; **phlehng lûuk
thûng** N เพลงลูกทุ่ง (Thai)
popular country music;
also used for 'country
music' more generally

M

máa N ม้า horse (NOTE: **máa
laai** ม้าลาย zebra)

măa N หมา dog

maa v, N มา to come; also
indicates time up to the
present; direction

maa jàak v มาจาก to come
from, originate

maa jàak năi มาจากไหน
common question form:
'Where do you come from/

where does it come from?' etc.

maa láew v (COLLOQUIAL) มาแล้ว to have arrived, to have come already: e.g. **khǎo maa láew** เขามาแล้ว 'He's/she's come; he's/she's already here.'

maa nîi (COLLOQUIAL) มานี่ Come here

maa sǎai (COLLOQUIAL) มาสาย to be late (e.g. for school, work, etc.)

maa sî (COLLOQUIAL) มาสิ Come on, come along there

mǎi lêhk thoh-rásàp N หมายเลขโทรศัพท์ telephone number

mâak ADJ มาก many, much, a lot ADV very

màak N หมาก betel nut (which was widely used/chewed in Thailand in the past, leaving a dark reddish stain on the lips, gums, teeth)

màak fàràng N หมากฝรั่ง chewing gum

mâak khûehn ADJ มากขึ้น more, increasing (e.g. the

cost of living, the number of tourists)

mâak koehn pai ADJ มากเกินไป too much

mâak kwàa ADJ มากกว่า more than (something else), e.g. to like something more than another thing

màak rúk N หมากรุก chess

mâak thîi sùt ADJ มากที่สุด (the) most

maa-lehsia N มาเลเซีย Malaysia, Malaysian

mâan N (pronounced 'marn' with a falling tone) ม่าน curtains, drapes

maandaa N มารดา (FORMAL) mother

maa-rá-yâat N มารยาท conduct, behavior, manners, etiquette

maa-rá-yâat dii ADJ มารยาทดี to have good manners, to be well-mannered

mâat-trà-thǎan N มาตรฐาน standard, specification(s) (e.g. of goods/services, etc.)

mâeh N แม่ mother

mâeh bâan N แม่บ้าน house-

keeper, housewife, lady of
the house

mâeh khrua N, FEM แม่ครัว
cook

mâeh kunjaeh N แม่กุญแจ a
padlock

mâeh mâai N แม่ม่าย a
widow

mâeh náam N แม่น้ำ river

mâeh sǎa-mii N แม่สามี
mother-in-law; also **mâeh
yaai** N แม่ยาย

máeh tàeh แม้แต่ even
(though), not even

máeh wâa แม้ว่า though, if,
no matter

maew N แมว a cat

maew náam N แมวน้ำ a seal

má-hǎa-chon N มหาชน the
public, the masses

má-hǎa sà-mùt N มหาสมุทร
ocean

máhǎa sèht-thǐi N มหาเศรษฐี
millionare, a very wealthy
person

má-hǎa witthá-yaa-lai
N มหาวิทยาลัย university
(COLLOQUIAL) **máhǎalai**
มหาลัย

mâi ADV ไม่ no, not (used with

verbs and adjectives)

mǎi ไหม common question
particle used at the end of
an utterance, e.g. 'is it good/
is it any good?' (written with
a rising tone but commonly
pronounced with a high
tone) **dii mǎi** ดีไหม

mài ADJ ใหม่ new

mái N ไม้ wood

mǎi N ไหม silk

mai N ไมล์ (from English) mile

mâi V ไหม้ to burn

mâi châi ADV ไม่ใช่ is not,
are not, am not, No, it's
not!, No!

mâi châwp V ไม่ชอบ not
to like (something/
somebody), to dislike

mâi hâi V ไม่ให้ not to give,
not to let, not to, without

mâi hěn dûai V ไม่เห็นด้วย to
disagree

mâi jampen ADJ ไม่จำเป็น
to be unnecessary, not
necessary

mái jîm fan N ไม้จิ้มฟัน
toothpick(s)

mái khwǎen sûea N ไม้แขวน
เสื้อ coat hanger

mái khìit fai N ไม้ขีดไฟ
matches

mâi khít ngoehn ADJ
(COLLOQUIAL) ไม่คิดเงิน free
of charge

mâi khoei ADV ไม่เคย never

mâi khôi mii ADJ (COLLOQUIAL)
ไม่ค่อยมี there's hardly any,
hard to find, scarce

mâi kìi... ADJ ไม่กี่ few..., e.g.
mâi kìi khon ไม่กี่คน few
people

mái kwàat N ไม้กวาด broom

mâi mâak kâw nói
(COLLOQUIAL) ไม่มาก
ก็น้อย more or less

mâi mii ADJ ไม่มี no (in
response to questions such
as 'have you a.../have you
got any?'), there's none/
there isn't any (NOTE: when
translated literally **mâi
mii** means 'no have' – an
expression you commonly
hear in Thailand from
those who haven't really
studied English)

mâi mii àrai ไม่มีอะไร
(COLLOQUIAL) 'no/nothing'
in response to such questions

as 'what's the matter?',
'what's on you mind?',
'what are you thinking?'

mâi mii khâw phùuk mát
EXP ไม่มีข้อผูกมัด to be free
of commitments

mâi mii khrai ไม่มีใคร
nobody (e.g. there is
nobody at home/I don't
have anyone [to help me
etc.])

mâi mii khwaam sùk ADJ
ไม่มีความสุข to be unhappy

mâi mii prà-yòht ADJ ไม่มี
ประโยชน์ to be of no use, to
be useless

mâi mii thaang
(COLLOQUIAL) ไม่มีทาง no
way (I'm doing that)

mâi nâa chûeah ADJ
(COLLOQUIAL) ไม่น่าเชื่อ
unbelievable, incredible

mái pàa diao kan ไม้ป่า
เดียวกัน EXP (SLANG)
homosexual (male) – i.e.
'wood from the same
jungle/forest'

mâi pen rai (common
idiomatic Thai expression)
ไม่เป็นไร don't mention

it!, never mind!, you're
welcome!, it doesn't
matter, it's nothing

mâi phaehng ADJ ไม่แพง to
be inexpensive

mâi phèt ADJ ไม่เผ็ด mild (not
spicy)

mâi prà-sòp phŏn sămrèt
V (SOMEWHAT FORMAL)
ไม่ประสบผลสำเร็จ to fail, to
be unsuccessful

mâi run raehng ADJ ไม่รุนแรง
mild (not very strong, e.g.
taste), (or, alternatively)
not violent (**run raehng**
รุนแรง means 'violent')

mâi rúu-jàk V ไม่รู้จัก (pronounced something like
'roo-juck') (COLLOQUIAL)
not to know someone or
something

mâi sà-baai ADJ ไม่สบาย
sick, ill

mâi sà-baai jai ADJ ไม่สบายใจ
(to feel) upset, unhappy

mâi săm-khan ADJ ไม่สำคัญ
not important, unimportant

mái sìap N ไม้เสียบ skewer
(e.g. a satay stick)

mâi sùk ADJ ไม่สุก (to be)

unripe

mâi su-phâap ADJ ไม่สุภาพ
impolite, rude

mâi tâwng V ไม่ต้อง not to
have to

mái tháo N ไม้เท้า walking
stick, cane

mák jà ADV ... มักจะ often,
usually, regularly

mák ngâai ADJ มักง่าย
careless, sloppy

má-kà-raa-khom N มกราคม
January

má-kàwk N มะกอก olive

má-khăam N มะขาม
tamarind (fruit)

má-khŭea mûang N มะเขือ
ม่วง eggplant, aubergine

má-khŭea thêht N มะเขือเทศ
tomato

mák-khú-thêht N มัคคุเทศก์
guide (i.e. tour guide)

má-laehng N แมลง insect
(general term)

má-laehng wan N แมลงวัน
fly (insect)

má-laeng-sàap N แมลงสาป
cockroach

má-lá-kaw N (kaw
pronounced like 'gore')

267

มะละกอ papaya, pawpaw

málí N มะลิ jasmine

má-mûang N มะม่วง mango

má-naow N มะนาว lemon, lime (citrus fruit)

má-phráow N มะพร้าว coconut

má-reng N มะเร็ง cancer

man ADJ มัน (SLANG) excellent, most enjoyable, to be fun, that's great

man PRON, N, ADJ มัน it; potato-like vegetables; shiny, brilliant

măn ADJ หมัน to be sterile, barren

mân V มั่น to engage (promise to marry)

man fá-ràng N มันฝรั่ง potato(es)

màn sâi V (COLLOQUIAL) หมั่น ไส้ to be disgusted (with), to be put off (by)

man thêht N มันเทศ yam(s)

mâng khâng ADJ มั่งคั่ง to (be) wealthy

mang sà-wí-rát N, ADJ มังสวิรัติ vegetarian

mang-khút N มังคุด mangosteen (fruit)

mân jai ADJ มั่นใจ confident, certain

mân-khong ADJ มั่นคง to be firm, definite, secure

mánút N มนุษย์ human (being)

máo N (from English) เมาส์ mouse (computer)

mao ADJ เมา drunk, intoxicated, stoned, wasted

mao kháang V (COLLOQUIAL) เมาค้าง to have a hangover

máruehn níi N, ADV มะรืนนี้ (the) day after tomorrow

màt N หมัด flea, fist, punch

mâw N (pronounced 'mor' with a falling tone) หม้อ (cooking) pot

măw N (pronounced 'mor' with a rising tone) หมอ doctor

maw-rà-dòk N มรดก inheritance, legacy

maw-rà-kòt N มรกต emerald

maw-rà-sŭm N มรสุม monsoon

màw sŏm ADJ เหมาะสม to be suitable/appropriate

màwk N หมอก mist, fog

măwn N หมอน pillow, cushion

mawng v มอง to watch, stare at

mawng mâi hěn v มอง ไม่เห็น to be invisible, unable to see

mâwp hâi v มอบให้ to hand over, bestow (e.g. power to incoming government/a university degree to a graduate)

mâwp tua v มอบตัว to give oneself up, surrender (to the police); to report (for duty, work etc.)

mawtoehsai N (from English) มอเตอร์ไซค์ motorcycle

mêhk mâak ADJ เมฆมาก overcast, cloudy

meh-nuu N (from English) เมนู menu

meh-sǎa-yon N เมษายน April

méht N เมตร meter

měn v, ADJ เหม็น to stink; to be stinky (NOTE: in Thai just this one word can be a whole sentence – the equivalent of 'It stinks/It smells foul' etc.)

mét N เม็ด (also pronounced **má-lét** เมล็ด) seed; classifier for small seed-like objects, e.g. pills

mí nâa là มิน่าล่ะ EXP (COLLOQUIAL) no wonder!

mia N เมีย (COLLOQUIAL) wife, defacto partner, sometimes simply 'girlfriend'

mia nói N เมียน้อย mistress

mii N หมี a bear

mii N หมี่ vermicelli, fine noodles

mii v มี to have, own; there is, there are; **khun mii... mái?** คุณมี...ไหม Do you have...?

mii amnâat ADJ มีอำนาจ to have power, to be powerful

mii chii-wít ADJ มีชีวิต live (be alive), living

mii chûeh ADJ มีชื่อ to be famous, to be well-known

mii chúu v มีชู้ (for a married person) to have a lover

mii ìt-thí-phon v มีอิทธิพล to have influence (to get things done), to have connections

mii jèht-tà-naa v มีเจตนา to

269

intend, have the intention (to)

mii khâa v มีค่า to be valuable, precious, to have worth/be useful

mii khon thoh maa (COLLOQUIAL) มีคนโทรมา someone's on the phone (i.e. someone's called me/you)

mii khun khâa v มีคุณค่า to have value (e.g. for a medicine to be useful)

mii khwaam mân-jai v มีความมั่นใจ to have confidence, to be confident

mii khwaam sùk v มีความสุข to be happy

mii klìn v มีกลิ่น to have an odor, smell bad

mii laai ADJ มีลาย patterned (to have a pattern on it), striped; (COLLOQUIAL) **tháwng laai** ท้องลาย for a woman to have 'stretch marks'

mii-naa-khom N มีนาคม March

mii phit v มีพิษ to be poisonous

mii phŏn tàw v มีผลต่อ... to affect

mii pràjam duean v มีประจำ เดือน (SOMEWHAT FORMAL) to menstruate, have one's period

mii prà-sòpkaan v มีประสบ- การณ์ to have experience, be experienced

mii prà-yòht v มีประโยชน์ to be useful

mii sà-maa-thí v มีสมาธิ to concentrate, be mindful

mii sà-nèh v (COLLOQUIAL) มีเสน่ห์ to be personable, alluring, appealing, to have charm

mii sên v มีเส้น (COLLOQUIAL) to have influence/ connections

mii sùan rûam v มีส่วนร่วม to participate/co-operate

mii tháksà v มีทักษะ skilful, to be skilled, to have skills

mii thúrá v มีธุระ to be busy, to have something to do

mîit N (pronounced like 'mead' with a falling tone) มีด knife

mít N มิตร (SOMEWHAT

270

FORMAL) friend

mít-chăa-chîip N มิจฉาชีพ wrongful/unlawful occupation; a person who makes their living from some form of criminality

mí-thù-naa-yon N มิถุนายน June

míti N มิติ dimension (e.g. as in 3D – **săm míti** สามมิติ)

mòeh ADJ เหม่อ inattentive

móh V โม้ to boast, brag

moh-hŏh ADJ โมโห to be cross/angry

mohng N โมง o'clock, e.g. 6 **mohng** 6 o'clock, hours

mŏi N หมอย (RUDE) pubic hair

mon-lá-phaa-wá N มลภาวะ pollution, also **mon-lá-phít** มลพิษ

mòt aàyú หมดอายุ V to expire (e.g. a license, a passport), past its use-by date (e.g. milk, etc.)

mòt láew ADJ (COLLOQUIAL) หมดแล้ว used up, all gone, none left

mót lûuk N มดลูก uterus, womb

mòt raehng ADJ (COLLOQUIAL) หมดแรง to have no energy left, tired out

mòt tua V หมดตัว have nothing left, be broke

mŭa ADV, ADJ (COLLOQUIAL) มั่ว haphazardly, indiscriminately; chaotic, erratic

muai N มวย boxing (general term)

muai săa-kon N มวยสากล Western-style boxing

muai thai N มวยไทย Thai boxing

mùak N หมวก hat, cap

mûang/sĭi mûang N (สี) ม่วง purple

mûea khuehn níi ADV เมื่อคืน นี้ (or simply) **mûea khuehn** เมื่อคืน last night

mûea kîi níi ADV (COLLOQUIAL) เมื่อกี้นี้, (or simply) **mûea kîi** เมื่อกี้ just a moment ago

mûeà rài เมื่อไร when?

mûeà rài kâw dâi เมื่อไร ก็ได้ (a common response to the question 'when?') whenever, any time

mûea waan níi ADV เมื่อวานนี้, (or simply) **mûea waan** เมื่อ

271

วาน yesterday

mûea waan suehn nii ADV
เมื่อวานซืนนี้ the day before
yesterday

mǔean ADJ เหมือน to
resemble, be similar to,
like, as

mueang N เมือง town,
city; also 'country' as in
the common name for
Thailand **mueang thai** เมือง
ไทย

mǔeang N (COLLOQUIAL)
เหมือง, (more fully)
mǔeang râeh เหมืองแร่ a
mine

mueang jiin N เมืองจีน China

mueang nâwk N
(COLLOQUIAL) เมืองนอก
foreign country, abroad

mueang thai N เมืองไทย
Thailand (NOTE: the most
common way Thai people
refer to their own country)

mǔean-kan ADJ, ADV เหมือนกัน
to be identical; too, either,
(in conversation if you are
of the same view as the
person you are talking to
you can say) likewise

mueh N มือ hand

múeh N มื้อ mealtime, a meal
(also commonly used when
referring to the number of
meals eaten)

mueh thǔeh N มือถือ cell
phone, mobile phone

mùehn NUM หมื่น ten
thousand

mûeht ADJ มืด dark

mûeht khrúem ADJ มืดครึ้ม to
be cloudy, overcast

mùek N หมึก ink

múk N มุก pearl

mum N มุม corner, angle

mum maam ADJ มุมมาม
sloppy, messy, uncouth in
manner

mǔn V หมุน to turn, rotate
(e.g. a knob/dial)

múng N มุ้ง mosquito net

múng lûat N มุ้งลวด fly
screen

mûng pai V, PREP มุ่งไป to
head for, towards

mút-sàlim N มุสลิม Muslim

mǔu N หมู pig, hog, boar

mùu bâan N หมู่บ้าน a village

mǔu haem N (from English)
หมูแฮม ham

272

N

ná นะ a particle used at the end of a sentence to convey a number of different meanings, e.g. 'right?' **mâi dii ná** ไม่ดีนะ 'That's no good, right?'; 'okay/OK?'; **tòk-long pai dûai kan ná** ตกลงไปด้วย กันนะ 'Agreed, let's go together, OK?'

năa ADJ หนา thick (of things)

naa N นา (irrigated) rice field, paddy field

náa N น้า aunt, uncle (a younger brother or sister of one's mother)

nâa N หน้า face, page, front (ahead); e.g. season – **nâa ráwn** หน้าร้อน summer (Feb–April); **nâa năaw** หน้า หนาว winter/cool season (Nov–Jan); **nâa fŏn** หน้าฝน rainy season (May–Oct)

nâa น่า a prefix used with verbs/adjectives to form words with endings such as -ful, -able, -y, -ing; also used to suggest that

something's worth doing, trying, sampling etc., e.g. **nâa kin** น่ากิน– appetizing, tempting, delectable, to look delicious

nâa bùea ADJ น่าเบื่อ boring, dull

nâa duu ADJ น่าดู worth seeing/watching

nâa fang ADJ น่าฟัง worth listening to

nâa itchăa ADJ น่าอิจฉา envious

nâa jà V น่าจะ ought to, might like to, would be

nâa jùup ADJ น่าจูบ kissable

nâa kàak N (pronounced 'gark' with a low tone) หน้า กาก a mask

nâa kàwt ADJ น่ากอด huggable, cuddlesome

nâa khăi nâa ADJ น่า ขายหน้า to be shameful (COLLOQUIAL) **khăi nâa** ขาย หน้า to lose face

nâa khít ADJ น่าคิด worth thinking about

nâa kliat ADJ น่าเกลียด ugly – can refer to both a person or thing as well as unseemly behavior

nâa klua ADJ น่ากลัว scary, frightening

nâa lá-aai ADJ น่าละอาย (to be) ashamed, embarrassed; to be embarrassing

nâa láeng N หน้าแล้ง dry season

nâa múet V หน้ามืด to black out, have a dizzy spell, lose control of oneself, be blind with passion

nâa òk N หน้าอก chest; also breast(s), chest

nâa phàak N หน้าผาก forehead

nâa plàehk jai ADJ น่าแปลกใจ surprising, weird

nâa prà-làat jai ADJ น่า ประหลาดใจ unusual, strange, wonderful

nâa rák ADJ น่ารัก cute, appealing, lovely, pretty (NOTE: this term is used in Thai to refer not only to people or animals, but also behavior)

nâa rák mâak ADJ น่ารักมาก very cute

nâa ram khaan ADJ น่ารำคาญ annoying

nâa rang-kiat ADJ น่ารังเกียจ disgusting

nâa sà-nùk ADJ น่าสนุก to be fun, to look like fun (i.e. it looks like fun)

nâa sàp sŏn ADJ น่าสับสน to be confusing

nâa sŏn-jai น่าสนใจ to be interesting

nâa sŏng săan ADJ น่า สงสาร to feel/express pity/ sympathy for someone else: Oh, what a pity!

nâa taa N หน้าตา countenance, look

nâa tàang N หน้าต่าง window (in house)

khăw thîi-nâng rim thaang-doen ขอที่นั่งริมหน้าต่าง Can I get a window seat?

nâa thîi N หน้าที่ duty (responsibility)

naa thîi N นาที a minute

nâa tùehn tên ADJ น่าตื่นเต้น to be exciting

nâa wái jai ADJ น่าไว้ใจ trustworthy, dependable, reliable

naai N นาย Mr, Mister, Sir, owner, employer, chief, boss

naai jâang N นายจ้าง employer

naai phâet N (FORMAL TERM) นายแพทย์ doctor

naai phon N นายพล general (in the armed forces)

naai rueah N นายเรือ captain (of a ship/vessel)

naai tamrùat N นายตำรวจ police officer

naai thá-hǎn N นายทหาร army officer

naai thun N นายทุน capitalist

naalí-kaa N นาฬิกา wristwatch, clock; o'clock in 24 hour system (i.e. **1 naalí-kaa** = one o'clock in the morning; **13 naalikaa** = one o'clock in the afternoon)

náam N น้ำ water, liquid, fluid (also see entries under **náam… below**)

náam àt lom N น้ำอัดลม soft drink, fizzy drink (Coke, Pepsi, etc.)

náam chaa N น้ำชา tea

náam hǎwm N น้ำหอม perfume

náam jai N น้ำใจ (an important Thai word expressing a very desirable trait – someone with): spirit, heart, goodwill, thoughtfulness, a willingness to help

náam jîm N น้ำจิ้ม sauce (for dipping, e.g. spring rolls, curry puffs, etc.)

náam jùet N น้ำจืด fresh water

náam khǎeng N น้ำแข็ง ice

náam khûen N น้ำขึ้น high tide

náam long N น้ำลง low tide

náam man N น้ำมัน gasoline, petrol

náam man khrûeang N น้ำมันเครื่อง engine oil

náam man ngaa N น้ำมันงา sesame oil

náam nàk N น้ำหนัก weight

náam nàk khûen V น้ำหนัก ขึ้น to gain weight, put on weight

náam nàk lót V น้ำหนักลด to lose weight

náam phǒn-lámái N น้ำผลไม้ fruit juice

náam phrík N น้ำพริก hot chili paste sauce

náam phú N น้ำพุ a spring/fountain

náam phú ráwn N น้ำพุร้อน hot spring

náam phûeng N น้ำผึ้ง honey

náam plaa N น้ำปลา fish sauce

náam prà-paa N น้ำประปา piped water, tap water, water supply (e.g. in a town/city)

naam sà-kun N นามสกุล surname, last name

náam sôm N น้ำส้ม orange juice; also (Thai) vinegar used as a condiment that can used to flavor such things as noodle soup

náam súp N น้ำซุป soup, broth

náam taa N น้ำตา tear(s)

náam taan N น้ำตาล brown (color), sugar

náam thá-leh N น้ำทะเล seawater

náam thûam N, V น้ำท่วม a flood; to flood

náam tòk N น้ำตก a waterfall

náam wăn N น้ำหวาน soft drink, flavored syrup

naan ADJ, ADV นาน long, lasting; for a long time, ages

naan thâo-rài นานเท่าไร (for) how long?

naa-naa châat ADJ นานาชาติ international

naang N นาง woman, lady; Mrs (title)

naang èhk N นางเอก leading actress, female lead, heroine

naang fáa N นางฟ้า angel, fairy

naang ngaam N นางงาม a beauty queen

naang ngaam jàkkrawaan N นางงามจักรวาล Miss Universe

naang săow N นางสาว unmarried woman, Miss/Ms (title)

naa-yók N นายก chairman, president (of a company)

naa-yók rát-thà-montrii N นายกรัฐมนตรี prime minister (COLLOQUIALLY) as **naa-yók** นายก

nâeh jai ADJ แน่ใจ certain, sure

276

nâeh nawn ADV แน่นอน certainly!, of course, exactly

nâen ADJ แน่น to be crowded; solid, tight

náe-nam V แนะนำ to suggest, advise, recommend

náe-nam tua V แนะนำตัว to introduce someone

náe-nam tua ehng V แนะนำ ตัวเอง to introduce oneself

naew N แนว line, row (e.g. of chairs etc.)

năi ADV ไหน where? which?

nai PREP ใน in, at (space), inside, within

nai à-diit ADV ในอดีต in the past

nai à-naakhót ADV ในอนาคต in the future

nai-lâwn N (from English) ไนลอน nylon

nai lŭang N (COLLOQUIAL) ในหลวง the King (of Thailand)

nai mâi cháa ADV ในไม่ช้า soon, shortly, before long

nai mueang ADJ ในเมือง downtown, urban

nai prá-thêet ADJ ในประเทศ

domestic, local

nai ra-wàng ADV ในระหว่าง during (e.g. the trip to the coast), between

nai rôm ADJ ในร่ม in the shade, indoor

nai thîi sùt ADV ในที่สุด finally, eventually, in the long run

nàk ADJ หนัก to be heavy

nàk jai ADJ หนักใจ depressed, heavy-hearted, anxious

nák นัก used as a prefix to form a word meaning – an expert, one skilled (in), or -er, fancier (see the following entries)

nák bin N นักบิน a pilot, aviator

nák doehn thaang N นักเดิน ทาง traveler

nák don trii N นักดนตรี musician

nák khàow N นักข่าว journalist

nák khĭan N นักเขียน writer

nák-lehng N นักเลง tough guy, hoodlum, ruffian

nák ráwng N นักร้อง a singer

nák rian N นักเรียน a student

nák thâwng thîao N นักท่องเที่ยว a tourist

nák thúrákìt N นักธุรกิจ businessperson

ná-khawn N นคร city, metropolis, the first part of the name in a number of Thai towns/cities/provinces, e.g. Nakhon Pathom, Nakhon Sawan, Nakhon Phanom, Nakhon Naiyok, Nakhon Sithammarat

nam v นำ to guide, lead; to head, escort

nam khâo v นำเข้า to import

nam pai v นำไป to lead (guide/take someone somewhere)

nam thîao v นำเที่ยว to guide, take (a person) around, lead a tour

nán PRON นั่น that

nân lâe! (COLLOQUIAL) นั่น แหละ exactly! just so!

nâng v นั่ง to sit: **nâng thîi-nîi dâi-mái** นั่งที่นี่ได้ไหม Do you mind if I sit here?

năng N หนัง leather

năng N หนัง film, movie

(NOTE: the same word as 'leather', this being related to a perceived likeness between the screening of early films and traditional shadow puppets whose images were illuminated on a thin leather/parchment type of screen)

nâng long v นั่งลง to sit down

nâng rót v นั่งรถ to ride (in a car, van, etc.)

năngsŭeh N หนังสือ book

năngsŭeh doehn thaang N หนังสือเดินทาง passport (the English word 'passport' is commonly used in Thailand, pronounced something like 'pars-port')

năngsŭeh nam thîao N หนังสือนำเที่ยว guidebook (such as Lonely Planet)

năngsŭeh phim N หนังสือพิมพ์ newspaper

nâo ADJ เน่า to be rotten, spoiled, (for food, etc.) to have gone off, decayed, corrupted

năow ADJ หนาว cold weather, to be cold (body

278

temperature)

nǎow sàn v หนาวสั่น to shiver

náp v นับ to count, reckon

náp thǔeh v นับถือ to respect, hold in high regard, believe in (a particular religion/faith)

nárók N นรก hell, purgatory

nát v (pronounced similar to 'nut' with a high tone) นัด to fix/set a time, make an appointment; also to sniff or snort (a substance) up the nose

nát-mǎai N นัดหมาย an appointment

nàw mái N หน่อไม้ bamboo shoot(s)

ná-wá-níyaai N นวนิยาย novel

nâwk ADJ นอก outside, beyond, outer, external

nâwk jàak PREP นอกจาก apart from, besides, except, unless

nâwk jàak níi PREP นอกจากนี้ besides, in addition, for another thing

nâwk jai v นอกใจ to be

unfaithful, adulterous

nâwk khâwk ADJ นอกคอก to be unconventional, offbeat, eccentric, non-conformist

nǎwn N หนอน worm, maggot

nawn v นอน to lie down, recline; to go to bed

nawn khwâm v นอนคว่ำ to lie face down, sleep on one's stomach

nawn làp v นอนหลับ to sleep, be asleep; the opposite – **nawn mâi làp** นอนไม่หลับ – to be unable to sleep

nawn lên v นอนเล่น to take a rest, lay about, repose

nawn ngǎai v นอนหงาย to lie/sleep on one's back

nâwng N น่อง calf (lower leg)

náwng N น้อง (COLLOQUIAL) younger brother or sister (also commonly used by Thais when speaking to an 'inferior' such as the staff in a restaurant, etc.)

náwng chaai N น้องชาย younger brother

náwng khŏei N น้องเขย

younger brother-in-law

náwng mia N น้องเมีย wife's younger sibling

náwng săamii N น้องสามี husband's younger sibling

náwng săow N น้องสาว younger sister

náwng sà-phái N น้องสะใภ้ younger sister-in-law

náwt N น็อต a bolt, nut (for building etc.)

ná-yoh-baai N นโยบาย policy (e.g. government policy)

nékthai N (from English) เน็คไท necktie

nian rîap ADJ เนียนเรียบ to be smooth (of surfaces)

nĭao ADJ เหนียว sticky, tough (e.g. chewy); (COLLOQUIAL) stingy – more fully **khîi nĭao** ขี้เหนียว

nîi PRON นี่ this; also (COLLOQUIAL; calling attention to something) hey!

nĭi V หนี to flee, run away, escape, get away

níi นี้ ADJ this: e.g. **yàang níi** อย่างนี้ 'like this'; **wan níi**

วันนี้ 'today' (i.e. this day)

nîi sĭn N หนี้สิน debt, obligation

nin thaa V นินทา to gossip about

nîng ADJ นิ่ง still, quiet

ní-săi N นิสัย habit, disposition, character

nithǎn N นิทาน fable, tale, story

nít nòi ADV นิดหน่อย slightly, a little bit

níu N นิ้ว finger; also part of the word for 'toe' **níu tháo** นิ้วเท้า; the names of the different fingers: **níu pôhng** นิ้วโป้ง thumb; **níu chíi** นิ้ว ชี้ index finger; **níu klaang** นิ้วกลาง middle finger; **níu naang** นิ้วนาง ring finger; **níu kôi** นิ้วก้อย little finger/pinky

niu-sii-laehn N นิวซีแลนด์ New Zealand

ní-yom ADJ นิยม to be interested in (e.g. fast cars); **rótsàni-yom** N รสนิยม taste, preference (e.g. in fashion, music etc.)

noehn khǎo N เนินเขา a hill

noei N เนย butter

noei khǎeng N เนยแข็ง cheese

nôhn ADV โน่น yonder, over there

nóhn ADV โน้น there, way over there (further than **nôhn**)

nói ADJ น้อย little, small, not much, few

nói kwàa ADJ น้อยกว่า less (smaller amount)

nói nàa N น้อยหน่า custard apple (fruit)

nói thîi sùt ADJ น้อยที่สุด least (the smallest amount)

nók N นก bird

nom N นม milk; breasts

nom khôn N นมข้น condensed milk

nonthá-bùrii N นนทบุรี Nonthaburi, provincial capital northwest of central Bangkok on the east bank of the Chaopraya River. Nowadays it is virtually a part of the greater Bangkok metropolitan area

nùat N หนวด mustache

nûat V นวด to massage

nǔea ADV, N เหนือ above, beyond; north

núea N เนื้อ beef, meat

núea kàe N เนื้อแกะ lamb, mutton

núea mǔu N เนื้อหมู pork (NOTE: when ordering food – simply **mǔu** หมู)

núea sàt N เนื้อสัตว์ meat, flesh

núea wua N เนื้อวัว beef

nùeay ADJ เหนื่อย to be exhausted, weary

núek V นึก to recall, to think of; (COLLOQUIAL) **nùek àwk láew** นึกออกแล้ว 'I've remembered it/I can recall it now'

nùeng NUM หนึ่ง one

nûeng V นึ่ง to steam

nùeng khûu หนึ่งคู่ a pair of

nùeng thii ADV หนึ่งที่ once

nûm ADJ นุ่ม soft

nùm ADJ, N หนุ่ม young, youthful; young man, adolescent

nùm sǎow N หนุ่มสาว teen-agers, young men and women

nûng V นุ่ง to wear, put on, be

281

clad in; **nûng phâa thǔng** นุ่งผ้าถุง to be wearing a sarong

nǔu N หนู a mouse or rat (NOTE: this word is also used by, generally, younger women as a first person [i.e. 'I'] pronoun)

NG

NOTE: '**ng**' ง is a distinct letter in Thai quite separate from '**n**' น, although here words beginning with this letter are grouped together under 'N'.

ngaa N งา sesame seeds

ngaa cháang N งาช้าง elephant tusk, ivory

ngâai ADJ ง่าย to be simple, easy

ngǎai tháwng ADJ หงายท้อง overturned, upside down (e.g. a vehicle that has rolled over onto its roof)

ngaam ADJ งาม to be beautiful, attractive; fine, good

ngaan N งาน job, work; also a party (as in 'a birthday party'), ceremony; a measure of land the equivalent of 400 sq. m.

ngaan àdìrèhk N งานอดิเรก a hobby

ngaan bâan N งานบ้าน housework

ngaan líang N งานเลี้ยง banquet

ngaan pii mài N งานปีใหม่ new year festival

ngaan sòp N งานศพ funeral

ngaan tàeng-ngaan N งานแต่งงาน wedding

ngaan wát N งานวัด a fair held within the Buddhist temple grounds

ngaan wí jai N งานวิจัย research work

ngâeh N แง่ (an) angle

ngai (COLLOQUIAL) ไง what; how; (COLLOQUIAL EXPRESSIONS) **pen ngai** เป็นไง 'How are things?', 'How are you?', 'And then what?'; **láew ngai** แล้วไง 'So?', 'So what'; 'And then?'; **wâa ngai** ว่าไง

'What did you say?', 'What did he/she say?'

ngán-ngán ADJ (COLLOQUIAL) งั้นๆ average (so-so, just okay)

ngáp v งับ to snap, snap at, nip, clamp, close, shut

ngát v งัด to pry out, force up, raise with a lever

ngăo ADJ เหงา lonely

ngao N, ADJ เงา shadow, reflection; glossy, shiny, lustrous

ngáw N (áw pronounced very short) เงาะ rambutan (fruit)

ngaw ngae ADJ งอแง fussy, childish, crying like a baby, clumsy

ngâwk v งอก to sprout, shoot, germinate;
thùa ngâwk ถั่วงอก beansprout(s)

ngawn v งอน to pout, show displeasure (esp. women, children), feign displeasure

ngîan N, ADJ เงี่ยน (a) strong urge (for), craving (for); horny, randy, having the hots for (someone)

ngîap ADJ, v เงียบ to be quiet, silent; (also used to say – rather brusquely) 'be quiet!'

ngoehn N เงิน money, silver, cash

ngoehn duean N เงินเดือน salary

ngoehn fàak N เงินฝาก deposit (money deposited in a bank)

ngoehn mát-jam N (pronounced 'mutt-jum') เงิน มัดจำ a deposit (e.g. on a car, etc)

ngoehn sòt N เงินสด cash, money

ngoehn traa N (FORMAL) เงิน ตรา currency

ngôh ADJ โง่ to be stupid

ngôi N ง่อย having a disability

ngók ADJ งก greedy, gluttonous, avaricious, stingy, mean

ngom-ngaai v งมงาย to be credulous, believe in something blindly

ngong ADJ งง to be puzzled, stunned, befuddled

ngòp-prà-maan N งบ ประมาณ budget

ngûang ADJ ง่วง, ง่วงนอน to be sleepy, tired

ngûea N เหงื่อ sweat

ngûea àwk V เหงื่อออก to perspire, sweat

ngûean kǎi N เงื่อนไข a condition/proviso (e.g. a pre-condition for something to take place)

nguu N งู snake

nguu-nguu plaàplaa EXP (COLLOQUIAL) งูๆปลาๆ a little bit, not much, rudimentary (e.g. to speak a language, be able to do something requiring a degree of skill)

nguu sà-wàt N งูสวัด shingles, *herpes zoster*

O

ôh hoh (exclamation expressing surprise) โอ้โฮ Wow! Gosh! Oh!

oh-kàat N โอกาส chance, opportunity

oh-líang N โอเลี้ยง iced black coffee (Thai-style)

oh-thii ADJ (from English) โอ ที overtime (work)

oh-yúa N โอยั๊วะ hot black coffee (Thai-style)

ohn V โอน to transfer (e.g. money to another bank account/overseas, etc.)

ohn ngoehn V โอนเงิน to transfer money

ohn sǎn châat V โอนสัญชาติ to become naturalized, change one's citizenship

òhng N โอ่ง earthen jar, (large) water jar

ohy/óhy EXCLAM โอย, โอ๊ย Ouch! Oh!

ôi N อ้อย sugarcane

òk/nâa òk N อก, หน้าอก breast, chest

om V อม to keep in the mouth, suck (e.g. a lolly/lozenge)

ong-kaan/ong-kawn N องค์การ/องค์กร (an) organization

ongsǎa N องศา degree(s) (of temperature)

òp V, ADJ อบ to bake, roast; baked

òp choei N อบเชย cinnamon

òp ùn ADJ อบอุ่น warm

òp-phá-yóp V อพยพ to migrate, evacuate

òt V อด to give up, abstain from

òt aa-hǎan V อดอาหาร to fast, go without food, abstain from food

òt taai V อดตาย to starve to death

òt thon V อดทน to be patient, have tenacity, stamina

P

NOTE: this letter should not be confused with the English 'p'. This Thai '**p**' ป is not a sound commonly found in English although it is similar to the 'p' sound in the word 'spa'.

pá V ปะ to patch (a tire/inner tube of bicycle/a piece of clothing)

pâa N ป้า aunt, the older sister of either parent

pàa N ป่า forest, jungle ADJ wild (of animals)

pâai N ป้าย sign, signboard

pâai rót N ป้ายรถ, ป้ายรถเมล์ bus stop

pàak N ปาก mouth, entrance

pàak sǐa ADJ (COLLOQUIAL) ปากเสีย to say unpleasant things, (to have) a big mouth

pàak soi N ปากซอย the entrance of a **Soi** (laneway, side road)

pàak-kaa N ปากกา pen

pâehng N แป้ง flour, (talcum) powder

pàeht NUM แปด eight

pàeht sìp NUM แปดสิบ eighty

páep diao EXP (COLLOQUIAL) แป๊ปเดียว in a jiffy, in a sec (second), (wait) just a second/moment

pai V ไป to go, depart, move; (COLLOQUIAL) to tell someone to 'Go, get out/ go away' simply say **pai** ไป with emphasis. One other sense for which the word is commonly used is to express the idea of 'too/too much', e.g. **phaehng pai** แพงไป *too expensive*; **dang pai** ดังไป *too loud*

pai ao maa v (COLLOQUIAL) ไปเอามา *to fetch, go and get* (literally, 'go'-'take'-'come')

pai doehn lên v (COLLO-QUIAL) ไปเดินเล่น *to go for a walk*

pai dûai v (COLLOQUIAL) ไปด้วย *to go along, to go as well*

pai kan v ไปกัน *to go together, let's go*; (COLLO-QUIAL) also **pai dûai kan** ไปด้วยกัน *let's go together*

pai...khá/khráp ไป...ค่ะ/ ครับ *I'd like to go to...,* *please.*

pai khâang nâa v ไปข้างหน้า *to go forward*

pai... kìi chûa-mohng? ไป...กี่ชั่วโมง? *How many hours is it to ...?*

pai kláp N ไปกลับ *round trip*

pai nǎi maa (COLLOQUIAL) ไปไหนมา *Where have you been?*

pai nawn v ไปนอน *to go to bed*

pai pen phûean v (COLLO-QUIAL) ไปเป็นเพื่อน *to accompany, go along with someone to keep them company*

pai sòng v ไปส่ง *to give (someone) a lift (home), see (someone) off (e.g. at the airport, etc.)*

pai súeh khǎwng v ไปซื้อ ของ *to shop, go shopping*

pai...thâo-rài? ไป...เท่าไร *How much is it to go to...?*

pai thát-sà-naa-jawn v (thát pronounced 'tat' with a high tone) ไปทัศนาจร (somewhat formal) *to go sightseeing*

pai thîi nǎi (QUESTION) ไป ที่ไหน *where are you going?*; (COLLOQUIAL – also used as a common greeting) **pai nǎi** ไปไหน

pai thîao v ไปเที่ยว *take a trip, travel*

pai yîam v ไปเยี่ยม *to go visit (e.g. a friend/relative etc.)*

pàk v ปัก *to embroider, implant*

286

pàkàtì ADJ ปกติ normal, regular, usual, ordinary

pám náam man N ปั๊มน้ำมัน gas/petrol station

pân V ปั้น to model (clay), mold, sculpt

panhǎa N ปัญหา problem; (COLLOQUIAL) **mâi mii panhǎa** ไม่มีปัญหา 'No problems'

pào V เป่า to blow (e.g. the candles out on a birthday cake)

pào hǔu V (COLLOQUIAL) เป่าหู to insinuate, whisper something in someone's ear (to get them on your side/believe you rather than someone else)

pâo mǎi N เป้าหมาย goal, objective

pàrin-yaa N ปริญญา a degree (i.e. a university/college degree)

pàtìbàt V ปฏิบัติ (FORMAL) to operate, perform

pàtìbàt tàw V ปฏิบัติต่อ (FORMAL) to behave towards

pàti-kìrí-yaa N ปฏิกิริยา reaction

pàtìsèht V ปฏิเสธ to decline, refuse, deny

pà-tì-thin N ปฏิทิน calendar

pàt-jù-ban nii ปัจจุบันนี้ (FORMAL) nowadays, these days, currently

pàwk V ปอก to peel (e.g. an orange)

pâwm N ป้อม fortress, citadel

pawn N ปอนด์ pound (money); also used to refer to a loaf of bread

pâwn V ป้อน to feed someone, spoonfeed

pâwng kan V ป้องกัน to prevent, protect; defend (in war)

pàwt N ปอด lung(s)

pêh N เป้ a backpack

pen V เป็น (the Thai equivalent to the verb 'to be') to be someone or something; to know how to do something

pen hèht hâi V เป็นเหตุให้ to be the cause or reason

pen ìtsàra ADJ เป็นอิสระ to be free, independent

pen jai V (COLLOQUIAL) เป็นใจ to favor, sympathize

287

(with), side (with); to be an accomplice (of)

pen jâo khǎwng v, N เป็นเจ้าของ to own; the owner

pen kan ehng ADJ (COLLOQUIAL) เป็นกันเอง to be friendly, outgoing; (COMMON EXPRESSION) 'make yourself at home/take it easy, just be yourself'

pen khǎwng... เป็นของ to belong to..., e.g. **pen khǎwng khǎo** เป็นของเขา 'It's his/hers'

pen man ADJ เป็นมัน oily (skin); shiny, glossy

pen mǎn ADJ เป็นหมัน to be sterile, infertile

pen nîi PHR เป็นหนี้ to owe, be in debt to someone

pen pai dâi EXP เป็นไปได้ to be possible

pen pai mâi dâi EXP เป็นไปไม่ได้ to be impossible

pen rá-biap ADJ เป็นระเบียบ to be orderly, organized

pen tham ADJ เป็นธรรม to be fair, just, equitable

pen thammá-châat ADJ เป็น

ธรรมชาติ natural

pen thammá-daa ADJ เป็นธรรมดา to be typical, normal

pen thîi niyom ADJ เป็นที่นิยม to be popular

pen thîi phaw jai ADJ เป็นที่พอใจ to be satisfying

pen wàt เป็นหวัด to have a cold

pèt N เป็ด duck

pìak ADJ เปียก to be wet, soaking

pii N ปี year, years old

pii nâa ADV ปีหน้า next year

pii thîi láew ADV ปีที่แล้ว last year

piik N ปีก wing (of a bird or aeroplane)

piin v ปีน to climb (e.g. a mountain)

pîng v, N ปิ้ง to grill/toast; to be grilled, toasted

pìt v ปิด to close, cover, shut off, to turn something off

pìt láew ADJ ปิดแล้ว turned off, closed

pìt prà-tuu v ปิดประตู to close the door

pìt ráan v ปิดร้าน to close the

288

shop/store

pìt thà‑nŏn v ปิดถนน to close the road

plaa N ปลา fish

plaa chà‑lăam N ปลาฉลาม shark

plaa mùek N ปลาหมึก squid (literally, 'fish'‑'ink')

plaai N ปลาย end (e.g. of the road), tip (e.g. of the tongue)

pláatsàtìk N (from English) พลาสติก plastic

plaeh v แปล to translate

plaeh wâa... แปลว่า it means...; a question to elicit the above response 'it means...': plaeh wâa arai แปลว่าอะไร 'what does it/ this mean?'

plàehk ADJ แปลก strange, unusual, odd; **khon plaehk nâa** คนแปลกหน้า a stranger

plàehk jai ADJ แปลกใจ surprised, puzzled

plák N (from English) ปลั๊ก plug (bath)

plák fai N ปลั๊กไฟ plug/ socket (electric)

plào ADJ เปล่า empty, void; one of the ways of saying 'no' in Thai, for example when someone asks a question assuming a positive reponse but instead gets a reply of 'no' (A: 'Do you want to go and see [name of film]? Everyone says it is great.' B: **plào** 'No')

plawm v ปลอม to forge, counterfeit, fake

plawm tua v ปลอมตัว to disguise oneself

plàwt phai ADJ ปลอดภัย to be safe (from harm)

plàwt pròhng ADJ ปลอดโปร่ง to be clear (the weather)

plìan v เปลี่ยน to change (e.g. clothes, plans, etc.)

plian jai v เปลี่ยนใจ to change one's mind

pling N ปลิง a leech

plòi v ปล่อย to free, release, drop/let go

plôn v ปล้น to rob (e.g. a bank), plunder

plòt kàsĭan ADJ ปลดเกษียณ to be retired

plùak N ปลวก termite, white ant

plueai ADJ เปลือย to be naked, nude

plùeak N เปลือก the peel (of an orange), the shell (of a nut)

plùk V ปลุก to awaken/wake up (someone); to arouse, excite

plùuk V ปลูก to plant, grow, build, construct

poehsen N (from English) เปอร์เซ็นต์ percent, percentage

pòeht V เปิด to open; turn or switch something on: **pòeht mí-têr mái?** เปิดมิเตอร์ไหม Is your meter on?

pòeht banchii V เปิดบัญชี to open an account (e.g. bank account)

pòeht phòei V เปิดเผย to reveal, make known

póh ADJ โป๊ indecent, revealing (clothing), scantily dressed; **nǎng póh** หนังโป๊ N an X-rated/pornographic film/ DVD etc.

pòk khrong V ปกครอง to take care of, govern, rule, administer

praa-kòt V ปรากฏ to appear, become visible

pràap V ปราบ to control, suppress (e.g. the drug trade), exterminate

praà-sàat N ปราสาท castle

pràat-sajàak ADV (FORMAL) ปราศจาก without

pràat-thànǎa V ปรารถนา (somewhat more formal than the colloquial **wǎng** หวัง) to wish (for something), to desire, to be desirous

prà-chaa-chon N ประชาชน the public, the people, populace

prà-chaa-kawn N ประชากร population

prà-chaakhom N (FORMAL) ประชาคม community (e.g. used for the EEC, or ASEAN Community)

pràchaa-sǎmphan N ประชาสัมพันธ์ public relations

prà-chót V ประชด to mock, ridicule, deride; to spite

290

(someone)

prà-chum v ประชุม to meet, hold a meeting, have a conference

prà-dàp v ประดับ to decorate, adorn

prà-dìt v ประดิษฐ์ to invent, make up, create

praehng n แปรง a brush

praehng sǐi fan n แปรงสีฟัน toothbrush

prai-sànìi n ไปรษณีย์ post office

prai-sànìi klaang n ไปรษณีย์กลาง GPO, central post office

prà-jaan v ประจาน (a traditional Thai practice) to humiliate publicly, disgrace, to shame (the modern version of this is for criminals to re-enact their crimes – usually in handcuffs – with the police and general public looking on. Photographs are taken and published in the popular press together with details about the particular crime/offence)

pràjam ADJ, ADV ประจำ regular(ly); **prajam thaang** n ประจำทาง the regular/ scheduled (e.g. bus) route

pràjam duean n (formal medical term) ประจำเดือน (menstrual) period

pràjam pii ADJ, ADV ประจำปี annual

pràjam wan ADJ, ADV ประจำ วัน daily

pràjòp v ประจบ to flatter, fawn (on, over); to please or humor someone (i.e. to kiss ass/arse)

prà-kàat v ประกาศ to announce, proclaim, declare, give notice

prà-kàat-sànìi-yá-bàt n ประกาศนียบัตร a certificate (for completing a course of study)

prà-kan v ประกัน to guarantee, insure; to put up bail/security

prà-kan chii-wít n ประกัน ชีวิต life insurance

prà-kàwp v ประกอบ to assemble, put together

prà-kàwp dûai v ประกอบ

ด้วย be made up of, comprising, consist of

prà-kùat v ประกวด to show (in competition), enter a competition, contest

prà-làat ADJ ประหลาด strange, odd, unusual, extraordinary

prà-làat jai ADJ ประหลาดใจ to be surprised

prà-maan v, ADV ประมาณ to estimate; about, approximately, roughly

prà-màat ADJ ประมาท to be negligent, careless (e.g. doing something with a high risk of causing an accident)

prà-muun v ประมูล to bid/ tender/auction

prà-muun khǎi v ประมูลขาย (to be) auctioned off

pràp v ปรับ to adjust (e.g. airconditioning)

pràp aa-kaat ADJ ปรับอากาศ air-conditioned

pràp tua v ปรับตัว to adjust, adapt (e.g. oneself to a new situation)

prà-phêht N ประเภท class, category, type

prà-phrúet v (FORMAL) ประพฤติ to behave

prà-sàat N ประสาท nerve; **sên prà-sàat** N เส้นประสาท a nerve; (COLLOQUIAL) **prà-sàat** ประสาท to be nuts/ crazy

prà-sòpkaan N ประสบการณ์ experience

prà-thaa-na thíp-bawdii N ประธานาธิบดี president

prà-tháp jai ADJ ประทับใจ to be impressed; impressive

prà-thát N ประทัด fireworks, firecrackers

prà-thêht N ประเทศ country (nation)

prà-thúang v ประท้วง to protest, go on strike

prà-tuu N ประตู door, gate; goal in football/soccer

prà-tuu náam N ประตูน้ำ a water gate; a very busy, lively area in the central part of Bangkok commonly written 'Pratunam'

prà-wàt N ประวัติ history (i.e. a personal history), record, resumé

pràwàttì-sàat N ประวัติ

ศาสตร์ history (the formal discipline of the study of the past)

prà-yàt V, ADJ ประหยัด to economize; economical, to be thrifty, frugal

prà-yòhk N ประโยค a sentence (i.e. a sentence of text)

prà-yòht N ประโยชน์ usefulness, utility, (for the) benefit (of), advantage

prîao ADJ เปรี้ยว sour (to the taste); spirited, vivacious, wild, untamed (of people – generally women still in their prime)

prîao wǎn ADJ เปรี้ยวหวาน sweet and sour (e.g. fish, pork, etc.)

prìap kàp ADJ เปรียบกับ compared with

prìap thîap V เปรียบเทียบ to compare

prùek-sǎa V ปรึกษา to consult, talk over with

pùai ADJ ป่วย to be ill, sick

pùat V ปวด to ache (e.g. toothache), be sore (e.g. sore back)

pûean ADJ เปื้อน to be soiled, dirty

puehn N ปืน gun (general term)

pǔi N ปุ๋ย fertilizer

pûm pûi ADJ ปุ้มปุ้ย pudgy, a bit of a fatty (COLLOQUIAL playful)

pùu N ปู่ grandfather (paternal)

puu N, V ปู a crab: to lay, spread, put (sheets/mat) on (bed/floor)

pùu yâa taa yaai N ปู่ย่าตายาย grandparents, forebears, ancestors

puun N ปูน cement

PH

NOTE: 'ph' is very similar to the 'p' sound in English

phâa N ผ้า cloth, material, fabric, textile

phàa V ผ่า to split (e.g. a piece of wood with an ax)

phaa V พา to take or lead someone somewhere

293

phaa pai v พาไป to take someone to

phâa chét tua N ผ้าเช็ดตัว towel

phâa hòm N ผ้าห่ม blanket

phâa khîi ríu N ผ้าขี้ริ้ว a rag; tripe/offal

phâa mâan N ผ้าม่าน curtain(s), drapes

phâa puu N ผ้าปู sheet (for bed) (NOTE: the most common way of referring to bedsheets: **phâa puu thîi nawn** ผ้าปูที่นอน)

phâa puu tó N ผ้าปูโต๊ะ tablecloth

phâa sîn N ผ้าซิ่น long Thai one-piece sarong-like skirt

phàa tàt v ผ่าตัด to operate, perform an operation or surgery

phá-yung v พยุง to carry carefully

phaai N พาย a paddle; **phaai rueah** v พายเรือ to paddle/row a boat

phaai nai PREP ภายใน in (time, years), within

phaai nai pràthêht ADJ ภายในประเทศ internal, domestic, within the country

phàan v ผ่าน to pass, go past; (to go) via, through

phâap N ภาพ picture

phâap kwâang N ภาพกว้าง panorama

phâap wâat N ภาพวาด painting

phâap-pháyon N ภาพยนตร์ motion picture, film

phaa-rá N ภาระ obligation, responsibility, burden

phaa-sǎa N ภาษา language

phaa-sǎa angkrit N ภาษา อังกฤษ English (language)

phaa-sǎa jiin N ภาษาจีน Chinese (language)

phaa-sǎa kha-měhn N ภาษา เขมร Khmer/Cambodian (language)

phaa-sǎa thai N ภาษาไทย Thai (language)

phaa-sǎa thin N (pronounced 'tin', not 'thin') ภาษาถิ่น local language, dialect

phaa-sǐi N ภาษี tax(es)

phaa-wá N ภาวะ state, condition, status

phaa-yú N พายุ storm

294

phà-choehn v เผชิญ to meet, confront

phà-choehn nâa v เผชิญหน้า to meet, face up to (someone or something), confront

pháe N แพะ goat

phaeh N แพ a raft, houseboat

pháeh v แพ้ to lose, be defeated; to be allergic (e.g. to some types of food, medication)

phǎen N แผน a plan, scheme

phǎen bohraan ADJ แผนโบราณ traditional, old style, e.g. **nùat phǎehn bohraan** นวดแผนโบราณ traditional Thai massage

phǎen thîi N แผนที่ map

phaeng ADJ แพง expensive, dear, costly

phàen N แผ่น classifier used when counting flat objects, e.g. CDs/DVDs, sheets of paper etc.

phàen-din wǎi N แผ่นดินไหว an earthquake

phâet N (FORMAL TERM) แพทย์ doctor, physician

phâi N ไพ่ card(s) (game); (COLLOQUIAL) **lên phâi** เล่นไพ่ to play cards

phai N ภัย danger, peril

phài N ไผ่, (more fully) **mái phài** ไม้ไผ่ bamboo

phai phíbàt N ภัยพิบัติ disaster

phai-lin N ไพลิน sapphire

phà-jon-phai N ผจญภัย adventure

phàk N ผัก vegetable(s)

phák N พรรค party (political), group

phák v พัก to stay (at, over), to rest, stop for a while

phàk bûng N ผักบุ้ง Thai morning glory

phàk chii N ผักชี coriander, cilantro

phàk kàat khǎow N ผักกาดขาว Chinese cabbage

phák phàwn v พักผ่อน to relax, rest

phàk sòt N ผักสด fresh vegetables

phá-lang N พลัง energy, power (e.g. physical energy, solar energy, wind power, etc.)

phá-lang ngaan N พลังงาน energy

phà-lit v ผลิต to manufacture, produce

phá-mâa N พม่า Burma, Burmese

phan NUM พัน thousand

phan láan NUM พันล้าน billion

phà-nàehk N แผนก division, section (e.g. of a government department)

phá-naehng/kaehng phanaehng N พะแนง/แกง พะแนง name of mildish curry (often written in English as 'panang' – apparently originating in Penang, Malaysia)

phánák-ngaan N พนักงาน employee in a department store/large enterprise

phánák-ngaan khǎai N พนักงานขาย sales assistant

phá-nan v พนัน to gamble; **lên kaan phá-nan** เล่นการ พนัน to gamble; **phá-nan kan** (COLLOQUIAL) **mái** พนันกันไหม do you want to bet?

phà-nǎng N ผนัง wall,

(internal) partition in a building

phá-ùet-phá-om v พะอืดพะอม to feel nauseated

phang ADJ พัง (pronounced like 'hung' with a 'p' in front – 'phung') broken down, destroyed, in ruins, ruined

phanràyaa/phanyaa N (POLITE FORMAL TERM) ภรรยา wife

phansǎa N พรรษา rainy season retreat/Buddhist Lent: **khâo phansǎa** เข้า พรรษา to enter/begin the rainy season retreat/ Buddhist Lent

phào N เผ่า tribe, ethnic group

phǎo v เผา to burn, cremate, set fire (to)

pháp v พับ to fold, double over

pháp phîap v พับเพียบ sit with both legs tucked back to one side

phà-sǒm v ผสม to mix, combine

phàt v, ADJ ผัด to stir-fry; stir-fried

phát v พัด to fan, blow

phátlom N พัดลม fan (for cooling)

phátsàdù N พัสดุ supplies, things, stores

phát-thá-naa v พัฒนา to develop (e.g. a project); for a child to 'develop/progress' in their ability/knowledge or understanding

phaw ADV พอ (pronounced 'pour' with a mid tone) enough; as soon as, when

phâw N (pronounced 'pour' with a falling tone) พ่อ father

phaw dii ADV พอดี just right (i.e. just the right amount), just then (i.e. 'just then someone came to the door')

phaw jai ADJ พอใจ to be satisfied, contented, to be pleased

phâw kháa N, MASC พ่อค้า merchant

phaw khuan ADV พอควร enough, moderately, reasonably

phâw mâai N พ่อม่าย widower

phâw mâeh N พ่อแม่ parents

phaw phiang พอเพียง a notion closely associated with King Phumiphon Adunyadet which refers to what is generally called in English 'the sufficiency economy' (i.e. something along the lines of self sufficiency)

phaw sǎw N (pronounced 'por saw') พ.ศ. Buddhist era, B.E. A year in the Buddhist era (which begins from the year of the Buddha's 'passing') is calculated by adding 543 to a given year in the Christian Era

phaw sǒmkhuan ADJ พอสมควร reasonable (price), appropriate/sufficient

phaw thii EXP (COLLOQUIAL) พอที่ enough (already), stop (doing what you're doing)

phǎwm ADJ ผอม thin, lean, slim

phawn N พร (commonly

written in English 'porn' or 'phorn') blessing, benediction, good wishes

phá-yaa-baan N พยาบาล nurse

phá-yaan N พยาน witness

phá-yâat N พยาธิ worm, parasite (in the body)

phá-yaa-yaam V พยายาม to try, attempt, make an effort

peh-daan N เพดาน ceiling

phêht N เพศ gender, sex

phèt ADJ เผ็ด to be hot (spicy), sharp, peppery

phét N เพชร diamond

phiang ADV เพียง just, only

phiang phaw ADJ เพียง พอ enough, sufficient, adequate

phiang tàeh ADV เพียงแต่ only

phîi PRON พี่ older brother or sister; commonly used as a polite, somewhat deferential, second person pronoun (you) when talking with a friend, or a stranger, who is older (but often not much older), or in a position of greater power or authority

phîi N ผี ghost, spirit, ghoul, apparition

phîi chaai N พี่ชาย older brother

phîi khoei N พี่เขย older brother-in-law

phîi náwng N พี่น้อง brothers and sisters/siblings

phîi săow N พี่สาว older sister

phîi sà-phái N พี่สะไภ้ older sister-in-law

phîi sûea N ผีเสื้อ butterfly (literally, 'ghost'-'shirt')

phí-jaàránaa V พิจารณา to consider, have a considered opinion

phí-kaan ADJ พิการ to be disabled, handicapped

phim V พิมพ์ to print, publish; to write on a computer

phim diit V พิมพ์ดีด to type (with a typewriter)

phí-nai-kam N พินัยกรรม a will, testament

phí-phít thá-phan N พิพิธ ภัณฑ์ museum

phísèht ADJ พิเศษ special, exceptional, particular

298

phí-sùut v พิสูจน์ to prove, show, demonstrate

phit ADJ ผิด to be false (not true); guilty (of a crime); wrong (false)

phí-thii N พิธี ceremony, ritual

phit kòtmǎai ADJ ผิดกฎหมาย to be illegal

phit phlâat ADJ ผิดพลาด to be mistaken, to be wrong

phit wǎng ADJ ผิดหวัง to be disappointed

phǐu N ผิว skin, complexion; surface, covering

phlâat v พลาด to be mistaken, make an error/a mistake; to miss (i.e. the bus, a target)

phlǎeh N แผล scar, cut, wound

phlàk v ผลัก to push

phlehng N เพลง song, tune

phóeh ADJ เพ้อ to ramble on, to be delirious; (COLLOQUIAL) **phóeh jôeh** เพ้อเจ้อ to refer to utterances that are nonsensical, way over the top, inane

phôehm v, ADJ เพิ่ม to add, increase; extra

phôehm khûen v เพิ่มขึ้น to increase

phôehm toehm ADV เพิ่มเติม further, in addition

phôeng ADV เพิ่ง just now, e.g. khǎo phôeng klàp bâan เขาเพิ่งกลับบ้าน he's just now gone home

phían ADJ เพี้ยน differing just a little

phǒm N ผม hair (on the head only)

phǒm PRON, MASC ผม I, me

phǒn N ผล effect, result

phǒn prá-yòht N ผลประโยชน์ benefit (which accrues to someone)

phǒn-lá-mái N ผลไม้ fruit

phǒn-sùt-thái EXP ผลสุดท้าย finally, in the end

phǒng sák fâwk N ผงซักฟอก detergent

phóp v พบ to find, meet

phóp kan mài EXP (COLLOQUIAL) พบกันใหม่ see you later!

phót-jà naa-ànú-krom N (FORMAL TERM) พจนานุกรม

dictionary

phrá N พระ (a Buddhist) monk; (also colloquially used to refer to) Buddhist amulets, images

phrá aa-thít N พระอาทิตย์ the sun

phrá aa-thít khûen N พระอาทิตย์ขึ้น sunrise

phrá aa-thít tòk din N พระอาทิตย์ตกดิน sunset

phrá jâo N พระเจ้า, also **phrá phûu pen jâo** พระผู้เป็นเจ้า God

phrá má-hǎa kà-sàt N พระมหากษัตริย์ king, monarch

phrá raa-chí-nii N พระราชินี; (COLLOQUIAL) **raa-chí-nii** ราชินี queen

phrá râat-chá-wang N พระราชวัง royal palace

phráw CONJ เพราะ (or **phráw-wâa** เพราะว่า) because; ADJ mellifluous, to sound pleasing to the ear

phráwm ADJ, ADV พร้อม to be ready

phrík N พริก chilli, chilli pepper

phrík thai N พริกไทย pepper/

black pepper

phrom N พรม carpet

phrúet-sà-ji-kaa-yon N พฤศจิกายน November

phrúet-sà-phaa-khom N พฤษภาคม May

phrûng níi N, ADV พรุ่งนี้ tomorrow

phǔa N ผัว husband (colloquial but somewhat rude, better left unsaid in polite company)

phûak N พวก group

phûak khǎo PRON พวกเขา they, them

phûang V พ่วง to trail, trailing; to be attached to (e.g. a trailer)

phuang N พวง bunch, cluster

phuang kunjaeh N พวงกุญแจ key ring/bunch of keys

phuang maa-lai N พวงมาลัย garland; also steering wheel

phûea àrai เพื่ออะไร what for?

phûea thîi CONJ เพื่อที่ ในorder that, so that

phùeak N เผือก taro; also

300

cháang phùeak ช้างเผือก albino – white elephant

phûean N เพื่อน friend

phûean bâan N เพื่อนบ้าน neighbor(s)

phûean rûam ngaan N เพื่อนร่วมงาน co-worker, colleague

phúehn N พื้น floor

phúehn din N พื้นดิน ground, earth

phúehn thîi N พื้นที่ area

phûeng N ผึ้ง bee(s); **náam phûeng** น้ำผึ้ง honey

phút-thá sàat-sà-nǎa N พุทธ ศาสนา Buddhism/Buddhist religion

phûu N ผู้ a prefix meaning 'one who (is or does something in particular)'; also male, e.g. to refer to male animals **tua phûu** ตัวผู้; a male cat is a **maeo tua phûu** แมวตัวผู้

phûu aa-sǎi N ผู้อาศัย resident, inhabitant

phûu am-nuai-kaan N ผู้อำนวยการ director (of company)

phûu chaai N ผู้ชาย male, man

phûu chá-ná N ผู้ชนะ winner

phûu chûai N ผู้ช่วย assistant, helper

phûu-chûai-sàat-traa-jaan N ผู้ช่วยศาสตราจารย์ assistant professor

phûu dohy-sǎan N ผู้โดยสาร passenger

phûu fang N ผู้ฟัง (pronounced 'fung') listener (e.g. to a radio program)

phûu jàtkaan N (pronounced 'jut garn') ผู้จัดการ manager

phuu-khǎo N ภูเขา mountain

phuu-khǎo fai N ภูเขาไฟ volcano

phûu nam N ผู้นำ leader

phûu phí-phâak-sǎa N ผู้พิพากษา judge (in a court of law)

phûu thaen N ผู้แทน representative (e.g. of a company), delegate

phûu yài N ผู้ใหญ่ adult; (COLLOQUIAL) a person of consequence

phûu yài bâan N ผู้ใหญ่บ้าน village headman

phûu yǐng N ผู้หญิง woman

phùuk v ผูก to tie, fasten, secure

phuu-mí-phâak N ภูมิภาค region

phuum-jai ADJ ภูมิใจ to be proud (of accomplishing something)

phûut v พูด to speak, talk, say

phûut lên v พูดเล่น to be joking/kidding

phûut rûeang... พูดเรื่อง (to) talk about...

phûut wâa... พูดว่า say/said that, used as follows: **kháo phûut wâa kháo mâi sabaai** เขาพูดว่าเขาไม่สบาย 'he said he (was) sick'

R

raa-chaa N ราชา king, monarch, rajah

râa-roehng ADJ ร่าเริง cheerful

ráai ADJ ร้าย wicked, evil, malicious, ferocious; **khon ráai** คนร้าย a bad person

raai chûeh N รายชื่อ list (of names)

raai dâi N รายได้ income

raai jàai N รายจ่าย expense(s), expenditure

raai-kaan N รายการ list (of names), item, particulars

raai-kaan aa-hǎan N รายการ อาหาร menu

raai-kaan sòt N รายการสด (a live) show, performance

raai ngaan N, v รายงาน a report; to report

ráai raehng ADJ ร้ายแรง serious (severe), violent

râak v ราก root (of plant or a tooth); foundation; also to throw up, retch

raa-khaa N ราคา price, value, worth

raa-khaa khàat tua N (COLLOQUIAL) ราคาขาดตัว bottom price, lowest price, best price

ráan N ร้าน shop, store, vendor's stall

ráan aa-hǎan N ร้านอาหาร restaurant

ráan in-ter-nèt N ร้านอิน เตอร์เน็ต Internet café: **ráan in-ter-nèt yóu thîi-nǎi?** ร้านอินเตอร์เน็ตอยู่ที่ไหน

Where can I find an
Internet café?

ráan kaa fae N ร้านกาแฟ
coffee shop

ráan khǎi yaa N ร้านขายยา
pharmacy, drugstore, chemist

ráan nǎng sǔe N ร้านหนังสือ
bookstore

ráan sǒehm sǔai N ร้านเสริม
สวย beauty parlor/salon

râang kaai N ร่างกาย body

raangwan N รางวัล a prize,
reward (for the arrest of…)

râap ADJ ราบ flat, level, even,
smooth

râap rûehn ADJ ราบรื่น
harmonious (relations)

râat V ราด to pour (something) on (something else)
(e.g. curry over rice **khâaw
râat kaehng** ข้าวราดแกง)

râat-chá-kaan N ราชการ
government service, the
bureaucracy

râat-chá-wong N ราชวงศ์
dynasty, royal house

rábaai sǐi V ระบายสี to paint
(in the artistic sense)

rá-biang N ระเบียง verandah,
porch

rá-bìap N ระเบียบ order,
regulations, rules

rá-bòp N ระบบ a system (e.g.
of organizing/processing
things)

rá-dàp N ระดับ level
(standard), degree

rá-hàt N รหัส code

rá-hàt waai-faai N รหัสสวาย
ฟาย a Wi-Fi password

rá-khang N ระฆัง bell

rá-wàang PREP ระหว่าง
during, between, among,
while

rá-waeng ADJ ระแวง to
be wary, suspicious,
mistrustful

rá-wang ADJ, V ระวัง to be
careful; beware (of), watch
out (for)

rêeh N แร่ mineral, ore; **náam
rêeh** N น้ำแร่ mineral water

râehk ADJ แรก beginning,
starting, original, first,
initial

raeng N แรง strength, force,
power

raeng-ngaan N แรงงาน labor

râet N แรด rhinoceros

râi N ไร่ a Thai measurement

of land (**1 rái** = 1,600 sq m)

rái khâa ADJ ไร้ค่า worthless

rái sǎa-rá ADJ ไร้สาระ nonsensical

rák v รัก to love, be fond of

rák châat v รักชาติ to love one's country, be patriotic

rák ráeh N รักแร้ armpit(s)

ráksǎa v รักษา to care for (someone who is ill); to maintain, preserve (the peace etc.)

ráksǎa khwaam láp v รักษา ความลับ to keep a secret

ram v รำ (pronounced 'rum') to dance (also commonly say **tên ram** เต้นรำ), to perform a Thai traditional dance

ramkhaan v รำคาญ to be annoyed, irritated; to be annoying

rán ADJ รั้น to be stubborn, headstrong

rang N (pronounced like 'rung') รัง nest (e.g. a bird's nest)

rang-kaeh v รังแก to bother, annoy, bully, mistreat

rang khaeh N รังแค dandruff

rangkiat v รังเกียจ to mind (e.g. someone's (bad) behavior); dislike, have an aversion to/for

rao PRON เรา we, I, us, me

ráo jai v เร้าใจ to encourage, arouse

raow-raow ADV ราวๆ around (approximately)

ráp v รับ to receive; to take, get; to pick someone up (e.g. from the airport)

ráp chái v รับใช้ to serve

ráp jâang v รับจ้าง to take employment, to work for hire; to be employed/hired (to do something)

ráp ngoehn duean v รับเงิน เดือน to get/receive (one's) salary/wages

ráp phit châwp v รับผิดชอบ to be responsible

ráp rawng v รับรอง to guarantee

ráp thoh-rá-sàp v (**sàp** pronounced 'sup' with a low tone) รับโทรศัพท์ to answer the phone

rát N รัฐ (pronounced 'rut' with a high tone) state (of

a country), government (in the sense of 'the state')

rát-thà-baan N (the **rát** sound is pronounced like 'rut' with a high tone) รัฐบาล government

raw V รอ (pronounced 'raw') to wait (for, at, in, on)

ràwk หรอก a particle of speech used at the end of a statement meaning: on the contrary (to what the other party has said or expressed)

ráwn ADJ ร้อน hot (temperature)

rawng-à-thí-kaan-baw-dii N รองอธิการบดี vice president (of a college)

ráwng hâi V ร้องให้ to cry, weep

rawng-khá-ná-baw-dii N รอง คณบดี deputy dean

ráwng phlehng V ร้องเพลง to sing

rawng phôu-am-nuay-kaan N รองผู้อำนวยการ deputy director

rawng sàat-traa-jaan N รอง ศาสตราจารย์ associate professor

rawng tháo N รองเท้า shoe(s)

rawng tháo tàe N รองเท้าแตะ thongs, flip flops, sandals, slippers

râwp N รอบ (a) round (like a lap of the park), circuit, trip; also used to refer to the 12-year cycle (the Chinese zodiac)

râwp-râwp ADJ รอบๆ around (surrounding)

râwt chii-wít V รอดชีวิต to survive (e.g. a car crash)

ráyá N ระยะ interval, distance, bar (in music)

ráyá thaang N ระยะทาง distance (e.g. of a journey)

ráyá wehlaa N ระยะเวลา period (of time)

rêng V เร่ง to hurry, accelerate; (COLLOQUIAL) step on it

rêng dùan ADJ เร่งด่วน to be urgent

rew ADJ เร็ว fast, rapid, quick

rew kwàa pàkàti ADJ เร็ว กว่าปกติ earlier/faster than usual

rew pai ADV, ADJ เร็วไป too soon, too fast; premature

rew-rew EXP เร็วๆ hurry up!

rîak v เรียก to call, demand, summon

rîak chûeh v เรียกชื่อ to call (someone) by name

rîak ráwng v เรียกร้อง to urge, push for, demand

rian N เหรียญ a coin, dollar (initial consonant actually written with an 'r' but commonly pronounced with an 'l')

rian v เรียน to learn, study, take lessons

rian nǎngsǔeh v เรียน หนังสือ to go to school/ college etc.

riang khwaam N เรียงความ (university/college/school) essay

rîap ADJ เรียบ even (smooth), flat, level; plain (not fancy)

rîap rói ADJ เรียบร้อย neat, orderly, tidy

rîip v รีบ to hurry, rush

rîit v รีด to squeeze, wring, put through a wringer; to iron, press

rîit sûea v รีดเสื้อ to iron (clothing)

rim N ริม edge, rim

rim fàng mâeh náam N ริม ฝั่งแม่น้ำ bank (of river)

rim fǐi pàak N ริมฝีปาก lip(s)

rin v ริน to pour (a drink)

roeh v เรอ to belch, burp

rǒeh (NOTE: this word is actually written rǒeh but commonly pronounced with an 'l' rather than 'r') เหรอ really?, is that so?; a question word at the end of a sentence (often expressed with some doubt or surprise) that seeks confirmation

rôehm v เริ่ม to begin, start, commence, initiate; also **rôehm tôn** เริ่มต้น to begin, start; **rôehm tôn mài** เริ่ม ต้นใหม่ to make a fresh start, begin again

rôhk N โรค disease

rôhk káo N โรคเกาต์ gout

rohng N โรง building, house, hall, shed, factory, godown (general term)

rohng lá-khawn N โรงละคร theater, playhouse (drama)

rohng nǎng N โรงหนัง

306

cinema, movie house

rohng ngaan N โรงงาน factory

rohng phá-yaa-baan N โรงพยาบาล hospital

rohng raehm N โรงแรม hotel

rohng rian N โรงเรียน school

rohng rót N โรงรถ garage (for parking)

rói NUM ร้อย hundred

roi N รอย trace, mark, track (e.g. fingerprints, footprints)

roi pûean N รอยเปื้อน stain

rók ADJ รก (for a room to be) in a mess, untidy, cluttered; (for a garden to be) over-grown

rôm N ร่ม shade, umbrella

róp kuan V รบกวน to bother, disturb

rót N รถ car, automobile (wheeled vehicles in general)

rót N รส flavor, taste

rót V รด to water (plants); **rót náam tôn-mái** รดน้ำต้นไม้ to water the plants/garden

rót banthúk N รถบรรทุก truck

rót-dùan N รถด่วน express

train: **wan-níi mii rót-dùan pai...mái?** วันนี้มีรถด่วนไป...ไหม Are there express trains to ... today?

rót-dùan-phí-sèt N รถด่วนพิเศษ special express train

rót fai N รถไฟ train

rót-fai-fáa N รถไฟฟ้า skytrain (BTS)

rót fai tâi din N รถไฟใต้ดิน underground railway, subway (MRT)

rót jàk-kràyaan N รถจักรยาน bicycle, pushbike

rót këhng N รถเก๋ง car

rót khën N รถเข็น (super-market) trolley, pram, cart (of the type used by street hawkers)

rót meh N รถเมล์ bus

rót phá-yaa-baan N รถพยาบาล ambulance

rót phûang N รถพ่วง trailer; (COLLOQUIAL) used to refer to a motobike with some sort of attached trailer/sidecar

rót-reow N รถเร็ว rapid train

rót săai níi phàan...mái? รถสายนี้ผ่าน...ไหม Does

this bus/mini bus pass…?

rót-sŏng-thăew N รถสองแถว two-row minibus

rót tûu N รถตู้ van

rót tháeksîi N รถแท็กซี่ taxi (or simply **tháeksîi** แท็กซี่)

rót-tham-má-daa N รถ ธรรมดา ordinary train

rót thua N รถทัวร์ an air-conditioned tour bus/coach: **mii rót-thua/rót-fai pai… kìi-mong?** มีรถทัวร์/รถไฟ ไป…กี่โมง When is there a bus/train to …?; **rót-thua/ rót-fai àwk kii-mong?** รถ ทัวร์/รถไฟ ออกกี่โมง What time does the bus/train leave?; **rót-thua/rót-fai thŭeng kii-mong?** รถทัวร์/ รถไฟ ถึงกี่โมง What time does the bus/train arrive?

rót tìt N รถติด (a) traffic jam

rót túk-túk N รถตุ๊กตุ๊ก tuk-tuk/motorized trishaw (or simply **túk-túk** ตุ๊กตุ๊ก)

rót tûu N (COLLOQUIAL) รถตู้ minibus/minivan

rót yon N รถยนต์ automobile, car

rúa N รั้ว a fence

rûa V รั่ว to leak

ruai ADJ รวย to be rich, well off, wealthy

ruam V รวม to total, add together, join, altogether

rûam V ร่วม to live together, associate (with), participate (in)

rûam kan V ร่วมกัน (to do/ put) together

rûam phêht V (FORMAL/ POLITE) ร่วมเพศ to have sex, or sexual intercourse

ruam tháng V รวมทั้ง to include, including (e.g. service charges, etc.) CONJ as well as

rûap ruam V รวบรวม to assemble, gather

ruea N เรือ boat, ship

ruea khâam fâak N เรือข้าม ฟาก ferry

ruean N เรือน house, home, dwelling building; the classifier used for counting (i.e. the number of) watches or clocks

rûeang N เรื่อง story, record, account, issue (as in 'there are many issues he has to face')

rûeang lék N เรื่องเล็ก a small matter, an insignificant thing

rûeang mâak ADJ เรื่องมาก (COLLOQUIAL) to be fussy; someone who is hard to please (i.e. a pain in the arse/ass); to be picky

rúe-duu N (FORMAL TERM) ฤดู season (COLLOQUIAL) see **nâa** หน้า

rúe-duu bai mái phlì N ฤดู ใบไม้ผลิ spring (temperate climates)

rúe-duu bai mái rûang N ฤดูใบไม้ร่วง autumn/fall (temperate climates)

rúe-duu fŏn N (FORMAL) ฤดู ฝน rainy season

rúe-duu nǎaw N (FORMAL) ฤดูหนาว cool season, winter

rúe-duu ráwn N (FORMAL) ฤดู ร้อน hot season, summer

rǔeh หรือ or **rǒer** (COLLO-QUIAL) question particle that comes at the end of an utterance asking for confirmation (perhaps with

some doubt or surprise); e.g. jing rǔeh จริงหรือ 'is that so?/really?'. Sometimes it also serves as a sort of jaded response to a comment/statement made by someone else along the lines of 'oh?', or 'oh, yeah?'

rúeh CONJ หรือ or

rûn N รุ่น model (type), vintage; 'class' of people, e.g. the class of 2001 – those graduating from high school in 2001

run raeng ADJ รุนแรง severe, violent

rúng N รุ้ง a rainbow

ruu N รู a hole

rúu V รู้ to know, realize, be aware of

rúu-jàk V รู้จัก to know a person/place, be acquainted with

ruu jà-mùuk N รูจมูก nostril(s)

rǔu rǎa ADJ หรูหรา luxurious

rúu-sùek V รู้สึก to feel/sense, have a feeling (of, that)

rúu-sùek phit รู้สึกผิด to feel guilty

rûup N รูป shape, picture

rûup khài N รูปไข่ oval (shape – 'egg-shaped')

rûup pân N รูปปั้น sculpture, statue

rûup phâap N รูปภาพ picture

rûup râang N รูปร่าง form (shape), appearance

rûup thàai N รูปถ่าย photograph

rûup wâat N รูปวาด drawing

S

sà-àat ADJ สะอาด to be clean

sà-bùu N สบู่ soap

sà-daeng V แสดง to display, show; to express (an opinion)

sà-dueh N สะดือ navel, belly button

sà phŏm V สระผม to shampoo the hair

sà wâai náam N สระว่ายน้ำ swimming pool

săa baan V สาบาน to swear

săa-hàt ADJ (hàt pronounced like 'hut' with a low tone) สาหัส severe, serious, grave

(condition)

săa-hèht N สาเหตุ cause, reason (for)

săa-khăa N สาขา a branch (e.g. the branch of a bank/a particular junk food chain)

săa laa N ศาลา rest-house, public rest-house

săa laa klaang N ศาลากลาง city hall

săa-lii N สาลี่ wheat

săa-man ADJ สามัญ regular, common, ordinary

săa-mii N (polite term) สามี husband

săa-ràai N สาหร่าย seaweed

sáai ADJ, N (long vowel) ซ้าย left (direction)

saai N (long vowel) ทราย sand

sàai (long vowel) สาย ADJ (to be) late N classifier for connecting things, e.g. roads, routes and phone lines

sàai V ส่าย to swing, sway, swerve

sǎai mâi wâang (long vowel) สายไม่ว่าง (for the phone) line is engaged/ busy

310

sáai mueh ADV (long vowel) ซ้ายมือ on the left-hand side

săai kaan bin N สายการบิน airline

săai taa N สายตา eyesight

săam NUM สาม three

săam liam N สามเหลี่ยม triangle

săam sip NUM สามสิบ thirty

săa-mâat V สามารถ to be able to, be capable of, can

săn N ศาล court (of law)

săn jâo N ศาลเจ้า a (Chinese) temple, joss house

sâang V สร้าง to build, construct, create

sâang khwaam pràtháp jai สร้างความประทับใจ to create/make an impression

sàang mao V สร่างเมา to become sober

sâap V (pronounced 'sarp' with a falling tone) ทราบ to know (more polite/formal term **than rúu** รู้)

sâap súeng V, ADJ ซาบซึ้ง to appreciate, to be grateful (for); heartfelt

sàat-sà-năa N ศาสนา religion

sàat-sa-năa khrít N ศาสนา คริสต์ Christianity

sàat-sà-năa phút N ศาสนา พุทธ Buddhism

sàat-traa-jaan N ศาสตราจารย์ professor

sàbaai ADJ สบาย to feel comfortable/relaxed/good; **sàbaai-sàbaai** สบายๆ laid back

sàbaai dii rŭeh/mái EXP (COLLOQUIAL) สบายดีหรือ/ ไหม how are you?

sàbaai jai ADJ สบายใจ to be happy, satisfied

sàdùak ADJ สะดวก to be convenient

săen NUM แสน hundred thousand

saeng V แซง to overtake/ pass (e.g. another car/ vehicle)

săeng aa-thít N แสงอาทิตย์ sunlight

sàep V, N แสบ to sting, smart; a stinging sensation

saew V (COLLOQUIAL) แซว to tease (someone)

sàhà-râatchá-aa-naàjàk N สหราชอาณาจักร (formal name of the) United Kingdom; (COLLOQUIAL) **yuu kheh** ยูเค, (or more commonly) **ang-grìt** – i.e. England

sàhà-rát àmehríkaa N สหรัฐอเมริกา (formal name of the) United States

sài v (shortish vowel) ใส่ to wear, put on; to load; to put in, insert

sǎi ADJ ใส (shortish vowel) clear, bright, unclouded

sài phaw dii (shortish vowel) ใส่พอดี (e.g. for clothing) to fit

sǎiyá-sàat N ไสยศาสตร์ sorcery, magic (of the non-stage variety), supernatural arts

sàk ADV สัก about, at least, approxiamately

sàk N,v สัก (a) tattoo; to tattoo (someone)

sàk N สัก teak (wood) – more fully **mái sàk** ไม้สัก

sák v ซัก to wash, launder (clothing etc.); to question, interrogate

sàk khráng ADV สักครั้ง just this once

sàk khrûu ADV สักครู่ (in) just a moment

sák phâa v ซักผ้า to do the washing/laundry

sàk phák N สักพัก for a while

sák rîit v ซักรีด to wash and iron (clothing)

sǎ-kon ADJ สากล international, universal, western

sà-kòt v สะกด to spell (a word)

sàk-sǐi N ศักดิ์ศรี dignity, honor, prestige

sàksìt ADJ ศักดิ์สิทธิ์ sacred, holy, revered, hallowed

sàlàk v สลัก to carve, chisel out, engrave

sàlàp v สลับ to alternate

sàlàt N สลัด salad; **phàk salàt** ผักสลัด lettuce

sàlòp v สลบ to pass out, lose consciousness

sà-maa-chík N สมาชิก member

sà-maak-hom N สมาคม society/association

312

sà-măi N สมัย time, period, age, era

sà-măi kàwn ADV สมัยก่อน in the past

sà-măi mài ADJ สมัยใหม่ modern, contemporary

sà-măi níi ADV สมัยนี้ nowadays, these days

sà-măwng N สมอง brain, mind

sà-mĭan N เสมียน clerk

sămkhan ADJ สำคัญ important, significant

sămlii N สำลี cotton wool

sămnao N สำเนา photocopy, (a) copy

sămnuan N สำนวน an idiom, idiomatic expression; style of writing

sà-mŏeh ADV เสมอ always

sămphâat V, N สัมภาษณ์ to interview (someone); an interview

sămràp PREP สำหรับ for, to, intended for

sămrawng V สำรอง to reserve (for), to have in reserve, a spare (e.g. tire); put on a waiting list

sămrèt ADJ, V สำเร็จ to be finished, completed, accomplished, successful; to succeed

sà-mŭn-phrai N สมุนไพร medicinal herbs

sà-mùt N สมุด notebook, exercise book

sà-mùt dai aà-rîi N (from English) สมุดไดอารี่ a diary

sà-năam N สนาม a yard, field, empty space

sà-năam bin N สนามบิน airport

sà-năam yâa N สนามหญ้า lawn

sà-nèh N เสน่ห์ charm, attraction, appeal

sà-ngòp ADJ สงบ peaceful, calm

sà-nŏeh V เสนอ to bring up (topic), propose (a matter) present; to offer, suggest

sà-nùk ADJ, N สนุก fun, enjoyable, entertaining; to have a good time

sà-òht sà-ong ADJ สะโอดสะอง slender

sà-phaai V สะพาย to carry (on the shoulder)

sà-phaan N สะพาน bridge

sà-phaan loi N สะพานลอย a foot bridge (over a road), overpass

sà-phâap N สภาพ condition (of a house, car)

sà-phái N สะใภ้ female in-law

sà-pring N (from English) สปริง (a) spring

sà-rùp V สรุป to summarize, sum up, recapitulate

sà-sŏm V สะสม to accumulate, amass, save, collect (e.g. stamps), build up

sà-taang N สตางค์ old unit of Thai currency, money; (COLLOQUIAL) **tang** ตังค์ money

sà-tăa pàttà-yá-kam N สถาปัตยกรรม architecture

sà-táat V (from English) (pronounced 'sar-tart') สตาร์ท to start (e.g. a car; also used in the broader English sense – 'the sale starts tomorrow')

sà-taehm N (from English) แสตมป์ stamp (postage)

sà-tì N สติ consciousness, mind, thought

sà-thăa-nii N สถานี station (general term – used in conjunction with other words to form such terms as – radio station, television station, police station, space station, city bus station, etc.)

sà-thăa-nii-khŏn-sòng N สถานีขนส่ง bus station

sà-thăa-nii rót fai N สถานี รถไฟ train station

sà-thăa-nii rót fai hǔa lam-phohng N สถานีรถไฟ หัวลำโพง Hualampong, Bangkok's main railway station

sà-thăa-nii tam-rùat N สถานี ตำรวจ police station

sà-thăan-nákaan N สถานการณ์ situation

sà-thăan thîi N สถานที่ place

sà-thăan thûut N สถานทูต embassy

sà-tháwn V สะท้อน to reflect (off the glass, the water, the window, etc.), to rebound, bounce (up, back)

sà-wàang ADJ สว่าง bright, brilliant (light)

314

sà-wàt-dì-kaan N สวัสดิการ welfare

sà-wit N (from English) สวิทช์ switch

sân ADJ สั้น brief, short (concise)

sàn V สั่น to shake, vibrate, tremble

sănchâat N สัญชาติ nationality

sàng V (pronounced similar to 'sung' with a low tone) สั่ง to order, command; to order something

săngkèht V สังเกต to notice

săngkhom N สังคม society

sănti-phâap N สันติภาพ peace

sănyaa V, N สัญญา to promise; a contract

sănyálák N สัญลักษณ์ symbol, sign, token

sâo ADJ เศร้า sad, sorrowful

săo N เสา post, pole, column

săo aa-thít N เสาร์อาทิตย์ the weekend

săow N (long vowel) สาว young woman; (COLLO-QUIAL) **săow kàeh** สาวแก่ an old maid

sàp V สับ to chop, mince, e.g. **mŭu sàp** หมูสับ minced pork

sáp sáwn ADJ ซับซ้อน complicated, complex

sàp sŏn ADJ สับสน to be confused; disorderly

sàpdaa N (FORMAL) สัปดาห์ week

sàpdaa nâa N (FORMAL) สัปดาห์หน้า next week

sàppàrót N สับปะรด pineapple

sàt N สัตว์ animal (general term)

sàt líang N สัตว์เลี้ยง pet (animal)

sàttà-wát N ศตวรรษ (a) century

sàt-truu N ศัตรู enemy

săwăn N สวรรค์ heaven, paradise

sàwàt dii สวัสดี (common polite form of greeting at any time of day) hello (good morning/good afternoon, etc.); also (CASUAL/COLLOQUIAL) **wàt dii** หวัดดี 'Hi'

sâwm N ส้อม (a) fork (utensil)

315

sâwm v ซ่อม to repair, mend, fix

săwn v สอน to teach, instruct

sâwn v ซ่อน to hide, conceal

sâwn yùu ADJ ซ่อนอยู่ (to be) hidden

sawng N ซอง envelope

săwng NUM สอง two

sâwng N ซ่อง brothel, hiding place, den (of iniquity)

sâwng kà-rìi N ซ่องกะหรี่ (SLANG – rude, better left unsaid in polite company) whorehouse

săwng săam ADJ (COLLO-QUIAL) สองสาม a few

săwng thăew N (COLLOQUIAL) สองแถว common term for a pick-up truck with bench seats (the name **săwng thăew** means 'two rows [of seats] facing one another') in the back that is used to take paying passengers on shortish journeys – primarily found in provincial towns/cities

săwng thâo ADJ สองเท่า double (e.g. double the price), twice as much

sàwp v สอบ to examine, test, take an examination; to verify, inquire

sàwp phàan v สอบผ่าน to pass a test/an exam

sáwt N (from English) ซอส sauce

sáwt phrík N ซอสพริก chili sauce

sěh-rìi ADJ เสรี free, independent

sèht N เศษ remainder, what is left over, scrap(s), fraction

sèht nùeng sùan sìi N เศษหนึ่งส่วนสี่ (¼) one quarter (part of something)

sèht sà-taang N เศษสตางค์ small change

sèht-thà-kìt N (pronounced 'set-àgit') เศรษฐกิจ economy

sèht-thǐi N เศรษฐี a/an wealthy/rich/affluent man

sèht-thǐi-nii N เศรษฐินี a/an wealthy/rich/affluent woman

sen N เซ็นต์ centimeter

sen v เซ็น to sign

sên N เส้น thread, line

(mark), blood vessel; classifier for counting string-like things, e.g. noodles, hair

seng ADJ (COLLOQUIAL) เซ็ง to be bored, fed up (with)

séng V เซ้ง to sell, for sale; sublet

sèohp V (from English) เสิร์ฟ to serve

sèt V เสร็จ to finish; (SLANG) to climax, have an orgasm

sèt láew ADJ เสร็จแล้ว (something) to be done, finished, completed, ready

sèt sîn ADJ เสร็จสิ้น over, done, completed

sí ซิ a particle that is used at the end of an utterance to request/urge (with some force) or persuade the other party do something, e.g. **pòeht thii wii sí** เปิดทีวีซิ 'come on, turn on that TV will you'; **duu sí** ดูซิ 'Look at that!/do look, will you'

sǐa ADJ เสีย to be spoiled, broken, out of order, spoiled; to have gone off (food) V to spend, pay; to

be dead; to die

sǐa chii-wít V เสียชีวิต to die, pass away

sǐa chûeh V เสียชื่อ to get a bad name, spoil one's reputation, be discredited, look bad

sǐa daai EXP เสียดาย to regret, be sorry; 'what a shame', 'too bad'

sǐa jai V เสียใจ to feel sorry, regretful, be disappointed

sǐa ngoehn V เสียเงิน to waste money; to pay/spend

sǐa phaa-sǐi V เสียภาษี to pay tax(es)

sǐa sà-là V เสียสละ to sacrifice, give up (something)

sǐa tua V (COLLOQUIAL) เสียตัว (for a woman) to lose her virginity, to have sex the first time, to sleep with (a man)

sǐa wehlaa V เสียเวลา to waste time

sǐang N เสียง a sound, noise, tone; voice

sìang V เสี่ยง to risk, take a risk, take a chance

siang chii-wít v เสี่ยงชีวิต to risk one's life

siang dang ADJ เสียงดัง to be loud, noisy

sìao ADJ เสียว hair-raising, chilling; to feel a thrill of pleasure/pain; (sexually) exciting

sìi NUM สี่ four

sǐi N สี color, also the word for paint (Here is a list of common colors: white **sǐi khǎaw** สีขาว; black **sǐi dam** สีดำ (pronounced 'dum'); green **sǐi khǐao** สีเขียว; red **sǐi daeng** สีแดง; orange **sǐi sôm** สีส้ม; yellow **sǐi lǔeang** สีเหลือง; brown **sǐi náam-taan** สีน้ำตาล; (sky) blue **sǐi fáa** สีฟ้า; (navy/royal) blue **sǐi náam ngoehn** สีน้ำเงิน; pink **sǐi chomphuu** สีชมพู; gray/grey **sǐi thao** สีเทา)

sii dii N (from English) ซีดี CD

sii eíu N ซีอิ๊ว soy sauce (salty)

sii eíu wǎan N ซีอิ๊วหวาน soy sauce (sweet)

sìi lìam N สี่เหลี่ยม square (shape)

sìi sìp NUM สี่สิบ forty

sǐi tòk v สีตก (for the color of clothing, for example) to run

sìi yâehk N สี่แยก (four-way) intersection

sí-kâa N (from English) ซิการ์ cigar

sìng N สิ่ง item, individual thing

sǐng N สิงห์ a lion (NOTE: this is the name of the well-known Thai beer – written in English as Singha but which is actually pronounced **sǐng** or, more fully **bia sǐng** เบียร์สิงห์ (Singha beer)

sìng khǎwng N สิ่งของ thing(s), object(s)

sìng kìit khwǎang N สิ่งกีดขวาง (a) hindrance, (an) obstruction

sìng wâeht láwm N สิ่งแวดล้อม the environment, surroundings

sǐng-hǎa-khom N สิงหาคม August

sǐngkhá-poh N สิงคโปร์ Singapore

sĭnlá-pà N ศิลปะ art

sĭnlá-pin N (commonly pronounced **sĭnlapin**) ศิลปิน artist

sip NUM สิบ ten; the numbers 11–19 are as follows: **sìp èt** สิบเอ็ด eleven; **sìp sǎwng** สิบสอง twelve; **sìp sǎam** สิบสาม thirteen; **sìp sìi** สิบสี่ fourteen; **sìp hâa** สิบห้า fifteen; **sìp hòk** สิบหก sixteen; **sìp jèt** สิบเจ็ด seventeen; **sìp pàet** สิบแปด eighteen; **sìp kâo** สิบเก้า nineteen

sìrì mongkhon ADJ สิริมงคล (to be) auspicious, lucky, favorable

sitthí N (commonly pronounced 'sìt' with a low tone) สิทธิ rights (e.g. legal rights)

sôh N โซ่ chain

soh faa N (from English) โซฟา couch, sofa

sŏhm N โสม ginseng

sohm V, ADJ โทรม to deteriorate, decline (of a person); (to look) run down/worn out

sŏh-pheh-nii N (POLITE) โสเภณี prostitute

sòht ADJ โสด single, unmarried

soi N ซอย lane, side street (sometimes virtually a main road)

sôi N สร้อย bracelet

sôi khaw N สร้อยคอ necklace

sòkkàpròk ADJ สกปรก dirty, filthy

sôm N ส้ม orange (citrus fruit)

sŏm hèht phŏn ADJ สมเหตุผล reasonable, sensible, logical

sŏm khuan ADJ สมควร should, worthy (of), proper, appropriate

sôm oh N ส้มโอ pomelo (a type of tropical grapefruit)

sŏmbàt N (pronounced 'som-but') สมบัติ property, wealth

sŏmbuun ADJ สมบูรณ์ to be whole, entire, complete, plentiful; healthy V to have put on weight

sŏmmút V สมมติ to suppose,

319

assume, hypothetical; e.g. **sŏmmút wâa** สมมติว่า 'suppose (that)…'

son ADJ ซน naughty, mischievous, playful

sòng V ส่ง to send, deliver

sòng àwk V ส่งออก to export

sòng fáek V ส่งแฟกซ์ to send a fax

sòng ii-mehl V ส่งอีเมล์ to (send an) email

sŏng kraan N สงกรานต์ traditional Thai New Year (mid April – 13–15 April)

sŏngkhraam N สงคราม war

sŏngsăan V สงสาร to pity, feel sorry (for)

sŏngsăi V สงสัย to doubt, suspect

sŏn-jai ADJ สนใจ (to be) interested in

sòp N ศพ corpse, cadaver

sòt ADJ สด fresh

sòt chûen ADJ สดชื่น fresh, joyful

suai ADJ ซวย to be unlucky, accursed, (to have) bad luck; (mild expletive) Damn it!

sŭai ADJ สวย beautiful,

attractive, pretty (of places, things), beautiful

sûam N ส้วม toilet, lavatory

sùan N ส่วน a portion, share, section, piece, part (not the whole)

sŭan N สวน garden, orchard, plantation, park

sùan koehn N ส่วนเกิน (pronounced 'gurn') surplus, excess

sùan nùeng ADV, N ส่วนหนึ่ง partly; one part

sŭan săa-thaa-rá-ná N สวน สาธารณะ public garden/ park

sŭan sàt N สวนสัตว์ zoo

sùan tua ADJ ส่วนตัว private, personal (e.g. matters)

sùan yài ADV ส่วนใหญ่ mostly, for the most part

sùat mon V สวดมนต์ to chant/pray (Buddhist style)

sùea N เสื่อ mat

sûea N เสื้อ (general term for items of clothing/upper garments) shirt, blouse, coat

sŭea N เสือ tiger; (SLANG) bandit, gangster

320

sŭea bai N (COLLOQUIAL) เสื้อ
ไบ bisexual

sûea chán nai N เสื้อชั้นใน
underwear/underclothing
(general term)

sûea chóeht N (from
English) เสื้อเชิ้ต shirt

sŭea dam N เสื้อดำ (**dam**
pronounced similar to
'dum') leopard (literally,
'tiger'+'black')

sûea kák N เสื้อกั๊ก a vest,
waistcoat

sûea kan năow N เสื้อ
กันหนาว coat, jacket,
windcheater

sûea khlum N เสื้อคลุม robe,
cloak, cape; bathrobe

sûea klâam N เสื้อกล้าม
undershirt, muscle shirt

sûea nâwk N เสื้อนอก jacket,
coat

sûea nawn N เสื้อนอน
pajamas

sûea phâa N เสื้อผ้า clothes,
clothing, garments

sûea yûeht N เสื้อยืด T-shirt,
undershirt

súeh V ซื้อ to buy, purchase:
khăw súeh tŭa pai... ขอซื้อ

ตั๋วไป... May I buy a ticket
to ...?

sùeh V สื่อ to communicate

sùeh muanchon N สื่อมวลชน
mass media

sùeh-sàt ADJ ซื่อสัตย์ to be
honest

sùek-săa N, V ศึกษา
education; to educate, to
study

súeng ADJ ซึ้ง deep, profound

sùk ADJ สุก to be ripe, be
ready (e.g. to be eaten), be
cooked

sùk láew ADJ สุกแล้ว to be
done (cooked)

sùksăn wan kòeht
(FORMULAIC EXPRESSION
– not commonly used)
สุขสันต์วันเกิด happy
birthday!

sùksăn wan pii mài
(FORMULAIC EXPRESSION)
สุขสันต์วันปีใหม่ happy new
year!

su-nák N (FORMAL/POLITE)
สุนัข dog/canine

sù-phâap ADJ สุภาพ to be
polite, courteous, well-
mannered

321

sù-phâap sàtrii N สุภาพ สตรี lady

sù-rào N สุเหร่า mosque

sùt ADJ สุด end, utmost, most, -est, e.g. the tallest person – **khon** คน (person) **sŭung** สูง (tall) **thîi sùt** ที่สุด (-est)

sùt sàpdaa N (FORMAL) สุด สัปดาห์ weekend

sùt tháai ADJ สุดท้าย final, last

sùt yâwt EXP (COLLOQUIAL) สุดยอด That's cool/Great!/ Tops! The best!

sùu PREP สู่ to, towards

sûu V สู้ to fight (physically), fight back, oppose, resist

sùu khăw V สู่ขอ to ask for the hand (of someone) in marriage

sûu khwaam V สู้ความ to contest a legal action

suu-poehmaa-ket N (from English) ซูเปอร์มาร์เก็ต supermarket

sûu róp V สู้รบ to do battle, engage in combat

sûu taai V (COLLOQUIAL) สู้ตาย to fight to the bitter end

sŭun N ศูนย์ zero, naught

sŭun klaang ADJ ศูนย์กลาง center

sŭung ADJ สูง high, tall

sùup V สูบ to smoke (e.g. smoke cigarettes **sùup bùrii** สูบบุหรี่); to pump (in, out, up, away)

sùut N (from English) สูท suit (clothes)

sùut N สูตร formula, method, recipe

sùut aa-hăan N สูตรอาหาร recipe (for food)

T

NOTE: This letter should not be confused with the normal English 't' sound. It is pronounced somewhere between a 'd' and a 't', similar to the sound of the 't' in the word 'star'.

taa N ตา eye; (maternal) grandfather

taa bàwt ADJ ตาบอด to be blind, sightless

taa cháng N ตาชั่ง scales

taa daeng N, ADJ ตาแดง conjunctivitis; bleary eyed, red-eyed

taa tùm N ตาตุ่ม ankle bone

taai V ตาย to die, pass away EXCLAM 'Oh!', 'Damn!'

taai jai V ตายใจ to have implicit faith in, trust implicitly

taai tua ADJ ตายตัว to be fixed (e.g. a fixed or set price of something)

tàak V ตาก to dry, expose to the air

tàak hàehng V ตากแห้ง (to) dry out (in the sun)

tàak phâa V ตากผ้า to dry the clothing out (in the sun)

taa khàai N ตาข่าย net

taa khăow N, ADJ ตาขาว the white of the eye; cowardly

tàak dàet V ตากแดด to expose to the sun, spread out in the sun

taa khěh ADJ ตาเข slightly cross-eyed, squint-eyed

taam V ตาม to follow, accompany; in accordance with; along

taam doehm ADV ตามเดิม as before

taam jai V ตามใจ to go along with (whatever you think/want to do); to give in to; to please, indulge (someone)

taam khoei ADV ตามเคย as usual (as expected/as he/ she does habitually)

taam kòtmăai ADV ตาม กฎหมาย legally, according to the law

taam lamdàp ADV ตามลำดับ in order, respectively

taam lam phang ADV ตาม ลำพัง alone

taam lăng V ตามหลัง to follow behind

taam pàkatì ADV ตาม ปกติ ordinarily, usually, normally

taam thîi ADV ตามที่.... according to... (e.g. what he said)

tàang ADJ, V ต่าง each; other; different; to differ

tàang châat ADJ ต่างชาติ alien, foreign (e.g. people)

tàang dâow N ต่างด้าว alien

tàang hàak ADV ต่างหาก

323

extra, separately (i.e. additional/extra fees apply, etc.)

tàang hǔu N ต่างหู earring(s)

tàang jang-wàt N, ADJ ต่างจังหวัด out of town; provincial

tàang prà-thêht ADJ ต่างประเทศ overseas, abroad, international

tàang-tàang ADJ ต่างๆ different, diverse, various

taaràang wehlaa N ตารางเวลา timetable, schedule

taa-raang N ตาราง square (also used to refer to square meters **taa-raang méht** ตารางเมตร)

tà-bai N, V ตะไบ file (e.g. nail); to file (down)

tà-bai lép N ตะไบเล็บ nail file

tà-bawng-phét N ตะบองเพชร cactus

tàe V (pronounced with a very short vowel sound) แตะ to touch

tàeh CONJ แต่ but, however, only; (COLLOQUIAL) **tàeh wâa** แต่ว่า 'but (she said…)'

tàeh kàwn ADV แต่ก่อน formerly, previously

tàeh lá ADJ แต่ละ each, every: e.g. **tàeh lá pii** แต่ละปี each/every year; **tàeh lá khon** แต่ละคน each/every person

tàehk V, ADJ แตก to be broken, shattered, cracked

tàehk là-iat V แตกละเอียด to break, shatter into tiny pieces

tàehk ngâai ADJ แตกง่าย breakable

tàehk ngoehn V (COLLO-QUIAL) แตกเงิน to get change, to break (a bill)

tàehk yâek ADJ แตกแยก divided, disunited, broken apart

taen N แตน hornet

taeng N แตง melon (general term)

tàeng V แต่ง to write, arrange, compose (letters, books, music)

taeng kwaa N แตงกวา cucumber

taeng moh N แตงโม watermelon

tàeng nâa V แต่งหน้า to make up

tàeng ngaan v แต่งงาน to marry, get married

tàeng ngaan láew ADJ แต่งงานแล้ว to be married

tàeng phlehng v แต่งเพลง to write or compose a song

tàeng tua v แต่งตัว to get dressed

tâi PREP ใต้ under, below; south

tai N ไต kidney(s)

tài v ไต่ to go up, climb (hills, mountains)

tâi din ADJ ใต้ดิน underground

tài sǎn v ไต่สวน to interrogate (a witness or accused person)

tâifùn N ไต้ฝุ่น typhoon

tàk N ตัก lap (i.e. 'the baby is sitting on her lap')

tàk v ตัก (pronounced similar to 'tuck' with the 'star' sound and a low tone) to draw, scoop up – **tàk khâaw** v ตักข้าว to help oneself/others to rice; to dish out the rice

tà-kawn N ตะกอน sediment, silt

ták-kà-taen N ตั๊กแตน grasshopper, locust

tà-khàap N ตะขาบ centipede

tà-khǎw N ตะขอ hook

tà-khrâi N ตะไคร่ moss

tà-khrái N ตะไคร้ lemongrass

tà-khriu N ตะคริว cramp

tà-kìap N ตะเกียบ chopstick(s)

tà-kiang N ตะเกียง lamp, lantern

tà-kohn v ตะโกน to cry out, shout, yell

tà-krâa N ตะกร้า basket

tà-kraeng N ตะแกรง shallow basket used as a sieve or strainer, sieve

tà-krâw N ตะกร้อ rattan ball, kind of a Thai ball game

tà-kùa N ตะกั่ว lead

tà-làat N ตลาด market, bazaar

tà-làat hûn N ตลาดหุ้น stock market

tà-làat náam N ตลาดน้ำ floating market (the most notable being in Ratburi/ Ratchaburi province)

tà-làat nát N ตลาดนัด occasional market (common in Thailand)

325

– perhaps once or twice a week/month, etc. in different spots in a given locality

tà-làat sòt N ตลาดสด food market, market in which raw or perishable food stuffs are sold

tà-làp N ตลับ (very) small box, compact (for make-up), case

tà-làwt PREP, ADV ตลอด through, throughout, all the time, from beginning to end

tà-làwt chii-wít ADV ตลอด ชีวิต for life, throughout one's life

tà-làwt pai ADV ตลอดไป forever, always, all the time

tà-làwt thaang ADV ตลอดทาง all the way

tà-lìng N ตลิ่ง bank (of a river)

tà-lòk ADJ ตลก funny, comical, ridiculous

tàm ADJ ต่ำ low, inferior, base

tam V ตำ to pound, beat (part of the word for the Northeastern Thai dish

'green papaya salad' **sôm tam** ส้มตำ)

tambon N ตำบล sub-district: an administrative unit in Thailand, often spelled in English as 'tombol'. In the Thai spelling the final letter is the letter 'l' but it is pronounced as an 'n'

tam-lueng N ตำลึง old Thai monetary unit; a kind of Thai plant

tam-naan N ตำนาน legend, chronicle

tam-nàeng N ตำแหน่ง position (in an organization)

tam-rùat N ตำรวจ police

tan N ตัน ton ADJ clogged up, solid (not hollow), stopped up

tâng V ตั้ง to set, place, erect, establish, settle, locate, appoint, form

tang chûe V ตั้งชื่อ to give a name to

tâng jai V ตั้งใจ to intend; to pay attention

tâng sà-tì V ตั้งสติ to concentrate

tâng-tàeh conj ตั้งแต่ since

tâng tôn v ตั้งต้น start, beginning

tâng yùu v ตั้งอยู่ to be situated, located

tao N เตา a stove (gas/electric), a traditional-style charcoal cooker/brazier

tao pîng N เตาปิ้ง toaster

tao káet N เตาแก๊ส gas stove

tào N เต่า turtle

tào hûu N เต้าหู้ beancurd, tofu

tao òp N เตาอบ oven

tao rîit N เตารีด iron

tào tà-nù N เต่าตนุ (sea) turtle

tàp N (pronounced similar to 'tup' with a low tone) ตับ liver (vital organ)

tàp àwn N ตับอ่อน pancreas

tà-puu N ตะปู a nail (spike)

tàt v ตัด to cut, cut off, sever

tàt phŏm v ตัดผม to have a haircut

tàt sĭn jai v ตัดสินใจ to decide, make a decision

tàw v ต่อ to extend (e.g. a visa); to lengthen; to join, reconnect (e.g. a severed limb)

taw-lăe v ตอแหล to lie, talk a lot; (COLLOQUIAL) babble, chatter

tàw pai v ต่อไป next (in line, sequence)

tàw ráwng v ต่อรอง to bargain, negotiate

tàw tâan v ต่อต้าน to oppose

tàw waay-faay v ต่อวายฟาย connect to Wi-Fi

tà-wan àwk N ตะวันออก east

tà-wan àwk chĭang nŭea N ตะวันออกเฉียงเหนือ north-east

tà-wan àwk chĭang tâi N ตะวันออกเฉียงใต้ south-east

tà-wan tòk N ตะวันตก west

tà-wan tòk chĭang nŭea N ตะวันตกเฉียงเหนือ north-west

tà-wan tòk chĭang tâi N ตะวันตกเฉียงใต้ south-west

tàwm náam laai N ต่อมน้ำลาย saliva gland

tàwm náam lŭeang N ต่อมน้ำเหลือง lymph gland

tawn N ตอน part, period; episode

tâwn v ต้อน to castrate, geld, neuter, spay

tawn bàai ADV ตอนบ่าย in the afternoon

tawn klaang khuehn ADV ตอนกลางคืน at night, during the night

tawn nǎi ADV ตอนไหน when?, what time?

tawn níi ADV ตอนนี้ now

tawn lǎng ADV ตอนหลัง later on, subsequently

tawn rôehm tôn N ตอนเริ่มต้น (at the) beginning

tawn sǎai N ตอนสาย late morning

tawn tîi PREP ตอนที่ as

tawn thîang N ตอนเที่ยง at noon, noontime

tawn yen N ตอนเย็น evening

tâwng AUX V ต้อง have to, must

tâwng hâam ADJ, V ต้องห้าม to be forbidden, prohibited; taboo

tâwng kaan AUX V ต้องการ to want, desire, must have

tàwp V ตอบ to answer, respond; reply

tàwp sà-nǎwng ตอบสนอง to respond, react

tèh V เตะ to kick, boot (e.g. a football)

tem ADJ เต็ม to be full, complete, filled up

tem jai ADJ เต็มใจ willing

tên/tên ram V เต้น, เต้นรำ to dance

tîa ADJ เตี้ย to be short, low

tiang N เตียง bed, bedstead

tiang diao N เตียงเดี่ยว single bed

tiang khûu N เตียงคู่ double bed

tì-chom V ติชม to find fault with, find both good and bad points

tii V ตี to hit, strike, beat

tii klawng V ตีกลอง to drum

tiin N ตีน foot, paw (sometimes considered vulgar)

tiin kòp N ตีนกบ diving fins

tii phim V ตีพิมพ์ to print, publish

tii raa-khaa V ตีราคา to estimate the value/price, give an estimate; set the price (of something)

tii sà-nìt V (COLLOQUIAL)

ตีสนิท to get on familiar terms, get close (to), become 'mates/buddies'; to befriend (for ulterior motives)

tìng N ติ่ง outgrowth, appendage: **sâi tìng** ไส้ติ่ง appendix (body part)

tìt v (not pronounced like the English word 'tit') ติด to stick, get stuck; be addicted to; to be close to; to owe, be owed

tìt àang v ติดอ่าง to stutter, stammer

tìt kan ADJ ติดกัน next, adjoining; stuck together

tìt kàp v ติดกับ to be trapped; next to

tìt khúk v ติดคุก to be gaoled/ jailed, go to gaol/jail; to be imprisoned

tìt lâo ADJ ติดเหล้า alcohol addicted

tìt lòm v ติดหล่ม to get stuck in the mud

tìt rôhk v ติดโรค to catch a disease

tìt taam v ติดตาม to follow

tìt tâng v ติดตั้ง to install, put

in (e.g. air conditioning)

tìt tàw v ติดต่อ to communicate with, contact, get in touch with; contagious/ infectious (e.g. disease)

tìt jai v ติดใจ to like, be fond of, be attracted or impressed

tìt thúrá v ติดธุระ to be busy, tied up (with some other matter)

toehm v เติม to add, put in (e.g. petrol)

toehm náam man v เติม น้ำมัน to refuel (gasoline)

tì v ติ to criticize, blame

toh ADJ (pronounced with a long vowel sound) โต to be big, large, mature

tó! N (pronounced very short!) โต๊ะ desk, table

toh khûen v โตขึ้น to grow larger (e.g. a tree); growing up (e.g. children)

tôh tàwp v โต้ตอบ to reply to, retort, argue

tòi v ต่อย to punch, box, strike; (for a bee) to sting

tòk v ตก to fall, drop, diminish, decrease

329

tòk jai ADJ ตกใจ alarmed, startled

tòk ngaan V ตกงาน to be out of work, to lose one's job

tòk plaa V ตกปลา to fish

tòk rót V (COLLOQUIAL) ตกรถ to miss (a bus, train)

tòk yâak V ตกยาก to fall on hard times; to be impoverished; to suffer misfortune

tòk-long V ตกลง to agree; OK, agreed!

tòk-long tham V ตกลงทำ to agree to do something

tom N ตม bog, mud

tôm V ต้ม to boil (water); (COLLOQUIAL/SLANG) take (someone) for a ride, swindle; to be taken in, cheated (out of something)

tôm khàa N ต้มข่า mildish coconut/cream soup flavored with galangal, kaffir lime, etc.

tôm yam N (pronounced similar to 'tom yum') ต้มยำ a Thai (generally clear) soup with a spicy, lemony taste

tôn N ต้น classifier for trees or plants

tôn mai N ต้นไม้ plant, tree

tôn chà-bàp N ต้นฉบับ script, manuscript

tôn khǎa N ต้นขา thigh

tôn khaw N ต้นคอ neck

tôn náam N ต้นน้ำ spring (river)

tòp V ตบ to clap, slap

tòp mueh V ตบมือ to clap hands

tòp tàeng V ตบแต่ง to beautify, improve the appearance; to marry off one's daughter

tòt N, V ตด to fart; to fart, pass wind

traa N ตรา seal, stamp, chop, brand

traa châng N ตราชั่ง scale

trài trawng V ไตร่ตรอง to consider, think (something over), ponder

traeh N แตร horn, trumpet, bugle

trà-kuun N ตระกูล lineage, family

tràwk N ตรอก alley, narrow passage

triam v เตรียม to prepare, make ready

triam phráwm v เตรียมพร้อม to be prepared, ready for action

triam tua v เตรียมตัว to get ready

trong ADJ ตรง straight; accurate; direct, non-stop (e.g. flight)

trong khâam ADJ, PREP ตรง ข้าม opposite (facing): **trong kan khâam** ตรง กันข้าม on the contrary; conversely

trong kan v ตรงกัน to correspond, coincide

trong klaang ADJ ตรงกลาง in the middle/center

trong pai khâng nâa ADJ, ADV ตรงไปข้างหน้า (go/it's) straight ahead

trong wehlaa ADJ ตรงเวลา (to be) on time, punctual

trùat v ตรวจ to inspect, examine, check

trùat sàwp v ตรวจสอบ to check, verify, test

tua N ตัว body; thing classifier for counting animals, tables, chairs and clothes

tǔa N ตั๋ว ticket (for transport, entertainment)

tua àksǎwn N ตัวอักษร letter, character (written), alphabet

tua ehng PRON ตัวเอง oneself

tua jing N ตัวจริง original, (the) genuine (article), (the) real (thing)

tua lêhk N ตัวเลข number, numeral, figure

túk-kà-taa N ตุ๊กตา doll

tua mia N ตัวเมีย female (used for animals/plants)

tua nǎng sǔe N ตัวหนังสือ letter, character (of the alphabet)

tua nóht N ตัวโน้ต musical note

tǔa pai klàp N ตั๋วไปกลับ return ticket: **khâa-tǔa pai-klàp thâo-rài?** ค่าตั๋วไป กลับเท่าไร How much is a round-trip ticket?

tua phûu N ตัวผู้ male (used for animals/plants)

tua ráwn v ตัวร้อน to have a high temperature

tua sàn v ตัวสั่น to shake, tremble

tŭa thîao diao N ตั๋วเที่ยว เดียว one-way ticket

tua yàang N ตัวอย่าง example, sample

tua yàang chên ADV ตัวอย่างเช่น such as, for example

tua yâw N ตัวย่อ abbreviation

tuean v เตือน to remind, warn

tùek N ตึก building

tueng ADJ ตึง tight

tûehn ADJ ตื้น to be shallow, not deep, superficial

tùehn/tûehn nawn v ตื่น, ตื่น นอน to wake up, be awake, get up (from sleeping)

tùehn tên v, ADJ ตื่นเต้น to be excited; exciting

tù-laa-khom N ตุลาคม October

tûm hŭu N ตุ้มหู earring(s)

tûu N ตู้ cupboard, cabinet, closet, bogie (of train)

tûu e-thii-em N ตู้เอทีเอ็ม ATM machine: mii tûu-e-thii-em mái? มีตู้เอทีเอ็มไหม Is there an ATM machine around here?

tûu nâng N ตู้นั่ง passenger car (of train)

tûu nawn N ตู้นอน sleeping car (of train)

tûu prai-sà-nii N ตู้ไปรษณีย์ letter box

tûu-sà-biang N ตู้เสบียง dining car (of train)

tûu thoh-rá-sàp N ตู้โทรศัพท์ telephone box

tûu năngsŭeh N ตู้หนังสือ bookshelf

tûu yen N ตู้เย็น refrigerator

tùut N ตูด ass, bottom, anus (vulgar)

TH

NOTE: This 'th' sound is the same as the English 't'. For example, in the words 'tie–Thai' – spelled differently, but pronounced exactly the same way

thaa v ทา to coat, paint, apply (e.g. sunscreen)

thâa CONJ ถ้า if, although; suppose

thâa ruea N ท่าเรือ harbor, port; wharf, pier

thaa sǐi V ทาสี to paint (e.g. a house, a wall)

tháa thaai V ท้าทาย to challenge, defy; to provoke

thâa thaang N ท่าทาง appearance, manner, bearing

thàai V ถ่าย to decant, pour out, discharge, throw away (FORMAL/POLITE) to defecate

thàai rûup V ถ่ายรูป to take a picture, photograph

thàai sǎmnao V ถ่ายสำเนา to make a photocopy

thǎm V ถาม to ask, enquire

thǎm kìao kàp V ถามเกี่ยวกับ to ask about

thǎn N ฐาน base (e.g. military), foundation, basis

thâan PRON ท่าน (polite form of address directly to, or when talking about, a higher status individual) he, she; him, her, you; sir

thaan V, N (COLLOQUIAL/POLITE) ทาน to eat (also 'drink'; the colloquial equivalent is **kin**);

donation, charity

thaan aa-hǎan yen V (COLLOQUIAL/POLITE) ทาน อาหารเย็น to eat dinner

thaan khâaw thîang (COLLOQUIAL/POLITE) ทา นข้าวเที่ยง to eat lunch

thǎa-ná N ฐานะ position, status, standing

thaang N ทาง way, path, direction

thaang àwk N ทางออก exit, way out

thaang doenh N ทางเดิน aisle: **khǎw thîi-nâng rim thaang doenh** ขอที่นั่งริมทาง เดิน Can I get an aisle seat please?

thaang kaan ADJ ทางการ official, formal; **phaa-sǎa thaang kaan** N ภาษาทางการ official/formal language

thaang khâo N ทางเข้า entrance, way in

thaang lûeak N, ADJ ทางเลือก choice; alternative

thaang rótfai N ทางรถไฟ railroad, railway

thaa-rók N (FORMAL) ทารก baby, infant

333

thàat N ถาด a tray

thăa-wawn ADJ ถาวร permanent, fixed, enduring

thaa-yâat N ทายาท heir, descendant

thá-bian bâan N ทะเบียนบ้าน census registration

thaen V, ADV แทน to represent; to substitute (for), in place of, instead (of); **tua thaen** ตัวแทน an agent, a representative (e.g. of a company)

thaen thîi แทนที่ instead of

thaen thîi jà... แทนที่จะ rather than...

tháeksîi N (from English) แท็กซี่ taxi: **khăw tháek-sîi khâ/khráp** ขอแท็กซี่ ค่ะ/ครับ I need a taxi, please.

thăem V แถม to give something extra, give in addition (e.g department store giveaways that often go with purchases above a certain amount; when a vendor gives you something 'extra' when buying fruit/fish etc. in a market)

thaeng V แทง to stab, pierce, prick

tháeng V แท้ง to abort; **tham tháeng** ทำแท้ง to have an abortion; **tháeng lûuk** แท้ง ลูก to have a miscarriage

thăew N แถว a row, line; area

thăew níi ADJ แถวนี้ around here (e.g. 'where's the bike shop?' 'around here/in this area')

thá-hăan N ทหาร soldier; (COLLOQUIAL) general term for someone in the armed services

thá-hăan aa-kàat N ทหาร อากาศ airman, airwoman; (the) air force (in general)

thá-hăan bòk N ทหารบก soldier in the army; (the) army (in general)

thá-hăan ruea N ทหาร เรือ sailor; (the) navy (in general)

thai ไทย Thai, Thailand; **khon thai** คนไทย a Thai person/Thai people; **châat thai** ชาติไทย the Thai nation; **prà-thêht thai** ประเทศไทย (the country)

Thailand; **phaa-săa thai** ภาษาไทย (the) Thai language

thák thaai v ทักทาย to greet, say hello

thá láw v, n ทะเลาะ to argue; an argument

thá-leh n ทะเล sea

thá-leh saai n ทะเลทราย a desert

thá-leh sàap n ทะเลสาบ a lake

thâm n ถ้ำ a cave

tham n ธรรม Dharma, the Buddha's teaching, the Doctrine

tham v ทำ to do, perform an action, make, act, undergo; see **tham hâi** ทำให้ in the next column – a very important aspect of the Thai language – commonly these two words go together to express the idea of 'to do (something) to/for (someone else)'

tham aa-hǎan v ทำอาหาร to cook

tham bun v ทำบุญ to make merit, perform good deeds,

give to charity

tham dii thîi sùt v ทำดีที่สุด to do one's best

tham dûai ADJ ทำด้วย made of/made from; **tham dûai mueh** ทำด้วยมือ made by hand, handmade

tham dûai mái/tham jàak mái ทำด้วยไม้/ทำจากไม้ to be made from wood/timber; wooden

tham fan v ทำฟัน to go to the dentist

tham hǎai v ทำหาย to lose, mislay

tham hâi v ทำให้ to make/do something to/for someone; to cause: e.g. **tham hâi khǎo jep** ทำให้เขาเจ็บ to hurt him (to cause him pain/grief)

tham hâi chamrút v ทำให้ชำรุด to cause damage

tham hâi hâeng v ทำให้แห้ง to (make something) dry

tham hâi jom náam v ทำให้จมน้ำ (to cause someone – the cause, for example, being the rough sea) to drown

335

tham hâi lâa cháa v
ทำให้ล่าช้า to delay

tham hâi mâi phaw jai v
ทำให้ไม่พอใจ to offend; to
offend (someone else)

tham hâi pen rûup v
ทำให้เป็นรูป to form/make
into (the) shape (of)

tham hâi pháeh v ทำให้แพ้ to
defeat, (or, more precisely)
to make (someone) lose

tham hâi phráwm v
ทำให้พร้อม to make ready

tham hâi pùat v ทำให้ปวด
to (make) ache/to cause
(some bodily part) to ache

tham hâi ráwn v ทำให้ร้อน to
heat, make hot

tham hâi sèt v ทำให้เสร็จ to
complete, finish off

tham hâi yen v ทำให้เย็น to
(make) cool

tham jai v ทำใจ to accept
(e.g. unpleasant news),
manage one's emotions/
feelings; come to terms with
(it); make the best of (it, a
situation, etc.)

tham jing-jing v ทำ
จริงๆ to do seriously, do

(something) in earnest

tham khwaam sà-àat v
ทำความสะอาด to clean

tham ngaan v ทำงาน to
work, function

tham phìt ADJ ทำผิด (to do
something morally) wrong

tham ráai v ทำร้าย to harm,
injure, hurt; do violence to

tham sám v (sám
pronounced similar to
'sum' with a high tone) ทำ
ซ้ำ to repeat

tham sĭa v ทำเสีย to spoil
something, ruin; to break

tham sŏngkhraam v ทำ
สงคราม to wage war, make
war

tham sŭan N ทำสวน
gardening

tham tàw pai ทำต่อไป v
to continue on (doing
something), to keep doing
something

tham tua v ทำตัว to act,
behave

tham tua dii ADJ ทำตัวดี to be
well-behaved

tham tua hâi sà-nùk v ทำตัว
ให้สนุก to enjoy oneself

tham wí-jai v ทำวิจัย to research, to do research

thamlaai v ทำลาย to destroy, demolish, ruin

thamleh N ทำเล location (e.g. a good location for a business), district

thammá-châat N, ADJ ธรรมชาติ nature; natural

thammá-daa ADJ ธรรมดา ordinary, common, simple, normal, undistinguished

tham-mai (question word) ทำไม why?, what for?, what?

tham naa v ทำนา to grow rice

tham naai v ทำนาย to predict, foretell, prophesy

tham-niam N ธรรมเนียม custom, tradition, practice; **khâa tham-niam** N ค่าธรรมเนียม a fee (e.g. for a government/official service)

tham thôht v ทำโทษ to punish

than ADV, v ทัน in time (e.g. to get the bus), to have time (to do something); to catch, catch up with

than sà-mǎi ADJ ทันสมัย to be modern, contemporary

than thii ADV ทันที at once, immediately

thá-naai khwaam N ทนายความ; (COLLOQUIAL) **thanai** ทนาย lawyer

thá-naa-khaan N ธนาคาร bank (financial institution): **thá-naa-khaan pòeht kìi-mohng?** ธนาคารเปิดกี่โมง What time does the bank open?

thá-ná-bàt N ธนบัตร (bank) note

thà-nǎwm v ถนอม to take care of, treat with care, cherish, nurture, conserve (e.g. one's complexion, a vintage car, etc.)

thà-nǎwm aa-hǎan V, N ถนอมอาหาร to preserve food; food preservation

thà-nǒn N ถนน road, street, avenue

thá nuu N ธนู bow, arrow

tháng ADJ ทั้ง all, entire, the whole of

tháng khuehn N ทั้งคืน all night (long)

tháng khûu PRON ทั้งคู่ both, both of them

tháng mòt ADV ทั้งหมด altogether, all, the whole lot

tháng prà-thêht N ทั้งประเทศ the whole country

tháng wan ADV ทั้งวัน the whole day

than jai ADV ทันใจ as quickly as desired

thanwaa-khom N ธันวาคม December

thâo ADJ เท่า as much as, the same as, equal (to), equivalent (to)

tháo N เท้า foot/feet (used for humans only)

thâo kan ADJ เท่ากัน equal (e.g. amounts of something)

thâo nán ADV, ADJ เท่านั้น just, only (used at the end of a sentence)

thâo rài (question word) เท่าไร how much? (used at the end of a sentence)

thâo thiam ADJ เท่าเทียม to be equal

tháp-phii N ทัพพี a ladle, dipper

thàt pai ADJ ถัดไป (the) next, succeeding (e.g. client, government)

thátsà-ná-khá-tì N ทัศนคติ opinion, view, outlook (on particular matters), attitude

thaw V ทอ to weave

thá-waan nàk N (medical term) ทวารหนัก anus

thá-wìip N ทวีป continent

thá-yer-thá-yaan ADJ ทะเยอะทะยาน ambitious

thǎwn V ถอน to withdraw (e.g. money from the bank), retract; to uproot, extract, pull out, e.g. **thǎwn fan** ถอนฟัน to pull out a tooth

thǎwn-ngoehn V ถอนเงิน to withdraw money

thawng N ทอง gold

thawng N, ADJ ท้อง stomach, belly; to be pregnant

thawng daeng N ทองแดง copper

thawng samrít N ทองสัมฤทธิ์ bronze

thawrá-maan V ทรมาน to torture, punish, torment; to suffer agonizing pain

338

thàwt v ถอด to take off, remove (clothes, shoes)

thâwt v ทอด to (deep-)fry; fried

theh v เท to pour (e.g. water out of a container)

thehp n (from English) เทป adhesive tape

thêht-sà-kaan n เทศกาล festival

thennít n (from English) เทนนิส tennis

thiam ADJ เทียม artificial (e.g. leg), synthetic

thian n เทียน candle

thǐang v เถียง to argue, dispute, bicker

thîang khuehn n เที่ยงคืน midnight

thîang wan n เที่ยงวัน midday

thîao n เที่ยว trip, journey

thîao v เที่ยว to go out for fun/pleasure; to go around; to visit

thîao bin n เที่ยวบิน a flight (a trip on an airplane)

thîaw-bin-trong n เที่ยวบินตรง direct flight

thîao diao n เที่ยวเดียว a single trip; one-way ticket

khâa-tǔa thîao diao thâo-rài? ค่าตัวเที่ยวเดียวเท่าไร How much is a one-way ticket?

thîao phûu-yǐng v (COLLOQUIAL) เที่ยวผู้หญิง to go whoring, for a man to go out and have sex with a prostitute/prostitutes

thii n ที time, occasion; chance, opportunity; classifier for counting the number of times

thîi ที PREP in, at (space) n site, place, space; that, which, the one who; portion, serve (food)

thîi bâan ADV ที่บ้าน at home

thîi din n ที่ดิน land (a piece of land)

thîi jàwt rót n ที่จอดรถ (a) carpark, parking lot

thîi jing ADV ที่จริง in fact, actually

thîi kiao khâwng ที่เกี่ยวข้อง (that which is) involved; concerning

thîi kwâang ADJ ที่กว้าง spacious

thii lá khon (COLLOQUIAL) ที่

ละคน one by one (e.g. were given a vaccination shot one by one)

thii lá lék thii lá nói (COLLOQUIAL) ที่ละเล็กที่ละน้อย little by little, bit by bit; also (COLLOQUIAL) **thii la nit** ที่ละนิด gradually, bit by bit

thii láew ADV ที่แล้ว ago: e.g. **sǎwng pii thii láew** สองปีที่แล้ว two years ago

thii lǎng ADV ที่หลัง later (on), afterwards

thii lǔea ADJ, N ที่เหลือ left, leftover, remaining, the rest

thii maa N ที่มา origin, source

thii nǎi (question tag) ที่ไหน where?

thii nǎi kâw dâi (COLLOQUIAL) ที่ไหนก็ได้ anywhere (at all)

thii nân ADV ที่นั่น there

thii nâng N ที่นั่ง a seat, a place to sit

thii nawn N ที่นอน a mattress

thii nii ADV ที่นี่ here

thii nôhn ADV ที่โน่น over there

thii phák N ที่พัก accommodation

thii râap N ที่ราบ (a) plain,

flatland, flat area

thii rák N ที่รัก darling, dear

thii rawng jaan N ที่รองจาน tablemat

thii sǎam ADJ ที่สาม third (e.g. the third person to go, third place in a race, etc.); in Thai ordinal numbers (1st, 2nd, 3rd, etc.) are created by placing **thii** ที่ in front of a given number: first (1st) **thii nèung** ที่หนึ่ง; second (2nd) **thii sǎwng** ที่ สอง, etc.

thii sǎa-thaa-rá-ná N ที่ สาธารณะ public place

thii sìap plúk N ที่เสียบปลั๊ก socket (electric)

thii sùt ADV ที่สุด the end, finally; -est (superlative), most, extremely; e.g. **dii thii sùt** ดีที่สุด the best; **rew thii sùt** เร็วที่สุด the fastest; **sǔai thii sùt** สวยที่สุด the most beautiful

thii tham ngaan N ที่ทำงาน place of work, office, etc.

thii thǔeh N ที่ถือ (a) handle

thii wâang ที่ว่าง (to have) room, space

thii wii N (from English) ทีวี TV, television

thii yùu N ที่อยู่ address

thii yùu ii-mehl ที่อยู่อีเมล email address

thiim N (from English) (pronounced similar to the English word) ทีม team

thíng V (pronounced like 'ting' with a high tone) ทิ้ง to throw away; to desert, abandon

thíng wái V ทิ้งไว้ (to) leave something somewhere (with intent) (The form of use is as follows – **thíng** (object) **wái**, e.g. **khǎo thíng rót wái thîi bâan phûean** เขาทิ้งรถไว้ที่บ้านเพื่อน) she left her car at her friend's place

thíp N, V (from English) ทิป (to) tip (gratuity)

thoeh PRON (pronounced similar to 'ter') เธอ you (intimate)

thoehm N (from English) เทอม school term; **pit thoehm** ปิดเทอม the end of (the school) term

thohrá-sàp N โทรศัพท์ telephone

thohrá-sàp mueh thǔeh N โทรศัพท์มือถือ, (COLLOQUIAL) **mueh thǔeh** มือถือ mobile phone

thohrá-thát N โทรทัศน์ (somewhat formal) television

thôht V, N โทษ to blame; punishment, penalty, sentence

thǒi V ถอย to retreat, draw back; to back up

thǒi lǎng V ถอยหลัง to go in reverse, back up, backwards

thòk panhǎa V ถกปัญหา to discuss

thon V ทน to put up with, tolerate, bear, stand, endure

thon fai ADJ ทนไฟ fireproof

thon náam ADJ ทนน้ำ waterproof

thon thaan ADJ ทนทาน lasting, durable, sturdy

thon thúk V ทนทุกข์ to suffer

thonbùrii N ธนบุรี Thonburi, area opposite Bangkok on the west bank of

341

the Chaophraya River.
The capital of the Thai
kingdom before Bangkok
(**Krungthep**) assumed this
role in 1782

thong N ธง flag

thong châat N ธงชาติ
national flag

thót lawng V ทดลอง to try,
experiment, test, give
(something) a trial

thûa ADJ ทั่ว all over,
throughout

thùa N ถั่ว bean(s), pea(s)
(general term)

thùa daehng N ถั่วแดง
kidney bean(s)

thùa dam N ถั่วดำ black
bean(s)

thùa fàk yaow N ถั่วฝัก
ยาว (long) green bean(s),
stringbean(s)

thùa lantao N ถั่วลันเตา
snowpea(s)

thùa lí-sŏng N ถั่วลิสง
peanut(s)

thùa ngâwk N ถั่วงอก (mung)
bean sprout(s)

thûa pai ADV ทั่วไป in general,
generally

thûa prà-thêet ADV ทั่ว
ประเทศ all over the
country; throughout the
country

thûai N (pronounced 'two-
ay' with a falling tone)
ถ้วย cup

thûeh V ถือ to hold something (in the hands); to
believe in (e.g. a religion,
faith, set of ideas); to mind
(i.e. to be offended by
some form of behavior,
way of dress, etc.)

thûeh sĭin V ถือศีล to keep/
observe the rules/precepts
(of religion)

thûeh tua ADJ ถือตัว to be
aloof, reserved; to have a
high opinion of oneself

thŭeng V ถึง to reach, arrive
(at), get to

thŭeng láew ถึงแล้ว to have
arrived; (COLLOQUIAL) we're
here (at the destination)

thŭeng máeh wâa... CONJ
ถึงแม้ว่า although, even
though

thúk ADJ ทุก each, every, all

thúk chá-nít N ทุกชนิด every

type, every kind of

thúk khon PRON ทุกคน
everybody, everyone

thúk khuehn ADV, ADJ ทุกคืน
every night, nightly

thúk sìng PRON ทุกสิ่ง
everything

thúk sìng thúk yàng PRON
(COLLOQUIAL) ทุกสิ่งทุกอย่าง
everything

thúk thîi ADV ทุกที่ everywhere

thúk thîi ADV ทุกที every time,
also (more commonly)
thúk khráng ทุกครั้ง

thun N ทุน funds, funding,
capital

thǔng N ถุง bag (i.e. plastic
or paper bag)

thǔng mueh N ถุงมือ glove(s)

thǔng tháo N ถุงเท้า sock(s)

**thǔng yaang (à-naa-
mai)** N ถุงยาง (อนามัย),
(commonly) **thǔng yaang**
ถุงยาง condom

thú-rá N ธุระ business,
affairs, work, something
to do; **tìt thúrá** ติดธุระ to
be busy, tied up, engaged,
occupied

thú-rákìt N ธุรกิจ business;

nák thu-rakìt นักธุรกิจ
businessman/woman

thú-rian N ทุเรียน durian
(tropical fruit)

thút-jàrìt ADJ ทุจริต dishonest,
corrupt, crooked (e.g.
officials, etc.)

thǔu V ถู to rub, scrub, polish,
wipe, clean (e.g. the floor)

thùuk ADJ, V ถูก to be cheap,
inexpensive; to be right,
correct; to touch; also used
to create the passive form:
e.g. he was hit by a car
khǎo thùuk rót chon เขา
ถูกรถชน

thùuk jai ADJ (COLLOQUIAL)
ถูกใจ to be pleased,
satisfied, content (with the
outcome of something)

thùuk jàp V ถูกจับ (**jàp**
pronounced similar to
'jup' with a low tone)
(COLLOQUIAL) to be arrested,
apprehended, caught

thùuk láew ADJ (COLLOQUIAL)
ถูกแล้ว yes, that's right

thùuk làwk V (COLLOQUIAL)
ถูกหลอก to be duped,
conned

thùuk luehm v ถูกลืม (to be) forgotten

thùuk tâwng ADJ ถูกต้อง to be correct

thùuk tham laai v ถูกทำลาย (for something to be) destroyed, ruined

thûup N รูป incense, joss stick

thûut N ทูต diplomat

U

ûak v อ้วก (COLLOQUIAL) to be sick; to vomit, spew, puke

ûan ADJ อ้วน to be fat, stout

ùap ADJ อวบ to be chubby

ùat v อวด to show off, strut, flaunt

ùat dii v อวดดี to be vainglorious, put on airs

ùat kèng v อวดเก่ง to show off

ùat rúu v อวดรู้ to be a know-it-all; pretentious

ù-bàat ADJ อุบาทว์ evil, sinister

ù-battihèht N อุบัติเหตุ accident

ù-bohsòt N อุโบสถ temple, consecrated assembly hall

ùdom ADJ อุดม rich in (i.e. fertile); great, excellent

ù-mohng N อุโมงค์ tunnel

ù-thaan v อุทาน to exclaim, cry out

ùt-thá-yaan N อุทยาน garden, park, national park

ùe (pronounced very short) อี (COLLOQUIAL) v to defecate
N poop

ueam ADJ เอือม fed up

ùehn ADJ อื่น other; **khon ùehn** คนอื่น other people/another person

ùehn-ùehn PRON, N อื่นๆ others

ù-jàat ADJ อุจาด obscene, filthy, shameful

ûm v อุ้ม to carry (e.g. a baby), hold in one's arms; (COLLOQUIAL/SLANG) **dohn ûm** โดนอุ้ม to be illegally taken and (usually) secretly killed

ùn v, ADJ อุ่น to heat; warm

un-hà-phuum N อุณหภูมิ temperature

ùn kaehng v อุ่นแกง to warm up the curry

344

ù-pà-kaa-rá v อุปการะ to support, look after, take care (of)

ù-pà-kawn N อุปกรณ์ equipment, instrument, implement

ù-pà-sàk N อุปสรรค obstacle, difficulty, impediment

ù-pà-thǎm N, v อุปถัมภ์ patronage; support; to give patronage

ùt-jaà-rá N (FORMAL MEDICAL TERM) อุจจาระ feces, stool, excrement

ùt nǔn v อุดหนุน to support, aid, back (someone or something)

ùtsàa N อุตส่าห์ to take the trouble (to do something), make an effort (to)

ùt-sǎa-hà-kam N, ADJ อุตสาหกรรม industry; industrial

ùu N อู่ cradle; drydock, boathouse

ûu ngaan v อู้งาน to work with unnecessary delay

ùu rót N อู่รถ garage (for mechanical repairs)

ùut N อูฐ a camel

345

W

waa N วา a linear Thai measure equal to 2 meters; **taa-rang waa** ตารางวา 1 square *waa* (or 4 sq.m.)

wâa... ว่า to speak, say, state, tell; that (introducing a spoken comment, remark, or quotation) – **kháo phûut wâa kháo mâi sàbaai** เขาพูดว่าเขาไม่สบาย he said that he was sick; to scold, rebuke, criticize (someone)

waai N (from English) ไวน์ wine

wáai EXCLAM (COLLOQUIAL) ว้าย Eek!, Oh! Oh my God, etc.

waai-faai N วายฟาย Wi-Fi connection

wâai náam v ว่ายน้ำ to swim

wǎan ADJ หวาน sweet (taste); (COLLOQUIAL) **pàak wǎan** ปากหวาน a smooth talker who uses sweet words and flattery with another person

wàan v หว่าน to sow, cast

waang v วาง to lay (something) down, place

(something somewhere)

waang jai ADJ วางใจ confident

wâang v ว่าง to be unoccupied, vacant, free, available; (COLLOQUIAL) **wehlaa wâang** เวลาว่าง to have spare/free time

wâang ngaan ADJ ว่างงาน to be unemployed, jobless

waang phǎehn v วางแผน to lay plans; to plot, scheme

wâang plào ADJ ว่างเปล่า to be vacant, unoccupied (e.g. piece of land), empty

waa-rá-sǎan N วารสาร magazine, periodical, journal

wâat v วาด to draw, paint, sketch

wâat phâap v วาดภาพ to draw/paint a picture; to portray, depict

wâatsà-nǎa N วาสนา fortune, good luck

wáe v วะ (pronounced very short) to stop by, pay a (quick) visit: (COLLOQUIAL) **wáe pai hǎa** แวะไปหา to pop in/drop by and visit (someone)

wàeng ADJ แหว่ง chipped, partly broken

wǎehn N แหวน a ring (jewellery)

wǎehn phét N แหวนเพชร (a) diamond ring

wâen taa N แว่นตา, (COLLOQUIAL) **wâen** แว่น (eye) glasses, spectacles; **wâen kan** (pronounced like 'gun') **dàet** แว่นกันแดด sunglasses

wái v ไว้ an important 'function' word in Thai – meaning 'to place, put; to keep, preserve, reserve'. Some examples of usage: to keep (name of object) [for the foreseeable future] **kèp** (name of object) **wái** เก็บไว้; to do something (for some ongoing/continuing purpose) **tham wái** ทำ ไว้; to leave (something somewhere for a period of time – either for a short period or for an unspecified length of time) **thíng** (pronounced 'ting' with a high tone) **wái** ทิ้งไว้:

e.g. leave the bag at home (and come back and get it later) **thíng kràpǎo wái thíi bâan** ทิ้งกระเป๋าไว้ที่บ้าน

wǎi v ไหว to be able (to do something), capable (of doing), up to it (a job, task, doing something, etc.); (COLLOQUIAL) **wǎi mǎi** ไหว ไหม 'Can you do it?' 'Are you up to it?' 'Can you manage it?': (to respond in the negative) **mâi wǎi** ไม่ไหว 'It's too much', 'I give up', 'I don't think I can manage (it)'

wǎi-phríp n ไหวพริบ adroitness

wai n วัย age (general term used with other words to refer to a particular age demographic or grouping); e.g. **wai rûn** วัยรุ่น youth, adolescent(s), teenager(s); **wai dèk** วัยเด็ก childhood; **wai chá-raa** วัยชรา old age, geriatric

wâi v ไหว้ the traditional Thai form of greeting and fundamental aspect of Thai social relations – to raise the hands pressed together up to the head as a sign of respect (an indicator of the relative status/position of those interacting – a 'junior/inferior' will always 'wâi' a 'superior' – the height of the 'wâi' is a clear indicator of the social standing of the parties involved); pay homage to. The **wâi** is a practice that is best avoided until one has developed a good deal of familiarity with Thai society.

wái jai v ไว้ใจ to trust

wâi jâo v ไหว้เจ้า to make a spirit offering; **wâi phrá** ไหว้พระ to salute/pay homage to a monk; to do one's chanting (in homage of Buddhism's Triple Gems)

wan n (pronounced similar to 'one') วัน day of the week

wan aa-thít n วันอาทิตย์ Sunday

wan angkhaan N วันอังคาร
Tuesday

wan duean pii kòeht N วัน
เดือนปีเกิด date of birth
(literally, 'day'-'month'-
'year'-'birth')

wan jan N วันจันทร์ Monday

wan kàwn ADV (COLLOQUIAL)
วันก่อน the day before;
some days before

wan kòeht N วันเกิด birthday

wan níi ADV, N วันนี้ today

wan phà-rúe-hàt N วันพฤหัส
Thursday (the full word
for Thursday is **wan phà-
rúe-hàt sà-baw-dii** วัน
พฤหัสบดี)

wan phút N วันพุธ Wednesday

wan săo N วันเสาร์ Saturday

wan sùk N วันศุกร์ Friday

wan thîi… วันที่ (the) date (of
the month), on the (date)

wan wén wan ADV
(COLLOQUIAL) วันเว้นวัน
every other day

wan yùt N วันหยุด day off

wan yùt phák phàwn N
วันหยุดพักผ่อน holiday,
vacation

wan yùt râat-chá-kaan N วัน

หยุดราชการ public holiday

wan yùt thêht-sà-kaan N
วันหยุดเทศกาล festival
holiday

wang N วัง palace

wăng V หวัง to hope

wanná-khádii N วรรณคดี
literature

wâow N ว่าว (a) kite; **chák
wâow** V ชักว่าว to fly a kite;
(COLLOQUIAL/SLANG) to
masturbate (males only)

wát N วัด temple, monastery
(e.g.Thai, Hindu-Balinese)
V to measure (e.g. the
length of something); **wát
tua** วัดตัว to take someone's
measurements

wàt N หวัด (a) cold (i.e. to
catch a cold)

wát bohraan N วัดโบราณ (an
ancient) temple

wát phrá kâew N วัดพระ
แก้ว Temple of the Emerald
Buddha in the precincts
of the old Grand Palace in
Bangkok

wát-sàdù N วัสดุ material
(e.g. building material),
ingredient

348

wát-táná-tham N วัฒนธรรม culture

wátthù N วัตถุ (general term similar to **wát-sàdù** วัสดุ above) thing, object, material (e.g. building material), substance; **wát-thù dìp** N วัตถุดิบ raw material(s); **wát-thù níyom** N วัตถุนิยม materialism

wehlaa N เวลา time, at the time; when; **tà-làwt wehlaa** ตลอดเวลา all of the time, continuously, always; **than** (pronounced similar to 'ton') **wehlaa** ทันเวลา (to be) in time (e.g. to catch a flight)

wehlaa wâang N เวลาว่าง spare time, free time, leisure time

wehn N เวร turn, shift, fate

wehn-kam N เวรกรรม misfortune, ill fated; EXCLAM (COLLOQUIAL) How awful! God almighty! etc.

weh-thii N เวที a stage, ring (e.g. boxing ring)

wéhn PREP เว้น to skip; excepting; **yók wén** ยกเว้น except, excluding, with the exception of

wép sâi N (from English) เว็บไซต์ website

wiang V เหวี่ยง to hurl

wian hŭa ADJ เวียนหัว dizzy

wîat-naam N เวียดนาม Vietnam

wí-chaa N วิชา knowledge; subject/branch of study

wí-chaa chîip N วิชาชีพ profession, occupation

wí-hăn N วิหาร Buddhist assembly hall (often written in English as 'Vihear' or 'Viharn' – despite the fact that there is no 'v' sound in Thai)

wii N หวี comb

wii-sâa N (from English) วีซ่า visa

wí-jaan V วิจารณ์ to criticize, comment (on), review (e.g. a book, film, etc.); **nák wi-jaan** นักวิจารณ์ a (professional) critic, commentator

wí-naa-thii N วินาที a second (of time)

wínai N วินัย discipline,

orderly conduct; Buddhist disciplinary rules; **mii winai** ADJ มีวินัย (to be) orderly, disciplined

wín maw-ter-sai N วิน มอเตอร์ไซค์ motorbike taxis

wîng V วิ่ง to run

wing wian ADJ วิงเวียน dizzy

wîng nǐi V วิ่งหนี to run away, to flee

win-yaan N วิญญาณ (pronounced 'win yarn') spirit, soul (of the dead)

wít-tha-yaa N วิทยา knowledge, science

wít-tha-yaàkawn N วิทยากร speaker, lecturer; expert

wít-thá-yaa-lai N วิทยาลัย college

wít-thá-yaa-lai khruu N วิทยาลัยครู teachers' college

wít-thá-yaa-sàat N วิทยา ศาสตร์ science; **nák wít-thá-yaa-sàat** N นัก วิทยาศาสตร์ (a) scientist

wí-thii N วิธี way, method, means

wí-thii chái N วิธีใช้ directions (for use, e.g. medication)

wí-thii N วิถี path, way

wí-thii chii-wít N วิถีชีวิต way of life, lifestyle (NOTE: the English term 'lifestyle' has made its way into Thai, pronounced something like **lai sàtai**)

wít-thá-yú N วิทยุ radio

wiu N (from English 'view') วิว scenery, view, panorama

wòht N (from English and pronounced something like 'whoat') โหวต to vote; there are also a number of Thai words for 'to vote' such as **àwk sĭang** ออกเสียง and **long khà-naehn** ลง คะแนน

wohy waai V โวยวาย to make a fuss/make a big to do (about/over something), complain (in an animated fashion)

wói mehl N (from English) วอยซ์เมล voicemail

won V วน to whirl

wong N วง a ring, circle

wong dontrii N วงดนตรี (a musical) band/group, orchestra

wong jawn N วงจร (a) circuit (e.g. an electrical circuit)

wong klom N วงกลม (a round) circle

wong phâi N (COLLOQUIAL) วงไพ่ a circle of card players

wong wian N วงเวียน circle (e.g. a traffic circle), roundabout

wua N วัว cow

wún N วุ้น jelly, gelatin, agar

wún sên N วุ้นเส้น glass noodles

wûn waai ADJ วุ่นวาย to be busy (crowded); chaotic, turbulent

wùt wìt ADV หวูดหวิด almost, nearly, narrowly

Y

yaa N ยา drug, medicine, pills; **yaa bâa** N (literally, 'drug'-'crazy/mad') ยาบ้า methamphetamine (type of smokeable speed); **yaa thàai** N ยาถ่าย (a) laxative

yâa N หญ้า grass (of the lawn variety)

yâa N ย่า (paternal) grandmother

yàa INTERJ อย่า don't (do that)!

yàa V หย่า to divorce

yàa láew ADJ หย่าแล้ว to be divorced

yaa mét N ยาเม็ด tablet(s)

yaa phít N ยาพิษ poison

yaa raksǎa rôhk N ยารักษา โรค pharmaceutical(s)

yaa sà phǒm N ยาสระผม (hair) shampoo

yaa sàmǔn phrai N ยา สมุนไพร herbal medicine(s)

yaa sèp tìt N ยาเสพติด narcotic(s), addictive drug (in Thailand this term is used to refer to all illicit drugs from heroin and ice to marijuana)

yaa sǐi fan N ยาสีฟัน toothpaste

yaa sùup N ยาสูบ tobacco

yaai N ยาย (maternal) grandmother

yáai V ย้าย to move (from one place to another), transfer, shift

yáai bâan V ย้ายบ้าน to move house

yâak ADJ ยาก (to be) difficult, hard (to do, say, make, etc.), not so easy

yàak V อยาก to want, desire, need, require; to be thirsty/hungry (adventure, sex, etc.)

yàak dâi V อยากได้ would like to get (something), e.g. on seeing a flashy new car a young man/woman says 'I want one/to get one of those' **yàak dâi** อยากได้

yâak jon ADJ ยากจน poor, needy, impoverished, hard up

yàak yâi N หยากไย่ cobweb

yaam N ยาม watch (i.e. as in the military 'be on watch/guard duty'); time, era (in a general sense); watchman, sentry

yâam N ย่าม (a) shoulder bag (e.g. the type of cloth shoulder bag used by monks and, once upon a time – hippies, aka freaks)

yaam dùek ADV ยามดึก at night; late at night

yaam kháp khăn N ยามคับขัน time of emergency

yâan N ย่าน district; area, quarter (of a city/town)

yaan yon (formal term, rarely spoken) ยานยนต์ motor vehicle

yaang N ยาง rubber (substance); resin, sap, latex, tar

yàang N อย่าง kind, type, sort, variety; classifier for things

yâang V ย่าง to roast, grill, barbecue

yaang baen N ยางแบน a flat tire; also **yaang tàehk** ยางแตก to have a flat tire, have a blowout

yàang dii ADJ อย่างดี good quality (e.g. material); well (e.g. makes furniture)

yàang nán ADV อย่างนั้น (COLLOQUIAL; **nán** pronounced like 'nun' with a high tone) (do it) like that; that's right, correct

yàang níi ADV อย่างนี้ (COLLOQUIAL) อย่างนี้ (do it) like this

yàang nói ADV อย่างน้อย at least (e.g. they should try it)

yàang prà-yàt ADJ อย่าง

352

ประหยัด economical

yàang rai (question marker) อย่างไร how? (used at the end of an utterance); (COLLOQUIAL) **yang-ngai** (pronounced something like 'yang-ngai') ยังไง how?; (COLLOQUIAL – GREETING) **pen yang-ngai** เป็นยังไง how are you/how are you doing?

yàang rai kâw taam CONJ อย่างไรก็ตาม however

yaang rót N ยางรถ (a rubber) tire (on a vehicle)

yàang rûat rew ADV อย่าง รวดเร็ว quickly, speedily

yàap ADJ หยาบ rough, rude

yàap khaai ADJ หยาบคาย to be rude, crude

yâat N (pronounced like 'yart' with a falling tone) ญาติ relatives (family)

yâeh ADJ (pronounced like 'yair' or 'yeah' with a falling tone) แย่ terrible

yâeh v แหย่ to insert, poke, tease, provoke, disturb

yâeh long ADJ แย่ลง (to get) worse

yâeh thîi sùt ADJ แย่ที่สุด (the) worst

yâehk v แยก to separate, divide, split; spread apart

yâehk kan v แยกกัน to separate, split up, divide

yaehm N (from English) แยม jam

yâeng v แย่ง to grab, snatch; to scramble for; to vie/ compete (for)

yài ADJ ใหญ่ large, big, great; major (important); in charge, in command; **yài toh** ใหญ่โต very big, huge; formidable; powerful

yai N ใย filament, fiber; thread

yai maeng mum N ใยแมงมุม spider web, cobweb

yai sǎngkhráw N ใย สังเคราะห์ synthetic (thread)

yák N ยักษ์ a giant, ogre (frequently appearing in traditional Thai poetic literature and folk tales)

yák lài v ยักไหล่ to shrug

yam N (pronounced like 'yum') ยำ Thai-style spicy salad

353

yang ADV ยัง still, even now; not yet (as a reply)

yang dèk ADJ (COLLOQUIAL) ยังเด็ก (he/she is) still a child/still young

yang dii ADJ ยังดี (it's) still good

yang mii... (COLLOQUIAL) ยังมี there is still some left, remaining

yang mii chii-wít yùu ADJ ยังมีชีวิตอยู่, (or, more colloquially) **yang yùu** ยังอยู่ (to still be) alive

yaow ADV ยาว long (in length); **khwaam yaow** ความยาว length

yao-wáchon N เยาวชน youth (general term – plural)

yáp ADJ ยับ (pronounced similar to 'yup') wrinkled (clothing), crushed

yát V ยัด to stuff (in, with), cram (in, with), stuffed (with)

yâw V ย่อ to abbreviate, make shorter; to summarize

yaw V ยอ to flatter (somebody)

yâw tua V ย่อตัว to bow down

yáwm V ย้อม to dye, tint (cloth, hair, etc.)

yawm V ยอม to yield, give in, submit; to allow, consent

yawm hâi V ยอมให้ to permit, allow (someone to do something)

yawm pháeh V ยอมแพ้ to surrender, give up, give in (to)

yawm ráp V ยอมรับ to acknowledge, accept, agree; to admit, confess

yawm taai (COLLOQUIAL) ยอมตาย I'll never give in

yâwng V ย่อง to walk quietly, creep up, walk on tiptoes

yàwt V หยอด to drop

yâwt N ยอด summit, peak, top

yâwt yîam ADJ ยอดเยี่ยม to be excellent

yeh suu N เยซู (although this may seem somewhat odd, the name is pronounced 'yeah sue') Jesus; also **phrá yeh-suu** พระเยซู

yen ADJ เย็น to be cool, cold

yép V เย็บ to sew, stitch, pin;

354

to staple

yét v เย็ด (COLLOQUIAL – EXTREMELY RUDE) to fuck

yîam ADJ เยี่ยม first rate, great, tops; **yâwt yîam** ADJ ยอดเยี่ยม top, superb

yîam v เยี่ยม to visit, call on, go to see (someone)

yîao N, v (COLLOQUIAL) เยี่ยว urine; to urinate, piss, pee

yìap v เหยียบ to step on, put one's foot on

yìap brèhk v (**brèhk** from English) เหยียบเบรค to brake, put one's foot on the brakes (of a car)

yìat v เหยียด to look down on, hold in contempt, despise, be contemptuous (of)

yìat phǐu N เหยียดผิว (to be a) racist (literally, 'despise'+'skin')

yîi-pùn N ญี่ปุ่น Japan

yîi sìp NUM ยี่สิบ twenty; **yîi sìp èt** ยี่สิบเอ็ด twenty one, (COLLOQUIAL) **yíp èt** ยิบเอ็ด

yìk v หยิก to pinch: **phǒm yìk** ADJ ผมหยิก wrinkled/kinky/ curly/fuzzy hair

yím v ยิ้ม to smile

yím yaehm ADJ ยิ้มแย้ม (to be) cheerful

yin dii ADJ ยินดี to be glad, pleased, be happy (for, to)

yin dii tâwn ráp (formal public type of greeting) ยินดีต้อนรับ welcome!

yin dii thîi dâi rúu-jàk EXP ยินดีที่ได้รู้จัก 'glad to meet you'; 'it's a pleasure to meet you'

yíng ADJ หยิ่ง (to be) haughty, stuck-up, conceited, vain, proud, aloof

yîng ADV ยิ่ง exceedingly

yǐng N หญิง female (humans only)

ying v ยิง to shoot, fire (a gun/cannon)

yîng khûen ADV ยิ่งขึ้น more and more, increasingly

yîng yài ADJ ยิ่งใหญ่ grand, great, momentous

yóeh yáe (COLLOQUIAL) (both words pronounced with very short vowels) เยอะ แยะ lots of, many; (SLANG) heaps of/tons of (e.g. great music)

yôhk v โยก to rock, shake from side to side

yoh khá N โยคะ yoga

yohn v โยน to throw, toss

yôi v ย่อย to digest, crush, dissolve

yòk N หยก jade (semi-precious stone)

yók v ยก to raise, lift N also a round in boxing

yók lôehk v ยกเลิก to cancel (e.g. a contract)

yók rá-dàp v ยกระดับ to elevate, upgrade, raise the level/standard (e.g. of teaching)

yók song N ยกทรง a bra, brassiere (literally, 'lift'+'shape')

yók thôht v ยกโทษ to forgive, pardon (someone/a prisoner)

yók tua yàang ADV ยกตัวอย่าง for example, for instance; to give an example

yók wén v ยกเว้น to except, excluding, not including; exempt from

yók yaw v ยกยอ to flatter, praise

yók yâwng v ยกย่อง to praise

yót N ยศ rank (military, police); insignia of rank

yòt v หยด to drop

yú v ยุ to incite, provoke

yûa ADJ, v ยั่ว provocative; to provoke, arouse, entice

yûa yuan ADJ ยั่วยวน provocative, sexy, seductive

yùea N เหยื่อ prey, bait, victim

yùeak N เหยือก a jug, pitcher

yuehm v ยืม to borrow

yuehn v ยืน to stand, get on one's feet

yûehn ADJ ยื่น to project, stick out; to hand, offer, present

yûehn àwk maa v ยื่นออกมา to protrude

yuehn khûen v ยืนขึ้น to stand (up)

yuen yan v ยืนยัน to confirm

yûet ADJ ยืด to expand, stretch; **yûet wehlaa** ADV ยืดเวลา to prolong; to extend the time (for doing something)

yúet thŭeh v ยึดถือ to grasp
hold of; to seize

yúk N ยุค time; period, age:
e.g. **yúk hĭn** ยุคหิน the
Stone Age

yung N ยุง mosquito

yung kàt N ยุงกัด mosquito
bites

yûng v, ADJ ยุ่ง to be busy/
hectic (work, etc.); to
interfere/meddle (in
someone else's affairs);
to fool around (with);
troublesome, bothersome;
(COLLOQUIAL) **yàa yûng**
อย่ายุ่ง 'leave it/me/alone',
'don't interfere', 'don't
mess/fool around with
(someone or something)'

yûng yôehng ADJ ยุ่งเหยิง
tangled up; to be in a
muddle, in a state of

yú-rôhp N ยุโรป Europe

yùt v หยุด to stop, halt

yùt ná (COLLOQUIAL) หยุดนะ
stop it!

yút-ti-tham ADJ ยุติธรรม to be
just, fair, equitable

yùu v อยู่ to stay, remain; to
live, dwell; to be alive

yùu bâan v (COLLOQUIAL)
อยู่บ้าน to be at home, stay
home

yùu kàp thîi v อยู่กับที่ to
stay, remain

yùu kin ADJ (COLLOQUIAL)
อยู่กิน, (or, more fully)
yùu kin dûai/dûai kan
อยู่กินด้วย/ด้วยกัน to live
(together, with)

yùu pen phûean v (COLLO-
QUIAL) อยู่เป็นเพื่อน to keep
another company

yùu trong khâam ADV อยู่ตรง
ข้าม to be opposite (facing)
(e.g. the cinema)

ABOUT TUTTLE
"Books to Span the East and West"

Our core mission at Tuttle Publishing is to create books which bring people together one page at a time. Tuttle was founded in 1832 in the small New England town of Rutland, Vermont (USA). Our fundamental values remain as strong today as they were then—to publish best-in-class books informing the English-speaking world about the countries and peoples of Asia. The world has become a smaller place today and Asia's economic, cultural and political influence has expanded, yet the need for meaningful dialogue and information about this diverse region has never been greater. Since 1948, Tuttle has been a leader in publishing books on the cultures, arts, cuisines, languages and literatures of Asia. Our authors and photographers have won numerous awards and Tuttle has published thousands of books on subjects ranging from martial arts to paper crafts. We welcome you to explore the wealth of information available on Asia at **www.tuttlepublishing.com**.